EU Cross-Border Commercial Mediation

Global Trends in Dispute Resolution

VOLUME 9

Series Editor

Nadja Alexander is Director of the Singapore International Dispute Resolution Academy and Professor of Law at Singapore Management University. Professor Alexander is an award-winning author and educator in the field of negotiation and dispute resolution. She is known for the passion, energy and creativity she brings to her various roles as scholar, policy adviser, mediation practitioner and trainer. She has been identified by *Who's Who Legal* as a global thought leader in mediation.

Introduction

Global Trends in Dispute Resolution offers readers a garden rich in ideas and insights into contemporary dispute resolution principles, processes, and practices. The series leads the way in first-class debate and analysis of dispute resolution trends across our rapidly globalising world. More particularly, its volumes analyse dispute resolution developments in various geographical regions around the world and in relation to diverse transnational practice areas. These practice areas include not only well-established legal categories such as intellectual property, construction, and resources law, but also emerging dispute resolution trends ranging from dispute systems design to cross-border mediation in private and public law.

Objective

With a particular focus on new initiatives and dispute resolution practices, the *Global Trends in Dispute Resolution* series aims to provide practitioners, scholars, policymakers, and 'pracademics' (that elusive yet rapidly emerging category of practical academics and academically-oriented practitioners – you know who you are) with the resources both to cultivate the dispute resolution gardens of the world and to explore new paths within and beyond them.

Frequency of Publication

A volume is published whenever an interesting topic presents itself.

The titles published in this series are listed at the end of this volume.

EU Cross-Border Commercial Mediation

Listening to Disputants – Changing the Frame; Framing the Changes

Anna Howard

Wolters Kluwer

Published by:
Kluwer Law International B.V.
PO Box 316
2400 AH Alphen aan den Rijn
The Netherlands
E-mail: international-sales@wolterskluwer.com
Website: lrus.wolterskluwer.com

Sold and distributed by:
Wolters Kluwer Legal & Regulatory U.S.
7201 McKinney Circle
Frederick, MD 21704
United States of America
Email: customer.service@wolterskluwer.com

ISBN 978-94-035-1753-7

e-Book: ISBN 978-94-035-1804-6
web-PDF: ISBN 978-94-035-1852-7

To my family

About the Author

Dr Anna Howard is a researcher, lawyer and mediator.

Anna is currently a post-doctoral researcher at the Centre for Commercial Law Studies, Queen Mary University of London. Anna was awarded her PhD, upon which this book is based, in March 2020.

Anna qualified as a solicitor (England & Wales) in 2003 and practised EU and UK competition law at Freshfields Bruckhaus Deringer and Field Fisher before moving to Singapore where she started her academic career. In Singapore, Anna was Lecturer of Law at the School of Law, Singapore Management University, where she taught courses on Legal Writing and Ethics.

In 2014, Anna trained as a mediator (Core Solutions), and in 2016 Anna joined the editorial team of the Kluwer Mediation Blog as Associate Editor.

Anna studied Modern Languages at Oxford University (The Queen's College) and was then sponsored by Freshfields Bruckhaus Deringer to study Law as a postgraduate at The College of Law.

Table of Contents

Foreword

Back in the 1990s when working in Germany, I was struck that politicians, policymakers and other mediation prophets were relying on the same rhetoric as their new world common law counterparts in North America and Australia to incentivise lawyers and their clients to use mediation. 'Mediate first. Save time and money. Your dispute will be done and dusted before you can say "litigation".' This mantra seemed incongruous in Germany – a jurisdiction that was considered to have one of the most efficient and effective court systems in the world. On top of that, the accessibility of legal costs insurance and the structuring of legal fees on the basis of the value of the dispute meant that mediation, as presented, did not seem to be a compelling proposition for dispute resolution users.

This insight finds fertile ground in this remarkable and original work by Dr Anna Howard, *EU Cross-Border Commercial Mediation. Listening to Disputants – Changing the Frame; Framing the Changes.*

At one level, the book examines the use, and lack of use, of cross-border commercial mediation in the European Union through the lens of its users, in this case, senior in-house counsel of multinational companies. At a deeper level, it surfaces a fundamental truth, namely that the way we see mediation profoundly affects what we do (and don't do) with it. Echoing my personal experience in Germany and other EU states, the author empirically demonstrates not only how mediation is framed and promoted as an alternative to litigation, but also why this framing has not had the desired effect of promoting cross-border mediation practice in the EU.

Through her painstakingly thorough research, Anna Howard convincingly shows that *negotiation* is a key comparator for disputants in considering whether to use mediation. In other words, the EU's messaging about mediation has been placed in the wrong frame. It is anchored in an understanding of mediation as an alternative to litigation. Anna Howard shows us that this frame is too narrow. She recommends changing the frame to see mediation through the disputants' negotiation lens, so that mediation becomes an extension of the negotiating that parties are already doing rather than merely a new procedural step before getting to litigation, or a means to avoid litigation altogether.

When mediation is framed as 'towards something' (negotiation) rather than 'away from something' (litigation), there is a massive cognitive shift. And it affects behaviour. This book examines how framing mediation with negotiation paradoxically raises both opportunities and obstacles to the increased use of mediation, and what policymakers can do about it. To use Howard's terminology, after covering the terrain of how and why to 'change the frame', she then offers specific recommendations for how to 'frame the changes' in terms of policy, practice and the EU Directive on Mediation.

Drawn from the findings of Howard's PhD thesis, this book contains many gems – some surprising. For example, flying in the face of conventional (legal) wisdom, not a single interviewee in her qualitative study identified the lack of a direct enforcement mechanism for inter-EU mediated settlement agreements as a reason for not using mediation. These and other findings are deftly analysed with a view to the impact on practice and EU policy. But of course the implications go beyond the EU.

In 2020, mediation is the new darling of the international dispute resolution scene, especially with the coming into force of the Singapore Convention on Mediation. Expectations are high that mediation delivers, yet there is much that we do not know. Empirical research on international mediation is at a nascent stage, and it is here that Anna Howard's research offers a significant contribution to the international literature.

This is a thoughtful and thought-provoking work that will be of equal interest to scholars and practitioners. Anna Howard is a bold new voice in dispute resolution. I am honoured to write this foreword to her debut book.

Nadja Alexander
Singapore, October 2020

List of Abbreviations

CEDR	Centre for Effective Dispute Resolution
CPR	The International Institute for Conflict Prevention and Resolution
CPR Pledge	The International Institute for Conflict Prevention and Resolution's Pledge
EU	European Union
EU Mediation Directive	Council Directive 2008/52/EC of 21 May 2008 on certain aspects of mediation in civil and commercial matters [2008] OJ L136/3
GPC Series	Global Pound Conference Series 2016-2017
Green Paper	European Commission, 'Green Paper on Alternative Dispute Resolution in Civil and Commercial Law' COM (2002) 196
IMI	International Mediation Institute
Rebooting Report	European Parliament, 'Rebooting the Mediation Directive: Assessing the Limited Impact of its Implementation and Proposing Measures to Increase the Number of Mediations in the EU' (2014) PE 493.042
SIDRA	Singapore International Dispute Resolution Academy
Singapore Convention	The United Nations Convention on International Settlement Agreements Resulting from Mediation
WIPO	World Intellectual Property Organisation

List of Figures

List of Tables

Acknowledgements

This is both the easiest and the hardest part of the book to write: the easiest because those without whom this book would not have been possible come so easily to mind; and the hardest because words are insufficient to express my gratitude to them.

I am deeply grateful to the in-house counsel who responded to a request from a stranger and found time in their busy schedules to be interviewed for this book. Without their generosity, this book, and the PhD upon which it is based, would not have been possible.

Most of the work for this book was done during my PhD studies at the Centre for Commercial Law Studies, Queen Mary University of London. I am very grateful to Queen Mary University for that opportunity. In particular, my very special thanks to Dr Debbie De Girolamo and Prof. Stavros Brekoulakis, my PhD supervisors, for their generous guidance, encouragement and detailed review of many drafts of my thesis. My thanks also to Prof. Kate Malleson for her enriching PhD seminars and advice and to Dr Rachel Cahill-O'Callaghan, at Cardiff University, for her comments and support. I am also very grateful to Prof. Bryan Clark and Prof. Sue Prince, my PhD examiners, for their careful review of my PhD and helpful comments.

My interest in mediation started in 2010 in Singapore when I had the very good fortune to work with Ian Macduff. Ian nudged me into mediation's path and changed the path of my career. I would like to thank Ian for being been an endlessly generous and wise mentor and friend.

It was at Ian's suggestion, back in 2014, that I trained as a mediator at Core Solutions, led by John Sturrock Q.C. Ever since, John has mentored me and offered me numerous opportunities to learn and grow. I am grateful to John for his generosity and friendship.

Thank you as well to Prof. John Phillips and Prof. David Llewelyn, my former colleagues at Singapore Management University, who have remained interested in my path and have continued to guide and encourage me.

My thanks also to Michael Leathes and Annie Dunster who both responded warmly to emails when I had reached an impasse in my research. Annie and Michael's generosity and encouragement, when I was a stranger to them, helped me to overcome a particularly difficult stage in the research process.

At the Kluwer Mediation Blog, I would like to thank my colleagues on the editorial team, in particular Prof. Nadja Alexander and Bill Marsh, the regular contributors, Vincent Verschoor and Eleanor Taylor for their collegiality while I was writing this book. Particular thanks as well to Dr Rosemary Howell for her guidance and wise advice.

At Wolters Kluwer, I would like to thank Kiran Nasir Gore for her encouraging comments during the early stages of this book and her very helpful and swift guidance throughout the editorial process. My special thanks as well to Prof. Nadja Alexander, the editor of the series within which this book sits, for her helpful editorial comments and uplifting guidance.

A tribe of generous friends saw me through the ups and downs of writing this book. Particular thanks to my talented and humble friend, Fiona Mitchell, for our many conversations on writing and for her unfailing encouragement and support. Thank you to Pilar Ariño, Mia Forbes Pirie, Suzanne Innes-Kent, Susan and Andrew Kendall, Christina Menig, Angela Parkin, Louisa Shand and Raul Valtueña for cheering me on, and up. And many thanks to Dr Caroline Withall who always said just what I needed to hear.

Without the love, encouragement and support of my family, this book would not have been completed. Throughout the four and a half years of writing this book, my kind and generous parents, Luiza and David Parks, provided endless meals and lifts for their granddaughters so that I could have more time to write. My brother, Robert Parks, carefully reviewed chapters, accompanying his comments and encouragement with his searingly sharp wit. My husband, Jonathan Howard, always made this endeavour seem achievable with his consistent optimism, good humour and resolute belief in me. His quiet strength, wisdom and enviable ability to always see the funny side of things kept, and keep, me going. And to my daughters, Emma and Chloe: you inspire me to reach higher, you show me what really matters and the greatest lessons I have learnt are from you.

CHAPTER 1
Overview of the Book

> The fundamental problem about mediation is that it's a good idea and nobody uses it.[1]

§1.01 EXECUTIVE SUMMARY

The statement above from one of the interviewees who participated in the research for this book captures the continued conundrum faced by mediation as it seeks to establish its position as a recognised and respected dispute resolution process. Why, in spite of the frequently acknowledged qualities and virtues of mediation, does its usage appear to remain stubbornly low? Despite numerous national and international measures to foster the use of mediation, there seems to be little movement in mediation's uptake.

This book focuses on the use, and lack of use, of mediation in the European Union (EU) cross-border commercial context. By drawing on interviews with senior in-house counsel of multinational companies, this book expands the discussion on why mediation is, and is not, used for EU cross-border commercial disputes. The insights provided by these experienced users of cross-border dispute resolution processes enable the construction of a different frame through which new proposals for the promotion of mediation can be identified.

This chapter opens the book by briefly introducing mediation and some of the key developments in the cross-border mediation context. It then explains the research focus of this book and provides a brief summary of each chapter.

1. Interviewee 18 (in-house counsel of multinational company) during his interview for this book.

§1.02 INTRODUCING MEDIATION

Mediation has been described as 'both the oldest and newest form of dispute resolution'.[2] As Alexander has explained, mediation is 'new in terms of its emergence in the legal arena and old in terms of its timeless universality'.[3] Its ancient origins can be traced back to Chinese and African dispute resolution processes,[4] while the roots of modern-day mediation are considered by many to be the American dispute resolution movement of the 1970s and 1980s.[5] In particular, the use of mediation in urban unrest and specifically interracial community conflict in a number of cities in the United States (US) has been identified as the beginning of the modern-day mediation field.[6] Mediation was at that time 'seen not as an alternative to the courts but an alternative to the streets'.[7] Many of its early advocates saw mediation as a way for the disenfranchised to gain access to justice and for citizens to exercise control over decisions affecting them.[8] In its continued trajectory from being a marginal to a more mainstream dispute resolution process, mediation has been differentially regulated, institutionalised and legitimised across numerous countries and legal systems.[9]

By way of a brief overview, mediation is a dispute resolution process under which a neutral third party helps disputing parties to reach a consensual solution.[10] Mediation has, more specifically, been described as a third-party facilitated negotiation between parties in conflict.[11] Within these broad definitions lie the different ways in

2. Ian Macduff (ed.), *Essays on Mediation: Dealing with Disputes in the 21st Century* 3 (Wolters Kluwer 2016). *See also* Christopher Moore, *The Mediation Process* 61-105 (4th ed. Jossey-Bass 2014) on the history and contemporary use of mediation.
3. Nadja Alexander (ed.), *Global Trends in Mediation* 1 (2nd ed. Kluwer Law International 2006).
4. Carrie Menkel-Meadow, *Variations in the Uptake of and Resistance to Mediation Outside of the United States*, University of California, Irvine School of Law, Research Paper No. 2015-80, 189 [2015] <https://papers.ssrn.com/sol3/papers.cfm?abstract_id=2658903> (accessed 10 May 2020).
5. Robert Bush, *Staying in Orbit, or Breaking Free: The Relationship of Mediation to the Courts over Four Decades*, 84 North Dakota Law Review 705, 706 (2008); Menkel-Meadow, *supra* n. 4, at 189; Menkel-Meadow, *Mothers and Fathers of Invention: The Intellectual Founders of ADR*, 16(1) Ohio State Journal on Dispute Resolution 1, 1 & 2 (2000); Marian Roberts, *Developing the Craft of Mediation* 17 (Jessica Kingsley Publishers 2007); Simon Roberts and Michael Palmer, *Dispute Processes, ADR and the Primary Forms of Decision-Making* 45-77 (2nd ed. Cambridge University Press 2008). For a detailed overview of the growth of mediation *see* Robert Bush and Joseph Folger, *The Promise of Mediation* 7-39 (Revised ed. Jossey-Bass 2005).
6. Bush, *supra* n. 5, at 709-712. *See also* Christine B. Harrington and Sally Engle Merry, *Ideological Production: The Making of Community Mediation*, 22(4) Law & Society Review 709 (1988).
7. Bush, *supra* n. 5, at 711.
8. Amy Cohen, *Dispute Systems Design, Neoliberalism, and the Problem of Scale*, 14 Harvard Negotiation Law Review 51, 68 (2009).
9. For a summary of varying types of mediation regulation and the challenges associated with such regulation *see* Carrie Menkel-Meadow, *The Future of Mediation Worldwide: Legal and Cultural Variations in the Uptake and Resistance to Mediation* in Ian Macduff (ed.), *Essays on Mediation, Dealing with Disputes in the 21st Century* 30 (Wolters Kluwer 2016).
10. Hazel Genn, *Judging Civil Justice* 82 (Cambridge 2010); Penny Brooker, *Mediation Law* 1 (Routledge 2013).
11. Menkel-Meadow, *supra* n. 4, at 189; Debbie De Girolamo, *The Fugitive Identity of Mediation* 5 (Routledge 2013); Carrie Menkel-Meadow, *Lawyer Negotiations: Theories and Realities – What We Learn from Mediation*, 56 The Modern Law Review 361, 372 (1993); Bush and Folger, *supra* n. 5, at 8; Marian Roberts, *supra* n. 5, at 69; Moore, *supra* n. 2, at 8. For an analysis of the core

which mediators practise and therefore the differing ways in which they may help parties in their efforts to resolve their disputes.[12] The values underpinning mediation include self-determination, autonomy, respect, empowerment, voluntariness and flexibility.[13] Perhaps at its broadest, mediation has been described as 'a "sensibility" – a way of thinking about how we approach each other and live in the world'.[14]

Mediation is now recognised as an important method of dispute resolution in an increasing number of countries and legal systems.[15] It has been embraced for reasons which have been gathered into two classes: 'quantitative' and 'qualitative'.[16] The 'quantitative' reasons for mediation's adoption focus on those aspects which lend themselves more easily to measurement, including that it is a quicker, cheaper and therefore more efficient alternative to adjudication.[17] The 'qualitative' reasons are those arising from the nature of the mediation process and its outcomes, and which may prove elusive to measurement and quantification.[18] These include, as regards the mediation process, the opportunity to 'reorient the parties towards each other'[19] and thereby change the way in which the parties view their relationship,[20] more party involvement and influence in the proceedings, the opportunity to address more than the particular matter in dispute, and improved communication between the parties.[21] As regards the outcomes of the mediation process, such qualitative reasons include the opportunity to reach solutions which maximise the joint gains that the parties together can achieve, which satisfy the parties' underlying interests (not limited to those

components of the mediation process *see* Roberts and Palmer, *supra* n. 5, at 153-172. There is much literature which discusses the nature of mediation. For a summary of this literature *see* Debbie De Girolamo, *The Fugitive Identity of Mediation* 47-52 (Routledge 2013). For a summary of various definitions of mediation *see also* Jacob Bercovitch and Richard Jackson, *Conflict Resolution in the Twenty-First Century* 33-34 (The University of Michigan Press 2009).

12. Brooker, *supra* n. 10, at 1; Len Riskin, *Understanding Mediators' Orientations, Strategies and Techniques: A Grid for the Perplexed,* 1 Harvard Negotiation Law Review 7 (1996); Len Riskin, *Decision-Making in Mediation: the New Old Grid and the New New Grid System,* 79(1) Notre Dame Law Review 1 (2003); Nadja Alexander, *The Mediation Metamodel: Understanding Practice,* 26(1) Conflict Resolution Quarterly 97 (2008); Bercovitch and Jackson, *supra* n. 11, at 33.
13. Menkel-Meadow, *supra* n. 4, at 189, 195; Carrie Menkel-Meadow, *Alternative and Appropriate Dispute Resolution in Context: Formal, Informal, and Semiformal Legal Processes,* School of Law, University of California Irvine School of Law Research Paper No. 2015-26, 10 (2015) <https://papers.ssrn.com/sol3/papers.cfm?abstract_id=2584188> (accessed 10 May 2020); Marian Roberts, *supra* n. 5, at 17; Kenneth Cloke, *The Dance of Opposites* 323-324 (Goodmedia Press 2013); Nadja Alexander, *International and Comparative Mediation* 15 (Wolters Kluwer 2009).
14. Carrie Menkel-Meadow, *Chartered Institute of Arbitration 8th Symposium on Mediation, October 2015: The Case for Mediation: the Things that Mediators should be Learning and Doing,* 82(1) Arbitration 22, 23 (2016).
15. Menkel-Meadow, *supra* n. 4, at 189.
16. Carrie Menkel-Meadow, *When Dispute Resolution Begets Disputes of Its Own: Conflicts Among Dispute Professionals,* 44 UCLA Law Review 1871, 1871 & 1872 (1996). *See also* Menkel-Meadow, *Alternative and Appropriate Dispute Resolution in Context, supra* n. 13, at 2.
17. Menkel-Meadow, *When Dispute Resolution Begets Disputes of Its Own, supra* n. 16, at 1871.
18. *Ibid.*, 1872 for the grouping into quantitative and qualitative reasons for using mediation.
19. Lon Fuller, *Mediation: its Forms and Functions,* 44 Southern California Law Review 305, 325 (1971).
20. *Ibid. See also* Roberts and Palmer, *supra* n. 5, at 173.
21. Menkel-Meadow, *When Dispute Resolution Begets Disputes of Its Own, supra* n. 16, at 1872. *See also* Roberts and Palmer, *supra* n. 5, at 174-175.

relevant to the legal issues), which take into account the future as well as the past, and which avoid the win-lose scenarios commonly seen in adjudicative processes.[22]

§1.03 MEDIATION IN THE CROSS-BORDER CONTEXT

While mediation has emerged as a significant dispute resolution process in an increasing number of countries and legal systems,[23] its emergence into the cross-border arena has been tentative.[24] Mediation continues to be in its infancy in the cross-border forum in spite of measures by international bodies, such as the EU, and by nations vying to be international dispute resolution centres, such as Singapore and Japan,[25] to hasten mediation's entry into the cross-border forum.[26] The United Nations Convention on International Settlement Agreements Resulting from Mediation (Singapore Convention), which opened for signature on 7 August 2019 in Singapore and entered into force on 12 September 2020,[27] is expected to result in an increase in the use of international cross-border mediation.[28] This will, however, depend largely on the number of signatories to the Singapore Convention and, more broadly, the extent to

---

22. Menkel-Meadow, *When Dispute Resolution Begets Disputes of Its Own*, *supra* n. 16, at 1872. *See also* Roger Fisher and William Ury, *Getting to Yes* 42-57 and 58-81 (3rd ed. Random House Business Books 2012).
23. Menkel-Meadow, *supra* n. 4, at 189. *See also* Klaus Hopt and Felix Steffek (eds), *Mediation: Principles and Regulation in Comparative Perspective* (Oxford 2012) which describes and analyses the law and practice of mediation in twenty-two countries.
24. S.I. Strong, *Realizing Rationality: An Empirical Assessment of International Commercial Mediation*, 73 Washington & Lee Law Review 1973, 1983 & 1984 (2016).
25. In 2014 Singapore established the Singapore International Mediation Centre and in 2016 founded the Singapore International Academy of Dispute Resolution to further develop Singapore's role in international dispute resolution. Further information can be found at < http://simc.com.sg > and < https://sidra.smu.edu.sg > (accessed 10 May 2020). In 2018, Japan established the Japan International Mediation Center < https://www.jimc-kyoto.jp/about > (accessed 10 May 2020).
26. Menkel-Meadow, *supra* n. 4, at 207 & 218. Nadja Alexander, *Nudging Users Towards Cross-Border Mediation: Is it Really About Harmonized Enforcement Regulation?*, 7(2) Contemporary Asia Arbitration Journal 405, 408 (2014); Thomas W. Walde, *Efficient Management of Transnational Disputes: Mutual Gain by Mediation or Joint Loss in Litigation*, 22(2) Arbitration International 205, 211 (2006).
27. UNCITRAL, 'Singapore Convention Signing Ceremony' < https://uncitral.un.org/en/07.08.2019 > (accessed 10 May 2020). Following the ratification of the convention by Singapore, Fiji and Qatar, the convention entered into force on 12 September 2020 < https://www.singaporeconvention.org/convention/about-convention/ > (accessed 16 September 2020).
28. The United Nations Convention on International Settlement Agreements Resulting from Mediation (UN Convention on International Mediated Settlement Agreements) < https://uncitral.un.org/sites/uncitral.un.org/files/media-documents/uncitral/en/annex_i.pdf > (accessed 10 May 2020). For analysis of the convention *see*: Nadja Alexander and Shouyu Chong (eds), *The Singapore Convention on Mediation, A Commentary* (Wolters Kluwer 2019); Timothy Schnabel, *The Singapore Convention on Mediation: A Framework for the Cross-Border Recognition and Enforcement of Mediated Settlements*, 19(1) Pepperdine Dispute Resolution Law Journal 1 (2019); and Eunice Chua, *The Singapore Convention on Mediation: A Brighter Future for Asian Dispute Resolution*, 9(2) Asian Journal of International Law 195(2019). At the opening ceremony of the convention, forty-six countries signed up to the convention. Cara Wong, *46 Countries Sign International Mediation Treaty Signed after Singapore, The Straits Times* (Singapore, 7 August 2019) < https://www.straitstimes.com/singapore/key-facts-about-the-singapore-convention-on-mediation > (accessed 10 May 2020). Information on the latest number of signatories to the

which commercial disputants were not using international mediation due to the lack of an international enforcement mechanism.

As will be considered in detail in Chapter 2, the EU has demonstrated a keen and consistent interest in the promotion of cross-border mediation, with its implementation of Directive 2008/52/EC on certain aspects of mediation in civil and commercial matters (EU Mediation Directive),[29] followed by extensive research to determine how to enhance the efficacy and impact of the directive. However, in spite of the EU's efforts to endorse and encourage cross-border mediation with the invocation of arguments of access to justice, efficiency, the 'amicable'[30] settlement of disputes and the maintenance of relationships,[31] these endeavours appear to have met with little success. While data on the number of cross-border mediations is notoriously hard to obtain,[32] the EU has identified that there continue to be low levels of cross-border mediation within the EU, in spite of the implementation of the EU Mediation Directive. In particular, the European Parliament has found that 'the data confirms that EU corporations, on average, have failed to engage mediation in cross-border disputes'.[33] Similarly, the European Commission has found that 'stakeholders ... reported a very limited number or no cross-border cases'[34] and that 'the number of domestic cases exceeds that of cross-border cases by far'.[35] Academics in the field share the view that cross-border mediation in the EU, and indeed further afield, is used sparingly and continue to contemplate why.[36] In particular, Menkel-Meadow has noted that 'despite

---

convention and ratification by such signatories can be found at: <https://uncitral.un.org/en/texts/mediation/conventions/international_settlement_agreements/status> (accessed 10 May 2020).

29. Council Directive 2008/52/EC of 21 May 2008 on Certain Aspects of Mediation in Civil and Commercial Matters [2008] OJ L136/3 (EU Mediation Directive).
30. EU Mediation Directive, Article 1(1).
31. European Commission, *Green Paper on Alternative Dispute Resolution in Civil and Commercial Law*, COM (2002) 196 final (Green Paper) section 1.2 at 7-9; EU Mediation Directive, Recitals 5 and 6 and Article 1(1). *See also* European Commission, *Study for an Evaluation and Implementation of Directive 2008/52/EC- the Mediation Directive* (16 March 2016) at IV <https://publications.europa.eu/en/publication-detail/-/publication/bba3871d-223b-11e6-86d0-01aa75ed71a1> (accessed 10 May 2020).
32. De Palo and D'Urso note that there are currently no comprehensive, comparable data on mediations, either domestic or cross-border, for the EU as a whole. De Palo and D'Urso, *Achieving a Balanced Relationship Between Mediation and Judicial Proceedings' in European Parliament, 'The Implementation of the Mediation Directive, Workshop 29 November 2016'*, (2016) PE 571.395, 20.
33. European Parliament, *Quantifying the Cost of Not Using Mediation – a Data Analysis*, (2011) PE 453.180, 18.
34. European Commission, *Study for an Evaluation and Implementation of Directive 2008/52/EC, supra* n. 31, at VII.
35. European Commission, *Report from the Commission to the European Parliament, the Council and the European Economic and Social Committee on the Application of Directive 2008/52/EC of the European Parliament and of the Council on Certain Aspects of Mediation in Civil and Commercial Matters*, COM (2016) 0542, 5. Further, a recent report commissioned by the European Parliament into the impact of the EU Mediation Directive captures the lack of success of this directive in the report's title: European Parliament, *'Rebooting' the Mediation Directive: Assessing the Limited Impact of its Implementation and Proposing Measures to Increase the Number of Mediations in the EU*, (2014) PE 493.042 (Rebooting Report) and *see also* page 11 of this report.
36. Guiseppe de Palo and Romina Canessa, *Sleeping? Comatose? Only Mandatory Consideration of Mediation Can Awake Sleeping Beauty in the European Union*, 16 Cardozo Journal of Conflict

the increased amount of legal and regulatory support for mediative processes, especially in the EU and especially in cross-border disputing, there remain cultural and legal resistances to the use of mediation in many areas'.[37]

§1.04 THE RESEARCH FOCUS OF THIS BOOK

In light of the low take-up of cross-border mediation and the EU's continued efforts to promote it, this book explores why parties do, and do not, use EU cross-border mediation in order to identify what they might need if they are to increase their use of such mediation. The research for this book adopts a different approach to that seen in the EU's research to date. In particular, it engages with a key category of stakeholder which has not received discernible attention in the EU's research, namely the users of dispute resolution processes,[38] and does so through the use of the qualitative research method of in-depth interviews. In so doing, this book offers insights regarding disputants' use, and lack of use, of mediation for their EU cross-border commercial disputes and, more broadly, into their views of mediation. These insights reveal a number of notable barriers to the increased use of mediation which have not been considered in the EU's efforts to date to increase the use of mediation. In particular, the identification of these barriers suggests that the EU's recent measures are insufficient to address fully users' concerns and needs regarding EU cross-border commercial mediation. The book then identifies further recommendations for the EU in its continued initiatives to promote the use of mediation.

The focus of this book's research on cross-border mediation does not assume that mediation is appropriate for all conflicts. The suitability of a particular form of dispute resolution depends on the type of the dispute and the needs of the disputants.[39] Rather, the chosen focus stems from an interest in how cross-border mediation might be promoted in a manner which engages with, and is responsive to, the particular needs

---

Resolution 713, 713-717 (2014-15); European Parliament, *Rebooting Report*, *supra* n. 35, 10; Jacqueline Nolan-Haley, *Evolving Paths to Justice: Assessing the EU Directive on Mediation*, Fordham Law Legal Studies Research Paper No. 1942391, 16 (2011) <http://ssrn.com/abstract=1942391> (accessed 10 May 2020); Kimberlee K. Kovach, *The Mediation Coma: Purposeful or Problematic*, 16 Cardozo Journal of Conflict Resolution 755, 755 and footnote 3 (2014-15); Alexander, *supra* n. 26, at 408; S.I. Strong, *Use and Perception of International Commercial Mediation and Conciliation: A Preliminary Report on Issues Relating to the Proposed UNCITRAL Convention on International Commercial Mediation and Conciliation* University of Missouri, School of Law Legal Studies Research Paper Series 2014-28, (2014) <http://ssrn.com/abstract=2526302> (accessed 10 May 2020). In particular, at page 16 Strong refers to data from her empirical research that 'suggests that international commercial mediation and conciliation are still relatively rare'. *See also* Thomas Stipanowich, *The International Evolution of Mediation: A Call for Dialogue and Deliberation*, 46 Victoria University of Wellington Law Review 1191, 1199 (2015) which states: 'although mediation is an increasingly visible part of the landscape of international commercial disputes, it has not achieved the status it enjoys in the United States'.

37. Menkel-Meadow, *supra* n. 14, at 27.
38. The limited involvement of disputants in the relevant empirical research to date is explained in Chapters 2 and 3. *See also* Chapter 4 which further explains the choice to focus on disputants.
39. Felix Steffek, *The Relationship Between Mediation and Other Forms of Alternative Dispute Resolution* in European Parliament, *The Implementation of the Mediation Directive, Workshop 29 November 2016*, *supra* n. 32.

of disputants. Providing disputants with what they need – rather than with what others think they might need – will give them real choice when selecting the appropriate dispute resolution process for their various and varied disputes.[40] A brief summary of each of the chapters in this book now follows.

§1.05 OVERVIEW OF EACH CHAPTER

Chapter 2 explores the EU's continued efforts to promote the use of cross-border mediation within the EU. In particular, it examines the history and the content of the key piece of legislation on such mediation: the EU Mediation Directive.[41] It also considers the empirical research conducted by the European Commission and Parliament to identify how to improve the directive. The analysis of this research identifies a number of noteworthy methodological features of the key empirical studies used to identify proposals to enhance the directive. The chapter also considers the suitability of the proposals arising from such empirical research to the particular cross-border scope of the directive. The examination of the empirical research and the proposals arising from such research identifies areas which would benefit from further empirical research.

Chapter 3 builds on the review in Chapter 2 of the research conducted to date by the European Commission and Parliament by considering further empirical research which, though not specific to the EU Mediation Directive, addresses cross-border commercial mediation. It therefore offers a comprehensive summary of the relevant research in the cross-border commercial mediation field. The review of the relevant research identifies that it is predominantly quantitative research, conducted by way of surveys, and there is a lack of qualitative research on cross-border mediation. In addition, as regards the respondents to such research, there is a limited involvement of the users of dispute resolution processes whose contributions and insights are of particular value, as is explained in Chapter 4.

Chapter 4 explains the choice of qualitative research for this study and, in particular, the use of semi-structured interviews, including how this choice of approach was influenced by the elicitive approach used by the mediator, John Paul Lederach. The chapter also explains the choice to focus on users of cross-border dispute resolution processes, and in particular in-house counsel. It then sets out the research process. This includes the way in which the research participants were identified and approached, the data collection process and the method of analysis of the data.

Chapter 5 provides key information on the twenty-one interviewees, and their organisations, who took part in this study. The information provided in this chapter

---

40. Menkel-Meadow has noted that the use of mediation should be encouraged when it is the most appropriate dispute resolution process. *See* Carrie Menkel-Meadow, *The Future of Mediation Worldwide: Legal and Cultural Variations in the Uptake of or Resistance to Mediation* in Ian Macduff (ed.) *Essays on Mediation, Dealing with Disputes in the 21st Century* (Wolters Kluwer 2016) 45.
41. *See supra* n. 29 for the full citation of the EU Mediation Directive.

demonstrates that those interviewed for this study occupy senior legal roles in their companies and are well placed to offer insights into their companies' experience of EU cross-border commercial disputes and the dispute resolution methods used for such disputes. Further, the data shows that the interviewees represent large companies which operate across numerous EU Member States and business sectors and which have considerable experience of EU cross-border commercial disputes. It should be emphasised here that the research for this book was conducted before the UK left the EU. Therefore, some of the interviewees referred to the UK in their answers to questions on EU cross-border disputes and mediation.

Chapter 6 is the first of three chapters which examine the insights provided by the interviewees. This chapter identifies the connection made by the interviewees between the dispute resolution processes of mediation and negotiation and considers the relevance of that connection for those seeking to promote the use of mediation, such as the EU. The interviewees highlighted the fundamental importance of negotiation in cross-border dispute resolution. Further, the interviewees viewed mediation not as an independent dispute resolution process but rather as assisted and extended negotiation. This is in contrast to how mediation is understood and portrayed in the EU Mediation Directive as an alternative to litigation, which has led to the EU's continued reliance on litigation for ideas of how to promote mediation. Further, this chapter also examines how the role of negotiation as a cross-border dispute resolution process has been overlooked in the empirical research to date.

Chapter 7 explores the key themes which emerged from the interview data regarding why disputants use mediation for their EU cross-border commercial disputes, including the triggers for their use of such mediation. The reasons identified confirm, challenge and expand upon the empirical research to date on why parties use mediation. In particular, the interviewees identified the preservation of relationships as a factor which influences their choice to use cross-border mediation. As considered in Chapter 7, arguably, the EU's approach to date of focusing on the relationship between mediation and litigation,[42] with the consequent association of mediation with the adversarial and adjudicative process of litigation, does not assist in emphasising this important characteristic of mediation.

In addition, a notable theme which emerges from the data is the efforts by the users themselves to bring about the use of mediation, whether by using dispute resolution clauses in their commercial contracts or at their ad hoc suggestion. This chapter then explains how, taken together, the insights from Chapters 6 and 7 suggest that, in its efforts to identify ways to promote mediation, the EU should consider expanding upon its current sole focus on the relationship between mediation and litigation to also consider the relationship between mediation and negotiation. A focus on the relationship between mediation and negotiation brings with it the opportunity to both identify and address barriers to the use of the mediation which have not previously been identified without exploring such a relationship. Indeed, the findings in Chapter 8 (which examines why parties do not use mediation) demonstrate that the

42. The EU Mediation Directive's focus on the relationship between mediation and litigation is considered in Chapter 2. *See*, in particular, text to (n. 78)-(n. 85) in Chapter 2.

association which disputants draw between mediation and negotiation is the backdrop for important reasons why they do not use mediation.

Chapter 8 then considers the key themes in the interview data regarding why parties do not use mediation for their EU cross-border commercial disputes. The key themes identified further reorient us away from the EU's sole focus on mediation's relationship with litigation towards an appreciation of the relationship between mediation and negotiation. In particular, reasons are identified as to why disputants do not use mediation which have not been explored in the EU's research to date. These include a scepticism as to what mediation can add to negotiation, an associated concern about being regarded as having failed for having been unable to resolve the dispute in unassisted negotiations, a reluctance to maintain responsibility for the resolution of the dispute and an associated fear of being criticised by others for failing to get a good deal in the mediation. These novel findings stem from the association which the interviewees draw between mediation and negotiation.

While the mediation literature has acknowledged the relationship between mediation and negotiation, with mediation being described as assisted or extended negotiation, what has not been considered to date is how the relationship which disputants draw between mediation and negotiation can affect their proclivity to use mediation. This is an important finding which has emerged from this qualitative study. In Chapter 8, this book demonstrates that the relationship between mediation and negotiation reveals a paradox: such a relationship raises both an opportunity and an obstacle to the increased use of mediation. The opportunity is that mediation is associated with a dispute resolution process which is familiar to and favoured by disputants. And the obstacle is that mediation's association with negotiation leads to barriers to the use of mediation, including a scepticism as to what mediation can add to negotiation and an associated concern about being regarded as having failed for having been unable to resolve the dispute in unassisted negotiations. The EU's focus on mediation's exclusive relationship with litigation means that the further reasons identified in this book regarding why parties do not use mediation have been missed in the EU's research to date. An awareness of these reasons is the first step in determining how those who seek to promote mediation might respond to them. Finally, Chapter 8 also draws upon the relationship between mediation and negotiation to identify a further suggestion for the promotion of cross-border mediation, namely an enhanced confidentiality provision in the EU Mediation Directive.

Chapter 9 draws on the themes identified in Chapters 6, 7 and 8 to argue that the EU's continued focus on mediation's relationship with litigation, to the exclusion of other methods of dispute resolution, has resulted in recommendations which are insufficient to address fully the barriers to the increased use of mediation. In particular, by changing the frame to view the use of mediation through the disputants' perspective, this in turn leads to a change in the framing of mediation from an alternative to litigation (as has been the EU's focus to date) to an extension of what parties already do (i.e., negotiation).

In changing the frame, both as regards the perspective through which the use of mediation is viewed and how mediation is framed, this leads to the framing of changes to the EU's continued efforts to promote mediation. With a recognition of the prominent role that negotiation can play as a cross-border dispute resolution process, together with an understanding of mediation as assisted and extended negotiation, novel obstacles to the increased use of mediation (as mentioned above) can be identified.

Crucially, such obstacles also highlight what is required of disputants when they pursue mediation. Rather than simply being the avoidance of something, i.e., litigation, as mediation has been presented by the EU, these obstacles demonstrate that mediation asks a considerable amount of disputants. It asks that they: assume continued responsibility for the resolution of their disputes; assume the risk that they may be regarded as having failed either for having been unable to resolve the dispute themselves through unassisted negotiations or for reaching a solution in mediation which others deem unsatisfactory; and accept that, with the assistance of a mediator, they may be able to achieve more than in unassisted negotiations. With this focus on what mediation *asks of* disputants rather than on what it allows them to *avoid* (i.e., litigation), different types of recommendations for the promotion of mediation can be identified.

Chapter 9 then identifies recommendations for the EU in its continued efforts to promote mediation and concludes with a call for more nuanced research and responses.

This book demonstrates that the way in which mediation has been presented and promoted by the EU is at odds with the way in which it is viewed by disputants. In particular, the EU's continued focus on mediation's relationship with litigation, to the exclusion of other methods of dispute resolution, has resulted in recommendations which are insufficient to address fully the barriers to the use of mediation. Changing the frame to view the use, and lack of use, of mediation through the disputants' perspective, as this book does, provides the opportunity for the EU to promote cross-border mediation in a way which resonates more deeply with disputants and responds more fully to their concerns and needs.

CHAPTER 2
The EU's Efforts to Promote Cross-Border Mediation

Improving how we respond to differences is not a simple matter.[1]

§2.01 EXECUTIVE SUMMARY

This chapter examines the EU's continued efforts to promote the use of cross-border mediation within the EU. It sets out the history, and examines the content, of the key piece of legislation on such mediation: the EU Mediation Directive.[2] It also reviews the empirical research conducted by the European Commission and Parliament to identify how to improve the directive and examines the suitability of the proposals arising from such research for the directive's cross-border scope. The examination of the empirical research conducted to date and the proposals arising from such research leads to the identification of areas which would benefit from further empirical research.

§2.02 OVERVIEW OF THE EU'S MEASURES TO PROMOTE CROSS-BORDER MEDIATION

The EU has long been interested in means of settling cross-border disputes other than by way of litigation.[3] The EU's interest in this field was first evidenced in 1998 in

1. Tim Hicks, *Embodied Conflict* 155 (Routledge 2018).
2. *See* Chapter 1 at n. 29 for the full citation of the EU Mediation Directive.
3. European Commission, *Green Paper on Alternative Dispute Resolution in Civil and Commercial Law* COM (2002) 196 final (Green Paper) 9 para. 14. For the history of the European Mediation Directive *see* Jacqueline Nolan-Haley, *Evolving Paths to Justice: Assessing the EU Directive on Mediation* (October 2011) Fordham Law Legal Studies Research Paper No. 1942391, 2-5 <http://ssrn.com/abstract=1942391> (accessed 5 June 2020); Jacqueline Nolan-Haley, *Is Europe Headed Down the Primrose Path with Mandatory Mediation?*, 37 North Carolina Journal of International Law & Commercial Regulation 981, 989-991 (2012). *See also* John M. Bosnak, *The*

Vienna when, as part of the European Commission and European Council's action plan on how best to implement the provisions of the Treaty of Amsterdam on an area of freedom, security and justice, the mediation of transnational family conflicts was identified as an area meriting further examination.[4] Then, in Tampere in 1999, the European Council endorsed the Council and Commission's further action plan on how best to implement the provisions of the Treaty of Amsterdam on an area of freedom, security and justice which included, in the context of cross-border cases, a recommendation that 'alternative, extra-judicial procedures should ... be created by Member States'.[5] In 2000, in Lisbon, the European Council acknowledged the role which could be played by so-called alternative dispute resolution (ADR) in fostering consumer confidence in electronic commerce.[6] Then, in 2002, with the publication of the Green Paper on Alternative Dispute Resolution in Civil and Commercial Law[7] (Green Paper), the Commission's attention focused on cross-border civil and commercial law disputes.[8]

In the Green Paper, the European Commission noted that with the creation of the internal market, and the consequent increase in trade and the mobility of EU citizens, came a steady increase in the number of cross-border disputes being brought before the courts.[9] It acknowledged the role which ADR could play in offering access to justice against this backdrop of an increasing number of cross-border disputes.[10] ADR was, in this paper, described as no less than 'a political priority'.[11] The Green Paper was followed by the publication in 2004 of the European Code of Conduct for Mediators which sets out a number of principles, including independence, impartiality and confidentiality, by which mediators can choose to be bound.[12] Then, following a consultation on the Green Paper and the issuance of a draft directive, the EU Mediation Directive[13] was published in 2008.[14]

European Mediation Directive: More Questions than Answers? in Arnold Ingen-Housz (ed.), *ADR in Business* Vol. II 627-629 (Wolters Kluwer 2011); Guiseppe de Palo and Mary Trevor (eds), *EU Mediation, Law and Practice* 1-2 (Oxford 2012).

4. European Council and Commission, *Action Plan of the Council and the Commission on How Best to Implement the Provisions of the Treaty of Amsterdam on an Area of Freedom, Security and Justice* [1999] OJ C 19/01, para. 41(b).
5. European Council, *Tampere European Council 15 and 16 October 1999, Presidency Conclusions*, para. 30 <http://www.europarl.europa.eu/summits/tam_en.htm> (accessed 5 June 2020).
6. European Council, *Lisbon European Council 23 and 24 March 2000, Presidency Conclusions*, para. 11 <http://www.europarl.europa.eu/summits/lis1_en.htm≥ (accessed 5 June 2020).
7. Green Paper, *supra* n. 3.
8. *Ibid.*, 7, paras 5 & 6. *See also* Nolan-Haley, *Evolving Paths to Justice, supra* n. 3, at 3.
9. Green Paper, *supra* n. 3, at 7, para. 6.
10. *Ibid.*, paras 5 & 6. *See also* Nolan-Haley, *Evolving Paths to Justice, supra* n. 3, at 3.
11. Green Paper, *supra* n. 3, at 5.
12. The European Code of Conduct for Mediators (2004) <http://ec.europa.eu/civiljustice/adr/adr_ec_code_conduct_en.pdf> (accessed 20 July 2019).
13. Council Directive 2008/52/EC of 21 May 2008 on Certain Aspects of Mediation in Civil and Commercial Matters [2008] OJ L136/3 (EU Mediation Directive).
14. For an overview of the history of the EU Mediation Directive *see*: European Commission, *Study for an Evaluation and Implementation of Directive 2008/52/EC- the Mediation Directive* (16 March 2016) at 24 <https://publications.europa.eu/en/publication-detail/-/publication/bba3871d-223b-11e6-86d0-01aa75ed71a1> (accessed 5 June 2020); Simone White, *Directive 2008/52*

The broad objective of the EU Mediation Directive (which is considered in detail later in this chapter) is, through the promotion of mediation, to improve access to justice (which includes access to both judicial and extrajudicial dispute resolution methods) and thereby 'contribute to the proper functioning of the internal market'.[15] The EU Mediation Directive affords mediation special attention as the EU Mediation Directive is currently the only EU instrument on so-called ADR which addresses one particular type of ADR.[16] The EU Mediation Directive was followed by two further legislative instruments which address ADR for consumer disputes: (i) 2013/11/EU on Alternative Dispute Resolution for Consumer Disputes;[17] and (ii) Regulation (EU) No. 524/2013 on Online Dispute Resolution for Consumer Disputes.[18] These later EU instruments on ADR in the consumer sector do not make a distinction between the various processes captured within the umbrella categories of 'alternative dispute resolution' (as used in Directive 2013/11/EU) or 'out-of-court resolution' (as used in Regulation (EU) No. 524/2013). The EU Mediation Directive continues to be the only EU instrument to specifically address mediation. As with all EU directives, it prescribes the results which all EU Member States have to achieve though leaves it to each individual Member State to determine how to achieve those results.[19]

In 2011, the European Parliament raised its concerns that the EU Mediation Directive 'appeared to have produced modest results'.[20] In 2013, research commissioned by the European Commission on the implementation of the directive noted that 'stakeholders ... reported a very limited number or no cross-border mediation cases'.[21] Subsequently, in 2013, the European Parliament commissioned a study to identify the reasons why mediation is not used more frequently in cross-border (and domestic)

---

on Certain Aspects of Mediation in Civil and Commercial Matters: A New Culture of Access to Justice?, 79(1) Arbitration 52, 53 (2013).

15. EU Mediation Directive, Recital 5. *See also* European Commission, *Study for an Evaluation and Implementation of Directive 2008/52/EC*, *supra* n. 14, at 'Executive Summary'; White, *supra* n. 14, at 52: 'The EU internal market and the linked need to ensure access to justice for cross-border disputes was probably the most important impetus behind the adoption of the Directive.' *See* further European Parliament, *A European Framework for Private International Law: Current Gaps and Future Perspective* (2012) PE 462.487, 20, which describes the EU Mediation Directive as 'containing measures that are necessary for the proper functioning of the internal market'.
16. Felix Steffek, *The Relationship Between Mediation and Other Forms of Alternative Dispute Resolution* in European Parliament, *The Implementation of the Mediation Directive, Workshop 29 November 2016* (2016) PE 571.395, 47.
17. Council Directive 2013/11/EU on Alternative Dispute Resolution for Consumer Disputes and amending Regulation (EC) No. 2006/2004 and Directive 2009/22/ EC (Directive on Consumer ADR) [2013] OJ L165/63.
18. Council Regulation 524/2013 on Online Dispute Resolution for Consumer Disputes [2013] OJ 165/1.
19. Article 288, (Part 6, Title I, Chapter 3 – Legal acts of the Union) Consolidated Version of The Treaty of the Functioning of the European Union [2012] OJ C326. Article 288 states: 'A directive shall be binding, as to the result to be achieved, but shall leave to the national authorities the choice of form or methods.'
20. European Parliament, *'Rebooting' the Mediation Directive: Assessing the Limited Impact of its Implementation and Proposing Measures to Increase the Number of Mediations in the EU* (2014) PE 493.042 (Rebooting Report), 12.
21. European Commission, *Study for an Evaluation and Implementation of Directive 2008/52/EC*, *supra* n. 14, at VII & 79.

disputes.[22] That study resulted in a detailed report published in 2014, namely, 'Rebooting the Mediation Directive: Assessing the Limited Impact of Its Implementation and Proposing Measures to Increase the Number of Mediations in the EU'[23] (Rebooting Report) which included proposals to bolster the directive. Then, in August 2016, in accordance with Article 11 of the EU Mediation Directive, the Commission issued a report on the application of the directive in which – perhaps surprisingly given the acknowledged limited impact of the directive – the Commission concluded that it was not necessary to revise the directive.[24] In this report, the Commission welcomed the directive's 'EU added value'[25] of increasing national legislators' awareness of the benefits of mediation and the introduction, or extension, of mediation systems. It also acknowledged the paucity of cross-border mediations noting that 'the number of domestic cases exceeds that of cross-border cases by far'.[26] In spite of this recognition, the Commission concluded that no revisions to the directive were needed.

However, the discussions on the limited impact of the EU Mediation Directive have continued. Following the Commission's report in August 2016, in November 2016 the European Parliament published a collection of papers commissioned for a workshop on the implementation of the directive.[27] Topics addressed in this compilation include: how to achieve a balanced relationship between mediation and litigation; the relationship between mediation and the courts, and mediation and other forms of ADR; how to improve the free circulation of mediation agreements across the EU; and online mediation and dispute resolution.[28] This was then followed by the European Parliament's 'own initiative report'[29] published in 2016 which included a motion for a Parliament resolution which notes that the EU Mediation Directive's objective of encouraging the use of mediation has 'clearly not been achieved'.[30] The European Parliament's resolution arising from this report was published on 12 September 2017. The resolution directs Member States to 'step up their efforts to encourage the use of mediation in civil and commercial disputes, including through appropriate information

22. Rebooting Report, *supra* n. 20, at 11.
23. For the full citation of this report *see supra* n. 20.
24. European Commission, *Report from the Commission to the European Parliament, the Council and the European Economic and Social Committee on the Application of Directive 2008/52/EC of the European Parliament and of the Council on Certain Aspects of Mediation in Civil and Commercial Matters* COM (2016) 0542, 11.
25. *Ibid.*
26. *Ibid.*, 5.
27. European Parliament, *The Implementation of the Mediation Directive, Workshop, supra* n. 16.
28. The compilation was comprised of the following papers: Guiseppe de Palo and Leonardo D'Urso, *Achieving a Balanced Relationship Between Mediation and Judicial Proceedings*; Geoffrey Vos, *The Relationship Between Formal and Informal Justice: The Courts and Alternative Dispute Resolution*; Felix Steffek, *The Relationship Between Mediation and Others Forms of Alternative Dispute Resolution*; Carlos Esplugues and Jose Luis Iglesias, *Mediation and Private International Law: Improving Free Circulation of Mediation Agreements Across the EU*; Jin Ho Verdonschot, *Online Mediation and Dispute Resolution: Legal and Practical Issues*. *See supra* n. 16 for the full citation.
29. European Parliament, *Report on the Implementation of Directive 2008/52/EC of the European Parliament and of the Council of 21 May 2008 on Certain Aspects of Mediation in Civil and Commercial Matters* A8-0238/2017, 4.
30. *Ibid.*, 7, para. F.

campaigns ... in order to boost awareness of how useful mediation is'.[31] The resolution also directs the Commission to undertake further research in certain areas. These include the need for EU-wide quality standards for mediation, the creation of national registers of mediation proceedings and the obstacles to the 'free circulation of foreign mediated agreements'[32] across the EU.[33] Then, in November 2018, the European Parliament published a briefing requested by the JURI (Legal Affairs) Committee which continues the calls for a form of mandatory mediation.[34]

Following this summary of the EU's initiatives to promote cross-border mediation, it is clear that the EU has exerted considered effort in promoting mediation and continues to explore further ways in which to do so. This chapter now turns to consider in detail the EU Mediation Directive, the recommendations to revise the directive and the research upon which such recommendations are based.

§2.03 THE EU MEDIATION DIRECTIVE

The EU Mediation Directive, which was published in 2008, has been described as a 'light-touch, workable directive'[35] that seeks to achieve 'a minimum of harmonisation between Member States'.[36] It has also been described as providing 'a minimum legal framework to protect clients and mediators, to the benefit of mediation and without "judicializing" it'.[37] The key components of the directive will now be considered.

---

31. European Parliament, *Resolution of 12 September 2017 on the Implementation of Directive 2008/52/EC of the European Parliament and of the Council of 21 May 2008 on Certain Aspects of Mediation in Civil and Commercial Matters (the 'Mediation Directive')* [2018] OJ C337/2, para. 11.
32. *Ibid.*, para. 14.
33. *Ibid.*, paras 12-14.
34. European Parliament, *A Ten-Year Long 'EU Mediation Paradox'. When an EU Directive Needs to be More ... Directive* (2018) PE 608.847. This is discussed further later in this chapter. At the close of this section on the European Union's efforts to promote cross-border mediation, it should briefly be noted that The Council of Europe, an international human rights organisation with forty-seven Member States including the EU Member States and which is entirely separate from the European Union, has recently developed a mediation development toolkit for its members. The toolkit contains a number of standard form documents which can be used in mediation, guidance on various topics such as establishing a pilot court mediation project, judicial referral to mediation, mediator training, conduct of mediation providers and forms which can be used to gather basic data on the number and settlement rates of mediations. As this book focuses on the European Union's measures to promote cross-border mediation and the Council of Europe is entirely separate to the European Union, the work by the Council of Europe is not considered further. Further, unlike the European Union the Council of Europe cannot make laws which are binding on its Member States. More information can be found at: <https://www.coe.int/en/web/about-us/who-we-are> (accessed 5 June 2020), and <https://www.coe.int/en/web/portal/-/the-cepej-adopts-a-toolkit-to-strengthen-the-implementation-of-the-cepej-guidelines-on-mediation> (accessed 5 June 2020).
35. European Parliament, *Report on the Proposal for a Directive of the European Parliament and of the Council on Certain Aspects of Mediation in Civil and Commercial Matters* A6-0074/2007, 22.
36. European Parliament, *Lessons Learnt from the Implementation of the EU Mediation Directive: the Business Perspective* (2011) PE 453.173, 8.
37. Bosnak, *supra* n. 3, at 657. For a more recent review of the EU Mediation Directive *see* Karen Vandekerckhove, *Mediation of Cross-Border Commercial Disputes in the European Union*, in

[A] The Directive's Scope

[1] Cross-Border Disputes

An appropriate place to commence the overview of the EU Mediation Directive is its scope. The directive sets out general principles regarding the mediation of *cross-border* commercial and civil disputes, with EU Member States permitted to apply such provisions to their domestic mediation processes should they choose to do so.[38] Member States therefore are required to apply the principles in the directive to *cross-border* civil and commercial disputes, and may choose whether or not to apply such principles to their *domestic* disputes.[39]

A cross-border dispute is defined on the basis of domicile or residency: 'a cross-border dispute shall be one in which at least one of the parties is domiciled or habitually resident in a Member State other than that of any other party'.[40] Most Member States chose to apply the directive to both cross-border and domestic civil and commercial disputes. Only three Member States confined the application of the directive to cross-border disputes, namely Ireland, the UK and the Netherlands.[41] This approach was 'deplore[d]'[42] by the European Parliament in spite of the specific *cross-border* jurisdictional basis of the EU Mediation Directive.

The jurisdictional basis of the directive is found in the reference, in the opening sentence of the directive, to Article 61(c) of the Treaty establishing the European Community (EC Treaty) (now Article 67 of the Treaty of the Functioning of the European Union (TFEU)) which allows the Council of the European Union to 'adopt measures in the field of judicial cooperation in civil matters as provided for in Article 65'.[43] Article 65 of the EC Treaty (now Article 81 of the TFEU) limits such measures to those 'in the field of judicial cooperation in civil matters having cross-border implications ... in so far as necessary for the proper functioning of the internal market'.[44] A

Catherine Titi and Katia Fach Gómez (eds), *Mediation in International Commercial and Investment Disputes* 182 (Oxford University Press 2019).

38. EU Mediation Directive, Recital 8.
39. The cross-border scope of the directive was emphasised in Neil Andrews, *Mediation: International Experience and Global Trends*, 4(2) Journal of International and Comparative Law 217, 231 (2017).
40. EU Mediation Directive, Article 2. In its recent empirical study on international commercial dispute resolution, the Singapore International Dispute Resolution Academy has noted that 'International dispute resolution involves different considerations compared to domestic settings'. SIDRA, *International Dispute Resolution Survey: 2020 Final Report*, 1 <https://sidra.smu.edu.sg/sidra-international-dispute-resolution-survey-final-report-2020> (accessed 10 August 2020).
41. European Parliament, *Report on the Implementation of Directive 2008/52/EC, supra* n. 29, at 3.
42. *Ibid.*, 8.
43. Consolidated Version of The Treaty Establishing the European Community, Article 61(2) [2002] OJ C325.
44. *Ibid.*, Article 65. Machteld W. De Hoon acknowledges that under Article 65 of the EU Treaty, the EU is only allowed to take measures in civil matters that have cross-border effects. Machteld W. De Hoon, *Making Mediation Work in Europe, What's Needed Is a New Balance Between Mediation and Court Proceedings*, 20 Dispute Resolution Magazine 23 (2013-2014). Further, the European Parliament's report, *The Mediation Directive – European Implementation Assessment* (2016) PE 593.789 at 6 states 'because of the legal basis available to European legislators, only

brief journey back to the earliest draft of the directive is instructive on the directive's jurisdictional basis. The first proposal for the EU Mediation Directive was not confined to cross-border disputes and applied to 'civil and commercial matters' irrespective of their geographical reach.[45] However, the report on this first proposal noted that a majority of Member States thought that the directive should be limited to cross-border disputes due to the scope of Article 65 of the EC Treaty (now Article 81 of the TFEU) being 'measures on judicial cooperation in civil matters having cross-border implications'.[46] Accordingly, the scope of the proposed directive was altered at this early stage in the legislative process to cross-border disputes only[47] and this approach remained through to the enacted directive.

The cross-border scope of the EU Mediation Directive is one of its defining characteristics. An 'in-depth analysis' on the directive written by the European Parliamentary Research Services[48] emphasised that measures taken under Article 81 of the TFEU (formerly Article 65 of the EC Treaty), which is the jurisdictional basis of the directive, can only address civil matters having cross-border implications.[49] It notes that, in contrast, later legislation on ADR for consumer disputes is not confined to disputes with a cross-border impact due to its different jurisdictional basis, namely Article 114 of the TFEU.[50] The TFEU (also known as the Lisbon Treaty), which entered into force after the EU Mediation Directive, allows, under Article 114, for the approximation of Member States' laws for the purpose of the establishment and functioning of the internal market. Notably, this provision is not limited, in contrast to Article 81 of the TFEU, to civil matters having a cross-border impact.

[2] Civil and Commercial Disputes

While the cross-border scope of the directive is clearly defined, a detailed definition of the other key element of the directive's scope, 'civil and commercial matters', is not provided in the directive. Rather, the directive defines 'civil and commercial matters' by what this category does not include. Article 1(2) of the EU Mediation Directive states:

> This Directive shall apply, in cross-border disputes, to civil and commercial matters except as regards rights and obligations which are not at the parties'

---

cross-border disputes were covered by the Mediation Directive, although Member States were free to extend the application of its rules to purely domestic cases'.

45. European Commission, *Proposal for a Directive of the European Parliament and of the Council on Certain Aspects of Mediation in Civil and Commercial Matters* COM(2004) 718, section 1.2.
46. European Parliament, *Report on the Proposal for a Directive of the European Parliament and of the Council on Certain Aspects of Mediation in Civil and Commercial Matters* A6-0074/2007, explanatory statement at 22.
47. *Ibid.*, Amendment 4 to Recital 7(a) at pages 6-7, and Amendment 5 to Recital 8 at page 7.
48. European Parliament, *The Mediation Directive: European Implementation Assessment*, *supra* n. 44.
49. *Ibid.*, 7.
50. Council Directive 2013/11/EU of 21 May 2013 on Alternative Dispute Resolution for Consumer Disputes and amending Regulation (EC) No. 2006/2004 and Directive 2009/22/EC [2013] OJ L165/63.

disposal under the relevant applicable law. It shall not extend, in particular, to revenue, customs or administrative matters or to the liability of the State for acts and omissions in the exercise of State authority (*acta iure imperii*).

Some have rephrased Article 1(2) positively: 'The scope of this Directive is limited to cross-border disputes of civil and commercial nature concerning rights and obligations which are at the parties' disposal to decide under the relevant applicable law.'[51] Phrased in this way, the breadth of the directive's scope becomes more easily apparent. If parties are free to decide on a particular civil or commercial matter under the relevant law, then such a matter falls within the scope of the directive.

An example of the breadth of the directive's scope is its application to family disputes for matters which are at the parties' disposal to determine under the relevant law.[52] While some have stated that the directive does not apply, in any way, to family disputes,[53] the correct interpretation of Article 1(2) is that the civil and commercial scope of the directive includes family matters to the extent that parties are free to decide the particular matter.[54]

The above explanation of the directive's scope of 'civil and commercial matters' draws attention to the great breadth of the scope of the directive. The term 'cross-border civil and commercial matters' gathers together neatly, and perhaps somewhat artificially, an assortment of matters ranging from certain family law matters to more abstruse commercial matters. An awareness of this expansive scope is important for two reasons.

First, this diversity should be kept in clear sight when considering ways in which to amend and enhance the directive. In particular, it is important to consider whether such approaches would be suitable for all types of dispute which fall within this broad grouping. In short, is a one-size-fits-all approach to the promotion of mediation appropriate?[55]

---

51. Philippe Billiet and Ewa Kurlanda, *An Introduction to the Directive on Certain Aspects of Mediation in Civil and Commercial Matters* in Association for International Arbitration (ed.), *The New Directive on Mediation, First Insights* 14 (Maklu 2008).
52. Phillip Howell-Richardson, *The European Mediation Directive and some thoughts on the Principles Involved in Dealing with the Problems Surrounding Mediation Confidentiality* in Association for International Arbitration, *supra* n. 51, at 47.
53. Danny McFadden, *Developments in International Commercial Mediation: US, UK, Asia, India and EU*, 8 Contemporary Asia Arbitration Journal 299, 308 (2015): 'The Directive only applies to cross-border disputes which concern civil and commercial matters and it excludes, amongst other things, disputes in family, community law and administrative actions.' *See also* White, *supra* n. 14, at 54 which states: 'The Directive excludes family law aspects.'
54. The application of the EU Mediation Directive to family disputes is confirmed in European Commission, *Study for an Evaluation and Implementation of Directive 2008/52/EC*, *supra* n. 14, at VI: 'The Directive applies to civil and commercial matters, including family and labour disputes.' In addition, De Palo and D'Urso acknowledge that the directive includes family disputes for which the parties' rights are fully disposable. De Palo and D'Urso, *supra* n. 28, at 8. Further confirmation that the scope of the directive includes certain family matters is provided by De Hoon, *supra* n. 44, at 24 and Bosnak, *supra* n. 3, at 635.
55. By way of an example of an important difference between commercial mediation and other types of civil mediation such as consumer or employment mediation, the use of alternative dispute resolution clauses plays a far greater role in triggering the use of such types of dispute resolution processes for commercial disputes compared to consumer or employment disputes. Thomas Stipanowich and J. Ryan Lamare, *Living with ADR: Evolving Perceptions and Use of*

Secondly, the breadth of the directive's scope means that it would be unfeasible, given time and resource constraints, to address the directive's full scope in the empirical research conducted for this book. Out of the categories of civil and commercial disputes, the category of commercial disputes was chosen as this book's focus. 'Commercial' disputes are not defined in the EU Mediation Directive therefore, drawing on the definition of 'commercial' in UNCITRAL's Model Law on International Commercial Mediation and International Settlement Agreements Resulting from Mediation and also the definition used in the Global Pound Conference Series 2016-2017 (GPC Series), 'commercial' disputes are, for the purposes of this book, understood to be business-to-business disputes whether contractual or not and excluding consumer (i.e., between a business and a consumer), family, employment or criminal disputes.[56]

The choice to focus on commercial disputes has been made for a number of reasons. First, as noted earlier in this chapter, the EU Mediation Directive was adopted pursuant to Article 65 of the EC Treaty which provides that the Council of the European Union can adopt measures which are 'necessary for the proper functioning of the internal market'. As commercial activities are a key aspect of the internal market, it is reasonable to focus on disputes in this particular sector. Further, the importance of the commercial (or business-to-business) sector is suggested by the attention afforded to it by the EU. In particular, the European Commission and Parliament have commissioned four studies on the use of ADR for business-to-business disputes.[57] One of these studies, which was part of the Commission's preparation for possible new initiatives on ADR in business-to-business disputes to complement the EU Mediation Directive,[58] notes that 'addressing B2B disputes is essential as part of the improvement of Europe's business climate'.[59] In addition, in a 2011 European Parliament resolution on the

Mediation, Arbitration, and Conflict Management in Fortune 100 Corporations, 19 Harvard Negotiation Law Review 1, 35 (2014).

56. Footnote 1 UNCITRAL Model Law on International Commercial Mediation and International Settlement Agreements Resulting from Mediation (adopted 20 December 2018) states: 'commercial should be given a wide interpretation so as to cover matters arising from all relationships of a commercial nature, whether contractual or not ...'. In the Core Questions of the Global Pound Conference Series, 'commercial disputes' is defined as 'includes disputes between business entities, business partners, or business entities and public sector entities, whether arising from contract, tort or any other grounds. They include disputes between individual entrepreneurs, small and medium-size enterprises, multinationals and state-owned enterprises. It is not the intention of this GPC Series to cover family, consumer, criminal or other types of disputes': *see* cover page of the Core Questions: <https://www.imimediation.org/research/gpc/series-data-and-reports/> (accessed 5 June 2020). For more information on the Global Pound Conference Series, *see* Chapter 3 and the section 'Research by the IMI.'
57. Ecorys, *Study on the Use of Alternative Dispute Resolution for Business to Business Disputes in the European Union* JUST/2011/CONT/FW/0078/A4; European Commission, Business-to-Business Alternative Dispute Resolution in the EU (November 2012) <http://ec.europa.eu/commfront office/publicopinion/flash/fl_347_en.pdf> (accessed 5 June 2020); European Parliament, *Lessons Learnt from the Implementation of the EU Mediation Directive: the Business Perspective* (2011) PE 453.173, 8; *European Parliament, Quantifying the Cost of Not Using Mediation – a Data Analysis* (2011) PE 453.180 which sought 'to show the usefulness and cost-saving impact of mediation in commercial settings, with the ultimate goal being to ensure the growth of commercial transactions within the EU' at 10.
58. Ecorys, *supra* n. 57.
59. *Ibid.*, 3.

implementation of the EU Mediation Directive, the European Parliament specifically called for further action on increasing mediation uptake by businesses.[60]

Secondly, the scope of the EU Mediation Directive is, as explained earlier, cross-border disputes and it is this specific context with which the research conducted for this book seeks to engage. This is more feasible to do for commercial disputes than for civil (excluding commercial) disputes due to the following reasons:

- for commercial disputes, these are disputes between one type of party: businesses. For civil disputes, these would include disputes between individuals and companies and also disputes between individuals. There would therefore be a greater range of disputants with which to engage;
- a greater range of disputes falls under the category of civil disputes which could include, for example, family disputes and employment disputes. The variety of disputes is, arguably, less marked in the category of commercial disputes; and
- on an important practical note, a feasible way to explore the particular context of EU cross-border commercial disputes is to engage with multinational companies which have activities in a number of European countries and therefore may be able to offer insights into cross-border disputes involving parties from a range of European countries.[61] For civil disputes, it is less likely that one party would have such a range of experience across borders.

[3] The Reasons for the EU Mediation Directive's Broad Scope

Given the EU's choice to adopt a far-reaching scope in the directive, it would be helpful to understand the reasons for such a choice. As the analysis below will demonstrate, the Commission did not clearly identify the reasons for the directive's broad scope.

The issue of the scope of the EU Mediation Directive was identified in the Commission's Green Paper.[62] One of the questions for public consultation addressed the scope of the directive:

> Question 2: Should the initiatives to be taken be confined to defining the principles applicable to one single field (such as commercial law or family law) – field by field

60. European Parliament, *Resolution of 13 September 2011 on the Implementation of the Directive on Mediation in the Member States, its Impact on Mediation and its Take-Up by the Courts* [2013] OJ CE51/17, point 18. Consistent with the EU's focus on business disputes is the recognition by commentators that: 'the ultimate goal [of the EU Mediation Directive] being to ensure the growth of commercial transactions within the European Union'. ADR Centre, *The Cost of Non-ADR – Surveying and Showing the Actual Costs of Intra-Community Commercial Litigation* (June 2010), 5 <https://www.adrcenterfordevelopment.com/wp-content/uploads/2018/06/Survey-Data-Report.pdf> (accessed 5 June 2020).
61. Such an approach has been adopted in empirical studies on international arbitration. Empirical studies on users' attitudes towards and use of international arbitration targeted general counsel or heads of legal of corporations with cross-border activities. *See* Loukas Mistelis, *International Arbitration: Corporate Attitudes and Practices – 12 Perceptions Tested: Myths, Data and Analysis*, 15 The American Review of International Arbitration 525, 531 (2014).
62. Green Paper, *supra* n. 3.

> – and in this way *discriminate* between these different fields, or should they as far as possible extend to all the fields governed by civil and commercial law?[63] (emphasis added)

An attentive reader will note that the use of the word 'discriminate' in this question suggests the answer which the Commission was inviting. The negative connotations of the word 'discriminate' may encourage the respondent to opt for the 'non-discriminatory' approach of applying the initiative to all fields governed by civil and commercial law. It therefore appears that from the early stages of preparing the directive the Commission favoured a broad scope for the directive.

The summary of the responses to the Green Paper contains conflicting accounts of the answers to this question on the directive's scope. The 'General comments' section states:

> The Commission took an overarching approach in the Green Paper as far as its scope is concerned (it covers both civil and commercial law). *Most respondents support this approach,* noting that similarities between ADR in the different domains exist and that, furthermore, the progress achieved in certain fields should be able to benefit others. Some, however, regret that the approach was as overarching as it was, arguing that it is difficult in this context to give responses which are truly workable and coherent, and that it would have been better to limit the work to one particular field.[64] (emphasis added)

However, the summary of the responses to Question 2 of the public consultation (as stated above) offers a contrary view:

> 1. *A majority agree that the different fields should be dealt with separately.* Distinctions should therefore be made not only on the basis of field but also the different characteristics of the different types of ADR ('one size does not fit all').
> 2. Others, however, declare themselves in favour of a comprehensive approach for all fields and propose to draw up general principles to which specific rules for each field could be added.[65] (emphasis added)

Accordingly, there is a contradiction between these two sections of the summary of the responses to the Green Paper. In the general comments section, the Commission notes that most respondents favoured an overarching approach which covers both civil and commercial law matters, as proposed by the Commission. However, in the response to the specific question on this issue, the Commission states that most respondents favoured an approach under which different fields were dealt with separately.[66]

---

63. *Ibid.*, 24 & 35.
64. European Commission, *Summary of Responses to the Green Paper on Alternative Dispute Resolution in Civil and Commercial Law* (31 January 2003) JAI/19/03, 1, para. 4.
65. *Ibid.*, 3, paras 1 & 2.
66. Interestingly, in the European Economic and Social Committee's opinion on the proposed EU Mediation Directive, the committee appears to acknowledge the value of a sector – specific approach. The committee notes that mediation in consumer matters was a useful precedent for civil and commercial matters as the practice of mediation in consumer matters 'has successfully adapted to new consumer habits'. European Economic and Social Committee, *Opinion of the*

Any elaboration on the reasons for the chosen scope of the EU Mediation Directive is also absent from the directive itself. Article 1 (Objective and Scope) of the directive simply states that the directive will apply to cross-border civil and commercial disputes.[67] Accordingly, as the analysis above demonstrates, it is not possible to determine the reasoning for the chosen scope of the directive. As will be identified later in this book, there may be some factors relevant to the specific field of commercial disputes which may best be addressed with a more tailored approach to the promotion of mediation.[68] In other words, one size may not fit all.

[4] Definition of Mediation

Within this section on the scope of the EU Mediation Directive, it is also appropriate to consider how mediation is defined in the directive.

Article 3(a) of the directive defines mediation as:

> a structured process, however named or referred to, whereby two or more parties to a dispute attempt by themselves, on a voluntary basis, to reach an agreement on the settlement of their dispute with the assistance of a mediator.

This definition has aptly been described by commentators as a 'broad' and 'general' definition.[69] At its core is the focus on the efforts by the parties themselves to resolve their dispute, assisted in doing so by a mediator.[70] The central role of the parties is also conveyed in the explanation of the voluntary nature of mediation provided in Recital 13 of the directive. This recital explains that mediation is a voluntary process 'in the sense that the parties are themselves in charge of the process and may organise it as they wish and terminate it at any time'. Central to the definition of 'mediation' in the directive is the principle of party self-determination, placing parties at the helm of the process.[71]

European Economic and Social Committee on the Proposal for a Directive of the European Parliament and of the Council on Certain Aspects of Mediation in Civil and Commercial Matters [2005] OJ C286/01, para. 1.6.

67. EU Mediation Directive, Article 1(2).
68. Chapters 6, 7 and 8 identify key themes which emerged in the interviews conducted for this research regarding why disputants do and do not use mediation for their EU cross-border commercial disputes. As is identified in those chapters, some of those themes are specific to the commercial context and may not be equally applicable to the broader category of civil disputes.
69. Elizabeth Birch, *The Historical Background to the EU Directive on Mediation,* 72(1) Arbitration 57, 59 2006; Nadja Alexander, *International and Comparative Mediation* 16 (Wolters Kluwer 2009).
70. Bosnak has noted that under this definition of mediation if 'the essence of the decision rests with a third party, it is no longer a matter of mediation but of arbitration or another form of third-party decision'. Bosnak, *supra* n. 3, at 637.
71. On the principle of self-determination *see*: Nancy Welsh, *The Thinning Vision of Self-Determination in Court-Connected Mediation: The Inevitable Price of Institutionalization?,* 6 Harvard Negotiation Law Review 1, 4 (2001); Robert Bush and Joseph Folger, *Reclaiming Mediation's Future: Re-Focusing on Party Self-Determination,* 16 Cardozo Journal of Conflict Resolution 741 (2014-2015) and in particular 742; Jacqueline Nolan-Haley, *Self-Determination in International Mediation: some Preliminary Reflections,* 7 Cardozo Journal of Conflict Resolution, 277 (2005-2006); Penny Brooker, *Mediation Law* 10 (Routledge 2013). It should be noted

Linked to the definition of mediation is the definition of a 'mediator' as the definition of mediation refers to 'the assistance of a mediator'. Article 3(b) states:

> 'Mediator' means any third person who is asked to conduct a mediation in an effective, impartial and competent way, regardless of the denomination or profession of that third party in the Member State concerned and of the way in which the third person has been appointed or requested to conduct the mediation.

The role of the mediator is similarly described in broad terms as being 'effective, impartial and competent'. The European Parliament has explained that 'specific provisions would need to expressly regulate how to apply these terms'[72] (i.e., effective, impartial and competent) and that the directive 'only portrays the reasonable expectation of the parties rather than conditions for being considered a mediator'.[73]

The European Parliament has further explained that the breadth of both the definition of mediation and the associated definition of mediator 'reflect[s] the reality of the various ways in which a number of Member States had already regulated this matter'.[74] The breadth also allows for a wide application of the directive to the diversity of mediation practices.[75]

[B] The Directive's Further Substantive Provisions

Turning to the further provisions of the directive, as is standard with this particular type of legislation, the directive identifies broad objectives and leaves it to the Member States to determine how to meet these objectives.[76] The provisions of the directive can be broadly grouped into two types: (i) those which seek to enhance the quality and accessibility of mediation; and (ii) those which address the relationship between the courts and mediation.[77] The directive does not regulate the mediation process itself.[78]

---

that the definition of mediation in Article 3(a) of the European Mediation Directive excludes attempts made by the court or judge to settle the dispute during judicial proceedings.

72. European Parliament, *The Mediation Directive, European Implementation Assessment*, *supra* n. 44, at 9.
73. *Ibid.*
74. *Ibid.*
75. Billiet and Kurlanda note that '"Mediation" and "mediator" for the purposes of this Directive are broadly defined. The intention is for a wide application of the Directive and the definitions have therefore been left rather general.' Billiet and Kurlanda, *supra* n. 51, at 16. *See also* Nadja Alexander who notes 'A lack of specific and meaningful definitions in mediation regulation may not only reflect but encourage diverse mediation practices ... .' Alexander, *International and Comparative Mediation*, *supra* n. 69, at 14.
76. Treaty for the Functioning of the European Union, Article 288 states: 'A directive shall be binding, as to the result to be achieved, but shall leave to the national authorities the choice of form or methods.'
77. Phillip Howell-Richardson identifies a similar grouping for the provisions of the EU Mediation Directive. Howell-Richardson's grouping is 'those that facilitate or promote the greater use of mediation (Articles 4, 5, 9 and 10); and those that seek to establish a sound framework for the relationship between the courts and the mediation process (Articles 6, 7 and 8)'. Howell-Richardson, *supra* n. 52, at 49. However, Articles 5 and 10 arguably also fall within the second category of establishing a sound framework for the relationship between the courts and the mediation process. For a detailed review of the provisions of the EU Mediation Directive *see* Bosnak, *supra* n. 3, at 629-656.
78. This has been applauded as a wise approach. *See* Steffek, *supra* n. 16, at 66.

Regarding the first grouping (of provisions which seek to enhance the quality and accessibility of mediation), these include Article 4 (Ensuring the Quality of Mediation) and Article 9 (Information for the General Public). Article 4 calls for 'effective quality control mechanisms' including the development of, and adherence to, voluntary codes of conduct for mediators. It further calls for both the 'initial and further' training of mediators so that they may mediate in an 'effective, impartial and competent way', leaving it to the Member States to determine the type of training which may be suitable, though acknowledging the valuable contribution of the European Code of Conduct for Mediators and the importance of making this widely available to both mediators and the general public.[79]

Article 9 requires Member States to ensure that the general public can access contact information for mediators and mediation organisations. With its focus on the provision of contact information (rather than any further information on the mediators' experience and expertise), Article 9 adopts a decidedly practical, rather than promotional, approach. This approach seems rather tentative given the directive's overarching aim of promoting mediation.[80]

Regarding the second category of provisions which addresses the relationship between the courts and mediation, these form the focus of the directive. They include Article 5 (Recourse to Mediation), Article 6 (Enforceability of Agreements Resulting from Mediation) and the related Article 10 (Information on Competent Courts and Authorities), Article 7 (Confidentiality of Mediation) and Article 8 (Effect of Mediation on Limitation and Prescription Periods).

Article 5 provides that courts may 'when appropriate' invite parties to use mediation. They may also invite parties to attend an information session on the use of mediation. The directive therefore acknowledges the key role which courts can play in directing disputants to mediation, though does not require courts to mandate mediation for cross-border disputes.[81] The directive however notes that it does not prevent Member States from enacting national legislation which mandates mediation.[82] As is discussed later in this chapter, mandatory mediation, a proposal which has frequently

79. European Mediation Directive, Recital 17 states: 'The mechanisms should aim at preserving the flexibility of the mediation process and the autonomy of the parties, and at ensuring that mediation is conducted in an effective, impartial and competent way. Mediators should be made aware of the existence of the European Code of Conduct for Mediators which should also be made available to the general public on the Internet.' *See also* Jacqueline Nolan-Haley, *Is Europe Heading Down the Primrose Path with Mandatory Mediation?,* 37 North Carolina Journal of International Law and Commercial Regulation 981, 994 (2012); Bosnak, *supra* n. 3, at 643.

80. Bosnak has noted that this requirement was 'already to a large extent in place by the realization of the new EU E-Justice Portal'. Bosnak, *supra* n. 3, at 656. However the portal currently only appears to provide information on cross-border family mediators: <https://e-justice.europa.eu/content_find_a_mediator-117-en.do> (accessed 5 June 2020).

81. Nolan-Haley, *Evolving Paths to Justice, supra* n. 3, at 7; Nolan-Haley, *Primrose Path, supra* n. 79, at 994.

82. EU Mediation Directive, Recital 14 and Article 5(2). Nolan Haley, *Primrose Path, supra* n. 79, at 994. The lack of congruence between domestic and international mediation legal frameworks for cross-border mediation has been identified as potentially problematic for the use of mediation. *See* Nadja Alexander, Sabine Walsh, Martin Svatos (eds), *EU Mediation Law Handbook* 6 (Wolters Kluwer 2017).

been suggested as a way in which to improve the directive, may be less problematic for domestic disputes than for cross-border disputes which is the scope of the directive.

Article 6 on enforceability stems from the aim noted in Recital 19 that 'Mediation should not be regarded as a poorer alternative to judicial proceedings in the sense that compliance with agreements resulting from mediation would depend on the good will of the parties'. Article 6 therefore provides that Member States shall ensure that an agreement resulting from mediation may be made enforceable by a court or 'other competent authority'. Article 10 is associated with Article 6 as it requires the provision of publicly available information on the courts and competent authorities referred to in Article 6. Article 6 and Article 10 therefore address the perceived weakness of mediation as against judicial proceedings, and the court's or competent authority's role in remedying this.

Articles 7 and 8 regulate the relationship between mediation and any subsequent judicial or arbitral proceedings. Article 7 addresses confidentiality and ensures that those taking part in the mediation will not be called to give evidence in judicial or arbitral proceedings regarding information on the mediation. However, this protection does not cover all of those present at the mediation. The protection is limited to mediators and 'those involved in the administration of the mediation process'.[83] Article 7 does not expressly extend to the parties to the mediation. This limited approach to confidentiality has been criticised, such as by Kallipetis who notes: 'The inexplicable omission in Article 7 is that it is utterly silent as to the position between the parties themselves in respect to the confidentiality of the mediation process.'[84] Others, however, have recognised the significant development which the directive brings for some countries by protecting mediators from being called to give evidence in any subsequent court or arbitral proceedings, and recognise that for certain countries extending such protection to the parties would have been too ambitious.[85]

Article 8 addresses the effect of mediation on limitation and prescription periods for initiating judicial or arbitral proceedings. This seeks to ensure that parties are not prevented from pursuing judicial or arbitral proceedings due to the time spent attempting to settle their disputes by using mediation.

---

83. EU Mediation Directive, Article 7(1).
84. Michel Kallipetis, *Mediation Privilege and Confidentiality and the EU Directive* in Arnold Ingen-Housz (ed.), *ADR in Business, Practice and Issues Across Countries and Cultures* 205 (Wolters Kluwer 2011). *See also* Brooker, *supra* n. 71, at 208-213. Further, Nolan-Haley notes that the EU Mediation Directive's provision on confidentiality falls short of the confidentiality provision in the United States' Uniform Mediation Act. Nolan Haley, *Primrose Path, supra* n. 79, at 995. In addition, the minimalist approach of the directive's provision on confidentiality was criticised by many respondents to the Green Paper. Bosnak, *supra* n. 3, at 651. The directive's provision on confidentiality is considered further in Chapter 8 in light of the theme from the interview data of the importance which disputants place on confidentiality.
85. Bosnak explains: 'in view of the tradition in countries where privilege is granted to only a very small, specific group of professionals, the addition of mediated parties to the group of privileged persons was too great a leap forward. Privilege for mediators is already a considerable step, for instance, in the Netherlands, where it is considered by some to be imposed by the directive, because only recently the Supreme Court had refused it'. Bosnak, *supra* n. 3, at 651.

While Articles 7 and 8 refer to another form of dispute resolution other than judicial proceedings, namely arbitration, the emphasis in the directive is clearly on the relationship between judicial proceedings and mediation. As Steffek notes:

> The Mediation Directive defines and regulates mediation with an emphasis on the dichotomy between mediation and judicial proceedings. The relationship between mediation and other forms of alternative dispute resolution has almost no relevance in the Mediation Directive.[86]

As will be shown later in this chapter, the continued binary focus on mediation as compared to judicial proceedings continues to be seen in the limited range of proposals to improve the directive identified by the empirical research conducted to date, with these proposals continuing to focus on court-related measures to increase the use of mediation, including mandatory mediation.[87] As explained in later chapters (and principally Chapter 8), this continued focus on the relationship between mediation and litigation means that certain obstacles to the increased use of mediation appear to have been missed in the EU's continued efforts to promote the use of mediation.

§2.04 RECOMMENDATIONS TO ENHANCE THE EU MEDIATION DIRECTIVE

As stated earlier, the aim of the EU Mediation Directive was to encourage cross-border mediation in civil and commercial matters, an aim which appears to remain unaccomplished.[88] In the European Parliament's and the Commission's continued efforts to determine how to achieve this aim, a significant amount of research has been commissioned, including empirical research. Such research has focused predominantly on: (i) determining whether the directive has been transposed in Member States; and (ii) identifying proposals to achieve the directive's aim of increasing mediation across the EU.

Regarding the transposition of the directive, this is comprehensively addressed in the European Commission's 'Study for an evaluation and implementation of Directive 2008/52/EC – the Mediation Directive', originally published in October 2013 and updated in March 2016.[89] The conclusion of this study on the quality of the transposition of the directive is generally positive, noting that 'the national legal frameworks in place to regulate the mediation systems do not pose important issues of conformity

86. Steffek, *supra* n. 16, at 49.
87. As is addressed later in the chapter, in addition to the proposal of mandatory forms of mediation, a further proposal is a quota of the number of mediations compared to judicial proceedings.
88. The European Parliament's, Rebooting Report, *supra* n. 20, captures the lack of success of this directive in the report's title: 'Rebooting the Mediation Directive: Assessing the *Limited* Impact of its Implementation and Proposing Measures to Increase the Number of Mediations in the EU' (emphasis added). *See also* page 11 of this report and European Commission, *Study for an Evaluation and Implementation of Directive 2008/52/EC, supra* n. 14, at VII which states: 'stakeholders ... reported a very limited number or no cross-border mediation cases'.
89. In addition, for detailed reviews of the mediation laws in the EU Member States *see* Alexander, Walsh and Svatos, *supra* n. 82, and De Palo and Trevor, *supra* n. 3.

with the Mediation Directive'.[90] A similar conclusion was also offered by the European Parliament which acknowledged that 'its [the Mediation Directive's] implementation throughout the European Union has been rather successful and unproblematic'.[91] The Parliament also acknowledged that in some countries the directive brought about limited changes given that provisions for mediation already existed in such countries, while in other countries which did not have a framework for mediation the directive resulted in more significant change.[92] As the transposition of the directive into the legal systems of the Member States was satisfactory, the EU's attention turned to identifying proposals to enhance the directive.

Engaging with stakeholders through empirical research plays an essential role in making good law[93] and empirical research has played a significant role in identifying proposals to improve the EU Mediation Directive. The most notable pieces of empirical research conducted to date on how to enhance the directive are the Rebooting Report[94] and the Commission's public online consultation conducted from 18 September to 18 December 2015.[95] A continued focus emerging from this body of empirical research is on court encouragement of mediation and, in particular, calls for mandatory mediation. These calls have continued to be made in the more recent collection of analyses on the implementation of the Mediation Directive requested by the European Parliament[96] and in a European Parliament briefing on the EU Mediation Directive[97] and therefore continue to be relevant for consideration.

---

90. European Commission, *Study for an Evaluation and Implementation of Directive 2008/52/EC, supra* n. 14, at VI.
91. European Parliament, *The Mediation Directive – European Implementation Assessment, supra* n. 44, at 1.
92. *Ibid.*, 26.
93. Steffek, *supra* n. 16, at 62.
94. Rebooting Report, *supra* n. 20. The European Commission's, *Study for an Evaluation and Implementation of Directive 2008/52/EC, supra* n. 14 also includes empirical research conducted but its focus is on evaluating the implementation of the directive (*see* IV). Earlier empirical work was also conducted for the Rebooting Report by the European Parliament, *Quantifying the Cost of Not Using Mediation – a Data Analysis, supra* n. 57. The same organisation which authored the European Parliament's, Rebooting Report, *supra* n. 20, authored this research, namely ADR Centre. It adopts a similar approach to the Rebooting Report in that it focuses on the cost and time savings which mediation can offer compared to litigation and involved a survey of 'Mediation experts' (*see*, in particular, page 11 of the report, and on the meaning of this term *see* later in this chapter at pages 59-60). However it does so on a smaller scale, focusing on two EU Member States (Belgium and Italy) rather than all of the EU Member States, as the Rebooting report does. As such, it can be regarded as a precursor to the European Parliament's Rebooting Report, *supra* n. 20.
95. The link to the Commission's consultation document is no longer available but the questions are available in Law Society of England & Wales, *Response of the Law Society of England and Wales to the Public Consultation on the Application of Directive 2008/52/EC* <http://www.lawsocieties.eu/download?ac=19208> (accessed 5 June 2020).
96. European Parliament, *The Implementation of the Mediation Directive, Workshop, supra* n. 16. *See* in particular Guiseppe de Palo and Leonardo D'Urso, *Achieving a Balanced Relationship Between Mediation and Judicial Proceedings, supra* n. 28, at 7. As is discussed later in this chapter, this paper recommends a 'required initial mediation session'.
97. European Parliament, *A Ten-Year-Long 'EU Mediation Paradox', supra* n. 34. The author of this report, Guiseppe De Palo, is the same author of the Rebooting report. For discussion on the proposal of mandatory mediation *see*: Carrie Menkel-Meadow, *Variations in the Uptake of and Resistance to Mediation Outside of the United States,* [2015] University of California, Irvine

[A] The Main Recommendations of the Rebooting Report

[1] Mandatory Mediation

The main proposal suggested by the Rebooting Report to 'reboot' the EU Mediation Directive is a form of mandatory mediation:

> the overall suggestion coming out of the study, to increase significantly the use of mediation in the EU, appears relatively straightforward: a regulatory intervention introducing, not simply allowing, a mitigated model of mandatory mediation, at least in certain categories of cases.[98]

The report elaborates on what is meant by 'mitigated' in this context. It refers to two types of 'mitigated forms of mandatory mediation':[99] 'compulsory attendance at information sessions and mandatory mediation with the ability to opt-out if litigants do not intend to continue with the process'.[100] Of these two types of 'mitigated' models of mandatory mediation, the report favours mandatory mediation with an opt-out[101] under which the first meeting between the parties and the mediator is already part of the mediation process.[102] This model has more recently been described as a requirement:

> that litigants make a serious and reasonable initial effort at mediation. During this initial stage, they will be allowed the freedom to decide whether or not to continue their effort at mediation (so called 'required mediation with easy opt-out').[103]

In essence, entry into the mediation process is mandated and parties are free to leave the mediation process, should they wish to do so. Perhaps the word 'opt-out' is included to make what may be considered by some to be an unpalatable proposal more appetising, with mandatory mediation being a controversial and polarising topic.[104]

School of Law, Research Paper No. 2015-80, at 189 <https://papers.ssrn.com/sol3/papers.cfm?abstract_id=2658903> (accessed 5 June 2020). At 196 Menkel-Meadow, citing the Rebooting report states: 'the European Union may soon debate whether to mandate mediation ... in some contexts'; James R. Coben, *Barnacles, Aristocracy and Truth Denial: Three Not So Beautiful Aspects of Contemporary Mediation*, 16 Cardozo Journal of Conflict Resolution 779, 780 (2014-2015); Guiseppe de Palo and Romina Canessa, *Sleeping? Comatose? Only Mandatory Consideration of Mediation Can Awake Sleeping Beauty in the European Union*, 16 Cardozo Journal of Conflict Resolution 713, 724 (2014-15); Kimberlee K. Kovach, *The Mediation Coma: Purposeful or Problematic*, 16 Cardozo Journal of Conflict Resolution 755, 773 at footnote 93 (2014-2015).

98. Rebooting Report, *supra* n. 20, at 9.
99. *Ibid.*, 163.
100. *Ibid.*
101. *Ibid.*,164.
102. European Parliament, *A Ten-Year-Long 'EU Mediation Paradox'*, *supra* n. 34, at 5.
103. *Ibid.*, 1 and 5.
104. For example, Nolan-Haley stated: 'Europe should step back, and be more cautious about following what could end up to be a primrose path to justice. The central ideology of mediation is voluntariness. Tampering with this principle could play havoc with access to justice'. Nolan-Haley, *Primrose Path, supra* n. 79, at 985. *See also* Hazel Genn, *What Is Civil Justice for? Reform, ADR, and Access to Justice*, 24 Yale Journal of Law and the Humanities 397, 406 & 415-417 (2012); Trina Grillo, *The Mediation Alternative: Process Dangers for Women*, 100(6)

However, the inclusion of the word 'opt-out' does little to soften the mandatory nature of this proposal. The word 'opt-out' is redundant as this is the very nature of the mediation process: parties can withdraw from the mediation at any stage they choose.[105] All that can be mandated is entry into the process and not how the process will conclude.[106] In an apparent attempt to address this point, the latest reference to this proposal in a briefing for the European Parliament refers to an 'easy' opt-out as it is described as 'required mediation with easy opt-out'.[107] In explaining the addition of 'easy', the report states:

> Of course, every participant in any mediation can opt out ... But under ordinary circumstances, opting out can result in such costs as accusations of bad faith or loss of fees paid up front. In an easy opt-out model, such consequences would not result from opting out.[108]

However, no explanation is provided for how such consequences might be avoided, i.e., how this *easy* opt-out could be achieved. Perhaps the point regarding the avoidance of a loss of fees paid upfront is suggesting that mandatory mediation should be free to the parties, which then raises the question of who would fund such mediation. Or, with the emphasis on 'fees paid upfront' is the proposal suggesting that the fees be paid after the parties opt-out of the mediation? The emphasis on 'upfront' fees rather than fees in general is perplexing – presumably to the parties the key issue is a loss of fees whether they are paid before or after the mediation. Further, as regards the point about an 'easy' opt-out approach avoiding any accusations of bad faith, how this could be achieved – if indeed it can be – is not clear.

It is interesting to note that in presenting the proposal for mandatory mediation with opt-out, frequent references are made to the Italian system as a positive example of such a model.[109] There is, however, an aspect of the Italian system which is troubling. As explained in the country summary of Italy in the Rebooting Report:

The Yale Law Journal 1545, 1549, 1581 and 1610 (1991); Nancy Welsh, *The Thinning Vision of Court Annexed Mediation: The Inevitable Price of Institutionalization?*, 6 Harvard Negotiation Law Review 1, 18, footnote 68 (2001) (citing various commentators). *See* Debbie De Girolamo, *Rhetoric and Civil Justice: A Commentary on the Promotion of Mediation Without Conviction in England and Wales*, 35(2) Civil Justice Quarterly 162, 164 (2016) for a summary of the arguments for and against mandatory mediation. *See also* Bryan Clark, *Lawyers and Mediation* 144-148 (Springer 2012).

105. Nolan-Haley notes: 'The central ideology of mediation is voluntariness'. Nolan-Haley, *Primrose Path*, *supra* n. 79 at 985. This point is acknowledged by the author of the Rebooting report who states 'Of course, every participant in any mediation can opt out; that idea is not, in itself, new or revolutionary.' *See* European Parliament, *A Ten-Year-Long 'EU Mediation Paradox'*, *supra* n. 34, at 5.
106. Sue Prince, *Mandatory Mediation: the Ontario Experience*, 26 Civil Justice Quarterly 79, 91 (2007). Numerous writers have been critical of the Rebooting report's proposal of mandatory mediation, including Coben, *supra* n. 97 at 780 and Bush and Folger, *supra* n. 71, at 741.
107. European Parliament, *A Ten-Year-Long 'EU Mediation Paradox'*, *supra* n. 34, at 1 and 3.
108. *Ibid.*, 5, footnote 17.
109. *See*, for example, European Parliament, *Rebooting Report*, *supra* n. 20, at 162; De Palo and D'Urso, *Achieving a Balanced Relationship Between Mediation and Judicial Proceedings*, *supra* n. 28, at 13, though in this document the term 'required initial mediation session' is used rather

> Pursuant to the new mediation rules that recently went into effect, parties are given an incentive to continue with the mediation process. Upon a party's withdrawal from the mediation, a mediator has the authority to propose a solution to the dispute. If this is rejected by one of the parties and the case subsequently goes to trial, the judge may shift all mediation and litigation costs onto the rejecting party if the judgment is consistent with the mediator's proposed solution.[110]

The potential penalties of having to pay all of the mediation and litigation costs, should the judge's decision concur with the mediator's rejected proposed solution,[111] sit very uncomfortably with the softener implied by the term 'mandatory mediation with *opt-out*' and indeed, more recently, *easy* opt-out.[112] This aspect of the Italian model is particularly disconcerting given the potential cost penalties which could be imposed on parties for simply choosing to withdraw from the mediation. It restricts one of the fundamental principles of mediation, as recognised in the EU Mediation Directive, that mediation is a voluntary process which parties may choose to terminate at any time.[113] A model of mandatory mediation with opt-out which, inspired by the Italian approach, were to include the type of potential penalties for rejecting a mediator's proposal outlined above would clearly be incompatible with the EU Mediation Directive's recognition of the parties' right to terminate the mediation at any time.

In addition, the continued calls for mandatory mediation as a way in which to boost the directive raise, more broadly, a number of concerns in relation to the directive's cross-border scope, as will now be considered.

than 'mandatory mediation with opt-out'; European Parliament, *A Ten-Year-Long 'EU Mediation Paradox'*, *supra* n. 34, at 1 and 6. In particular, at 6 it is stated: 'It is also important to note that the Italian mechanism has been lauded as a model to follow.'

110. Rebooting Report, *supra* n. 20, at 41. The 'new mediation rules' referred to in this quotation are understood to be the mediation rules under Legislative Decree 28. It is not known whether these rules provide for costs sanctions should all parties (rather than only one party) reject the mediator's proposal and proceed to trial.
111. As an official translation of Legislative Decree 28 is not available in English this section draws upon the summary offered in the Rebooting Report and quoted at text to (n. 110). *See also* Rafal Morek, *Mandatory Mediation in Italy – Reloaded* <http://mediationblog.kluwerarbitration.com/2013/10/09/mandatory-mediation-in-italy-reloaded/?doing_wp_cron=1591807975.751749038696289062500> (accessed 5 June 2020), which confirms the summary provided in the Rebooting Report regarding the cost penalty should the judge's opinion be consistent with the mediator's proposal. *See also* Alexander, Walsh, and Svatos, *supra* n. 82, at 479-480.
112. Interestingly, the lead author of the various documents which propose the model of mandatory mediation with opt-out, Guiseppe de Palo, has described this potential penalty as 'a controversial mechanism to ensure that parties think twice before withdrawing from mediation without reaching a settlement'. Guiseppe de Palo, *Mandatory Mediation Is Back in Italy with New Parliamentary Rules*, 22 October 2013 <http://www.mondoadr.it/cms/articoli/mandatory-mediation-italy-parliamentary-rules.html> (accessed 5 June 2020).
113. EU Mediation Directive, Recital 13 states: 'The mediation provided for in this Directive should be a voluntary process in the sense that the parties are themselves in charge of the process and may organize it as they wish and terminate it at any time.'

[a] *Problematic Nature of Mandatory Mediation Proposal to Increase EU Cross-Border Mediation*

While the continued proposals of mandating mediation in order to reboot the directive do not specify the type of mediations to which they will apply (i.e., cross-border or domestic), given the cross-border scope of the directive, its jurisdiction under Article 65 of the EC Treaty (now Article 81 of the TFEU)[114] and the fact that some Member States have only implemented the directive for cross-border mediations, the suitability of this proposal for *cross-border* mediations in particular must be considered. Put another way, any revision to the EU Mediation Directive which provides for mandatory mediation could only apply to cross-border mediation given the directive's specific cross-border scope. There are a number of reasons why such a proposal for mandatory mediation is particularly problematic for cross-border disputes.

First, in order for mediation to be mandated it must first reach the realms of the court. Under the mandatory mediation proposal to enhance the EU Mediation Directive, before filing a dispute with the courts, parties would be required to take part in an initial mediation session.[115] Accordingly, the courts would play a key role as they would direct parties to attempt mediation before registering their dispute with the court. It is this reliance on the courts to direct parties to mediation which raises concern regarding the suitability of such a measure for cross-border disputes, and in particular cross-border commercial disputes which are the focus of this book, given doubt as to the extent to which courts are used for such disputes.[116] International arbitration is recognised as being the most popular dispute resolution method for cross-border commercial disputes.[117] Indeed, empirical research by the Singapore International Dispute Resolution Academy (SIDRA) on international commercial dispute resolution found that 'International commercial arbitration remained the dispute resolution mechanism of choice.'[118] Similarly, research by Queen Mary University of London has identified that the preferred method – and by a significant margin – of dispute resolution for cross-border disputes is international arbitration, and has identified that corporations are the main users of international arbitration.[119] If corporate parties

114. *See* §2.03[A][1] on the EU Mediation Directive's scope for more detail on the jurisdictional basis of the directive.
115. *See* European Parliament, *A Ten-Year-Long 'EU Mediation Paradox'*, *supra* n. 34, at 6.
116. *See* §2.03[A][2] for the reasons why this study focuses on cross-border commercial disputes.
117. S.I. Strong, *Realizing Rationality: An Empirical Assessment of International Commercial Mediation*, 73 Washington & Lee Law Review 1973, 1976 (2016).
118. SIDRA, *supra* n. 40, at 5.
119. In the 2018 study on international arbitration by the School of International Arbitration, Queen Mary University of London, 97% of respondents identified arbitration as their preferred method of dispute resolution, either on its own (48%) or together with ADR (49%). In marked contrast, only 1% of respondents identified litigation as their preferred method of cross-border dispute resolution. School of International Arbitration, Queen Mary University of London, *2018 International Arbitration Survey: The Evolution of International Arbitration*, 5 <http://www.arbitration.qmul.ac.uk/research/2018/> (accessed 5 June 2020). *See also* School of International Arbitration, Queen Mary University of London, *International Arbitration: Corporate Attitudes and Practices 2008*, 3 <http://www.arbitration.qmul.ac.uk/research/2008/#d.en.493188> (accessed 5 June 2020) where the report states that 74% of arbitral proceedings involved only private corporations.

largely rely on arbitration rather than on the courts for the resolution of their cross-border commercial disputes, a system of mandatory mediation may not be particularly effective at increasing the use of cross-border commercial mediation. This suggests again that a one-size-fits-all approach for both commercial and civil disputes may not be effective.

Secondly, the proposal to mandate mediation for *cross-border* disputes may also be problematic in light of its consistency with Article 6(1) of The European Convention for the Protection of Human Rights and Fundamental Freedoms (ECHR). Article 6(1) of the ECHR guarantees the right to a fair and public hearing within a reasonable time by an independent and impartial tribunal established by law. In *Rosalba Alassini v Telecom Italia SpA*[120] the Court of Justice of the European Union considered whether a compulsory mediation scheme (under which parties had to mediate before commencing court proceedings) required under Italian law would infringe Article 6(1) of the ECHR. The court held that such a scheme did not infringe Article 6(1) of the ECHR. It is important to emphasise that in reaching this conclusion, the court noted that compatibility of a mandatory mediation procedure with Article 6(1) of the ECHR was dependent on a number of conditions, including that the procedure does not 'result in substantial delay for the purposes of bringing legal proceedings'[121] and that the costs for such a procedure are not 'significant'.[122] If the EU were to mandate mediation across the broad category of civil and commercial matters and across all the Member States, there would be a considerable challenge in ensuring that the multitude of mandatory cross-border mediation schemes across the various EU Member States did not result in substantial delay nor significant costs in order to be compatible with Article 6(1) of the ECHR.

First, these two conditions of no substantial delay and no significant costs may prove more difficult to satisfy in the cross-border context given that cross-border mediation, involving parties from different jurisdictions, may well be more costly and time-consuming than domestic mediation.[123] Secondly, in those countries in the EU where the court systems are efficient, such as Germany[124] and

120. Joined Cases C-317/08 and C320/08 *Rosalba Alassini and others v Telecom Italia SpA and others* [2010] ECR 1- 02213. For a summary of this case *see* Lorna McGregor, *Alternative Dispute Resolution and Human Rights: Developing a Rights-Based Approach through the ECHR*, 26(3) European Journal of International Law 607, 624 (2015). *See also* De Palo and D'Urso, *Achieving a Balanced Relationship Between Mediation and Judicial Proceedings*, *supra* n. 28 at 25.
121. *Rosalba Alassini*, *supra* n. 120, at para. 55.
122. *Ibid.*, para. 57. The conditions established in Alassini regarding the compatibility of a mandatory mediation scheme with Article 6(1) of the ECHR were later applied by the Court of Justice of the European Union in Case C-75/16 *Livio Menini & another v Banco Popolare Società Cooperativa* Judgment of the Court (First Chamber) (14 June 2017).
123. Strong notes: 'savings of time and money may be even less likely to occur in international commercial matters, where there is a tendency for counsel to conduct mediations like "mini arbitrations."' S.I. Strong, *Beyond International Commercial Arbitration? The Promise of International Commercial Mediation*, 45 Washington University Journal of Law & Policy 11, 16 (2014).
124. Nadja Alexander (ed.), *Global Trends in Dispute Resolution*, Vol. 1 (Kluwer 2006). In Chapter 9 on Germany, reference is made to Germany's efficient legal system. At 256 the authors state 'In fact in Germany it may, in some cases, be more expensive to mediate a case successfully than to take it to court.'

Belgium,[125] a mandatory mediation scheme may, under the conditions established in *Alassini*, breach Article 6(1) of the ECHR given that it would be easier to establish that mandatory mediation resulted in 'substantial' delay or 'significant' cost relative to the efficiency of the court proceedings. This is all the more likely for the mandating of cross-border mediation in such countries where the court systems are efficient given that, as noted above, cross-border mediations can be more lengthy and costly than domestic disputes.

Thirdly, it should be noted that even if forms of mandatory mediation were not to be in breach of Article 6(1) of the ECHR, they might breach individual Member State's constitutions. Romania offers a relevant recent example where a requirement to simply attend a mediation information session was held to be unconstitutional.[126] In order for mandatory mediation to be an effective way in which to increase the use of cross-border mediation in the EU, mandatory mediation would have to apply in all of the EU Member States from which parties may engage in cross-border dealings.

The issues identified above regarding the compatibility of mandatory mediation schemes with Article 6(1) of the ECHR and also the constitutions of certain Member States suggest that the proposal of mandatory mediation is unlikely to be implementable across all EU Member States. Accordingly, the main proposal arising from the

---

125. Menkel-Meadow notes: 'Belgium ... has had a relatively efficient legal system with less delay in litigation time.' Menkel-Meadow, *Variations in the Uptake of and Resistance to Mediation*, *supra* n. 97, at 205.

126. European Parliament, *A Ten-Year-Long 'EU Mediation Paradox'*, *supra* n. 34, at 10. *See also*, Augustin Farcas, *Implications of the Constitutional Court Decision No. 266/2014 in the Field of Dispute Resolution Through Mediation* (10 November 2014). Romanian Case Law Review issue 5/2014 <https://ssrn.com/abstract=2520935> (accessed 5 June 2020). Further, in Greece an earlier law requiring mandatory mediation was held to be unconstitutional because of the disproportionate costs it would impose on the disputants, however a further law requiring mandatory mediation has more recently been implemented. *See* European Parliament, *A Ten-Year-Long 'EU Mediation Paradox'*, *supra* n. 34, at 10. *See also* regarding the later law on mandatory mediation in Greece, Vassiliki Koumpli, *Greece: Institutionalizing Mediation Through Mandatory Initial Mediation Session (Law 4640/2019)*, Kluwer Mediation Blog (20 January 2020) <http://mediationblog.kluwerarbitration.com/2020/01/20/greece-institutionalizing-mediation-through-mandatory-initial-mediation-session-law-4640-2019/?doing_wp_cron=1591811097.9079520702362060546875> (accessed 5 June 2020). *See also* Haris Meidanis, *Greece: Mediation Going Compulsory: And They Lived Happily Ever After?* Kluwer Mediation Blog (19 February 2020) <http://mediationblog.kluwerarbitration.com/2020/02/19/greece-mediation-going-compulsory-and-they-lived-happily-ever-after/?doing_wp_cron=1591810847.3130519390106201171875> (accessed 5 June 2020). In addition, in the UK, the Civil Justice Council ADR Working Group has noted that it does not support the introduction of mandatory mediation (*see* Civil Justice Council, *ADR and Civil Justice Final Report* (November 2018) at section 2.6 <https://www.judiciary.uk/wp-content/uploads/2018/12/CJC-ADR-Report-FINAL-Dec-2018.pdf> (accessed 5 June 2020). It is also interesting to note that the compulsory use of mediation has only been introduced in a very small number of Member States and for specific cases. Compulsory mediation has been introduced in Croatia for family matters, Hungary for child-custody, Austria for the anticipated termination of apprenticeship contracts, and Italy for some disputes. *See* European Parliament, *The Mediation Directive – European Implementation Assessment*, *supra* n. 44, at 14 & 15. The disputes for which mandatory mediation applies in Italy are disputes on: 'condominium, real rights, division, inheritance, family agreements, lease, loan, rental companies, damages resulting from medical and sanitary liability and from defamation by means of press or other means of advertising, insurance, banking and financial contracts'. *See* European Commission, *Study for an Evaluation and Implementation of Directive 2008/52/EC*, *supra* n. 14, at 32.

report, of mandating mediation (which has been repeated in more recent publications), raises particular challenges for the *cross-border* context of the EU Mediation Directive.

Fourthly, it is interesting to note that data obtained in an empirical study on international commercial mediation suggests that 'judicially mandated mediations were particularly rare in the international commercial context'.[127] The study does not elaborate on the reasons for this particular rarity and it would be helpful to conduct further research to identify and explore these. However, this finding could suggest that there might be more difficulty in mandating mediation at a cross-border level, such as a greater reluctance from the judiciary to mandate mediation for commercial cross-border disputes compared to national disputes.

Fifthly, a further challenge arising from a proposal to mandate mediation at cross-border level in Europe is the variation in how mediation is practised across Member States. As discussed above, the EU Mediation Directive defines mediation broadly which enables it to cover a variety of approaches to mediation.[128] As identified by Stipanowich, this broad approach means that the directive 'did not clarify whether mediation was a clearly understood process, or whether it may have varied in practice from country to country and if so, how'.[129] This point is further illustrated by the use of the terms 'mediation' and 'conciliation' across Europe which may be used interchangeably though can have the same or very different meanings.[130] Nolan-Haley notes that some consider conciliation to be an evaluative form of mediation while others view it as a type of facilitative mediation,[131] identifying this 'definitional concern' as a challenge to the establishment of mandatory mediation regimes in Member States.[132]

This is a challenge which is particularly relevant to mandatory mediation regimes for cross-border disputes given the parties' potential exposure to a variety of types of mediation. If there were to be a requirement on parties to mediate their EU cross-border disputes, parties are unlikely to welcome disparate approaches to mediation. In other words, they would presumably appreciate consistency in the type of process in which they are required to participate. For example, should a party be compelled to mediate in a country where the common approach is of facilitative mediation (e.g., Austria)[133] and then find itself compelled to mediate in another country where a more evaluative process may be more common (e.g., Estonia),[134] such inconsistency may well frustrate the parties and do little for the promotion of cross-border mediation. Accordingly, the

---

127. S.I. Strong, *Use and Perception of International Commercial Mediation and Conciliation: A Preliminary Report on Issues Relating to the Proposed UNCITRAL Convention on International Commercial Mediation and Conciliation*, University of Missouri, School of Law Legal Studies Research Paper Series 2014-28 (2014), 19 <http://ssrn.com/abstract=2526302> (accessed 5 June 2020).
128. *See* §2.03[A][4] on the definition of mediation in the EU Mediation Directive.
129. Thomas Stipanowich, *The International Evolution of Mediation: A Call for Dialogue and Deliberation*, 46 Victoria University of Wellington Law Review 1191, 1197 at footnote 33 (2015).
130. Nolan-Haley, *Primrose Path*, *supra* n. 79, at 1009.
131. *Ibid.*, 1010.
132. *Ibid.*, 1009.
133. Alexander, Walsh and Svatos, *supra* n. 82, at 39.
134. *Ibid.*, 243.

different understandings across Member States of 'mediation' present a further challenge in the cross-border context for the continued calls to mandate mediation.

In addition, even if the proposal for mandatory mediation relates to domestic rather than cross-border disputes, though it must be emphasised that domestic disputes do not fall within the specific scope of the directive, it is not clear how a system of mandatory mediation for domestic disputes would necessarily lead to an increased usage of mediation in cross-border disputes. Here it should be acknowledged that while proposals to encourage the use of domestic mediations might be a helpful, and general, starting point for the promotion of mediation across borders, such proposals appear to have been insufficient to date to achieve a notable uptake in cross-border mediations, as is addressed later in this chapter.[135] It cannot therefore be assumed that an increase in the use of domestic mediation as a result of mandatory mediation would necessarily lead to an increase in the levels of cross-border mediation. In any event, mandating mediation for domestic disputes is beyond the scope of the directive and therefore any proposal for mandatory mediation as a proposal to enhance the directive could only apply to cross-border disputes.

Finally, and on a more philosophical note, some have cautioned against a move to mandatory mediation, be it for cross-border or domestic disputes, due to the departure this would bring from mediation's core principle of voluntariness.[136] In particular, concern has been expressed that compulsion into mediation could extend to compulsion to settle.[137] Such a concern appears relevant given that the proposal to mandate mediation in order to enhance the EU Mediation Directive has been inspired by the Italian model of mandatory mediation[138] with, as described earlier, its troubling mediator settlement proposal approach and its associated penalties. The inclusion of such an approach in any mandatory mediation regime at EU level would raise

135. *See* later in this chapter at text to (n. 171)-(n. 175) which discusses the EU Mediation Directive's impact on raising awareness of mediation at the national level though the number of cross-border mediation remains low. It also identifies literature which suggests that context matters and that there may be factors which affect the use of mediation which are specific to cross-border mediation and which do not equally apply to domestic mediation.

136. Nolan-Haley, *Primrose Path, supra* n. 79, at 985; Menkel-Meadow, *Variations in the Uptake of and Resistance to Mediation, supra* n. 97, at 208; Jacqueline Nolan-Haley, *Consent in Mediation,* 14 Dispute Resolution Magazine 4 (2007-2008). *See also* Marian Roberts, *Developing the Craft of Mediation* (Jessica Kingsley Publishers 2007) 101. Roberts' research on mediators' perspectives revealed that there was a unanimous consensus among the mediators who were interviewed that mediation should only be voluntary. However, others argue that mandatory mediation would not be counter to mediation's core principle of voluntariness as compelling parties to mediate does not force them to continue with the mediation nor to settle. *See* Sue Prince, *Mandatory Mediation: The Ontario Experience,* 26 Civil Justice Quarterly 79, 91 (2007); De Girolamo, *Rhetoric and Civil Justice, supra* n. 104, at 164; Further, for a summary of the arguments for and against mandatory mediation *see* De Girolamo, *Rhetoric and Civil Justice, supra* n. 104, at 164.

137. Lucy V. Katz, *Compulsory Alternative Dispute Resolution and Voluntarism: Two-Headed Monster or Two Sides of the Coin?,* 1 Journal of Dispute Resolution 22, 41 (1993).

138. *See* Rebooting Report, *supra* n. 20, at 162; De Palo and D'Urso, *Achieving a Balanced Relationship Between Mediation and Judicial Proceedings, supra* n. 28, at 13, though in this document the term 'required initial mediation session' is used rather than 'mandatory mediation with opt-out'; European Parliament, *A Ten-Year-Long 'EU Mediation Paradox', supra* n. 34, at 1 and 6.

significant concerns about parties being compelled not only to enter into the mediation but to settle for an outcome not of their free choice. This is an example of how the details of any mandatory mediation scheme must be carefully considered in order to determine whether compulsion is confined to entry into the mediation or whether it extends in any way beyond entry into mediation to settling during the mediation process.

The above points demonstrate that one of the key proposals arising from the empirical research conducted for the Rebooting Report, namely mandatory mediation with opt-out, is particularly problematic for the specific cross-border scope of the EU Mediation Directive. The same issue also arises for the alternative proposal arising from such empirical research, as will now be addressed.

[2] Target Number of Mediations

A further key suggestion arising from the empirical research conducted for the Rebooting Report, which has more recently been proposed again to the European Parliament,[139] is the imposition of a 'Balanced Relationship Target Number'.[140] Such a target number would prescribe the number of mediations compared to court cases to be achieved by each Member State, with a suggested ratio of at least one mediation for every two court cases.[141] It is a proposal which has attracted emphatic criticism. For example, Menkel-Meadow has noted:

> The recommendations of the report actually go so far as to suggest possible 'quotas' or specific guidelines for the ratios of mediated cases to litigated cases within any legal system. I am deeply opposed to and sceptical of these suggestions.[142]

The imposition of such a target is drawn from a literal, and seemingly forced, interpretation of Article 1(1) of the EU Mediation Directive. Article 1(1) states:

> The objective of this Directive is to facilitate access to alternative dispute resolution and to promote the amicable settlement of disputes by encouraging the use of mediation and *by ensuring a balanced relationship between mediation and judicial proceedings.* (emphasis added)

The proponents of the 'balanced relationship target number' argue that the EU Mediation Directive therefore requires Member States to achieve this balanced relationship between mediation and judicial proceedings.[143] They add that a failure to

139. European Parliament, *A Ten-Year-Long 'EU Mediation Paradox'*, *supra* n. 34, at 6-8.
140. Rebooting Report, *supra* n. 20, at 10. *See also* De Palo and D'Urso, *Achieving a Balanced Relationship Between Mediation and Judicial Proceedings*, *supra* n. 28; European Parliament, *A Ten-Year-Long 'EU Mediation Paradox'*, *supra* n. 34, at 6-8.
141. European Parliament, *A Ten-Year-Long 'EU Mediation Paradox'*, *supra* n. 34, at 7.
142. Menkel-Meadow, *Variations in the Uptake of and Resistance to Mediation*, *supra* n. 97, at 195 at footnote 19.
143. Rebooting Report, *supra* n. 20, at 10; De Palo and D'Urso, *Achieving a Balanced Relationship Between Mediation and Judicial Proceedings*, *supra* n. 28, at 8 & 18; European Parliament, *A Ten-Year-Long 'EU Mediation Paradox'*, *supra* n. 34, at 6.

determine a clear target number for that relationship and/or the failure to meet that target would amount to a lack of compliance with the directive.[144] However, a review of the history of the directive casts doubt on this interpretation of the directive. One of the early documents in the directive's history states:

> The proposed directive contributes to this objective [of promoting access to adequate dispute resolution processes] by facilitating access to dispute resolution through two types of provisions: first provisions that aim at ensuring a sound relationship between mediation and judicial proceedings *by establishing minimum common rules in the Community on a number of key aspects of civil procedure.*[145] (emphasis added)

The Commission therefore explains how the relationship between mediation and court proceedings will be achieved, namely through the establishment of minimum common rules on key aspects of civil procedure. It should be noted here that 'sound' was changed to 'balanced' and no reasons were given for this change.[146] It therefore appears that the Commission envisaged a certain level of harmonisation of civil procedure rules in order to achieve the desired relationship between mediation and court proceedings and an argument that Article 1(1) enables the implementation of a quota system is not supported by the directive's documentary history.

[a] Problematic Nature of Target Number Proposal for Cross-Border Disputes

Even if this quota system were to have a basis in the directive, it raises some significant problems regarding its implementation for the directive's scope of cross-border disputes.

First, and on a more general note, one might query why there is a quota simply of mediations as against judicial proceedings given the wider range of available dispute resolution processes such as adjudication, ombuds schemes and arbitration.[147] For cross-border disputes, international arbitration plays a prominent role, as noted earlier, and its omission from any quota is therefore surprising.

Secondly, there would be significant difficulty in obtaining reliable data on the number of mediations in order to determine whether the quota has been met. Indeed, the proponents of this proposal acknowledge that there is:

---

144. De Palo and D'Urso, *Achieving a Balanced Relationship Between Mediation and Judicial Proceedings*, *supra* n. 28, at 8; Rebooting Report, *supra* n. 20, at 10. Further information on the 'Balanced Relationship Target Number' can be found in Chapter 1 of De Palo and Trevor, *supra* n. 3, at 8-10.
145. European Commission, *Proposal for a Directive of the European Parliament and of the Council on Certain Aspects of Mediation in Civil and Commercial Matters* COM (2004) 0718, 2 at 1.1.1. This paragraph continues: 'Secondly by providing the necessary tools for the courts of the Member States to actively promote the use of mediation without nevertheless making mediation compulsory or subject to specific sanctions.'
146. European Parliament, *Report on the Proposal for a Directive of the European Parliament and of the Council on Certain Aspects of Mediation in Civil and Commercial Matters* A6-0074/2007, *see* Amendment 12 at 11. The explanatory statement at 22 does not provide the reason for this change from 'sound relationship' to 'balanced relationship'.
147. *Steffek, supra* n. 16, at 53.

> currently no comprehensive, comparable data on mediations, either domestic or cross-border, for the European Union as a whole. Additionally, almost no member state has an official count of mediations; as a result, it is difficult to obtain reliable data.[148]

For cross-border mediations, obtaining data is likely to be even more challenging than obtaining data for domestic mediations. Cross-border mediations might, for impartiality concerns, be conducted on neutral territory in a country which, and with a mediator who, has no association with the countries which the disputants are from, making the recording of this data all the more problematic. This leads to the third and associated problem: how would a mediation for a cross-border dispute be attributed to a particular country? Would it be where the mediation occurs, the nationality of the parties to the mediation or the nationality of the mediator, or to all of these?

The reasons identified above demonstrate that the proposal of a quota of the number of mediations compared to court proceedings presents significant challenges in its implementation for EU cross-border disputes.

The above review of recommendations arising from the Rebooting Report demonstrates that they are problematic for the specific EU cross-border scope of the EU Mediation Directive. Further, consistent with the directive's emphasis on the relationship between mediation and litigation, the Rebooting Report also focuses on the relationship between mediation and litigation in order to identify ways in which to increase mediation's use. Similarly, the proposal emerging from empirical research conducted by the European Commission in its public consultation, and which will now be considered, also relies on the relationship between mediation and litigation in order to increase the use of mediation.

[B] The Recommendations from the Public Consultation Questionnaire

The second key piece of empirical research conducted by the EU in its efforts to determine how to improve the EU Mediation Directive was the Commission's public consultation on the directive. On 18 September 2015, the Commission launched a public consultation, by way of a questionnaire, which closed on 11 December 2015. The questions in the questionnaire correspond to the topics addressed in each article of the EU Mediation Directive, with a catch-all question at the end asking how the directive could be improved.[149]

While the results of the public consultation have not been made public, the Commission's 2016 report to the European Parliament on Directive 2008/52, as required under Article 11 of the EU Mediation Directive, draws on the results of this

148. De Palo and D'Urso, *Achieving a Balanced Relationship Between Mediation and Judicial Proceedings*, *supra* n. 28, at 20.
149. The Commission's public consultation questionnaire on the application of Directive 2008/52/EC is no longer available on the EU's public consultation website <https://ec.europa.eu/info/consultations_en> (accessed 5 June 2020). However, the questions in the questionnaire can be seen in the response by the Law Society of England and Wales, *supra* n. 95.

consultation.[150] Though the report concludes that no changes are required to the directive, the Commission encourages Member States to improve the application of the directive by, in particular, increasing the number of cases in which courts invite parties to use mediation.[151] As considered earlier in the analysis of the mandatory mediation proposal of the Rebooting Report, a proposal which relies on the courts to direct parties to mediate is dependent on the disputes reaching the vicinity of the court. For commercial cross-border cases given, as identified earlier, the significant use of international arbitration for such disputes, it is likely that a significant portion of these disputes does not reach the courts.[152] Accordingly, such a proposal may therefore not be as effective for encouraging the use of cross-border mediation, which is the scope of the directive, as it might be for domestic disputes.

The problematic nature for the *cross-border* context of the recommendations resulting from the European Commission's public consultation questionnaire and the Rebooting Report may be attributable to certain methodological characteristics of those studies, as will now be considered.

§2.05 METHODOLOGY OF THE KEY EMPIRICAL RESEARCH

The two methodological features of both the Rebooting Report and the European Commission's public consultation which may explain why the principal proposals arising from these studies appear to be problematic for the particular context of EU cross-border mediation are: (i) the lack of a specific engagement with the cross-border context; and (ii) the absence of detail on the respondents to the questionnaires, and in particular the extent of their experience or expertise in mediation.

[A] Lack of Specific Engagement with EU Cross-Border Context

As regards the Rebooting Report, the two aims of this report were: (i) 'to obtain national-level feedback regarding the experience gained from transposing the Directive into national legal orders';[153] and (ii) 'to identify reasons why mediation is not used more frequently for both internal and cross-border disputes within the European Union'.[154] The focus of the report is, however, on the national context rather than the cross-border context and the report therefore lacks an engagement with the specific context to which the directive applies.[155]

150. European Commission, *Report from the Commission to the European Parliament, the Council and the European Economic and Social Committee on the Application of Directive 2008/52/EC*, *supra* n. 24, at 3.
151. *Ibid.*, 12.
152. *See* text to (n. 115)-(n. 119).
153. Rebooting Report, *supra* n. 20. A further study by the European Commission, *Study for an Evaluation and Implementation of Directive 2008/52/EC*, *supra* n. 14 has also been undertaken on the transposition of the directive into national legal systems.
154. Rebooting Report, *supra* n. 20, at 11.
155. It should be noted that there is an earlier empirical study which, though not specific to the topic of how the EU Mediation Directive might be enhanced, does in places address the EU

The focus on the domestic context, and the lack of engagement with the cross-border context, is evidenced in the methodology of the research which underpins the Rebooting Report. The report's research is comprised of two parts. First, in-depth analyses of the mediation legislation in eleven EU Member States were conducted, with a short analysis for the remaining seventeen countries.[156] These analyses offer a detailed overview of the mediation legislation in each country and identify how the EU Mediation Directive has been implemented. Secondly, and crucially - given that the recommendations of the report are based on the results of this questionnaire[157] - a questionnaire was used to obtain information from 'EU mediation experts'.[158]

While the scope of the EU Mediation Directive is limited to EU cross-border disputes and one of the stated aims of the report is to understand why mediation is not more frequently used for cross-border[159] disputes, the questionnaire does not specifically address the cross-border context. For example, the title of the questionnaire refers to 'exploring legislative and non-legislative measures to encourage the use of mediation in EU Member States'.[160] There is no reference to encouraging cross-border mediation in particular.

Further, there are no questions in the questionnaire which specifically address cross-border mediation. The questionnaire contains questions which are grouped into three parts, none of which has a clear cross-border focus.[161] For example, Part I of the questionnaire includes questions on estimates of the current mediation market. The opening sentence states: 'For the purposes of this questionnaire, the "mediation market" is defined as the total number of civil and commercial mediations falling within the scope of the 2008 Mediation Directive (Directive 2008/52/EC).'[162] The scope of the EU Mediation Directive, as stated in Article 1(2), is *cross-border* civil and commercial disputes.[163] However, no suggestion of the *cross-border* scope is provided

cross-border context. In 2010, empirical research was conducted on the costs of commercial litigation across the EU in the EU-funded study by ADR Centre, *The Cost of Non-ADR – Surveying and Showing the Actual Costs of Intra-Community Commercial Litigation*, *supra* n. 60. Parts of this study address EU cross-border disputes including (i) the amount of cross-border disputes the respondents are currently engaged with and how many of those are subject to each of mediation, arbitration or litigation (page 17) and (ii) the respondents' perceptions of the time and cost involved in each of EU cross-border litigation, arbitration and mediation (pages 46-47). The information obtained is, however, of limited value as the study does not state how many respondents took part and the information on the time and cost of each of the methods of dispute resolution processes is based on perception rather than experience. Further, the study does not provide any detail of who took part in the study. It simply states at page 5 that the study 'surveyed companies, lawyers and legal researchers'.

156. Rebooting Report, *supra* n. 20, at 14.
157. *Ibid.*, 162-164 for the legislative and non-legislative proposals identified from the data obtained from the questionnaire.
158. *Ibid.*, 14. The term 'EU mediation experts' is not defined in the Rebooting Report, *supra* n. 20.
159. *See* the earlier section on the scope of the EU Mediation Directive for the definition of cross-border.
160. Rebooting Report, *supra* n. 20, at 226.
161. *Ibid.*, 226, Annex 3.
162. *Ibid.*, 226, Annex 3: The Study Questionnaire, Part I – Estimate of the Current Mediation Market.
163. EU Mediation Directive, Article 1(2) provides: 'This Directive shall apply, in cross-border disputes, to civil and commercial matters ... .'

to respondents in this opening sentence of the questionnaire. Respondents are then asked to provide estimates regarding mediations 'in your country'.[164] There are no questions on the number of cross-border mediations. This suggests that when answering the questions in this part the respondents were doing so as regards domestic mediations rather than cross-border mediations in particular.

Similarly, Part III of the questionnaire contains a list of legislative proposals (Part IIIA) and non-legislative proposals (Part IIIB) which respondents are asked to rank according to their 'ability or inability, to make more mediations happen in your country'.[165] Respondents are therefore asked to consider the impact of such proposals on mediation in their country and are not directed to think, in particular, of the impact which such proposals might have on cross-border mediations.[166] In order to engage specifically with the EU cross-border context, the questionnaire could, for example, have made a clear distinction between domestic and EU cross-border mediation and asked which proposals might be particularly effective to increase the use of EU cross-border mediation.[167]

As with the empirical research for the Rebooting Report, notably absent from the European Commission's public consultation questionnaire are any questions which engage with the directive's particular context of cross-border mediation.

The questionnaire includes questions which are grouped into ten numbered sections with, generally, each section addressing the topic of the article in the EU Mediation Directive with the equivalent number. As Article 1 of the directive addresses the scope of the directive, one would expect any questions on the cross-border nature of the directive to be found in section 1 of the questionnaire.[168] However, surprisingly absent from the description of the directive's objective as provided in the questionnaire is a reference to the cross-border scope of the directive. Question 1 states:

164. Rebooting Report, *supra* n. 20, at 226, Part I, questions 2, 3 & 4.
165. *Ibid.*, 226, in particular the opening paragraphs of the questionnaire. For Part IIIA and Part IIIB see *ibid.*, 229.
166. While there are two proposals in Part III which may be of relevance to cross-border mediation in the EU (the creation of a uniform certification of mediators at the EU level (point 38 of Part IIIB) and the creation of an EU Alternative Dispute Resolution Agency to promote mediation (point 39 of Part IIIB), the respondents have, as mentioned above, been asked to rank the likely impact that such proposals would have in *their countries*. Further, as mentioned above, the start of Part I of the questionnaire defines the mediation market with regard to civil and commercial mediations and makes no specific reference to cross-border mediations. The respondents' attention has therefore not been directed to the cross-border context.
167. Similarly, the lack of a specific engagement with the cross-border context is seen in Part II of the questionnaire which contains questions on the assessment of the existing law in the respondent's country. At the beginning of this part, the questionnaire states: 'Please note: the following questions are only for mediation in civil and commercial matters as covered by the Directive.' Rebooting Report, *supra* n. 20, at 227. There is no reference to the specific cross-border scope of the directive.
168. The other sections of the questionnaire address the following topics: section 2: mediators, section 3: quality of mediation, section 4: mediation and courts, section 5: compulsory mediation, incentives, sanctions, section 6: enforceability, section 7: confidentiality, section 8; limitation and prescription periods, section 9: information for the general public, section 10: possible improvements, section 11: general context.

> The objective of the Mediation Directive is to facilitate access to alternative dispute resolution and to promote the amicable settlement of disputes by encouraging the use of mediation and by ensuring a balanced relationship between mediation and judicial proceedings (Article 1(1)) of the Directive ... Do you consider that the Directive has reached its objective?[169]

There is no mention of the aim being to promote 'cross-border' mediation. Accordingly, when asked whether the directive has achieved its objective, respondents are not directed to its cross-border scope. This suggests that the information obtained through the public consultation is not specific to the directive's cross-border scope. In addition, it directs respondents to focus on the relationship between mediation and litigation.

The analysis above demonstrates that the questionnaires used to obtain data for each of the Rebooting Report and the European Commission's public consultation lack a clear reference to the cross-border context which is the scope of the EU Mediation Directive. This absence suggests that the data obtained from the responses to these questionnaires primarily relates to domestic mediations (and even if the data contained within it data on cross-border mediation such data cannot specifically be identified). The question which this then raises is whether data obtained on domestic mediation is equally relevant to the different context of cross-border mediation. Caution has been expressed against assuming that research on domestic mediation necessarily applies to cross-border mediation.[170] Such caution appears warranted given that the principal proposals arising from this research (mandatory mediation, courts inviting parties to use mediation and a ratio of the number of mediations to the number of judicial proceedings) appear to be particularly problematic for the cross-border context, as explained earlier in this chapter.

At this juncture, it is important to acknowledge that proposals to encourage the use of domestic mediations might be a helpful and general starting point for the promotion of mediation across borders in the EU. The Commission's study on the EU Mediation Directive, updated in 2016,[171] concludes that the directive has raised awareness among national legislators on the advantages of mediation, by introducing domestic mediation systems or by triggering the extension of existing domestic mediation systems.[172] However, it appears that such proposals have not led to a notable uptake in EU cross-border mediations. The same study notes that its research reports 'a very limited number or no cross-border mediation cases'.[173] This suggests that raising awareness in national contexts has not been sufficient to lead to an increase in cross-border mediation. Indeed, as is addressed in more detail in Chapter 3, research by the International Institute for Conflict Prevention and Resolution (CPR) found a marked decrease in the preference for mediation for cross-border disputes compared to

169. *See supra* n. 149.
170. Strong, *Use and Perception of International Commercial Mediation*, *supra* n. 127, at 20. *See also* Chapter 3 which explains why engagement with the specific cross-border context is necessary.
171. European Commission, *Study for an Evaluation and Implementation of Directive 2008/52/EC*, *supra* n. 14.
172. *Ibid.*, 79.
173. *Ibid.*, VII.

domestic disputes.[174] This finding suggests that context matters and that there may be factors which affect the use of mediation which are specific to cross-border mediation and which do not equally apply to domestic mediation. Indeed, SIDRA has recently noted that 'International dispute resolution involves different considerations compared to domestic settings.'[175] Accordingly, in order to increase cross-border mediation, measures tailored to the specific cross-border context may be needed. A notable example of such a tailored measure at the international level is the Singapore Convention which addresses the enforcement of mediation settlement agreements for the cross-border context.[176] Further, the recommendations identified in Chapter 9 which draw upon the key themes identified in the interview data obtained for this book demonstrate that measures which are specific to the EU cross-border context may be needed in order to promote the use of EU cross-border mediation.[177]

[B] Respondents to the Questionnaires

The second methodological characteristic regarding the Rebooting Report and the EU's public consultation is the lack of information on the respondents to the questionnaires, and in particular the extent of their experience or expertise in mediation.

Regarding the Rebooting Report's questionnaire, it is unclear whether the respondents to the questionnaire had experience of cross-border or domestic mediation, whether as mediators or as parties. The term 'EU mediation experts', which is not defined, refers to the targeted audience for the questionnaire.[178] Respondents were only asked to state their profession and were not required to state whether they had any experience of mediation, cross-border or otherwise.[179] It is therefore not possible to

---

174. *See* CPR and CEDR, 'Insights in Alternative Dispute Resolution', Winter 2018-19, at 4 <https://www.cpradr.org/news-publications/reports/2019-04-04-cpr-cedr-joint-insights-report-on-the-use-of-adr/_res/id=Attachments/index=0/CEDR%20CPR%20report%20040419.pdf> (accessed 5 June 2020) and also *see* further Chapter 3.
175. SIDRA, *supra* n. 40, at 1.
176. The United Nations Convention on International Settlement Agreements Resulting from Mediation (UN Convention on International Mediated Settlement Agreements) <https://uncitral.un.org/sites/uncitral.un.org/files/media-documents/uncitral/en/annex_i.pdf> (accessed 5 June 2020). For analysis of the convention *see*: Nadja Alexander and Shouyu Chong (eds), *The Singapore Convention on Mediation, A Commentary* (Wolters Kluwer 2019); Timothy Schnabel, *The Singapore Convention on Mediation: A Framework for the Cross-Border Recognition and Enforcement of Mediated Settlements*, 19(1) Pepperdine Dispute Resolution Law Journal 1 (2019); and Eunice Chua, *The Singapore Convention on Mediation – a Brighter Future for Asian Dispute Resolution*, 9(2) Asian Journal of International Law 195 (2019). The convention is considered further in Chapters 3 and 8.
177. The recommendations include, for example: a heightened confidentiality regime for EU cross-border mediation; greater, and coordinated, information on cross-border mediators and the outcomes of cross-border mediations; an enhanced mediation pledge; and a body in the EU dedicated to cross-border mediation similar to the bodies focusing on cross-border mediation in other regions such as in Asia.
178. Rebooting Report, *supra* n. 20, at 14.
179. *Ibid.*, 230, in particular question 43 of the questionnaire. Further, one of the authors of the Rebooting report, Guiseppe De Palo, acknowledges that there was no request in the questionnaire for information regarding the respondents' experience in mediation. De Palo and Canessa, *supra* n. 97, at 724.

determine the type or level of experience and expertise of this group of 'EU Mediation Experts'. This therefore calls into question the value of their responses to identifying proposals to enhance the EU Mediation Directive.

Further, the data provided on the questionnaire responses does not break down the responses by profession.[180] It is therefore not possible to determine the role of the respondents, for example, whether they were mediators, mediation organisations, lawyers or users of mediation. However, in spite of this lack of a breakdown of participants by profession, the report notes that 'the participation from ADR experts and practitioners was highly satisfactory' and adds that because of this 'the study team has been attentive to possible biases in the study findings'.[181] No further information is offered on what these biases are, how they were identified nor how such possible biases were addressed. The report adds that: 'The team members have done their utmost to address these wherever they could occur, but they cannot be fully excluded.'[182] Accordingly, one particular category of stakeholder, the undefined category of 'ADR experts and practitioners', may have significantly influenced the data.

The only categorisation of the respondents provided is by country[183] and this reveals a further methodological issue. Of the 816 responses to the questionnaire, 210 were from Romania.[184] Romania therefore accounts for roughly a quarter of the respondents. Accordingly, there is a disproportionate influence by respondents from one EU Member State on the results of this quantitative study on the use of mediation across the EU Member States.

In summary, as regards the respondents to the questionnaire for the Rebooting Report, it is not possible to determine in detail who the respondents were and, in particular, whether the respondents to the questionnaire had expertise or experience in mediation (whether cross-border or domestic), and there is a disproportionate contribution to the data from one EU Member State.

Turning to the questionnaire for the European Commission's public consultation, similarly, it is not possible to determine the extent of respondents' experience or expertise in mediation, nor indeed in other methods of dispute resolution. The Commission's report to the European Parliament on Directive 2008/52 which draws on the results of this consultation only states that '562 answers were submitted by interested individuals, mediators, judges, attorneys, other legal practitioners, academics, organisations, public authorities and Member States'.[185] Further, it is not possible to determine whether the views of the users of dispute resolution processes, who are an important category of stakeholder because they are the consumers of such processes and also have the ability to influence the dispute resolution field,[186] were obtained as

180. Rebooting Report, *supra* n. 20, at section 3.2.
181. *Ibid.*, 16.
182. *Ibid.*
183. *Ibid.*, 119.
184. *Ibid.*
185. European Commission, *Report on Certain Aspects of Mediation in Civil and Commercial Matters*, *supra* n. 24, at 3.
186. *See* further Chapters 3 and 4 regarding why the users of dispute resolution processes are a particularly important category of stakeholder.

part of the consultation process. In short, little is known about the respondents and why they were suitable respondents for the questionnaire.

The methodological features outlined above, particularly the lack of engagement with the cross-border context of the directive, may explain why the main recommendations for the enhancement of the EU Mediation Directive arising from the empirical research to date (mandatory mediation, courts inviting parties to use mediation and a ratio of the number of mediations to the number of judicial proceedings) appear to be problematic for achieving the aim of encouraging the use of cross-border mediation in the EU, as was explored earlier. The recommendations regarding mandatory mediation and the ratio of mediations against judicial proceedings have continued to be made in the more recent collection of analyses on the implementation of the Mediation Directive requested by the European Parliament[187] and in a European Parliament briefing on the EU Mediation Directive,[188] and therefore continue to be relevant for consideration.

§2.06 CONCLUSION

As the EU continues to consider how to promote mediation following the implementation of the EU Mediation Directive, it has a limited body of empirical research upon which to draw, as has been explored in this chapter. In particular, the available data lacks a discernible engagement with both the cross-border scope of the directive and an important category of stakeholder: the users of dispute resolution processes. Further, the problematic nature, as explained above, of the proposals identified in such research for cross-border mediation in particular suggests that further research which engages with the specific cross-border context would be a worthwhile addition to the EU's current body of research on the EU Mediation Directive. Accordingly, the research conducted for this book seeks to contribute to this ongoing enquiry by engaging with the users of dispute resolution processes and asking them specifically about EU cross-border mediation. In so doing, its aim is to identify proposals which might address users' needs for the specific context of EU cross-border commercial mediation.

187. European Parliament, *The Implementation of the Mediation Directive, Workshop, supra* n. 16. *See* in particular Guiseppe de Palo and Leonardo D'Urso, *Achieving a Balanced Relationship Between Mediation and Judicial Proceedings, supra* n. 28, at 7. As is discussed later in this chapter, this paper recommends a 'required initial mediation session'.

188. European Parliament, *A Ten-Year-Long 'EU Mediation Paradox', supra* n. 34. The author of this report, Guiseppe De Palo, is the same author of the Rebooting report. For discussion on the proposal of mandatory mediation *see*: Menkel-Meadow, *Variations in the Uptake of and Resistance to Mediation, supra* n. 97, at 189. At 196 Menkel-Meadow, citing the Rebooting report states: 'the European Union may soon debate whether to mandate mediation ... in some contexts'; Coben, *supra* n. 97, 780; De Palo and Canessa, *supra* n. 97, at 724; Kovach, *supra* n. 97, at 773 at footnote 93.

CHAPTER 3

Literature on Cross-Border Mediation

> We never think entirely alone: we think in company, in a vast collaboration; we work with the workers of the past and of the present. [In] the whole intellectual world ... each one finds in those about him the initiation, help, verification, information, encouragement, that he needs.[1]

§3.01 EXECUTIVE SUMMARY

Following the review in Chapter 2 of the EU's empirical research, it is important to place such research in a wider context and explore research on cross-border mediation generally. This chapter considers the small, but growing, body of empirical research on cross-border mediation in the wider international context. The purpose of this chapter is to identify the research which has been conducted in the field of international commercial cross-border mediation and which serves as an important backdrop for the empirical research conducted for this book.

§3.02 LITERATURE ON CROSS-BORDER MEDIATION

Before considering the empirical research on cross-border mediation which has been conducted to date, to place this research in context, this chapter will briefly consider the wider, non-empirical literature in the field.

There appears, at first glance, to be a considerable body of literature on the topic of cross-border mediation at both European and international levels. The use of the words 'global', 'international' or 'Europe', for example, in the titles of numerous works on mediation suggests that these texts might examine the cross-border context of

1. Antonin D. Sertillanges, *The Intellectual Life: Its Spirits, Conditions and Methods* 145 (Mary Ryan tr, Mercier Press 1978).

mediation.[2] On closer inspection, it appears that the 'global', 'international' and 'Europe' focus of these texts stems largely from the range of countries – rather than the type of mediation – examined. Put another way, the tendency in the literature is to consider and, in some texts, compare domestic mediation in a number of countries, for example, in light of differing mediation regulations and differing legal systems (notably whether a civil or common law system) rather than to address mediation across borders. This approach offers valuable and detailed insights into the mediation landscape in various countries and enables the transfer, and transformation, of expertise and experience between countries. However, to better understand the use, or lack of use, of cross-border mediation, it is the cross-border intersection with which we must engage further.

Another approach seen in the academic literature on the cross-border context is to compare and contrast the cross-border dispute resolution processes of arbitration and mediation. In particular, a topic which received much attention was the lack of an international enforcement mechanism for cross-border mediation compared with international arbitration's enjoyment of the Convention on the Recognition and

2. These include: (i) at the international/global level: Carlos Esplugues and Louis Marquis (eds), *New Developments in Civil and Commercial Mediation, Global Comparative Perspectives* (Springer 2015); Nadja Alexander, *International and Comparative Mediation, Global Trends in Dispute Resolution*, Vol. 4 (Kluwer Law International 2009); Nadja Alexander (ed.), *Global Trends in Mediation* (Kluwer Law International 2006); Klaus Peter Berger, *Private Dispute Resolution in International Business: Negotiation, Mediation, Arbitration* (3rd ed. Kluwer Law International 2015); *William Herbert and others, International Commercial Mediation*, 45(1) International Legal Developments in Review 111 (2011); Penny Brooker and Suzanne Wilkinson (eds), *Mediation in the Construction Industry: An International Review* (Spon Press 2010); Carrie Menkel-Meadow, *Correspondences and Contradictions in International and Domestic Conflict Resolution: Lessons from General Theory and Varied Contexts*, Journal of Dispute Resolution 319 (2003); Carrie Menkel-Meadow, *The Future of Mediation Worldwide: Legal and Cultural Variations in the Uptake of or Resistance to Mediation* in Ian Macduff (ed.) *Essays on Mediation: Dealing with Disputes in the 21st Century* (Wolters Kluwer 2016); Manon Schonewille and Fred Schonewille (eds), *The Variegated Landscape of Mediation: A Comparative Study of Mediation Regulation and Practices in Europe and the World* (Eleven International Publishing 2013); Danny McFadden, *Developments in International Commercial Mediation: U.S., UK, Asia, India and EU*, 8 Contemporary Asia Arbitration Journal 299 (2015); Nadja Alexander, *Mediation in Perspective: Common Law and Civil Law Perspectives Compared*, 6 International Trade and Business Law Annual 1 (2001); Nadja Alexander, *What's Law Got to do With It? Mapping Modern Mediation Movements in Civil and Common Law Jurisdictions*, 13(2) Bond Law Review 335 (2001); and (ii) at the European level: Guiseppe de Palo and Mary B. Trevor (eds) *EU Mediation, Law and Practice* (Oxford University Press 2012); Nadja Alexander, Sabine Walsh and Martin Svatos (eds) *EU Mediation Law Handbook* (Wolters Kluwer 2017); Guiseppe de Palo and Linda Costabile, *Promotion of International Commercial Arbitration and Other Alternative Dispute Resolution Techniques in Ten Southern Mediterranean Countries*, 7 Cardozo Journal of Conflict Resolution 303 (2005); Ewald Filler, *Commercial Mediation in Europe, An Empirical Study of the User Experience* (Wolters Kluwer 2012). In addition to the texts listed which include 'global', 'international' or 'Europe' in their titles, other key texts which illustrate the differences between a selection of domestic mediation systems are Felix Steffek and Hannes Unberath in cooperation with Hazel Genn, Reinhard Gregor and Carrie Menkel-Meadow (eds), *Regulating Dispute Resolution – ADR & Access to Justice at the Crossroads* (Hart Publishing 2013); Klaus J. Hopt and Felix Steffek (eds), *Mediation – Principles and Regulation in Comparative Perspective* (Oxford University Press 2013).

Enforcement of Foreign Arbitral Awards, also known as the New York Convention.[3] This difference has been addressed by the Singapore Convention which opened for signature in Singapore on 7 August 2019 and entered into force on 12 September 2020.[4] Further, there are also texts of a more practical genre which explain, and contrast, international mediation and arbitration drawing on real-life examples to do so.[5]

There is, however, one aspect of cross-border mediation which has received considerable attention in the literature: its cross-cultural nature.[6] While this characteristic may also be seen in domestic mediation, it is an aspect which is particularly

3. United Nations Convention on the Recognition and Enforcement of Foreign Arbitral Awards, (adopted 10 June 1958, entered into force 7 June 1959). Regarding the literature on the lack of a comparable convention for international mediation *see*: Brette Steele, *Enforcing International Commercial Mediation Agreements as Arbitral Awards under the New York Convention*, 54 UCLA Law Review 1385 (2007); Winnie Jo-Mei Ma and others, *Enforcing Cross-Border Mediated Settlement Agreements: Colloquium Held at Bond University Faculty of Law on November 2013*, 7(1) Contemporary Asia Arbitration Journal 3 (2014); Bobette Wolski, *Recent Developments in International Commercial Dispute Resolution: Expanding the Options*, 13(2) Bond Law Review 1 (2001); Edna Sussman, *The Final Step: Issues in Enforcing the Mediation Settlement Agreement* <http://www.sussmanadr.com/docs/Enforcement_Fordham_82008.pdf> (accessed 20 May 2020); Chang–Fa Lo, *Desirability of a New International Legal Framework for Cross-Border Enforcement of Certain Mediated Settlement Agreements*, 7(1) Contemporary Asia Arbitration Journal 119 (2014); Laurence Boulle, *International Enforceability of Mediated Settlement Agreements; Developing the Conceptual Framework*, 7 Contemporary Asia Arbitration Journal 35 (2014); Edna Sussman, *A Path Forward: A Convention for the Enforcement of Mediated Settlement Agreements 1*, Transnational Dispute Management <https://www.transnational-dispute-management.com/article.asp?key=2295> (accessed 20 May 2020); Winnie Jo-Mei Ma, *Enforcing Mediated Settlement Agreements under the New York Convention: from Controversies to Creativities*, 7 Contemporary Asia Arbitration Journal 69 (2014); Bobette Wolski, *Enforcing Mediated Settlement Agreements (MSAs): Critical Questions and Directions for Future Research*, 7(1) Contemporary Asia Arbitration Journal 87 (2014); Edna Sussman, *The New York Convention through a Mediation Prism*, 15 Dispute Resolution Magazine 10 (2009); Chang-Fa Lo, *Desirability of a New International Legal Framework for Cross-Border Enforcement of Certain Mediated Settlement Agreements*, 7(1) Contemporary Asia Arbitration Journal 119 (2014); S.I. Strong, *Beyond International Commercial Arbitration? The Promise of International Commercial Mediation*, 45 Washington University Journal of Law and Policy 11 (2014); Eunice Chua, *The Future of International Mediated Settlement Agreements: of Conventions, Challenges and Choices*, Tan Pan Online: A Chinese-English Journal on Negotiation 1 (2015).
4. United Nations Convention on International Settlement Agreements Resulting from Mediation <http://www.uncitral.org/pdf/english/commissionsessions/51st-session/Annex_I.pdf> (accessed 20 May 2020). UNCITRAL, 'Singapore Convention Signing Ceremony' <https://uncitral.un.org/en/07.08.2019> (accessed 20 May 2020). Following the ratification of the convention by Singapore, Fiji and Qatar, the convention entered into force on 12 September 2020 <https://www.singaporeconvention.org/convention/about-convention/> (accessed 16 September 2020). For a list of the signatories to the Singapore Convention *see* <https://uncitral.un.org/en/texts/mediation/conventions/international_settlement_agreements/status> (accessed 20 May 2020). *See also*: Nadja Alexander and Shouyu Chong, *The Singapore Convention on Mediation, A Commentary* (Wolters Kluwer 2019); Timothy Schnabel, *The Singapore Convention on Mediation: A Framework for the Cross-Border Recognition and Enforcement of Mediated Settlements*, 19(1) Pepperdine Dispute Resolution Law Journal 1 (2019).
5. Michael McIlwrath and John Savage, *International Arbitration and Mediation: A Practical Guide* (Kluwer Law International 2010); Eileen Carroll and Karl Mackie, *International Mediation – The Art of Business Diplomacy* (Tottel Publishing 2006); Eileen Carroll and Karl Mackie, *International Mediation: Breaking Business Deadlock* (Bloomsbury Professional 2016).
6. Many authors have written on the topic of the cross-cultural nature of cross-border disputes including John Paul Lederach, Kevin Avruch, Carrie Menkel Meadow, Jacob Bercovitch, John Barkai. *See* John Paul Lederach, *Preparing for Peace, Conflict Transformation Across Cultures*

noticeable in cross-border mediations given that parties are from different countries and therefore cultures or, to be more precise, national cultures.[7] Within the literature on cross-cultural mediation, considerable attention has been given to the particular challenges associated with practising cross-cultural mediation and the particular skills which cross-border mediators may need.[8] International mediation organisations have also issued guidance and specific training and certification for cross-cultural mediation.[9]

The review of the relevant literature suggests that two aspects of cross-border mediation have received notable attention: the cross-cultural nature of such mediations and the challenges which this can present; and the issue of enforcement across borders of mediated settlement agreements resulting from cross-border mediations. It is only this latter topic of enforcement which has received notable attention in the empirical research to date on cross-border commercial mediation (which will be considered in the following section on empirical research). In contrast, while the issue of culture has received considerable attention in the non-empirical literature, it has not received comparable attention in the relevant empirical research on cross-border commercial mediation considered later in this chapter. This may be because the issue

(Syracuse University Press 1995); Kevin Avruch, *Context and Pretext in Conflict Resolution* (Paradigm Publishers 2013); Kevin Avruch, *Culture as Context, Culture as Communication: Considerations for Humanitarian Negotiators*, 9 Harvard Negotiation Law Review 391 (2004); Kevin Avruch, *Culture and Conflict Resolution* (United States Institute of Peace Press 1998); Kevin Avruch, *Type I and Type II Errors in Culturally Sensitive Conflict Resolution Practice*, 20 Conflict Resolution Quarterly 351 (2003b); Kevin Avrich and PeterW. Black, *A Generic Theory of Conflict Resolution Theory*, 3(1) Negotiation Journal 87 (1987); Carrie Menkel-Meadow, *Mediating Multi-Culturally: Culture and the Ethical Mediator* in Ellen Waldman (ed.) *Mediation Ethics: Cases and Commentaries* 305 (Jossey-Bass 2011); Carrie Menkel-Meadow, *The Future of Mediation Worldwide: Legal and Cultural Variations in the Uptake of or Resistance to Mediation* in Ian Macduff (ed.) *Essays on Mediation: Dealing with Disputes in the 21st Century* (Wolters Kluwer 2016); Carrie Menkel-Meadow, *Variations in the Uptake of and Resistance to Mediation Outside of the United States*, University of California, Irvine School of Law, Research Paper No. 2015-80 [2015], 189 <https://papers.ssrn.com/sol3/papers.cfm?abstract_id=2658903> (accessed 20 May 2020); Jacob Bercovitch, *Theory and Practice of International Mediation* (Routledge 2011); John Barkai, *What's a Cross-Cultural Mediator to do? A Low-Context Solution for a High-Context Problem*, 10 Cardozo Journal of Conflict Resolution 43 (2008); Rebecca Golbert, *An Anthropologist's Approach to Mediation*, 11 Cardozo Journal of Conflict Resolution 81 (2009-2010); Howard Gadlin, *Conflict Resolution, Cultural Differences, and the Culture of Racism*, 10(1) Negotiation Journal 33 (1994); Sally Engle Merry, *Disputing without Culture*, 100 Harvard Law Review 2057 (1987).

7. On the point that domestic mediation may also be of a cross-cultural nature, Avruch has identified multiple 'containers for culture' beyond national culture and including profession, occupation, class, religion and region. Accordingly, Avruch has warned against a monolithic concept of culture deriving solely from nationality. Kevin Avruch, *Culture & Conflict Resolution* 44 (United States Institute of Peace 2006).
8. *See supra* n. 6 and in particular Barkai, *What's a Cross-Cultural Mediator to do?;* Menkel-Meadow, *Mediating Multi-Culturally: Culture and the Ethical Mediator*; Avruch, *Type I and Type II Errors in Culturally Sensitive Conflict Resolution Practice.*
9. *See*, for example, the criteria for The International Mediation Institute's Inter-cultural certification: <https://imimediation.org/intercultural-certification-criteria> (accessed 20 May 2020).

of culture does not lend itself easily to empirical research given the complex nature of culture with its multiple meanings.[10]

§3.03 EMPIRICAL RESEARCH ON EU CROSS-BORDER MEDIATION

As regards the European context, in the empirical research which has been conducted for the EU's continued review of the EU Mediation Directive there is, as explained in Chapter 2, a lack of empirical research which focuses specifically on the EU cross-border context.[11] Rather, the empirical research focuses on the use of mediation in individual EU Member States. A similar approach is also seen in Filler's empirical study on commercial mediation in Europe.[12] The empirical research in Filler's study involved questionnaires and interviews with mediators and business executives regarding mediation in each of a number of European countries.[13] Filler's comparative study explores both mediators' and business executives' perspectives and experiences of mediation in each of these countries.[14] Indeed, there is a growing body of empirical studies of domestic mediation in European countries which addresses a variety of issues and sectors[15] with the following topics receiving considerable attention: mandatory mediation; the recording and analysis of the intricacies of the mediation process; and mediation in the construction sector.

---

10. Avruch argues that culture does not only encompass 'quasi- or pseudo-kinship grouping (tribe, ethnic group, and nation are the usual ones) but also groupings that derive from profession, occupation, class, religion or region'. Avruch, *Culture and Conflict Resolution, supra* n. 6, at 5. Such an approach to culture acknowledges that individuals carry multiple cultures which raises challenges in conducting empirical research on the concept of culture. Indeed, Bercovitch and Elgström have noted that the complexity of the concept of culture raises difficulties for the empirical assessment of the influence of culture in mediations Jacob Bercovitch and Ole Elgström, *Culture and International Mediation: Exploring Theoretical and Empirical Linkages*, 6 International Negotiation 3, 4 (2001). It should be added that, as will be seen in Chapters 7 and 8, the theme of culture was not a notable theme which emerged in the empirical research conducted for this book.
11. *See* Chapter 2 for a detailed review of the empirical research conducted as part of the EU's efforts to increase the use of cross-border mediation.
12. Filler, *supra* n. 2.
13. *Ibid.*, 5, para. 1.01.
14. For an overview of Filler's study *see ibid.*, 5-7.
15. For example, the following studies are empirical studies on domestic mediation and address a variety of issues: *in the UK*: Charlie Irvine, *What Do 'Lay' People Know about Justice? An Empirical Enquiry*, 16(2) International Journal of Law in Context 146 (2020); Debbie De Girolamo, *The Fugitive Identity of Mediation* (Routledge 2013); Andrew Agapiou, *The Factors Influencing Mediation Referral Practices and Barriers to Its Adoption: A Survey of Construction Lawyers in England and Wales*, 7(3) International Journal of Law in the Built Environment 231 (2015); Andrew Agapiou and Bryan Clark, *A Follow-Up Empirical Analysis of Scottish Construction Clients' Interaction with Mediation*, 32(3) Civil Justice Quarterly 349 (2013); Andrew Agapiou and Bryan Clark, *Scottish Construction Lawyers and Mediation: An Investigation into Attitudes and Experiences*, 3(2) International Journal of Law in the Built Environment 159 (2011); Varda Bondy, Linda Mulcahy, Margaret Doyle and Val Reid, *Mediation and Judicial Review: An Empirical Research Study (2009)* <*http://www.nuffieldfoundation.org/sites/default/files/files/MediationandJudicialReview.pdf*> (accessed 20 May 2020); *In Ireland:* Deirdre Curran, *The Role of Mediation in the Resolution of Two Industrial Disputes in Ireland*, 36(5) Employee Relations 496 (2014); in *The Netherlands*: Bert Niemeijer and Machteld Pel, *Court-Based Mediation in the Netherlands: Research, Evaluation and Future Expectations*, 110(2) Penn

Given this book's focus on EU cross-border commercial mediation, any previous empirical research on cross-border mediation, and in particular cross-border commercial mediation, is of greatest interest and is therefore the focus of this chapter.[16] Empirical research on domestic mediation is of lesser interest given that cross-border mediation differs in certain respects to domestic mediation and therefore it cannot be assumed that the findings of empirical research on domestic mediation apply equally to cross-border mediation.[17] In its recent empirical study on international commercial

---

State Law Review 345 (2005). Beyond Europe, a considerable amount of empirical research on mediation has been conducted including: *In the U.S.A*: Douglas A. Henderson, *Mediation Success: An Empirical Analysis,* 11 Ohio State Journal on Dispute Resolution 105 (1996); Daniel Klerman and Lisa Klerman *Inside the Caucus: An Empirical Analysis of Mediation from Within,* 12(4) Journal of Empirical Legal Studies 686 (2015); Roselle Wissler, *Judicial Settlement Conferences and Staff Mediation: Empirical Research Findings,* 17 Dispute Resolution Magazine 18 (2011); Roselle Wissler, *Representation in Mediation: What We Know from Empirical Research,* 37 Fordham Urban Law Journal 419 (2010); Craig McEwen and Roselle Wissler, *Finding Out If it's True: Comparing Mediation and Negotiation Through Research,* 1 Journal of Dispute Resolution 131 (2002); Thomas Stipanowich and John Lamare, *Living with ADR: Evolving Perceptions and Use of Mediation, Arbitration and Conflict Management in Fortune 1000 Corporations,* 19(1) Harvard Negotiation Law Review 44 (2014); Roselle Wissler, *The Effects of Mandatory Mediation: Empirical Research on the Experience of Small Claims and Common Pleas Courts,* 33 Willamette Law Review 565 (1997); E. Patrick McDermott and Ruth Obar, *What's Going on in Mediation: An Empirical Analysis of the Influence of a Mediator's Style on Party Satisfaction and Monetary Benefit,* 9 Harvard Negotiation Law Journal 75 (2004); Bobbi McAdoo, Nancy Welsh and Roselle Wissler, *Institutionalization: What Do Empirical Studies Tell us about Court Mediation?,* 9 Dispute Resolution Magazine 8 (2003); John M. Lande, *Getting the Faith: Why Business Lawyers and Executives Believe in Mediation,* (5) Harvard Negotiation Law Review 138 (2000); Nancy Welsh, *Stepping Back Through the Looking Glass: Real Conversations with Real Disputants about Institutionalized Mediation and Its Value,* 38 Ohio State Journal on Dispute Resolution 573 (2004); *In Canada*: Tamara Relis *Perceptions in Litigation and Mediation: Lawyers, Defendants, Plaintiffs and Gendered Parties* (Cambridge University Press 2009); Julie Macfarlane, *Culture Change? A Tale of Two Cities and Mandatory Court-Connected Mediation,* 2 Journal of Dispute Resolution 241 (2002); Julie Macfarlane and Michaela Keet, *Civil Justice Reform and Mandatory Civil Mediation in Saskatchewan: Lessons from a Maturing Program,* 42 Alberta Law Review 677 (2004-2005); *In Australia*: Mary Anne Noone and Lola Akin Ojelabi, *Ensuring Access to Justice in Mediation Within the Civil Justice System,* 40(2) Monash University Law Review 528 (2014); *In New Zealand,* Grant H. Morris and Daniella Schroder, *LEADR/Victoria University Commercial Mediation in New Zealand Project Report* (June 2015) <https://papers.ssrn.com/sol3/papers.cfm?abstract_id=2650261> (accessed 20 May 2020); Grant H. Morris and Amanda Lamb, Resolution Institute/Victoria University, *Lawyers as Gatekeepers to Commercial Mediation in New Zealand Report* (June 2016) <https://papers.ssrn.com/sol3/papers.cfm?abstract_id=2797995.> (accessed 20 May 2020); Grant Morris and Freya McKechnie, Resolution Institute/Victoria University of Wellington, *Users of Commercial Mediation in New Zealand – Insurance Industry Report* (July 2017) <https://www.resolution.institute/documents/item/2442> (accessed 20 May 2020).

16. It should be mentioned here that, for completeness, where key themes emerged in the data obtained in the research conducted for this book, any relevant domestic empirical research on such themes is also considered. The empirical data arising from the research for this book is considered in Chapters 6, 7 and 8.
17. S.I. Strong, *Realizing Rationality: An Empirical Assessment of International Commercial Mediation,* 73 Washington & Lee Law Review 1973, 1984 (2016); S.I. Strong, *Beyond International Commercial Arbitration? supra* n. 3, at 18-19; Paul E. Mason, *What's Brewing in the International Commercial Mediation Process,* 66(1) Dispute Resolution Journal 64, 66 (2011). *See also* Mauro Rubino-Sammartano, *Domestic, Transnational, Foreign and International Mediations: Legal Issues,* 81(4) Arbitration 381, 381 (2015), who distinguishes between domestic and international mediations.

dispute resolution, SIDRA noted that 'International dispute resolution involves different considerations compared to domestic settings.'[18] A key consideration is obviously that parties to cross-border mediation come from, or are based in, different countries and therefore different jurisdictions. This characteristic raises issues specific to cross-border mediation, for example, the potential need to enforce a mediated settlement agreement across borders, as previously discussed.[19]

Further, numerous other ways in which cross-border mediation may differ from domestic mediation have been identified in the literature. The cross-cultural nature of cross-border mediation can make such mediations more challenging as, for example, parties may have different perceptions of the same behaviour.[20] While there may be a cross-cultural element to domestic mediation, this may not always be the case, nor be as pronounced, as it would be for cross-border mediations.[21] There may also be language differences in cross-border mediations, which can add further complexity.[22] Another difference is that in the international context the range of types of mediation which parties may encounter is wider and likely to be less familiar to parties than for domestic mediation.[23] Finally, a further difference identified in the literature between cross-border and domestic mediation is that cross-border mediation tends to be more complex, involving multiple parties and contracts.[24]

These differences between cross-border and domestic mediation are supported by empirical research which has identified differing results, when the same question was asked, for domestic mediation compared to cross-border mediation, and notably a significant decrease in the preference for mediation for cross-border disputes compared to domestic disputes.[25] This further confirms the view that the different contexts raise different considerations.

In addition, it is instructive to note that the arbitration field distinguishes between international and domestic arbitration, with a considerable body of empirical research dedicated to the particular international context. The lack of data specifically on international arbitration prompted the series of empirical studies into international arbitration by the School of International Arbitration of Queen Mary University of

18. SIDRA, *International Dispute Resolution Survey: 2020 Final Report*, 1 <https://sidra.smu.edu.sg/sidra-international-dispute-resolution-survey-final-report-2020> (accessed 10 August 2020).
19. *See supra* n. 3 which lists some of the key literature on the issue of an enforcement mechanism for international commercial mediated settlement agreements.
20. Thomas Gaultier, *Cross-Border Mediation: A New Solution for International Dispute Settlement?*, 26(1) New York State Bar Association International Law Practicum 38, 50 (2013); Mason, *supra* n. 17, at 66.
21. Barkai, *supra* n. 6, at 43 recognises the cross-cultural nature which may be present in domestic mediations. *See also* Avruch, *Culture & Conflict Resolution*, *supra* n. 6, at 44.
22. Mason, *supra* n. 17, at 66.
23. Harold Abramson, *Time to Try Mediation of International Commercial Disputes*, 4 Journal of International Law and Comparative Law 323, 325 (1998).
24. Mason, *supra* n. 17, at 66; Strong, *supra* n. 3, at 18-19.
25. CPR and CEDR, *Insights into Alternative Dispute Resolution*, Winter 2018-2019, at 3 <https://www.cpradr.org/news-publications/reports/2019-04-04-cpr-cedr-joint-insights-report-on-the-use-of-adr/_res/id=Attachments/index=0/CEDR%20CPR%20report%20040419.pdf> (accessed 20 May 2020). This research is considered in detail later in this chapter.

London.[26] There is now an established body of empirical research on the specific field of international arbitration[27] and it seems that international mediation is following suit with Strong's empirical research on international commercial mediation and SIDRA's research which also specifically addresses international commercial mediation.[28] The empirical research conducted for this book, though on the narrower context of EU cross-border commercial mediation, seeks to contribute to this growing body of empirical research which specifically addresses cross-border mediation.

Turning to the empirical research conducted to date on cross-border mediation, such research falls broadly into two categories: research conducted by academics and research conducted by mediation institutions.[29] Each of these categories of research is considered in turn below.

§3.04 EMPIRICAL RESEARCH AT INTERNATIONAL LEVEL

Given the lack of relevant empirical research on cross-border mediation in the EU, it is necessary to consider empirical research conducted at the broader international level as such research may, within its wider reach, encompass the European context. In this broader international context there is a small number of empirical studies on international cross-border commercial mediation. Given the paucity of such studies and their value in informing the approach selected for the empirical research conducted for this book, each study is considered below.

As will be seen, the review of the empirical research conducted to date on international mediation demonstrates that the focus in such research to date has been quantitative research under which a number of responses are given to respondents from which they can choose. In addition, in such research there tends to be a limited engagement with the users of mediation. There is also a focus on an international convention on the enforceability of mediated settlement agreements as the principal way in which to increase the use of international cross-border commercial mediation.

26. Loukas Mistelis, *International Arbitration: Corporate Attitudes and Practices – 12 Perceptions Tested: Myths, Data and Analysis*, 15 The American Review of International Arbitration 525, 530-531 (2004).
27. In addition to the empirical studies conducted by Queen Mary University *see also* Christopher Drahozal and Richard Naimark (eds), *Towards a Science of International Arbitration: Collected Empirical Research* (Kluwer 2005).
28. *See* SIDRA, *supra* n. 18, at 2 & 46.
29. A similar categorisation is seen in the empirical work on international arbitration which has been conducted by either arbitration institutions or independent experts. *See* Mistelis, *supra* n. 26, 532. On a broader note, McConville and Wing Hong Chui identify a distinction 'between academic legal research, that is, that carried out by academics and students, as compared to legal research for professional (legal practice) purposes or research conducted by government and non-government agencies'. Mike McConville and Wing Hong Chui, *Research Methods for Law* 17 (Edinburgh University Press 2007).

[A] Empirical Research by Academics

[1] Research by the School of International Arbitration, Queen Mary University of London

Since 2006, the School of International Arbitration of Queen Mary University of London has conducted extensive empirical research on various topics regarding international arbitration. While the focus of such research is on international arbitration, some of the studies also offer interesting data on, or of potential relevance to, cross-border mediation.[30] Of particular note for the data obtained on cross-border mediation or 'ADR'[31] are Queen Mary's 2018, 2015 and 2006 studies. The data relevant to cross-border mediation from each of these studies is considered in turn below.

Queen Mary's 2018 study *The Evolution of International Arbitration*[32] offers data that is of potential relevance to cross-border mediation. Respondents were asked to select their preferred method of resolving cross-border disputes. The options from which respondents could choose were 'international arbitration together with ADR', 'international arbitration', 'cross-border litigation together with ADR', and 'cross-border litigation'.[33] The most popular choice was 'international arbitration with ADR' with 49% of respondents identifying this category as their preferred method for resolving cross-border disputes. Of particular interest, given its focus on the preference of the users of dispute resolution processes, is how this percentage increases when only the data from in-house counsel is considered. In-house counsel demonstrated a clear preference for the option of 'international arbitration with ADR', with 60% identifying it as their preferred method compared to 32% who identified arbitration alone as their preferred method.[34] This suggests a keen appetite for, and possibly use by, in-house counsel of ADR processes (other than arbitration) for their cross-border disputes.[35] In light of this appetite for 'ADR' for cross-border disputes, further research to explore the

30. Another notable study which focuses on international arbitration but also considers international mediation is Christian Buhring-Uhle, Lars Kirchhoff and Gabriele Scherer, *Arbitration and Mediation in International Business* (2nd ed. Kluwer Law International 2006). This study is not considered in this review as its research on mediation focuses on mediation within arbitration and specifically the use of mediation 'windows' in the arbitration process. The predominant focus of the study is arbitration, *see* page 105.
31. In its 2018 study, The School of International Arbitration uses the undefined term 'ADR' which excludes arbitration as arbitration is referred to specifically and separately from 'ADR'. *See* question 1 (What is your preferred method of resolving cross-border disputes?) on page 5 of the report. School of International Arbitration, Queen Mary University of London, *2018 International Arbitration Survey: The Evolution of International Arbitration* <http://www.arbitration.qmul.ac.uk/media/arbitration/docs/2018-International-Arbitration-Survey---The-Evolution-of-International-Arbitration-(2).PDF> (accessed 20 May 2020).
32. *Ibid.*
33. *Ibid.*, 5. The term 'ADR' is not defined in the study.
34. *Ibid.*
35. *Ibid.* The relevant question addresses preference rather than usage hence my reference to 'suggests ... *possibly* use by ...'. Regarding the interest in ADR processes other than arbitration, the report explains: 'even though arbitration continues to be the go-to dispute resolution mechanism, parties are increasingly resorting to various forms of ADR in the hope that a swifter and more cost-efficient resolution can be found to disputes before having them resolved by arbitration'.

extent of parties' preferences for, and indeed usage of, the specific types of dispute resolution which fall within this broad category of 'ADR', including mediation, would be a valuable addition to the empirical research on cross-border dispute resolution already conducted.

In Queen Mary's 2015 study on *Improvements and Innovations in International Arbitration*,[36] respondents were asked which types of dispute resolution methods they had used for cross-border disputes in the past five years and, in addition to the general term of 'ADR', mediation was specifically listed. The options from which respondents could choose were: 'international arbitration', 'cross-border litigation', 'international arbitration together with (other) ADR', 'mediation', and 'cross-border litigation together with ADR'.[37] Thirty-one per cent of respondents had used mediation for their cross-border disputes during the past five years, while 90% of respondents had used international arbitration.[38] The use of the broad category of 'ADR' means that it is not possible to gain a complete picture of the respondents' use of mediation. It may be that those who chose the option of 'international arbitration together with (other) ADR' (39%)[39] or the option of 'cross-border litigation together with ADR' (22%)[40] had used mediation as an 'ADR' method. Accordingly, it is possible that more than 31% of respondents had used mediation for their cross-border disputes either as a standalone dispute resolution process or in conjunction with arbitration or litigation.

In addition to the data on the use of mediation for cross-border disputes, Queen Mary's 2015 study explores the appetite for a convention on the enforceability of international mediated settlement agreements.[41] In particular, respondents were asked whether they would be encouraged to use mediation more often if there were a convention on the enforcement of settlement agreements resulting from mediation.[42] Fifty-four per cent of respondents were of the view that a convention on the enforcement of settlement agreements resulting from a mediation would encourage them to use mediation more often.[43] However, this finding seems to sit uncomfortably with a further finding of the study that only 8% of respondents had experienced difficulties in the past five years in enforcing settlement agreements resulting from a mediation. If there are few difficulties in practice in enforcing settlement agreements resulting from

36. School of International Arbitration, Queen Mary University of London, *2015 International Arbitration Survey: Improvement and Innovations in International Arbitration* <http://www.arbitration.qmul.ac.uk/media/arbitration/docs/2015_International_Arbitration_Survey.pdf> (accessed 20 May 2020).
37. *Ibid.*, 53.
38. *Ibid.* Respondents could select multiple answers which explains why the total of the percentages of respondents who chose each option amounts to more than 100%.
39. *Ibid.*
40. *Ibid.*
41. *Ibid.*, 31. It should be noted that the study does not explicitly refer to a convention on the enforcement of *international* settlement agreements resulting from mediation (*see* pages 31-32). It is assumed that *international* settlement agreements are the focus of that part of the study and are what respondents had in mind when answering the relevant questions as the proposals for a UN convention for settlement agreements arising from mediation have only been for *international* settlement agreements.
42. *Ibid.*
43. *Ibid.*

mediation, one may question the need for a convention on such enforcement; however, on a more general note, the Singapore Convention has significantly raised the profile of mediation.[44] It is important to note – as the study does – the high proportion of respondents (56%) who chose the 'not applicable' option for this question regarding whether they had, in the past five years, experienced difficulties enforcing settlement agreements resulting from a mediation.[45] The popularity of the 'not applicable' option may suggest that a significant number of respondents did not have the requisite experience of mediation to answer this question.[46] In light of the high number of respondents who chose 'not applicable', the study concluded that its findings on the topic of such a convention were inconclusive.[47] Accordingly, further research on such a convention, and in particular research focused on those who have experience of cross-border mediation, and ideally the users of mediation, would be helpful to further explore this timely topic of a convention for the enforcement of mediated settlement agreements given that the Singapore Convention opened for signature on 7 August 2019 and entered into force on 12 September 2020.[48] Such research might be a valuable resource for countries who are considering whether to sign up to this convention.

Finally, in Queen Mary's 2006 study, as in the 2018 study, mediation did not receive individual attention and was grouped together with 'other ADR' in questions regarding the preference for, and experience of, the various dispute resolution processes. It is therefore not possible to gain a clear picture of respondents' preference for, nor experience of, mediation (or other individual methods of ADR). Respondents were asked for their preferred mechanism(s) for resolving cross-border disputes. The choices from which they could choose were: 'international arbitration & ADR', 'international arbitration', 'international mediation & other ADR', and 'transnational

---

44. Others have noted that a lack of compliance with cross-border mediated settlement agreements is unlikely. *See* Jo-Mei Ma and others, *supra* n. 3, at 8; Wolski, *Recent Developments in International Commercial Dispute Resolution*, *supra* n. 3, at 9; Sussman, *The Final Step*, *supra* n. 3, at 2 and 3. It has also been argued that that in spite of the likely high levels of compliance with international mediated settlement agreements an international enforcement convention would play an important role in encouraging parties to comply with their mediated settlement agreements, in reinforcing parties' confidence in mediation, and also in marketing and promoting international mediation. *See* Jo-Mei Ma and others, *supra* n. 3, at 8; Boulle, *supra* n. 3, at 57; Wolski, *Recent Developments in International Commercial Dispute Resolution: Expanding the Options*, *supra*, n. 3, at 9. *See also* IMI, Herbert Smith Freehills and PWC, *Global Pound Conference Series: Global Data Trends and Regional Differences* available at: <https://www.imimediation.org/research/gpc/series-data-and-reports/#909-reports> (accessed 20 May 2020) which states at 20 'enforcement of mediated settlement agreements could help optically to evidence the status and value of mediation, is perhaps the key point'.
45. School of International Arbitration, Queen Mary University of London, *2015 International Arbitration Survey*, *supra* n. 36, 32.
46. Another possible explanation for the high percentage of respondents who selected 'not applicable' may be because those who would be best placed to answer this question, namely the users of mediation, could account for, at most, 8% of the respondents, which was the percentage of in-house counsel which took part in the study. *See* School of International Arbitration, Queen Mary University of London, *2015 International Arbitration Survey*, *supra* n. 36, 51 for a breakdown of the respondents by role.
47. *Ibid.*, 32.
48. On the Singapore Convention *see supra* n. 4. This chapter later considers research by S.I. Strong on such a convention for the enforcement of international settlement agreements arising from mediation.

litigation'.[49] The term 'ADR' was not defined in the study. The most popular choice was 'international arbitration & ADR' at 44% followed by 'arbitration' with 29%, 'international mediation & other ADR' with 16% and 'transnational litigation' with 11%. As with the later 2018 study, the data suggests a notable interest in ADR processes. The study also includes a question on respondents' experience of various dispute resolution processes.[50] The categories of arbitration, litigation and ADR are used for this question, and mediation is not specifically listed.

As is to be expected in studies which focus on international arbitration, the above brief summaries of the relevant portions of Queen Mary's extensive empirical research demonstrate that mediation receives little specific attention. Mediation tends to find itself grouped together with other dispute resolution processes in the broad category of 'ADR'. Where it does receive specific attention, for example, the questions on a convention for the enforcement of international settlement agreements arising from mediation, it appears that the respondents did not have the requisite experience of mediation to answer. Further studies which explore the use of mediation as a cross-border dispute resolution process would therefore be a valuable addition to the current body of empirical research on cross-border dispute resolution. This seems particularly worthwhile given the notable appetite from in-house counsel for cross-border 'ADR' identified in Queen Mary's 2018 research.

[2] Research by S.I. Strong

The most extensive recent piece of academic empirical research dedicated solely to international commercial mediation is Strong's *Realizing Rationality: An Empirical Assessment of International Commercial Mediation*.[51] The research was conducted to assist participants in UNCITRAL's discussions on a new United Nations treaty on the enforcement of settlement agreements resulting from international commercial mediation.[52] The research explored the future of international commercial mediation and, in particular, whether there was a need for an international convention on international commercial mediation and, if so, what such a convention should address.[53] Strong's research found that a convention addressing each of the enforcement of an agreement

49. School of International Arbitration, Queen Mary University of London, *International Arbitration: Corporate Attitudes and Practices* (2006) 5 <http://www.arbitration.qmul.ac.uk/media/arbitration/docs/IAstudy_2006.pdf> (accessed 20 May 2020).
50. *Ibid.*
51. Strong has written two papers on her research into international commercial mediation. The first is S.I. Strong, *Use and Perception of International Commercial Mediation and Conciliation: A Preliminary Report on Issues Relating to the Proposed UNCITRAL Convention on International Commercial Mediation and Conciliation*, University of Missouri School of Law Legal Research Paper 2014-28 <https://papers.ssrn.com/sol3/papers.cfm?abstract_id=2526302> (accessed 20 May 2020). This paper was followed in 2016 by Strong, *Realizing Rationality: An Empirical Assessment of International Commercial Mediation, supra* n. 17. Regarding the lack of empirical research on international commercial mediation, Strong notes at 1984 and 1985 that while there is a significant body of both theoretical and empirical academic research on domestic mediation there is a lack of information on international commercial mediation.
52. Strong, *Realizing Rationality, supra* n. 17, 1985 & 1990.
53. *Ibid.*, 1999.

to mediate and the enforcement of settlement agreements resulting from international commercial mediation would encourage parties to use such mediation.[54]

The research was conducted by way of a questionnaire from which respondents could select from a number of possible answers. The 221 respondents to the study came from key stakeholder groups and included private practitioners (35%), neutrals (arbitrators, mediators or conciliators – 28%), academics (20%), those in 'other forms of employment (10%), which included work as judges, in government, in multiple types of employment (for example, as both a private practitioner and a neutral) and in institutional settings (such as an arbitral institution)',[55] and in-house counsel (7%).[56]

The study explores 'the use and perception of international commercial mediation in the international legal and business communities'[57] and provides insights into the views of 'the international business and legal communities'.[58] Such insights seem to be of particular relevance to the legal community given the composition of the respondents to the study. Of the categories of respondent to the study (as listed above), the in-house counsel group of respondents, which accounts for 7% of the respondents, appears to be the only group which falls within the category of the international business community.[59] An interest in further exploring the views of the international business community prompted the focus, in the research conducted for this book, on the category of in-house counsel of multinational companies.

For studies on international dispute resolution, responses from those who have experience of such dispute resolution are of particular value.[60] Accordingly, respondents to Strong's survey were categorised according to the percentage of time they had spent working on international commercial dispute resolution during the preceding three years, with the largest category of respondents (37% of respondents) having spent between 0% and 20% of their time on international commercial dispute resolution.[61] The grouping of 0%-20% could include respondents who had no experience of international commercial dispute resolution together with those who had some experience, albeit as a small proportion of their overall work.[62] In designing the empirical research conducted for this book, and building on Strong's empirical

54. *Ibid.*, 2051, 2055 & 2057.
55. *Ibid.*, 2017.
56. *Ibid.*
57. *Ibid.*, 1998.
58. *Ibid.*, 2055 & 2060.
59. The data is not broken down by the respondents' type of employment. It is therefore not possible to determine whether the responses differ across the various employment categories and in particular the legal and business communities.
60. SIDRA's study (considered later in this chapter) notes that one of its study's characteristics which makes it unique is that 'the views are based on user experiences'. SIDRA, *supra* n. 18, at 1.
61. *Ibid.*, 2018.
62. Strong notes that some may view it as problematic that 'more than one-third of the respondents did not have extensive experience with international dispute resolution' and addresses this potential concern at *ibid.*, 2018.

research, one of the criteria which respondents had to fulfil in order to take part in the research was prior experience of cross-border commercial disputes.[63]

Further, another categorisation of respondents in Strong's study relates to their experience of mediation. Fifty-nine per cent of respondents had experience in at least one international commercial mediation during the relevant period.[64] Such experience was defined as 'including any matter for which the respondent had prepared, even if the mediation was cancelled before actual proceedings began'.[65] Accordingly, respondents who were categorised as having experience in international commercial mediation may have included those who had prepared for a mediation though had not then taken part in a mediation. This categorisation is of particular interest given the direction of certain questions on the use of mediation only to those respondents who had experience of mediation given that such respondents were best placed to answer such questions.[66] For example, only those respondents who had experience of mediation were asked why they had used mediation for their international commercial disputes. When answering this question, those who had experience of participating in a mediation would be able to draw on their actual experience of mediation while those who had prepared for, but had not then used, mediation would be able to draw on the reasons why they had intended to use mediation and their perception of mediation, rather than their actual experience.[67] This point influenced the design of the empirical research conducted for this book which directed the question of why parties used mediation to those who had experience of using mediation.[68]

On a related note, when exploring the issue of why parties used mediation, users' insights are particularly valuable. The question of why parties used mediation is best answered by the actual users of mediation and therefore the responses by the in-house counsel who took part in Strong's survey are of particular interest.[69] To ask others why users use international commercial mediation is to ask the different question of why *do*

63. As this book focuses on EU cross-border commercial mediation rather than the wider context of international cross-border commercial mediation, experience in EU cross-border commercial disputes was a requirement for participation in the research. Such a point was emphasised in the pre-interview information document (*see* Appendix 1) sent to interviewees before the interviews.
64. Strong, *Realizing Rationality*, *supra* n. 17, 2020.
65. *Ibid.*
66. *Ibid.*, 2021 & 2022.
67. SIDRA's study (considered later in this chapter) notes that one of its study's characteristics which makes it unique is that 'the views are based on user experiences and not just preferences'. Respondents to SIDRA's study were only asked to respond to questions on a particular dispute resolution process if they had indicated that they had used that particular process. SIDRA, *supra* n. 18, at 1.
68. As noted at n. 67, the focus on user experience is also seen, at the wider international level, in the inaugural International Dispute Resolution Survey by SIDRA. *supra* n. 18, at 1. Chapter 7 of this book explores the reasons why the interviewees who had used mediation for their EU cross-border disputes had used such mediation.
69. A breakdown by employment category of respondent is not available for the answers to the question on why parties use international commercial mediation. Strong, *Realizing Rationality*, *supra* n. 17, 2030. In SIDRA's later study on international commercial dispute resolution, SIDRA provides a breakdown by respondent of the factors influencing their choice of mediation as a dispute resolution mechanism. This breakdown identifies interesting differences regarding the factors which influence the decision to use mediation between the respondent categories of

you think users use such mediation. An interest in further exploring the views of the users was the foundation for the empirical research conducted for this book.[70]

Finally, it is important to note that, as addressed earlier, the focus of Strong's research on international commercial mediation is on a convention on the enforcement of settlement agreements arising from international mediation.[71] This focus on an international convention may not be of equal relevance to the EU cross-border context, addressed by this book, given the enforcement regime provided for EU cross border mediated settlement agreements under Article 6 of the EU Mediation Directive.[72] Accordingly, empirical research which focuses on the specific EU cross-border context would be a valuable addition to research which has already been conducted at the wider international context, together with, as explained above, a focus on the users of dispute resolution processes.

[3] Research by SIDRA

In 2020, SIDRA published the final report on its inaugural International Dispute Resolution Survey.[73] The survey focused exclusively on dispute resolution processes for cross-border disputes given that 'International dispute resolution involves different considerations compared to domestic settings.'[74] It addressed three international dispute resolution processes: international commercial arbitration, international commercial mediation and international commercial litigation. Another key characteristic of SIDRA's survey is that all respondents were users of international dispute resolution mechanisms.[75] The term 'users' is defined to include both 'Client Users (corporate executives and in-house counsel) and Legal Users (lawyers and legal advisers)'.[76] Of the total number of respondents (304), 64% were lawyers and legal advisers and 36% were corporate executives and in-house counsel.[77]

SIDRA's research found that international commercial mediation was the least used method of international dispute resolution mechanism between 2016 and 2018. The final report explains: 'International commercial arbitration remained the dispute resolution mechanism of choice by a large majority of respondents, and was used by 74% of the respondents between 2016 and 2018. This was followed by international commercial litigation (49%), hybrid mechanisms involving arbitration and mediation (27%) and international commercial mediation (26%).'[78] These findings are consistent with earlier empirical research by the EU which also suggests a limited use of

'Client Users' (in-house counsel and corporate executives) and 'Legal Users' (lawyers and legal advisers). SIDRA, *supra* n. 18 at Exhibit 7.1.2 at 47, and 48.

70. Chapter 4 explains further the focus in the empirical research for this book on the users of dispute resolution processes.
71. Strong, *Realizing Rationality*, *supra* n. 17, 1999.
72. *See* Chapter 2 for a discussion of Article 6, EU Mediation Directive.
73. SIDRA, *supra* n. 18.
74. *Ibid.*
75. *Ibid.*
76. *Ibid.*, 2.
77. *Ibid.*, 3.
78. *Ibid.*, 5.

cross-border mediation, though in the narrower context of EU cross-border mediation.[79]

Regarding the key findings on international commercial mediation, SIDRA notes that 'International commercial mediation users did not rank enforceability very highly on their list of reasons to mediate.'[80] SIDRA explains that this ranking may be due to the lack of an 'internationally recognised expedited enforcement mechanism'.[81] Another possible explanation for this finding is that enforcement may not be an issue in practice (i.e., users do not need, nor see the need, to enforce their mediated settlement agreements) and users therefore attribute limited importance to enforceability as a reason to mediate.[82]

While enforceability was ranked low on the list of factors which influence users' decision to use international commercial mediation, the factors which were ranked highly were impartiality/neutrality, speed and confidentiality.[83] Given the important role which these factors play in influencing decisions to use international commercial mediation, those seeking to increase the use of cross-border mediation, such as the EU, should focus on emphasising these aspects of mediation and on exploring how such characteristics might be enhanced. In particular, it is interesting to note that SIDRA's data suggests that improvement is needed to international commercial mediation's characteristics of confidentiality and impartiality/neutrality. As regards confidentiality, while 55% of users identified confidentiality as an 'absolutely crucial' factor influencing their decision to use international commercial mediation, only 38% of users were 'very satisfied' with the confidentiality of such mediation.[84] Similarly, as regards

79. *See* Chapter 2, text to (n. 20)-(n. 26).
80. SIDRA, *supra* n. 18, at 46.
81. *Ibid.*
82. It has been noted that the consensual nature of mediation means that parties are likely to adhere to their mediated settlement agreements. *See* Simon Roberts and Michael Palmer, *Dispute Processes ADR and the Primary Forms of Decision-Making* (2nd ed. Cambridge 2005) 215; Sussman, *The Final Step: Issues in Enforcing the Mediation Settlement Agreements*, *supra* n. 3, 2 & 3; Boulle, *International Enforceability of Mediated Settlement Agreements: Developing the Conceptual Framework*, *supra* n. 3, 57. Further, Boulle has acknowledged that there is not a problem in practice regarding compliance with mediated settlement agreements, Jo-Mei Ma and others, *Enforcing Cross-Border Mediated Settlement Agreements: Colloquium held at Bond University Faculty of Law on November 2013*, *supra* n. 3, at 8. *See also* SIDRA, *supra* n. 18, at 51, para. 7.1.14 which notes that corporate executives and in-house counsel may have a 'perception that mediated settlement agreements are generally voluntarily complied with in practice'.
83. SIDRA, *supra* n. 18, at 46 & 47. A breakdown of the factors which influence the choice of mediation by respondent user profile is provided at 47.
84. SIDRA, *International Dispute Resolution Survey: Currents of Change, 2019 Preliminary Report.*, 11 <https://sidra.smu.edu.sg/international-dispute-resolution-survey-currents-change-2019-preliminary-report> (accessed 10 August 2020). Data from SIDRA's preliminary report is used here rather than from the final report as the preliminary report identifies those factors which were 'absolutely crucial' to the respondents' choice to use mediation whereas the final report groups together the factors which were 'absolutely crucial' with those which were 'important' to the choice to use mediation (*see* SIDRA, *supra* n. 18, at 46, Exhibit 7.1.1). It is informative to see those factors which respondents identified as 'absolutely crucial' to their choice of mediation given that those are the factors of greatest influence. The ranking of the 'absolutely crucial' factors was then compared with the data on the extent to which respondents were 'very satisfied' with these factors (the later final report groups together the categories of 'very satisfied' and 'somewhat satisfied' (*see* SIDRA, *supra* n. 18 at 49, Exhibit 7.1.3). It is informative

impartiality/neutrality, while 53% of users identified impartiality/neutrality as 'absolutely crucial' to their decision to use international commercial mediation, only 31% of users were 'very satisfied' with the impartiality/neutrality of such mediation.[85] These figures show that some users who identified confidentiality and impartiality/neutrality as 'absolutely crucial' factors in their decision to use international commercial mediation were not 'very satisfied' with these characteristics of such mediation. It seems, therefore, that there is room for improvement as regards these two important characteristics of international commercial mediation which have been notably absent from the focus of recent measures and discussions to increase the use of such mediation.

[4] Potential Relevance of Domestic Research by Stipanowich and Lamare

To conclude this review of academic empirical research on international mediation, a further piece of empirical research merits consideration in spite of its apparent domestic US focus. Stipanowich and Lamare's research of Fortune 1000 corporations[86] sought to obtain information, by way of survey, from leading counsel at Fortune 1000 companies regarding perceptions and experiences of mediation, arbitration, and other ADR approaches.[87] While the study notes that it is unlikely that its findings apply beyond domestic mediation in the US,[88] it is possible that its findings apply beyond those borders to cross-border mediation.[89] Stipanowich and Lamare explain that their findings are unlikely to apply to cross-border business disputes for the following reason:

> Given the strong reasons to use arbitration in cross-border business disputes (including broad international enforceability of awards and avoidance of foreign courts), the data *likely* does not reflect international trends. Arbitration in the U.S. domestic market, however, is another matter.[90] (emphasis added)

However, two aspects of the study when considered together suggest that its findings may be relevant to cross-border mediation. First, the companies surveyed are Fortune 1000 companies, many of which have international dealings and presence and

to determine how many users had high levels of satisfaction with the factors which they regard as 'absolutely crucial' to their choice of mediation. The data in SIDRA's final report also conveys a disparity between the importance to respondents of the factors of impartiality/neutrality and confidentiality compared to their levels of satisfaction with those factors, though the disparity is less marked due to the different categorisation used (*see* SIDRA, *supra* n. 18 at 46 & 49).

85. *Ibid.*, 11.
86. Thomas Stipanowich and J. Ryan Lamare, *Living with ADR: Evolving Perceptions and Use of Mediation, Arbitration, and Conflict Management in Fortune 1000 Corporations*, 19 Harvard Negotiation Law Review 1 (2014).
87. *Ibid.*
88. *Ibid.*, 52.
89. Hale notes that Stipanowich's and Lamare's study does not differentiate between domestic and international disputes. Thomas Hale, *Between Interests and Law: The Politics of Transnational Commercial Disputes* (Cambridge 2015) 43 footnote 11.
90. Stipanowich and Lamare, *supra* n. 86, at 52.

therefore are likely to have experienced cross-borders disputes. Indeed, these companies are described by Stipanowich and Lamare as 'many of the world's largest corporations'.[91] Secondly, the questions asked of the companies, as referred to in section IV,[92] do not distinguish between ADR or mediation in domestic and cross-border disputes.[93] The terms 'ADR' and 'mediation' are used in these questions with no distinction made between their domestic and international forms. Therefore, when asked about ADR and mediation, companies may have taken these terms to refer to the resolution of both domestic and international disputes.

Accordingly, it is possible that Stipanowich and Lamare's findings may be applicable to cross-border dispute resolution and therefore should be included in this review of empirical research on international mediation. Notably, Stipanowich and Lamare's research, which focuses on the users of dispute resolution processes, and which includes specific reference to mediation rather than only using the broad category of 'ADR',[94] suggests a 'pre-eminence'[95] of mediation not previously seen in earlier research. In particular, of the various forms of ADR, mediation was the process of which most respondents had experience (98%), followed by arbitration (83%).[96] Further, compared to the study of in-house counsel in 1997, the 2011 study demonstrates that many more companies had, over the three previous years, used mediation for most types of dispute.[97] This contrasted with the results for arbitration, with many fewer companies having used arbitration for many types of dispute over a comparable period.[98] The study therefore captured a difference in trends in the usage of mediation and arbitration, with the report noting that 'Mediation usage is expanding and arbitration usage contracting in most conflict settings.'[99] In addition, a similar divergence in trends for the use of mediation and arbitration was seen in the data regarding respondents' predictions for the future use of each of these processes.[100] 85.6% of respondents were 'very likely' or 'likely' to use mediation rather than litigation for future commercial disputes.[101] In contrast, only 50.2% of respondents were 'very likely' or 'likely' to use arbitration rather than litigation.[102]

91. *Ibid.*, 2.
92. *Ibid.*, 32-44 (section IV Conflict Resolution Policies, perspectives on and experience with ADR).
93. This observation has also been made by Hale who notes that Stipanowich and Lamare's: 'surveys did not differentiate international disputes from domestic ones'. Hale, *supra* n. 89, 43 at footnote 11.
94. *See also* Thomas Stipanowich, *The International Evolution of Mediation: A Call for Dialogue and Deliberation*, 46 Victoria University of Wellington Law Review 1191, 1195 (2015).
95. *Ibid.*, 1194.
96. Stipanowich and Lamare, *supra* n. 86, at 41 (Chart F).
97. *Ibid.*, 45 (Chart G).
98. *Ibid.*, 45 & 46 (Chart H).
99. *Ibid.*, 47.
100. *Ibid.*, 49.
101. *Ibid.*
102. *Ibid.*, 49, 51 (Table O). This was a notable decrease compared to the results of the earlier 1997 study which found that 71% of respondents considered it either 'very likely' or 'likely' that they would use arbitration instead of litigation (page 51 of 2014 study).

The data shows a notable increase in the use of mediation and enthusiasm for its future use.[103] As explained above, while the authors note that it is unlikely that their findings apply to the cross-border context, it is possible that they could also apply to that context. However, further research which continues to focus on the users of dispute resolution processes and explicitly addresses cross-border mediation would be a valuable addition to the current body of research.

[B] Empirical Research by Mediation Institutions

[1] Research by the International Mediation Institute (IMI)

In 2014, the IMI conducted a survey of in-house counsel and business managers for its study 'How Users View the Proposal for a UN Convention on the Enforcement of Mediated Settlements'.[104] The purpose of the survey was to assist UNCITRAL Working Group II as it considered a convention on the recognition and enforcement of international settlement agreements reached through mediation.[105] The forty-four respondents were all users of dispute resolution processes.[106] The four questions in the survey explored the appetite for such a convention. For most of these questions, respondents could choose from yes/no type answers. The responses to these questions suggested a firm appetite for such a convention with, for example, 52.4% of respondents being 'much more likely' to mediate a dispute with a party from another country if that country had ratified a UN Convention on the enforcement of mediated settlement agreements.[107] A further 40.5% were 'probably' more likely to do so.[108] The study therefore offered an important introduction to users' appetite for a convention of the enforcement of mediated settlement agreements and the impact which such a convention might have on the use of mediation. However, the study cannot offer insights into the reasons for support for such a convention given the yes/no nature of the answers from which respondents could choose.

Further, research on international mediation was conducted by the IMI in 2014 in collaboration with the idrgroup.org and the Centre for Effective Dispute Resolution (CEDR).[109] The research, on how both mediation and arbitration should develop, was

103. Regarding the greater use by companies of mediation, Stipanowich and Lamare suggest that their research captures a 'tipping point in the modern history of mediation and arbitration, because it marks the points at which reliance on mediation contributed to a drop-off in arbitration'. *Ibid.*, 51.
104. IMI, *How Users View the Proposal for a UN Convention on the Enforcement of Mediated Settlements*. Details of the survey and its results are available at: < https://www.imimediation.org/wp-content/uploads/2018/06/IMI-UN-Convention-on-Enforcement-Survey-Summary-final-27.11.14.pdf > (accessed 20 May 2020).
105. *Ibid.*, 1.
106. 51% of the respondents were in-house counsel, 29% were senior corporate managers and 20% were described as 'held other roles'. *Ibid.*, 1.
107. *Ibid.*
108. *Ibid.*
109. IMI, idrgroup.org and CEDR, *Shaping the Future of International Dispute Resolution* (29 October 2014) <https://www.imimediation.org/wp-content/uploads/2018/11/London-2014-Final-data.pdf> (accessed 20 May 2020). A summary of the findings of this research is

by way of a survey to which over 150 delegates from over 20 countries contributed.[110] Respondents included users (defined as 'e.g. business persons or in-house counsel')[111] of international dispute resolution services (18%), advisors of such services (28%), providers of such services (38%), educators of such services (8%) and others (9%).[112] A number of the questions specifically addressed international mediation. Of particular note is the users' response to the question of whether international dispute resolution institutions 'have been providing innovative solutions to respond proactively to users' needs'.[113] While the aggregated responses to this question found that 27% of all respondents agreed that such institutions have been providing such solutions, that 40% were neutral on this issue and that 32% disagree, a different trend is seen in the data just from the users. In response to this question, only 8% of users agreed that such solutions were being provided to meet their needs, 31% were neutral on this issue, and a notable 62% disagreed that solutions were being provided to meet their needs.[114] This suggests that users were of the view that their needs were not being met by service providers in the international dispute resolution field. Further explorative research to both identify the needs of the users and then determine how such needs might be met would therefore be a valuable contribution to the current body of research on international mediation.

The survey also enquired about the need for an UNCITRAL convention on mediated settlement agreements, asking whether such a convention was 'needed to ensure that any mediated settlement agreement reached ... could automatically be recognised and enforced in all signatory countries'.[115] Seventy-three per cent of respondents agreed with this statement. It may also be helpful to explore, beyond the discrete issue of whether a convention is needed to ensure automatic recognition and enforcement of mediated settlement agreements, the broader issue of the reasons for such a convention. Such insights may assist those countries which are considering whether to sign up to the Singapore Convention. Finally, the survey asked whether there was a need for a platform to be created to allow users to express their international dispute resolution needs. This question received a positive response, with 72% agreeing to such a proposal.[116] This was followed by the suggestion of a series of international 'pound conferences' which similarly received an enthusiastic response, with 79% agreeing to such a suggestion.[117] Such a series of conferences took place in

available in Deborah Masucci and Michael Leathes, *The Urgent Need for Data: Are the Needs of Users and the Dispute Resolution Market Misaligned?* (Kluwer Mediation Blog, 5 November 2014) < http://mediationblog.kluwerarbitration.com/2014/11/05/the-urgent-need-for-data-are-the-needs-of-users-and-the-dispute-resolution-market-misaligned-2/ > (accessed 20 May 2020).

110. Masucci and Leathes, *supra* n. 109.
111. IMI, idrgroup.org and CEDR, *Shaping the Future of International Dispute Resolution*, *supra* n. 109, at 5.
112. *Ibid.*
113. *Ibid.*, 20.
114. *Ibid.*, 21.
115. *Ibid.*, 49.
116. *Ibid.*, 67.
117. *Ibid.*, 69.

2017. The findings of this survey suggest that further in-depth exploration of international dispute resolution users' needs would be an important contribution to the field.

In 2016, the IMI published its '2016 International Mediation & ADR Survey: Census of Conflict Management Stakeholders and Trends'.[118] This survey's internationality derives from the range of countries of the respondents (from sixty-seven countries) rather than from the type of mediation. None of the questions asked in the survey specifically refers to international/cross-border mediation and therefore this study is not considered further in this review of the relevant literature.

Notably, the IMI conceived of and led the GPC Series 2016-2017.[119] Back in 2014, the IMI had the idea of surveying dispute resolution stakeholders in interactive conferences across the world.[120] The GPC Series involved more than 4,000 people at 28 conferences in 24 countries during 2016 and 2017.[121] The GPC Series sought to gain data to establish whether suppliers of dispute resolution services were fully meeting users' needs.[122] Its focus was therefore on identifying users' needs and determining whether, in light of these needs, any changes were needed to dispute resolution services.

Bearing in mind this book's focus on cross-border commercial mediation and on the users' perspective, there are a couple of observations to be made regarding the GPC Series' research. First, the questions addressed in the conferences do not specifically address *cross-border* dispute resolution.[123] Further, the questions mostly explore commercial dispute resolution in general rather than each of the different dispute resolution processes. There is therefore little specific focus in the questions on mediation in particular.[124] Secondly, the five stakeholder groups involved in the GPC Series were: parties (defined as 'end-users of dispute resolution, generally in-house counsel and executives'),[125] advisors, adjudicative providers, non-adjudicative providers and influencers (defined as 'academics, government officers, policymakers').[126] Given the GPC Series' emphasis, as mentioned earlier, on users' needs, the extent of the

118. IMI, *2016 IMI International Mediation and ADR Survey: Census of Conflict Management Stakeholders and Trends* <http://www.odreurope.com/assets/site/content/IMI_survey_2016.pdf> (accessed 20 May 2020).
119. IMI, Herbert Smith Freehills and PWC, *Global Pound Conference Series: Data Trends and Regional Differences* (2018), 5. The report and the core questions used in the conferences are available at: <https://www.imimediation.org/research/gpc/series-data-and-reports/> (accessed 20 May 2019).
120. *Ibid.*, 1.
121. *Ibid.*, 2. The questions were also available for online voting after the final event in London in July 2017 until 31 August 2017 (*see* page 7 of IMI, Herbert Smith Freehills and PWC, *supra* n. 119).
122. *See* '2016-2017 GPC Series' at <https://www.imimediation.org/research/gpc/gpc-about/#about-gpc-series> (accessed 20 May 2020).
123. The questions generally explore 'commercial dispute resolution'. *See* questions 1.1, 1.6, 2.1, 2.5, 2.6, 3.2, 3.3, 3.4, 3.5, 3.6, 4.1, 4.4, 4.5, 4.6.
124. There is one question specific to mediation, namely Question 2.3, though which also refers to conciliation: 'In commercial disputes, what is achieved by participating in a non-adjudicative process (mediation or conciliation) (whether voluntary or involuntary –e.g. court ordered)?'. The questions are available at <https://www.imimediation.org/research/gpc/series-data-and-reports/> (accessed 20 May 2020).
125. IMI, Herbert Smith Freehills and PWC, *supra* n. 119, 6.
126. *Ibid.*

users' involvement in the research seems an important factor. The final report on the GPC Series does not provide data on how many participants in the GPC Series were from each of the five stakeholder groups. Therefore, it is not possible from the final report to determine the extent of the involvement of users of dispute resolution processes nor, in particular, users of mediation. Research continues to be provided based on the data gathered in the GPC Series[127] and further information on the involvement of users may become available.

[2] Research by CPR and CEDR

CPR and CEDR's joint report, *Insights into Alternative Dispute Resolution,*[128] dated winter 2018-2019, draws on research conducted separately by each of CPR and CEDR. CPR's research focuses on research of in-house counsel regarding their use of mediation and arbitration for both their domestic and cross-border disputes. CEDR's research focuses on research of mediators in both the UK and US regarding their mediation practice, including the extent and nature of their workload, the way in which they obtain their work and their fees.[129] It is CPR's research with its focus on in-house counsel and cross-border mediation which is of particular interest given this book's focus on cross-border mediation and, specifically, from the users' perspective.

Before considering key findings from the research, it is important to note that it is not possible to determine from the report how many in-house counsel took part in CPR's research. The report states that 'Overall, this report is based on responses from 90 individuals'[130] and this total is not broken down between the two separate surveys conducted by each of CPR (which surveyed in-house counsel) and CEDR (which surveyed mediators). Accordingly, it is not possible to determine the statistical significance of the findings for the particular user context.

One of the questions asked of in-house counsel in CPR's research was 'What is your company's preferred method for resolving disputes?'[131] For each of the categories of domestic and cross-border disputes, respondents could select from 'direct negotiation', 'arbitration', 'mediation', 'litigation' and 'other'.[132] The results reveal a significant preference for 'direct negotiation', which was the preferred method of dispute resolution for domestic disputes for 57% of respondents. The preference for direct

127. For example, GPC reports for each of San Francisco, New York, Miami, Baltimore, Austin and Toronto were published in December 2019, <https://www.imimediation.org/research/gpc/series-data-and-reports/#909-reports> (accessed 20 May 2020) and the GPC's North America Report, which offers a comparative analysis of the seven local North American reports was published in January 2020, <https://www.imimediation.org/2020/02/11/north-america-report-release/> (accessed 20 May 2020).
128. CPR and CEDR, *Insights into Alternative Dispute Resolution*, Winter 2018-19, <https://www.cpradr.org/news-publications/reports/2019-04-04-cpr-cedr-joint-insights-report-on-the-use-of-adr/_res/id=Attachments/index=0/CEDR%20CPR%20report%20040419.pdf> (accessed 20 May 2020).
129. *Ibid.* CEDR's research is referred to at pages 6-9 of the report.
130. *Ibid.*, 2, which also explains that 'Respondents to CPR's corporate counsel survey were predominantly large businesses – average revenues exceeded $15 billion'.
131. *Ibid.*, 3.
132. *Ibid.*

negotiation increases slightly for cross-border disputes with 59% of respondents selecting direct negotiation as their preferred method of dispute resolution for such disputes. Arbitration is the next most popular preferred method, though with a significantly lower percentage of in-house counsel selecting it as their preferred method: 16% for domestic disputes and 27% for cross-border disputes. Mediation is the third most popular preferred method of dispute resolution, at 12% for domestic disputes and 6% for cross border disputes.

The data summarised above on preferred dispute resolution methods reveals a number of interesting patterns. Direct negotiation is by far the most preferred method of dispute resolution for in-house counsel for both domestic and cross-border disputes. Interestingly, the preference for direct negotiation increases slightly for cross-border disputes (from 57% for domestic disputes to 59% for cross-border disputes). The increase, slight as it is, is surprising given the challenges which cross-cultural negotiation can bring which may make negotiation across borders more challenging than within borders.[133] This raises the interesting and important question of why there is a slightly increased preference for negotiation as a dispute resolution process for cross-border disputes compared to national disputes. This is a question which we cannot answer with the survey's results.

Further, this pattern regarding negotiation's popularity is particularly interesting given the very different pattern seen with mediation, the popularity of which decreases for cross-border disputes. While 12% of respondents selected mediation as their preferred method of dispute resolution for domestic disputes, only 6% selected mediation as their preferred method of dispute resolution for cross-border disputes. Given that mediation is, in essence, assisted negotiation[134] it is surprising that while negotiation's popularity increases for cross-border disputes compared to domestic disputes, mediation sees the opposite trend with a marked decrease in the preference for mediation for cross-border disputes compared to domestic disputes. It would be interesting to know the reasons for this difference. While the report appears to attribute this difference to concerns over the enforcement of mediated settlement agreements,[135] the data does not seem to support such a conclusion because: (i) such concerns would presumably apply equally to settlement agreements reached through negotiation and in the report negotiation is by far the most popular method of dispute resolution for cross-border disputes (at 59% and an increased popularity compared to domestic disputes, at 57%); (ii) the report notes that only one respondent reported having any difficulties with the other party complying with a settlement agreement arising from mediation;[136] and (iii) in the section on the reasons why parties do not use mediation

133. *See* text to (n. 19)-(n. 21).
134. *See* Chapter 1 for an explanation of mediation.
135. The report states 'when it comes to cross-border international disputes, one can see in this Insights report that confidence in ADR is not uniform; it would appear that mediation is at somewhat of a disadvantage when it comes to concerns over enforcement, presumably due to the different status of mediation across jurisdictions'. CPR and CEDR, *supra* n. 128, at 6.
136. *Ibid.*, 5.

to resolve their disputes, the issue of concerns about enforcement does not appear in the five most popular reasons for not using mediation.[137]

It is not possible, therefore, to determine with any certainty from the data provided in the report why there is such a marked difference in the preference for mediation for domestic disputes compared to cross-border disputes. It is important to recognise that such a finding suggests that context matters. Put another way, there are issues regarding the use of mediation which may be specific to cross-border mediation and which do not equally apply to domestic mediation.[138] It should however be noted that some caution is necessary when considering these statistics as, as mentioned earlier, it is not possible to determine how many in-house counsel took part in the survey.

Another interesting insight from CPR's research relates to why parties do not use mediation. The most popular reason for not using mediation is 'Difficulty in convincing counterparty to use mediation.'[139] It would be interesting, particularly for those such as the EU who are keen to promote the use of mediation, to know the reasons why such respondents experienced such resistance to the use of mediation. An awareness of the reasons why parties are reluctant to use mediation would be the first step in addressing such concerns. It may be that the second most popular reason why parties do not use mediation - namely, 'Perception that it is waste of time and money'[140] offers an explanation for such resistance. It is important to note that the data on the reasons why parties do not use mediation does not differentiate between domestic and cross-border mediation. In light of the report's findings regarding the difference in popularity between mediation for domestic disputes compared to mediation for cross-border disputes, it would be helpful to gather data on why parties do not use mediation specifically for each of the domestic and cross-border contexts. Such data may be particularly useful for those seeking to promote mediation in the specific cross-border context given the opportunity such insights would give to address such reasons. As will be explained in Chapter 4, the research for this study adopts such a context-specific approach as it focuses, in particular, on the EU cross-border context.

Further, while CPR's research identified interesting and important patterns regarding the use of mediation, as considered above, such survey-based research cannot explore the reasons for such patterns. Accordingly, research which builds on such patterns and enables them to be explored, such as by way of further qualitative research, would be an important complement to such survey-based research.

137. *Ibid.*
138. *See also* SIDRA, *supra* n. 18, at 1, regarding the different considerations for international dispute resolution compared to domestic dispute resolution.
139. The report lists the five most popular reasons why parties do not use mediation. The percentage of respondents which chose each answer is not provided. CPR and CEDR, *supra* n. 128, at 5.
140. *Ibid.*

§3.05 CONCLUSION

While it is difficult to identify themes which are common to the various pieces of research reviewed in this chapter, such research appears to suggest both a growing use of and interest in cross-border commercial mediation, at least as regards research findings focused on in-house counsel users of mediation. It also captures a notable appetite for, and interest in, measures which may increase the use of cross-border commercial mediation such as an international convention on the enforcement of mediated settlement agreements.

It is important to note that the review in this chapter of the relevant research demonstrates that there is a limited amount of empirical research on the use of *cross-border* commercial mediation, particularly by academics. The research also suggests that context matters. Put another way, factors which are relevant to the use of cross-border mediation may not equally apply to the use of domestic mediation. In addition, the review of the relevant research both in this chapter and the research by the EU examined in Chapter 2 highlights that there is no empirical research which focuses specifically on the context of EU cross-border commercial mediation.

Further, the review in this chapter demonstrates that the research which has been conducted on cross-border commercial mediation has largely employed quantitative research methods, namely surveys. While of course of great value, quantitative data cannot provide insights into the reasons behind the respondents' selection of a particular answer. The identification of such reasons would enable a deeper understanding of the relevant matters. In addition, in quantitative research it is the researcher who prescribes the answers from which respondents can choose which results in an inquiry focused on the issues predetermined by the researcher.

As regards the respondents to the research to date, there is limited involvement of the users of dispute resolution processes whose contributions and insights are of particular value to research on the use of mediation, as is explained in Chapter 4. In addition, where users are involved, some studies do not distinguish users' views from those of other respondents.

It is also important to note that in the cross-border research conducted to date there has been a notable emphasis on the topic of a convention on the enforcement of settlement agreements resulting from international commercial mediation. Such a topic may well be of less significance in the narrower EU context given the harmonisation across EU Member States of the enforcement of settlement agreements arising from EU cross-border mediations provided by Article 6 of the EU Mediation Directive (as considered in Chapter 2). This further suggests the potential value of empirical research which focuses on the specific EU cross-border context.

To build upon the research which has gone before it, both that which has been considered in this chapter and the EU's research considered in Chapter 2, the empirical research conducted for this book seeks to open up the conversation regarding the use, and lack of use, of cross-border commercial mediation in the EU. As will be explained in detail in Chapter 4, this research will therefore be by way of qualitative research involving interviews with respondents. Such an approach offers the opportunity to be expansive and exploratory. Perhaps most importantly, this research will focus on the users of dispute resolution processes, and in particular in-house counsel of multinational corporations, in its aim to gain a richer understanding of why disputants do, and do not, use mediation for the particular context of EU cross-border commercial disputes.

CHAPTER 4
Methodology

> Approach the context with care and respect. Walk carefully. Watch and listen to those who know the setting. Do not presume to know solutions or to provide preconceived recipes.[1]

§4.01 EXECUTIVE SUMMARY

The choice of methodology has been informed by the analysis in Chapters 2 and 3, in particular: (i) the tendency towards a prescriptive approach by way of surveys where a set of possible answers and solutions are put to the respondents from which they can choose; and (ii) the limited involvement of users of dispute resolution processes in the relevant empirical research to date. In contrast, this research adopts an elicitive approach by engaging with users of EU cross-border commercial dispute resolution processes to explore how mediation is viewed and why it is, and is not, used in that particular context. It seeks to be 'research with rather than on people'.[2]

This chapter explains the choice of qualitative research for this study and, in particular, the use of semi-structured interviews. The chapter then sets out the research process. This includes the way in which the research participants were identified and approached, the data collection process and the method of analysis of the data.

1. John Paul Lederach, *The Moral Imagination* 107 (Oxford University Press 2005).
2. John Heron and Peter Reason, *The Practice of Co-operative Inquiry: Research With Rather Than On People* in Hilary Bradbury-Huang (ed.), *Handbook of Action Research, Participative Inquiry and Practice* (Sage 2000).

§4.02 THE CRITICAL ROLE OF EMPIRICAL WORK IN THE CONFLICT RESOLUTION FIELD

Before the description of the research process, it is helpful to step back and to briefly acknowledge the role of empirical work in the dispute resolution field. Some disquiet has been expressed regarding a growing distance between the concerns of academics and the reality in the conflict resolution field.[3] The irony has not been lost that a field born of a firm belief in collaboration may need to be better at practising what it preaches.[4] Empirical studies have been identified as 'critical to developing, testing, and correcting conflict resolution-related theories and findings'.[5] In a compilation of papers on the implementation of the EU Mediation Directive, Steffek identifies that good dispute resolution law should be centred upon the interests of the parties to disputes.[6] To that end, Steffek emphasises that listening to those parties through empirical research forms an essential ingredient in the making of good law, citing Naomi Creutzfeldt's research on users' perceptions of ombudsmen practices as one such example.[7] More broadly, Stipanowich has recently called for 'more active mutual engagement and discernment'[8] to accompany the widening international conversation on mediation. He offers an eloquent caution against an approach that is not founded on awareness and considered action:

> the mounting global hubbub surrounding mediation, and highly varied perceptions regarding the nature and value of mediation, underscore the need for thoughtful conversation and deliberate reflection on present trends and tendencies. The failure to periodically step back and take stock of where we are and where we are going increases the likelihood of behavioural 'drift' – that is, action that becomes increasingly reflexive as opposed to deliberate.[9]

This is a caution recently echoed by Howard Gadlin in posing the following question to the mediation community, 'To my mind, as we assess the current state and

3. Christopher Honeyman, Barbara McAdoo and Nancy Welsh, *Not Quite Protocols: Toward Collaborative Research in Dispute Resolution*, 19(1) Conflict Resolution Quarterly 75, 77 (2001). *See also* Thomas Stipanowich, *The International Evolution of Mediation: A Call for Dialogue and Deliberation*, 46 Victoria University of Wellington Law Review 1191, 1193 & 1200 (2015); Machteld W. De Hoon, *Making Mediation Work in Europe: What's Needed Is a New Balance Between Mediation and Court Proceedings*, 20(2) Dispute Resolution Magazine 22, 23 (2013-2014).
4. Honeyman, McAdoo, Welsh, *supra* n. 3, at 77.
5. *Ibid.*, 75.
6. Felix Steffek, *The Relationship between Mediation and other Forms of Alternative Dispute Resolution* in European Parliament, *The Implementation of the Mediation Directive, Workshop 29 November 2016* (2016) PE 571.395, 47 at 61.
7. *Ibid.*, 62. The reference for Creutzfeldt's work is: Naomi Creutzfeldt, *Trusting the Middle-Man: Impact and Legitimacy of Ombudsmen in Europe*, Westminster, 2016 <https://www.law.ox.ac.uk/trusting-middle-man-impact-and-legitimacy-ombudsmen-europe/project-reports> (accessed 20 May 2020).
8. Stipanowich, *supra* n. 3, at 1192.
9. *Ibid.*, 1200.

future prospects of mediation, strengthening the relationship between practice, research and theory is among the most important tasks we face because it poses the question "do we know what we are talking about".'[10]

Against the backdrop of these cautions, the research conducted for this book appears timely. As explored in Chapters 2 and 3, there remains a limited amount of empirical work on mediation to which users of cross-border commercial dispute resolution processes have contributed at both the EU cross-border level and the broader international cross-border level. Accordingly, further work would be valuable in order to gain a deeper perspective of the 'reality' in this cross-border field. The research for this book is a contribution to building such a perspective, through its engagement with commercial parties in interviews in order to gain a rich understanding of how they regard mediation and why they do, and do not, use mediation for their EU cross-border commercial disputes.

§4.03 THE CHOICE OF QUALITATIVE RESEARCH

Given the exploratory aim of the empirical research conducted for this book, the natural fit was qualitative research. Qualitative research affords the opportunity to gather rich, 'thick description'[11] on particular matters. It lends itself to research which is exploratory in nature, meaning 'research that is designed to examine whether an issue, situation, or problem exists and if so define it'.[12] Put simply, if you are asking why people do certain things or what factors influence their choices and if you want to truly understand those issues the appropriate tool is qualitative research.[13] Such research requires the researcher to set aside his/her views, to provide the opportunity for others to share their perspectives and to accurately record such insights. As Lofland has explained:

> the role of a qualitative researcher is not to interject one's own view but instead to describe accurately another's experience so as to elicit what the research participant believes or understands, and to provide quotes as evidence, rather than to judge through one's own lens what that person must think or feel.[14]

Further, in the particular context of the conflict resolution field, Stipanowich has highlighted the important contribution that qualitative research can make in shedding light on particular contexts, 'To appreciate the true value of ADR in operation, one

10. Howard Gadlin, *Remembrance of Pleasures Past: Reflections of a Practitioner* in Ian Macduff (ed.), *Essays on Mediation, Dealing with Disputes in the 21st Century* 16 (Wolters Kluwer 2016).
11. Clifford Geertz, *The Interpretation of Cultures* 6 (3rd ed. Basic Books 2017).
12. Lisa Webley, *Qualitative approaches to Empirical Legal Research* in Peter Cane and Herbert Kritzer (eds), *The Oxford Handbook of Empirical Legal Research* 928 (Oxford University Press 2010). Further, Patton has explained: 'It's not how many said something that matters. It's the import, wisdom, relevance, insightfulness, and applicability of what was said, by many or by a few.' Michael Quinn Patton, *Qualitative Research & Evaluation Methods* 632 (4th ed. Sage 2015).
13. Hazel Genn, *Hazel Genn and Paths to Justice* in Simon Halliday and Patrick Schmidt, *Conducting Law and Society Research* 231 (Cambridge 2009).
14. John Lofland and others, *Analyzing Social Settings: A Guide to Qualitative Observation and Analysis* 50 (4th ed. Wadsworth 2004).

cannot depend exclusively or even primarily on statistical data, however rich. Ultimately, we need to ... qualitatively illuminat[e] the evolution of ADR within various contexts and the experiences of those who play a part in it.'[15]

The research for this book seeks to add to the largely quantitative body of research in the cross-border context conducted to date by gaining detailed insights into the views and experiences of users, and potential users, of EU cross-border commercial mediation. It then identifies further ways in which to promote EU cross-border commercial mediation which reflect, and respond to, the insights provided by these cross-border commercial dispute resolution users. As explained in Chapter 3, the data obtained through the semi-structured interviews for this research is a first step in gaining insights on mediation from those who know and operate within the specific context of EU cross-border commercial disputes. This data begins to fill a gap in the literature.

It is appropriate here to mention that the choice to engage, via qualitative research, in depth with a particular context was also influenced by the work of the mediator, John Paul Lederach. Lederach employs an elicitive approach to practising mediation. Such an approach is 'a philosophy of interaction with people in settings of conflict'[16] which looks for unique characteristics of particular contexts that offer fresh and effective resources for conflict resolution.[17] It is a participative approach 'aimed primarily at discovery, creation, and solidification of models that emerge from the resources present in a particular setting and respond to the needs in that context'.[18] Accordingly, such an approach explores and engages with a particular setting to identify resources which are already present in that particular context, rather than transplant resources from another, different context.[19] It is an inquisitive and collaborative approach rooted in, respectful of and drawing from the particular context, and which looks for solutions that emerge from the specific context.[20]

15. Thomas Stipanowich, *ADR and the 'Vanishing Trial': The Growth and Impact of 'Alternative Dispute Resolution'*, 1(3) Journal of Empirical Legal Studies 843, 847 (2004). Similarly, Welsh has emphasised the value of qualitative research describing it as 'the "best strategy" for developing hypotheses, testing hypotheses against real-life evidence, and helping to explain, supplement, or dispute quantitative data. Even small qualitative studies and individual case studies have been instrumental in allowing the creation and testing of theories in a manner that is directly tied to evidence'. Nancy Welsh, *Stepping Back Through the Looking Glass: Real Conversations with Real Disputants about Institutionalized Mediation and its Value*, 19 Ohio State Journal on Dispute Resolution 573, 607 (2004).
16. John Paul Lederach, *Building Mediative Capacity in Deep-Rooted Conflict*, 26 The Fletcher Forum of World Affairs 91, 95 (2002).
17. *Ibid.*, 96.
18. John Paul Lederach, *Preparing for Peace*, 83 (Syracuse University Press 1995). Lederach's call for a bottom-up, participatory, context-specific approach to conflict resolution has been heeded, and advocated, by other writers on peacebuilding such as Nathan Funk, *Building on What's Already There, Valuing the Local in International Peacebuilding*, 67 International Journal 391 (2011-2012).
19. Lederach has also described an elicitive orientation as 'decidedly an orientation toward solidifying grounded and inside resources that support long-term change processes in a sustainable manner'. Lederach, *Building Mediative Capacity*, *supra* n. 16, at 96.
20. Lederach, *Preparing for Peace*, *supra* n. 18, at 10.

An example that illustrates this elicitive approach of finding resources present, though hidden, in the specific context is available from Lederach's work in peace initiatives in Somalia. In his work as a peacebuilder and mediator, by engaging with the particular context, Lederach identified an intriguing and powerful peacebuilding resource available in the particular conflict setting: the women of Wajir (Wajir is in the northeast of Kenya near the Somali and Ethiopian borders).[21] These women had a number of characteristics which meant that they had a unique potential and capacity to contribute to building peace in that particular environment.[22] These characteristics included their position in society as a result of cross-clan marriages, their responsibilities for their families' everyday needs, and their key role in being the holders of money in the marketplace.[23] For example, as a result of their cross-clan marriages, women experienced the war differently to men as the women's fathers and brothers could often be fighting their sons and husbands.[24] In addition, their cross-clan status meant that they could travel between clans with more safety and could therefore serve as informal diplomats.[25] Regarding women's responsibility for their families' everyday needs and survival, women were often in the market places where they mixed with women from other clans, and they were instrumental in bringing conflicts in the market places to an end so that they could continue with life in the market.[26] Finally, as regards women being the holders of money, given the lack of central banking and governance, the economy was conducted by informal means and the women working in the markets played a significant role in the economy.[27]

Lederach's elicitive approach looks for and supports resources such as the women of Wajir who offer the potential to bring about change to a particular context from within that particular context. The role of the external mediator, such as Lederach brought in to help to mediate the conflict, was not to insert him or herself into the particular context but rather to identify and support the women's unique peacebuilding capacity which was present in that particular context.[28]

An elicitive approach can further be explained by contrasting it with a prescriptive approach. Regarding his work as both a mediator and mediation trainer, Lederach describes a prescriptive approach as one with the 'unspoken motto of ... "We have just what you need"',[29] a 'menu approach'[30] with a 'predefined agenda designed to meet

21. Lederach, *The Moral Imagination*, *supra* n. 1, at 10.
22. *Ibid.*, 97; Lederach, *Building Mediative Capacity*, *supra* n. 16, at 96.
23. Lederach, *The Moral Imagination*, *supra* n. 1, at 99; Lederach, *Building Mediative Capacity*, *supra* n. 16, at 96.
24. Lederach, *Building Mediative Capacity*, *supra* n. 16, at 96.
25. *Ibid.*; Lederach, *The Moral Imagination*, *supra* n. 1, at 99.
26. Lederach, *Building Mediative Capacity*, *supra* n. 16, at 96; Lederach, *The Moral Imagination*, *supra* n. 1, at 99.
27. Lederach, *Building Mediative Capacity*, *supra* n. 16, at 96; Lederach, *The Moral Imagination*, *supra* n. 1, at 99 & 100.
28. Lederach, *Building Mediative Capacity*, *supra* n. 16, at 96; Lederach, *The Moral Imagination*, *supra* n. 1, at 99 & 100.
29. Lederach, *Preparing for Peace*, *supra* n. 18, at 47.
30. *Ibid.*, 48 & 49.

predefined need [sic]'.[31] It is an approach to mediating and to mediation training founded on the assumptions of transferability and universality, with an expert who determines and prescribes what parties need. In contrast to an elicitive approach, a prescriptive approach is not rooted in the particular context nor does it seek resources in the context itself.[32] Perhaps the focus to date in the field of international commercial mediation on an international enforcement mechanism, inspired by the enforcement system available to international arbitration under the New York Convention, may resemble such a prescriptive approach.[33] The focus has tended to be on transferring an element from the context of international arbitration (i.e., a direct enforcement mechanism) into the different context of international mediation.

Drawing on Lederach's quotation which opens this chapter and which emphasises, under an elicitive approach, the value of listening to those who know the particular context, and for those coming from outside the context not to presume to know solutions, the semi-structured interviews conducted for this book afforded an opportunity to listen to and engage with those who know the particular context of EU cross-border commercial disputes. In particular, the use of open questions – without a set of answers from which the interviewees could choose – allowed the interviewee to freely and fully determine his/her answers. Accordingly, the researcher was able to elicit from those who know the particular context of EU cross-border commercial disputes, important and novel themes regarding their views and use of EU cross-border commercial mediation, as are explored in Chapters 6, 7 and 8.

[A] The Choice of Semi-Structured Interviews

Of the various methods of qualitative research, semi-structured interviews were chosen. Inspired by Lederach's elicitive approach, as described earlier, such semi-structured interviews offered the opportunity to engage with the participants in order to gain insights into how they see the particular setting.[34] It is a method of research which emphasises the interviewees' own perspectives and understanding of issues[35] and allows for the gathering of rich, detailed answers.[36] Such a method has been used

31. *Ibid.*
32. *Ibid.*, 55.
33. Chapter 3 considered the research which focuses on an international convention for the enforcement of settlement agreements arising from mediation.
34. Webley, *supra* n. 12, at 934.
35. Alan Bryman, *Social Research Methods* 466, 467 & 468 (5th ed. Oxford University Press 2012).
36. *Ibid.*, 467. Further, in their empirical work on Scottish construction clients' interaction with mediation, and drawing on Geertz (*supra* n. 11), Agapiou and Clark note that interviews offer the opportunity to get a 'thicker description' of the relevant issues. Andrew Agapiou and Bryan Clark, *A Follow-Up Empirical Analysis of Scottish Construction Clients Interaction with Mediation*, 32(3) Civil Justice Quarterly 362, 366 (2013).

in recent research on mediation, though in a different context to that of this book, where the aim was to gain more insightful accounts into particular issues.[37] Notably, in Bondy et al.'s work,[38] the purpose of the research was similar to that of this study, though in a different context. In Bondy et al.'s research, the focus was the use of mediation in judicial review cases. However, the purpose was similar to that of this research: it sought to understand the lack of take-up of mediation in that context and whether it was possible, or desirable, to encourage a greater uptake.[39]

Further, the decision to use semi-structured interviews was in part prompted by the identification of interesting and novel findings resulting from the use of open questions in the most substantial piece of empirical research to date dedicated to international commercial mediation. In Strong's empirical research on international commercial mediation, the opportunity to offer additional answers other than those listed in the survey produced some particularly interesting information. For example, in response to a question regarding factors that affect parties' likelihood of using international commercial mediation, respondents raised issues regarding the level of trust which parties have of institutional providers of dispute resolution services and also identified a concern about qualified mediators being unable to break into the international mediation market.[40] This suggests that there could be interesting threads of inquiry which have not yet been teased out regarding the use, and lack of use, of cross-border commercial mediation. Using the exploratory forum offered by semi-structured interviews maximises the opportunity of not only discovering such threads but also of being able to examine them in detail. As Lande and Benner have explained, the research method of semi-structured interviews is 'especially useful for getting a more complete understanding than is possible with surveys'.[41]

Finally, semi-structured rather than unstructured interviews were chosen given that there were particular topics regarding the use of mediation for EU cross-border commercial disputes which the research sought to address.[42] Using guideline questions also ensured uniformity.[43]

---

37. Varda Bondy et al., *Mediation and Judicial Review: An Empirical Study*, 11 (The Public Law Project 2009); Deirdre Curran, *The Role of Mediation in the Resolution of Two Industrial Disputes in Ireland*, 36(5) Employee Relations 496 (2014); Mary Anne Noone and Lola Akin Ojelabi, *Ensuring Access to Justice in Mediation within the Civil Justice System*, 40(2) Monash Law Review 528, 534 (2014).
38. Bondy et al., *supra* n. 37.
39. *Ibid.*, 6.
40. S. I. Strong, *Use and Perception of International Commercial Mediation and Conciliation: A Preliminary Report on Issues relating to the Proposed UNCITRAL convention on International Commercial Mediation and Conciliation*, University of Missouri School of Law Legal Research Paper 2014-28, 1, 29 & 31 (2014) <https://papers.ssrn.com/sol3/papers.cfm?abstract_id=2526302> (accessed 20 May 2019).
41. John Lande and Peter Benner, *Why and How Business Use Planned Early Dispute Resolution*, 13 University of St. Thomas Law Journal 248, 295 (2017).
42. *See* later in this chapter for the particular topics which were covered in the interviews.
43. Loukas Mistelis, *International Arbitration: Corporate Attitudes and Practices – 12 Perceptions Tested: Myths, Data and Analysis*, 15 The American Review of International Arbitration 525, 534 (2014).

[B] The Choice of Interviewee

The interviewees are users of EU cross-border commercial dispute resolution processes.[44] Put another way, they are parties to EU cross-border commercial disputes who have chosen to use, or not to use, mediation to resolve such disputes.

The users of commercial dispute resolution processes have been chosen as the focus of this research for two reasons. First, as identified in Chapters 2 and 3, users have not played a significant role in the relevant research on mediation to date.

Secondly, and most importantly, the users' perspective is a distinct and important one.[45] In his paper for a workshop on the EU Mediation Directive, Steffek identified the primacy of the users' perspective. In arguing for a taxonomy ('a reference system of classification')[46] in order to improve the regulation of dispute resolution, Steffek notes that 'since it is the parties' interests and conflicts that matter, the best perspective for a dispute resolution taxonomy is the perspective of the parties'.[47] Put simply, the parties' perspective should play a key role in influencing and shaping any measures to develop dispute resolution. The value of the parties' perspective has further been emphasised by Stipanowich who notes, 'Though business clients and corporate counsel are notoriously difficult to convene or poll, their perspectives as users and consumers of dispute resolution services are naturally of exceptional value.'[48] In addition, the importance of the users' views was recognised in a recent IMI study involving stakeholders in conflict management in which 75% of the stakeholders surveyed noted that users' views on conflict management are 'extremely important' to them and notably more so than mediators' views and certain statistical data on mediation.[49] Further, as regards the specific dispute resolution field of mediation where self-determination is recognised as a fundamental tenet, the importance of the users' perspective has been widely recognised and emphasised.[50] With mediation's key

44. Chapter 2 explained why the focus of this research is on commercial mediation rather than the broader category of civil mediation. Accordingly, users of commercial dispute resolution processes were approached for this research.
45. For example, as regards the distinct perspective of users of dispute resolution processes, Lande found that the different groups of respondents in his study, namely outside counsel, inside counsel and executives, had 'remarkably different patterns of opinions about litigation'. John Lande, *Failing Faith in Litigation? A Survey of Business Lawyers' and Executives' Opinions*, 3 Harvard Negotiation Law Review 1, 48 (1998). This chapter later explains why the research for this book focused on in-house counsel rather than the business executives.
46. Steffek, *supra* n. 6, at 57.
47. *Ibid.*
48. Thomas Stipanowich, *What Have We Learned From The Global Pound Conferences?* (*Kluwer Mediation Blog*, 27 November 2017) <http://mediationblog.kluwerarbitration.com/2017/11/27/learned-global-pound-conferences/?doing_wp_cron=1589968951.4794659614562988281250> (accessed 20 May 2020).
49. International Mediation Institute, *The 2016 IMI International Mediation and ADR Survey: Census of Conflict Management Stakeholders and Trends* 23 <http://www.odreurope.com/assets/site/content/IMI_survey_2016.pdf> (accessed 20 May 2020).
50. Machteld W. De Hoon, *Making Mediation Work in Europe: What's Needed Is a New Balance Between Mediation and Court Proceedings*, 20 Dispute Resolution Magazine 23, 25 (2013-2014). Welsh, *supra* n. 15, at 578 & 605-606. *See also* the seminal work by Carrie Menkel-Meadow, *Whose Dispute Is it Anyway: A Philosophical and Democratic Defence of Settlement (in some cases)*, 83 Georgetown Law Journal 2663, 2669 (1995); Bondy at al., *supra* n. 37, at 13;

characteristic of party self-determination, it is the users who determine the outcome of their disputes and therefore, in this field, their views hold particular value and importance.

Having explained why the users' perspective is the focus of this study, the next point to consider is what the term 'user' of EU cross-border commercial dispute resolution processes means for the purpose of the research for this book. The users are the corporations who choose a method, or methods, of dispute resolution to address their EU cross-border commercial disputes. Further, while the term 'users' of EU cross-border commercial dispute resolution processes may include both the business and in-house counsel representatives of a corporation, for the purpose of the research for this book 'users' is defined as in-house counsel representatives.[51] This focus on in-house counsel rather than on the business representatives of the corporation is for two reasons.

First, qualitative research focuses on an in-depth study of a small number of data sources that are regarded to be data rich.[52] The question therefore to ask is who within those companies would be the most data-rich source. In light of their role in counselling their businesses on their disputes,[53] in-house counsel rather than their business colleagues were considered to be best placed to offer rich data given the greater exposure to disputes which the role of in-house counsel brings.[54] This is particularly relevant for the large multinational corporations that took part in this research. These companies have disputes across different countries and business sectors and, while a business representative may have had experience with some of these disputes, it is senior in-house counsel who has oversight of the company's various material disputes.[55] It should also be noted that, on an important practical note, as an outside researcher it would be very difficult, if not impossible, to identify the business representative in each company with the greatest experience of cross-border disputes. Accordingly, interviewing in-house counsel of multinational companies afforded the

Jacqueline Nolan-Haley, *Self-Determination in International Mediation: some Preliminary Reflections*, 7 Cardozo Journal of Conflict Resolution 277, 278 (2005-2006).

51. Chapter 3 refers to a number of empirical studies involving users of mediation. The description of these studies includes reference to the way in which the term 'users' was used.
52. Webley, *supra* n. 12, at 934.
53. Prashant Dubey and Eva Kripalani, *The Generalist Counsel: How Leading General Counsel Are Shaping Tomorrow's Companies* 5 (Oxford University Press 2013); Michael McIlwrath and John Savage, *International Arbitration and Mediation: A Practical Guide*, para. 1-002 (Kluwer 2010).
54. It should be acknowledged that there is an abundance of literature on the expanding role of in-house counsel with an increasing emphasis on not only the provision of legal advice but in adding value to the business. *See*, for example, Michael Leathes, *Negotiation: Things Corporate Counsel Need to Know But Were Not Taught* (Kluwer 2017) and in particular Chapter 1; Dubey and Kripalani, *supra* n. 53, and in particular Chapter 1; Lubomir Litov, Simone Sepe and Charles Whitehead, *Lawyers and Fools: Lawyer-Directors in Public Corporations* Cornell Law Faculty Publications 673, [2014] <https://scholarship.law.cornell.edu/facpub/673> (accessed 20 May 2020); Mari Sako, *General Counsel with Power?* Said Business School, University of Oxford, at 23 <http://eureka.sbs.ox.ac.uk/4560/1/General_Counsel_with_Power.pdf> (accessed 20 May 2020). Further, Lande has noted that in-house counsel offer a unique 'blend of the experience and perspective of both outside counsel and executives'. Lande, *Failing Faith*, *supra* n. 45, at 22.
55. The in-house counsel's oversight of the company's disputes is borne out by the data from the interviews in which the in-house counsel confirmed their involvement in their companies' disputes, including cross-border disputes. *See* further Chapter 5.

best and most practicable way of gaining rich data on this research topic. Indeed, numerous studies which have sought to gain insights into how and why businesses use dispute resolution processes (with a focus on arbitration and litigation) have recognised the data-rich source of in-house counsel and have chosen in-house counsel as the participants for their research.[56]

Secondly, given their role as participants in a variety of conflicts and their status as clients of law firms, in-house counsel has been recognised as being 'uniquely placed to help to bring about a sea change in the culture of conflict'.[57] Notably, a greater appetite for early dispute resolution for commercial disputes has been attributed to the increasing influence of in-house counsel.[58] They have extensive purchasing power which brings with it the opportunity to influence the legal market, including the way in which disputes are addressed.[59] Further, it appears that the power of in-house counsel is at an unprecedented high with companies seeking to take greater control of external legal fees and strategy.[60] Such power is also suggested by the data from the GPC Series 2016-2017 which identified in-house lawyers 'as the group with the potential to be most influential in bringing about change in commercial dispute resolution practice'.[61]

One prime example of the influence of in-house counsel in the dispute resolution field is the creation by leading corporate counsel of the non-profit organisation, CPR[62] which 'helps prevent and resolve legal conflict effectively and efficiently'.[63] Among its numerous initiatives, in the 1980s CPR developed its CPR Pledge (under which

---

56. Thomas Stipanowich and J. Ryan Lamare, *Living with ADR: Evolving Perceptions and Use of Mediation, Arbitration, and Conflict Management in Fortune 1000 Corporations*, 19 Harvard Negotiation Law Review 1, 4 (2014); David Lipsky and Ronald Seeber, *The Appropriate Resolution of Corporate Disputes: A Report on the Growing Use of ADR by U.S. corporations* Scheinman Institute on Conflict Resolution, Cornell University ILR School <http://digitalcommons.ilr.cornell.edu/cgi/viewcontent.cgi?article=1003&context=icrpubs> (accessed 20 May 2020); IMI, *2013 International Corporate Users ADR Survey* <https://www.imimediation.org/2013/04/06/imi-adr-users-survey-results/> (accessed 20 May 2020); School of International Arbitration, Queen Mary University of London, *Corporate Choices in International Arbitration* (2013) <http://www.arbitration.qmul.ac.uk/research/2013/#d.en.493207> (accessed 20 May 2020); School of International Arbitration, Queen Mary University of London, *International Arbitration: Corporate Attitudes and Practices 2008* <http://www.arbitration.qmul.ac.uk/research/2008/#d.en.493188> (accessed 20 May 2020); School of International Arbitration, Queen Mary University of London, *International Arbitration: Corporate Attitudes and Practices 2006* <http://www.arbitration.qmul.ac.uk/research/2006/#d.en.493194> (accessed 20 May 2020); Mistelis, *supra* n. 43. As explained in Chapter 3, there is however limited empirical research specifically on international mediation which involves the users of dispute resolution processes.
57. Stipanowich and Lamare, *supra* n. 56, at 4.
58. Julie Macfarlane, *The New Lawyer: How Settlement Is Transforming The Practice of Law* 85, 133 & 134 (UBC Press 2008).
59. Richard Susskind, *Tomorrow's Lawyers* 84 (2nd ed. Oxford 2017). *See also* Bryan Clark, *Lawyers and Mediation* 38 (Springer 2012) on the influence of in-house counsel on the general legal policy of their corporations.
60. Macfarlane, *supra* n. 58, at 8.
61. Report by IMI, Herbert Smith Freehills and PWC, *Global Pound Conference Series, Global Data Trends and Regional Differences*, 17 <https://www.imimediation.org/research/gpc/series-data-and-reports/> (accessed 20 May 2020).
62. *See* the history section on the website of CPR at <https://www.cpradr.org/about/history> (accessed 20 May 2020). *See also* Stipanowich and Lamare, *supra* n. 56, at 10.
63. *See* 'What We Do' section at <https://www.cpradr.org/about> (accessed 20 May 2020).

signatories pledge to explore the use of ADR before commencing court proceedings) to encourage the use of mediation in the corporate world.[64] This was followed, in the 1990s, by CPR's expansion into Europe with the creation of CPR Europe.[65]

In summary, in-house counsel have been selected as the research participants due to their *exposure* to dispute resolution processes and their ability to *influence* the dispute resolution field.

§4.04 THE RESEARCH PROCESS

[A] Identification of Potential Interviewees

A common approach used to gain access to interviewees is 'purposeful sampling'.[66] Under this approach the researcher will identify and approach key people who are likely to be rich sources of information.[67] They would be selected on the basis of their ability to answer the research questions.[68] This section explains how the in-house counsel interviewees were identified and approached.

Before explaining the researcher's approach to engaging with in-house counsel for the interviews, it should be noted that it was hoped that the qualitative research for this book could be supplemented with quantitative research. The study therefore initially adopted a mixed-methods approach comprised of both qualitative and quantitative research. The purpose of the quantitative research was to gain base-line data on the current use of EU cross-border commercial mediation, given the current lack of such empirical data. While international arbitration has been the focus of numerous international surveys,[69] far less empirical research has been done on international mediation.[70] To that end, a detailed questionnaire was prepared and circulated widely

64. Further information on the CPR pledge can be found at <https://www.cpradr.org/about/history> accessed 20 May 2020. The CPR pledge can be found at <https://www.cpradr.org/resource-center/adr-pledges> (accessed 20 May 2020).
65. Information on CPR's expansion into Europe can be found at <https://www.cpradr.org/strategy/international-initiatives/europe> (accessed 20 May 2020). It is also important to note that, more broadly, businesses have been credited for their key role in the development of mediation. In the context of England and Wales, 'mediation ... grew mainly out of the business environment, and not through the introduction of court reforms. In other words, it was essentially "demand-led" and not "supply-led"'. Bill Marsh, Alexander Oddy and Jan O'Neill *England and Wales* in Nadja Alexander, Sabine Walsh and Martin Svatos (eds), *EU Mediation Law Handbook* 208 (Wolters Kluwer 2017). By way of example, at footnote 1 of page 208, Marsh, Oddy and O'Neill add that the Centre for Effective Dispute Resolution was originally funded by UK businesses and the Confederation of British Industry.
66. Webley, *supra* n. 12, at 934.
67. Bryman, *supra* n. 35, at 415; Webley, *supra* n. 12, at 934.
68. Bryman, *supra* n. 35, at 410. Also *see* Nigel King and Christine Horrocks, *Interviews in Qualitative Research* 30-34 (Sage Publishing 2010) regarding practical guidance on how to gain access to interviewees.
69. These include the empirical research conducted by the School of International Arbitration, Queen Mary University of London <http://www.arbitration.qmul.ac.uk/research/index.html> (accessed 20 May 2020).
70. Notable exceptions are S.I. Strong's research on international commercial mediation: S.I. Strong, *Realizing Rationality: An Empirical Assessment of International Commercial Mediation*,

to corporate in-house counsel. The questionnaire included a request for the opportunity to speak with the respondents in order for qualitative research to also be conducted. Accordingly, the initial efforts to engage with in-house counsel for the research for this book were efforts to gain both quantitative and qualitative data and therefore for completeness those early efforts are also explained here.

With the generous support of many in-house counsel associations and social networks, the questionnaire was circulated widely to in-house counsel in Europe and beyond between March and May 2017.[71] Unfortunately, and in spite of offering anonymity to respondents, the wide circulation of the questionnaire to corporate counsel resulted in only seven responses, including one expression of willingness to speak with the researcher. Due to this low number of responses, the researcher decided to change her approach and offer an either/or approach under which respondents could either complete the questionnaire or speak with the researcher. In-house counsel associations kindly circulated a further request to their members offering this either/or approach. In addition, this request was also sent directly to in-house counsel. While it proved very difficult to obtain the direct email addresses of in-house counsel, directories of in-house counsel offered some, though limited, contact information. In particular, the Thomson Reuters Legal Hub In-House Lawyer Directory[72] offered email addresses for some of the in-house counsel listed. Where a direct email address was not provided for the in-house counsel listed, an email was sent to a general email address of the relevant organisation with a request for it to be forwarded to the counsel listed in the directory.

In spite of these further efforts to elicit engagement from in-house counsel, no further quantitative data nor expressions of interest to be interviewed were obtained.

A turning point occurred in May 2017. Given that the indirect means of reaching corporate counsel via associations – which had been the principal method of contacting potential respondents – was not proving fruitful, further research was conducted to find the direct email addresses of corporate counsel of multinationals operating across Europe. While it proved very difficult to obtain the direct email addresses of such corporate counsel, a list of leading in-house lawyers was eventually found in a directory.[73] This list referred to the in-house counsel of approximately 100 companies

---

73 Washington & Lee Law Review 1973 (2016) and SIDRA's research on international commercial dispute resolution which included international commercial mediation, SIDRA, *International Dispute Resolution Survey: 2020 Final Report*, 1 <https://sidra.smu.edu.sg/sidra-international-dispute-resolution-survey-final-report-2020> (accessed 10 August 2020). *See* further Chapter 3. The scope of this study differs to Strong's and SIDRA's as it addresses only EU cross-border commercial mediation.

71. Particular thanks to Michael Leathes who generously offered guidance on how to widen my efforts to reach in-house counsel and for directing me to many corporate counsel associations across the EU.

72. The Thomas Reuters Legal Hub In-House Lawyer Directory service closed on 3 October 2017.

73. As anonymity was given to the interviewees, in order to protect their anonymity the name of the directory has not been included. Further, the precise number of in-house counsel listed in the list has not been given (the text above refers only to an approximate number) as a further precaution to preserve anonymity. In addition, the list of in-house counsel from this directory has not been added as an appendix. This list, when combined with the general information on turnover and sector provided by the interviewees, could result in the identification of the interviewees.

and organisations, many of which were large multinational companies with activities across Europe. Crucially, the list included the direct email addresses of all the in-house counsel listed. An email request was sent directly to the in-house counsel listed asking them to either complete the questionnaire or to speak with the researcher. After sending out a small number of such requests, an enthusiastic response was received from one of the listed in-counsel who was a very senior in-house counsel for a large multinational financial services company. In his response, the in-house counsel emphasised his preference to take part in an interview rather than complete a survey. In light of this preference and given the lack of responses to the numerous earlier emails which had asked respondents to complete the questionnaire or speak with the researcher, the decision was taken to ask respondents to only take part in an interview in order to attempt to gain greater involvement from in-house counsel. Accordingly, further email requests to the in-house counsel listed in the directory included a request only to participate in an interview and no longer also referred to the survey as the earlier emails had done. The combination of direct correspondence and a request only to take part in the qualitative research proved successful. This list of in-house counsel with direct email addresses proved to be the principal means of identifying interviewees for this research.

It is important to emphasise that this list of in-house counsel allowed for the selection of potential interviewees in a transparent manner and, importantly, one which was free from any suggestion of the in-house counsel's or company's dispute resolution process preferences. This therefore provided a selection mechanism which was free of selection bias.[74] In addition, the list covered many business sectors. This allowed views to be obtained from in-house counsel operating in a variety of business sectors. The breadth of business sectors of the interviewees can be seen in the categorisation of interviewees in Chapter 5.

Eleven of this study's twenty-one interviewees came directly from this source. This study also employed the snowball method,[75] whereby at the end of the interview interviewees were asked whether they could provide the name and contact details of any further potential interviewees. This method resulted in the identification of one further in-house counsel of a multinational company who was willing to be interviewed. Accordingly, twelve of the respondents can be attributed directly or indirectly to this list of general counsel.

The remaining nine interviewees were identified by three further methods. First, six willing interviewees were identified due to their attendance at the GPC Series in London in July 2017. The GPC Series, conducted in numerous countries, 'considered how disputants in civil and commercial conflicts have access to appropriate dispute resolution processes that respond to users' needs'.[76] It did so by engaging with stakeholders in the global and local dispute resolution markets.[77] The GPC Series

74. Lee Epstein and Andrew Martin, *An Introduction to Empirical Legal Research* 87 (Oxford 2014).
75. *See* Webley, *supra* n. 12, at 934 for a summary of the snowball sampling technique.
76. *See* the '2016-2017 GPC Series' section at <https://www.imimediation.org/research/gpc/gpc-about/#about-gpc-series> (accessed 20 May 2020).
77. *Ibid.*

brought together many stakeholders in the dispute resolution field, including in-house counsel of multinational companies. The London conference of the GPC Series therefore offered the researcher an invaluable opportunity to identify potential participants for the research. It is important to emphasise that the conferences of the GPC Series were relevant to stakeholders in the dispute resolution field in general; their relevance was not confined to stakeholders in the mediation field as the GPC Series 'encompass[ed] all forms of dispute resolution, including litigation, arbitration, conciliation, and mediation'.[78] Accordingly the conferences appealed to stakeholders in the dispute resolution field in general and were not limited to stakeholders involved or interested only in the mediation field.

In addition to approaching potential participants in person at the London conference, which resulted in four interviewees for the research, the involvement of a further interviewee was the result of an email communication sent after the conference. Further, as regards email communication, attendees of the GPC Series could contact other attendees through the GPC online application. The opportunity was therefore taken to contact those who appeared to be in-house counsel of multinational companies via this application. This resulted in one positive response from a willing research participant. Further emails were also sent to in-house counsel of multinational companies suggested by a number of people involved in the GPC Series though unfortunately these did not generate any interest. In summary, email correspondence with participants of the GPC Series resulted in the involvement of two interviewees, with the other four interviewees agreeing to be interviewed following an in person request at the London conference.

Secondly, two interviewees were identified due to being speakers at a different conference in London in 2017 on dispute resolution.[79] Thirdly and finally, one interviewee was, as mentioned earlier, identified as a result of responding to the questionnaire which was circulated for the attempted quantitative research.

The above methods resulted in interviews, conducted between May and October 2017, with twenty-one senior in-house counsel from large companies which operate across Europe. It is acknowledged that the majority of respondents were identified either due to their listing on a UK directory of in-house counsel or attendance at a dispute resolution event in London. However, given England's, and specifically London's, status as the European headquarter capital for the world's largest businesses,[80] it is not surprising that these sources led to opportunities to speak with

78. *See* '2016-2017 GPC Series' section at <https://www.imimediation.org/research/gpc/gpc-about/#about-gpc-series> (accessed 20 May 2020). The GPC Series' focus on dispute resolution in general rather than on one specific method of dispute resolution is also reflected in the questions asked at the conferences. These questions have been discussed in Chapter 3. By way of very brief summary they cover both adjudicative and non-adjudicative methods of dispute resolution. As noted in Chapter 3, in the questions asked at the conference there was little specific focus on mediation.

79. Further details on this conference have not been provided in order to protect the participants' anonymity.

80. Research by Deloitte has identified that of the largest 250 companies in the world (measured by revenue) with global or regional headquarters in Europe, 40% of those headquarters are located in London. Deloitte LLP, *London Futures, London Crowned Business Capital of Europe* (2014)

in-house counsel with experience of and, in some cases responsibility for, cross-border commercial disputes across Europe. Indeed, as the categorisation of respondents in Chapter 5 demonstrates, the interviewees play a key role in managing their companies' disputes, including their EU cross-border disputes. It should be noted here that the research for this book was carried out before the UK left the EU and it remains to be seen whether the UK's departure will affect London's European headquarter status.

Finally, research involving interviews with twenty-one in-house counsel is a valuable contribution to the particular field of EU cross-border commercial mediation. Given the lack of empirical research in this field which provides in-depth interview data and, in particular, research focused on the corporate users and potential users of such mediation (as identified in Chapters 2 and 3), the interviews with twenty-one in-house counsel conducted for this book offer a meaningful contribution to the field.[81]

[B] Preparation for the Interviews

An interview guide, included at Appendix 2, was prepared for use in the interviews. This served as a guide and flexibility was adopted during the interviews, with some questions being added and some omitted depending on the information provided by the interviewees.[82]

<https://www2.deloitte.com/content/dam/Deloitte/uk/Documents/uk-futures/london-futures-london-crowned-business-capital-of-europe.pdf> (accessed 20 May 2020).

81. In addition, it is interesting to note that there are a number of qualitative studies involving in-depth interviews with in-house counsel on dispute resolution topics (including but not limited to mediation) for which roughly the same or slightly lower numbers of in-house counsel were interviewed. *See* John Lande and Peter Benner's qualitative study on how and why businesses use planned early dispute resolution for which fifteen in-house counsel of large corporations in the US were interviewed: John Lande and Peter Benner, *Why and How Business Use Planned Early Dispute Resolution,* 13 University of St. Thomas Law Journal 248, 255 (2017). *See also* John Lande's study on belief in mediation which involved qualitative in-depth interviews with thirteen interviewees in the US (including in-house counsel, external counsel and non-lawyer executives): John Lande, *Getting the Faith: Why Business Lawyers and Executives Believe in Mediation,* 5 Harvard Negotiation Law Review 138, 162 (2000). In Ewald Filler's empirical research on commercial mediation in Europe (considered in Chapter 3), qualitative in-depth interviews were conducted with twenty executives whose companies had experience of mediation in European countries: Ewald Filler, *Commercial Mediation in Europe* 7-8 (Wolters Kluwer 2012). As discussed in Chapter 3, such research does not focus on the EU cross-border context which is the focus of this book. Further, in Craig McEwen's qualitative study on barriers to the use of mediation for corporate disputing, in-house counsel and business executives in the US were interviewed from six companies (it is not stated how many individuals in total were interviewed): Craig Mc Ewen, *Managing Corporate Disputing: Overcoming the Barriers to the Effective Use of Mediation for Reducing the Cost and Time of Litigation,* 14 Ohio State Journal on Dispute Resolution 1, 4-5 (1998). Finally, while not specifically on dispute resolution, for *The Generalist Counsel* (*supra* n. 53) Dubey and Kripalani interviewed twenty US-based in-house counsel regarding how general counsel are shaping the future paths of their companies (*see* 171-181 for the list of their interviewees).
82. An interview guide was also used in a qualitative study by Lande on why business lawyers and executives believe in mediation. The scope of that study was the use of mediation in the US and therefore its scope differs to that of this study. Lande describes how he 'developed interview protocols to serve as a general guide for the interviews. Based on the flow of the interviews, I asked unscripted follow-up questions and skipped questions in the protocol'. Lande, *Getting the Faith, supra* n. 81, at 162.

At the outset of the interviews, general information was obtained from the interviewees so that the responses could be categorised by their companies' business sector, turnover and geographical reach. Information was also obtained on the interviewees' role within their companies and their involvement in their companies' EU cross-border commercial disputes.

Further, definitions of key terms frequently used by the interviewer were provided at the start of the interviews so as to ensure that all the interviewees had the same understanding of important terms.[83] The decision to provide brief definitions of the key terms was taken further to the review of the key literature in the field which is provided in Chapter 2. In addition to identifying the areas which would benefit from further exploration, the review also revealed useful practical information to be borne in mind when conducting the empirical research for this book. For example, some of the studies lacked definitions of key terms such as 'ADR', 'mediation', 'cross-border' and 'commercial'. Notably, in their empirical study on ADR, Stipanowich and Lamare identify the different ways in which the undefined term 'mediation – arbitration' could have been interpreted by respondents and attribute the unexpected results of a particular question to this ambiguity.[84] In light of the risk of varied interpretations, brief definitions of key terms were given to the interviewees.

The overriding purpose of the interviews was to gain rich insights into in-house counsel's use of, and views on, EU cross-border commercial mediation. At the outset, interviewees were asked about their experience of EU cross-border commercial disputes, including the extent to which they had used mediation to address such disputes. The questions which were subsequently asked varied depending on whether or not the interviewees had experience of EU cross-border commercial mediation.

Various topics were addressed in the interviews in order to gain an understanding of in-house counsel's use of, and views on, mediation as a dispute resolution method for EU cross-border commercial disputes. The topics addressed were:

- the preferred method/s of dispute resolution for EU cross-border commercial disputes;
- the organisation's dispute resolution policy and clauses;
- triggers for the use of EU cross-border commercial mediation;
- reasons for using, and for not using, EU cross-border commercial mediation;
- enforcement of the resolution of EU cross-border commercial disputes;
- trends in the use of EU cross-border commercial mediation both at individual and industry level;
- the obstacles and opportunities for an increased use of EU cross-border commercial mediation; and
- finally, recent proposals to improve the EU Mediation Directive were shared with the interviewees for their comments.

83. *See* page 2 of the interview guide, provided at Appendix 2, for the terms which were defined.
84. Stipanowich and Lamare, *supra* n. 56, at 41.

In addition, as noted earlier, further questions were asked during the interview as appropriate.

[1] Focus Group

In preparation for the interviews, the questions which formed the basis of the interviews were shared with a focus group of ten people. In order to obtain comments on these questions from a variety of stakeholders in the dispute resolution community, the focus group was comprised of members of the following stakeholder groups: in-house counsel, mediators, academics and lawyers practising in law firms.

[C] Conducting the Interviews

Once a positive response to the request to take part in the research was received, a short note about the research was sent to the interviewee. This is included in Appendix 1. Importantly, the note emphasised the requirement of experience with EU cross-border commercial disputes in order to take part in the research. The note also stated the purpose of the research and informed the participant that ethical approval had been obtained. The note added that verbatim notes of the interview would be taken which would then be shared with the interviewee for any comments that the interviewee might have on them. It also informed the interviewee that they would be afforded anonymity.[85]

Interviewees were afforded anonymity for two reasons. First, some parties may be reluctant to provide information which might in some way disclose the dispute resolution policy or strategy of their company. Secondly, parties to a mediation are subject to confidentiality commitments and some interviewees might not wish to take part in research which draws upon their experience of their confidential mediations. Accordingly, for these two reasons, the researcher felt that offering anonymity would be likely to increase participation in the research. Many of the interviewees welcomed the anonymity and sought confirmation that neither they nor their company would be referred to by name in any subsequent publications. Furthermore, the anonymity given to respondents would not lessen the value of the data as such data could be categorised in a detailed manner according to the background information provided by the interviewees, which included the sector, turnover, headquarters' location and geographical reach of the interviewees' companies.

Interviewees were offered the opportunity to be interviewed in person or over the telephone. While the researcher preferred to conduct interviews in person (and ten of the interviews were conducted in this way), the researcher appreciated that for some of the interviewees an interview over the telephone would be more convenient. For those interviews conducted with in-house counsel located overseas, given the prohibitive

85. Similar studies have also afforded participants anonymity. *See* Filler, *supra* n. 81 and Strong, *Realizing Rationality, supra* n. 70, for which participating representatives of commercial enterprises were given anonymity.

expense to the researcher of travelling to another country, such interviews were conducted over the telephone.

Given the very busy lives of the prospective interviewees and in order to encourage participation in the research, in the first email communication they were asked to give twenty minutes for the interview. With the exception of one interviewee who could only give ten minutes, after twenty minutes the interviewees were invited to either finish the interview or continue. All agreed to continue to varying degrees.[86] Many interviewees gave considerably more time than the suggested twenty minutes, with the longest interview lasting sixty minutes (Figure 4.1). The average interview time was thirty-six minutes. Many of the interviewees expressed an interest in, and enthusiasm for, the research. For those interviewees who were more pressed for time, the interviewer focused on those areas of the semi-structured interviews which were of most importance, including the reasons why parties did and did not use mediation for their EU cross-border commercial disputes.

Figure 4.1 Duration of Interviews

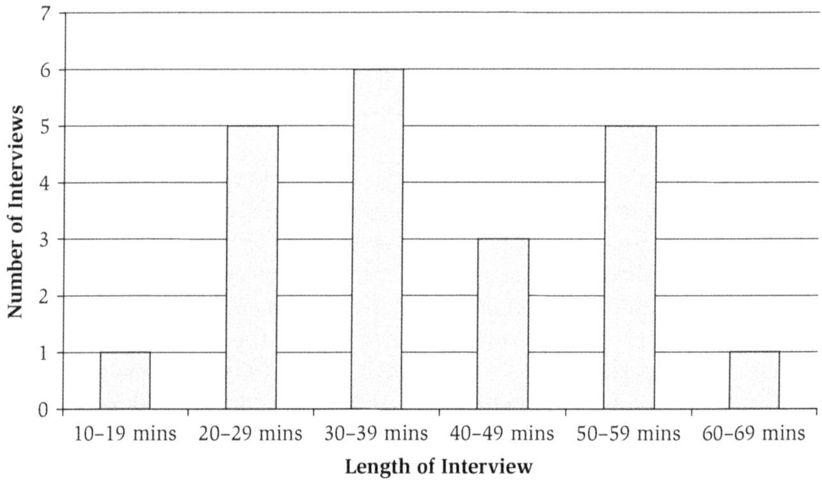

The researcher acknowledges that longer interviews would have allowed for further insights to be obtained into the particular context. However, the amount of time available for the interviews was determined by the interviewees. In other words, the researcher worked within the time parameters set by the interviewees.

During the interviews, the researcher took verbatim notes as best she could. After the interview, the researcher typed up the notes and sent these to the interviewee within twenty-four hours of the interview.[87] Interviewees were therefore given the

86. For example, some interviewees simply said they were happy to continue and did not state for how long, while others said they could continue for a certain amount of time.
87. There was only one exception to the provision of the record to the interviewees within twenty-four hours. On one day, three interviews were conducted which meant that it was not

opportunity to provide comments. Where comments were provided, they were minor.[88]

The interviews were recorded by way of verbatim notes rather than being recorded by a sound-recording device. There were two reasons for this approach. First, given the seniority of the respondents and the potentially sensitive and confidential topics on which they were speaking, the researcher thought that potential interviewees might be less willing to take part in the research if they were to be recorded. Secondly, the researcher was also concerned that the interviewees would not talk freely during the interviews if they were being recorded.[89] Taking verbatim notes, as best the researcher could, and sending them to the respondents within twenty-four hours ensured that an accurate record of the interview was obtained while also affording a method of recording which did not inhibit the interviewees while they were being interviewed.

[D] Analysis of Data

Thematic analysis was used to analyse the data. This is a common approach used to analyse qualitative data under which the data is scrutinised for themes and sub-themes which relate to the focus of the research.[90] As described by Braun and Clarke 'thematic analysis involves the searching across a data set – be that a number of interviews or focus groups or a range of texts – to find repeated patterns of meaning'.[91] The method of thematic analysis has been used, for example, in Bondy et al.'s research on the limited use of mediation in judicial review cases and also in Irvine's study on small claims mediation in Glasgow and Edinburgh Sheriff Courts, both of which involved semi-structured in-depth interviews.[92]

---

possible to complete the records of the three interviews within twenty-four hours. Two records were sent within twenty-four hours and the third was sent within two days.

88. By way of example, some of the comments provided on the notes included: in the description of the company adding a couple of further sectors in which the company was active; removing an adjective used to describe politicians; changing 'people' to 'agents'; and adding 'for example' before introducing a particular example.
89. Caution about being involved in the interviews was demonstrated by one in-house counsel who had to check with her compliance department before confirming that she could take part in the research. In addition, the interviewee sought firm assurances at the start of the interview regarding anonymity and also regarding how the data would be used. The interviewee asked to be contacted prior to the publication of any quotation taken from the record of her interview.
90. Bryman, *supra* n. 35, at 584 & 585.
91. Victoria Braun and Victoria Clarke, *Using Thematic Analysis in Psychology*, 3 Qualitative Research in Psychology 77, 86 (2006).
92. Bondy et al., *supra* n. 37, at 16. The thematic analysis method was used in Bondy et al.'s' project because the exploratory nature of the interviews meant that it was difficult to code responses into set categories. Charlie Irvine, *What Do 'Lay' People Know About Justice? An Empirical Enquiry*, 16(2) International Journal of Law in Context 146 (2020). Irvine explains at 153: 'the goal of this approach [thematic analysis] is to build theory rather than to test it, so as to remain open to new insights emerging from the data'.

The process for conducting the thematic analysis involved numerous steps.[93] First, it should be acknowledged that, as the researcher conducted the interviews and did the verbatim record herself, she was already familiar with the data before the formal data analysis commenced.[94] The researcher then read all of the interview records numerous times in order to immerse herself in the data. This ensured that the researcher had a firm familiarisation with the data.[95] After this thorough review, the researcher then read the interview records numerous further times to identify codes. A code is a label given to a portion of text which is of relevance to the broad research questions.[96] Examples of the codes used include 'Meaning of mediation', 'Awareness of EU Mediation Directive', 'Reasons for using cross-border mediation', 'Reasons for not using cross-border mediation' and 'Negotiation'. The codes were identified inductively, meaning that the coding scheme was developed after examining the data.[97] Such an approach tends to be associated with qualitative research.[98] The codes were listed in a Word document. The records were then examined further times in order to complete the coding process. The codes, together with the relevant text for each code, were recorded in Word documents with one document for each code. Once the coding process had been completed, the interview records were reviewed again to check the coding. The Word documents for all the codes were then carefully reviewed and themes were identified.[99] Themes were identified principally due to the repetition of particular topics across the data and also, though to a lesser extent, due to notable omissions in the data.[100] Further, the data was then examined to see whether there were links between the themes.[101] The themes became the focus of this study.

It should be emphasised that the analysis process was not linear. Rather, it was iterative and there was movement back and forth as required.[102] When an interesting

93. The approach summarised in this paragraph draws on guidance on conducting thematic analysis in Bryman, *supra* n. 35 and Braun and Clarke, *Using Thematic Analysis*, *supra* n. 91.
94. Braun and Clarke, *Using Thematic Analysis*, *supra* n. 91, 88. Braun and Clarke acknowledge that the time spent transcribing the interviews contributes to the early stages of the data analysis.
95. Victoria Braun and Victoria Clarke, *Teaching Thematic Analysis: Overcoming Challenges and Developing Strategies for Effective Learning*, 26(2) The Psychologist 120, 121 (2013).
96. Bryman, *supra* n. 35, at 588; Braun and Clarke, *Teaching Thematic Analysis*, *supra* n. 95, at 121.
97. Epstein and Martin, *supra* n. 74, at 96. The opposite approach, as also described at 96, is the deductive approach under which the coding schemes are developed before the data is collected and reviewed.
98. *Ibid.*
99. Bryman, *supra* n. 35, at 588; Braun and Clarke, *Using Thematic Analysis*, *supra* n. 91, at 89.
100. Bryman notes that repetition is the most commonly used way to identify themes in qualitative thematic analysis. Bryman explains 'a theme is more likely to be identified, the more times the phenomenon it denotes occurs in the course of coding' adding that 'In other words, a kind of implicit quantification may be in operation that influences the identification of themes and the elevation of some themes over others.' Bryman, *supra* n. 35, at 630. Bryman also identifies missing data (what interviewees have not included in their answers) as another way to identify themes. Bryman, *supra* n. 35, at 586 & 630. Patton also emphasises the importance of 'looking for recurring regularities in the data'. Michael Quinn Patton, *Qualitative Research & Evaluation Methods*, 555 (4th ed. Sage 2015).
101. Bryman, *supra* n. 35, at 588.
102. Braun and Clarke, *Using Thematic Analysis*, *supra* n. 91, at 86.

pattern emerged, the researcher would go back through the data again to see if anything further could be identified that was relevant to the pattern. It should also be added that all of the data was coded and analysed but, as is to be expected in in-depth interviews, not all of the data was relevant.[103]

Given the manageable number of interviews and the fact that the researcher had conducted the research herself, the researcher chose not to use a qualitative data analysis software system for the coding of the data.

Finally, it should be added that when analysing the data, the researcher also drew upon a concept identified by Lederach within his elicitive approach to mediation in conflict settings, as was discussed earlier. It is the concept of the critical yeast.

[1] Lederach's Concept of the Critical Yeast

In order to explain this concept, it is first necessary to provide some context. In his work in seeking sustainable change in protracted conflicts, Lederach recognised the emphasis which was being placed on effecting change by getting large numbers of people involved in social change.[104] Lederach saw that the commonly accepted view was that change was achieved by getting sufficient numbers of people to join a particular side regarding an issue or conflict, also referred to as 'arriving at the critical mass'.[105] The focus was therefore on mobilising large numbers in order to bring about a desired change.[106] However, Lederach recognised from his experience in helping to bring about change in protracted conflicts that often when there was the involvement of a critical mass of people those moments were 'fleeting, ephemeral and short-lived'.[107] While the activity of large numbers of people in the streets caught the media's attention, it was then not capable of creating sustainable change.[108] In contrast, Lederach noted that when sustainable and significant change was achieved this was not as a result of focusing only on the generation of a critical mass: 'In social change it is not necessarily the amount of participants that authenticates a social shift. It is the quality of the platform that sustains the shifting process that matters.'[109] The important role played by the 'quality of the platform' prompted Lederach's identification of the critical yeast concept.[110]

103. As noted by Wolcott, 'The major problem we face in qualitative inquiry is not to get data, but to get rid of it!', Harry Wolcott, *Writing Up Qualitative Research*, 18 (Sage 1990). Further Bryman explains 'much of the rich data you accumulate will have to be discarded. If you do not do this, the sense of an argument will be lost'. Bryman also highlights the importance of using your research questions to focus your analysis of the data. Bryman, *supra* n. 35, at 665.
104. Lederach, *The Moral Imagination*, *supra* n. 1, at 87; Lederach, *Building Mediative Capacity*, *supra* n. 16, at 98.
105. Lederach, *The Moral Imagination*, *supra* n. 1, at 88.
106. *Ibid.*, 100.
107. Lederach, *Building Mediative Capacity*, *supra* n. 16, at 98.
108. *Ibid.*
109. Lederach, *The Moral Imagination*, *supra* n. 1, at 89; Lederach, *Building Mediative Capacity*, *supra* n. 16, at 98.
110. Lederach, *Building Mediative Capacity*, *supra* n. 16, at 98; Lederach, *The Moral Imagination*, *supra* n. 1, at 91.

To elaborate on this concept of the critical yeast, Lederach explains that the concept of 'critical mass', as it is commonly used, has been misunderstood and misapplied.[111] Lederach notes that the term 'critical mass' was borrowed by the social sciences from the physical sciences and in that journey the original meaning was lost.[112] He explains that in the original context of the physical sciences, and in particular the topic of nuclear physics and the chain reactions of fission,[113] the term 'critical mass' referred to whether the neutrons in a reaction created sufficient fission to create a *self-sustained* process of reactions, i.e., reactions could reproduce themselves independently of the original reaction.[114] Lederach notes that critical mass originally meant 'that a self-sustained process is generated, meaning that one reaction can reproduce itself exponentially, independent of the original cause'.[115] He explains that somewhere in the trajectory from physics to the social sciences, and in particular the social sciences topic of how ideas move from birth to wide acceptance in society, the term 'critical mass' lost this meaning of the creation of a *self-sustained* process of change.[116] Lederach notes that when the term 'critical mass' is applied in the social sciences context it is used to refer to the point at which enough people accept an idea and social attitudes change.[117]

In response to the misapplication of the term 'critical mass' in the social sciences, Lederach coined the term 'critical yeast' (which he also refers to as strategic yeast)[118] to capture the original meaning of critical mass as a platform which generates exponential and self-sustaining growth. Lederach recognised from his experience in mediating protracted social conflicts that sustainable change often resulted not with a strategy focused on involving large numbers of people, but rather due to an ingredient - the yeast - which has the capacity to create and sustain growth.[119] The critical yeast which Lederach identified was 'the strategic who'.[120] Lederach's metaphor of the critical yeast asks the question of 'who' rather than 'how many' could be brought together who, due to their location in the particular conflict setting, could bring about sustainable change.[121] Reflecting the original meaning of critical mass in physics, he explains that his question asks: 'Who, though not liked-minded or like-situated in this context of conflict, would have a capacity, if they were mixed and held together, to make other things grow exponentially, beyond their numbers.'[122] It is a question concerned with the quality of the catalyst for change and the creation of sustainable change.[123] He adds that the key to achieving change was 'getting a small set of the right

111. Lederach, *The Moral Imagination, supra* n. 1, at 89.
112. *Ibid.*, 90.
113. *Ibid.*, 89.
114. *Ibid.*, 89 and 90.
115. *Ibid.*, 90.
116. *Ibid.*
117. *Ibid.*
118. *Ibid.*, 91.
119. Lederach, *Building Mediative Capacity, supra* n. 16, at 98.
120. *Ibid.*, 99.
121. Lederach, *Building Mediative Capacity, supra* n. 16, at 98; Lederach, *The Moral Imagination, supra* n. 1, at 91.
122. Lederach, *The Moral Imagination, supra* n. 1, at 91.
123. *Ibid.*, 89 & 90.

people involved at the right places. What's missing is not the critical mass. The missing ingredient is the critical yeast'.[124] He added:

> the principle of yeast is this: A few strategically connected people have greater potential for creating the social growth of an idea or process than large numbers of people who think alike. When social change fails, look first to the nature of who was engaged and what gaps exist in the connections among different sets of people.[125]

By way of examples of the critical yeast in conflict settings, this role of the 'strategic who' was played by the women of Wajir (described earlier in this chapter) who with their unique characteristics and connections could play a key and innovative role in peacebuilding far beyond their numbers.[126] Lederach also identifies that the role of the 'strategic who' was played by former paramilitaries in the Northern Ireland peace process and also by a conciliation commission in Nicaragua.[127] Regarding the former paramilitaries, they were inside peace brokers who helped to keep the process going, even when it was at its most fragile, through their contacts, conversations and a street-based crisis response.[128] Regarding the conciliation commission in Nicaragua, this small team of people mediated the conflict in the east coast of Nicaragua but due to their personal and institutional networks were able to have a positive impact on conciliation in the wider regional context.[129] As Lederach describes: 'In both cases fewer than a dozen people made the key links and held the mostly informal processes ... together.'[130] Lederach notes that the role of outside mediators, when that exists, is to support the small groups of key individuals located within the particular conflict setting.[131]

Returning to the context of the use of mediation for EU cross-border commercial disputes, Lederach's concept of the critical yeast offers a different way of considering how such mediation might be encouraged. In particular, there has been significant focus to date, as explained in Chapter 2, on increasing the amount of mediation through mandatory mediation, an approach which is reminiscent of Lederach's recognition of the emphasis on reaching a critical mass in order to effect change, i.e., by focusing on hastily increasing the number of mediations in order to bring about a wider uptake of mediation. However, the concept of the critical yeast invites us to look beyond such measures to explore whether there may be a more subtle and critical ingredient which could be a catalyst for a self-sustaining growth in the use of mediation. Here it should be emphasised that while Lederach identified the critical yeast in the context of

124. *Ibid.*, 91.
125. *Ibid.*, 92.
126. Lederach, *Building Mediative Capacity*, *supra* n. 16, at 99. The characteristics of the women of Wajir which enabled them to play a key role in peacebuilding are described earlier in this chapter.
127. Lederach, *Building Mediative Capacity*, *supra* n. 16, at 99.
128. *Ibid.*; Lederach, *The Moral Imagination*, *supra* n. 1, at 99.
129. Lederach, *Building Mediative Capacity*, *supra* n. 16, at 99; John Paul Lederach, *Building Peace*, 50-51 (United States Institute of Peace Press 1997).
130. Lederach, *The Moral Imagination*, *supra* n. 1, at 99.
131. Lederach, *Building Mediative Capacity*, *supra* n. 16, at 99 & 100.

peacebuilding as the ingredient of 'who' rather than 'how many', in other contexts (such as the EU's efforts to promote mediation which is the focus of this book) the critical ingredient which may result in significant and sustainable growth might not be a 'strategic who' but another factor. Accordingly, when analysing the data the researcher kept this concept of the critical yeast in mind and looked for whether there was any suggestion in the data of the type of ingredient described by Lederach which might generate growth in the use of mediation.

§4.05 CONCLUSION

This chapter has explained why the particular research method was chosen and how the research was executed. Inspired by Lederach's elicitive approach, as captured in the opening quotation of this chapter, the core motivation behind this research project has been to approach the context with curiosity, care and respect, to create an opportunity to listen carefully to those who know the setting and to move away from predetermined and standardised solutions.[132] Such an approach has led to the identification of important and interesting issues borne of the particular context and which will be examined in Chapters 6, 7 and 8.

132. Lederach, *The Moral Imagination*, *supra* n. 1, at 107.

CHAPTER 5

Key Information on the Interviewees and their Companies

§5.01 EXECUTIVE SUMMARY

This chapter provides key information on the interviewees who took part in the research for this book and their companies. It therefore offers an important backdrop to the analysis of the interview data provided in Chapters 6, 7 and 8.

§5.02 THE INTERVIEWEES

Figure 5.1 Interviewees' Legal Experience

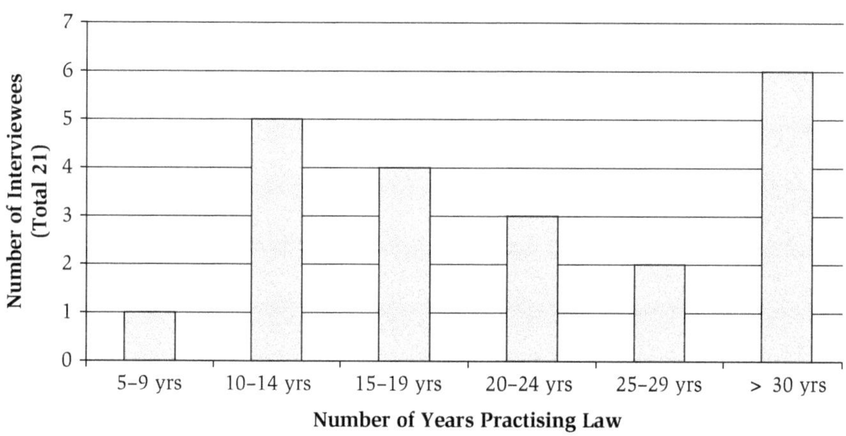

The most junior person among the interviewees had eight years of experience practising law. The term ' > 30 years' was used for the top-end category as, in response to the question of how many years he had been practising law, one interviewee answered: 'over 30 years'. Finally, it should be noted that one of the interviewees who had the title 'Head of claims'[1] was not a lawyer but, as he described, 'effectively head[s] up the legal department', and the number of years of experience is the number of years he has been working with claims.

Figure 5.1 shows the extensive legal experience of the interviewees. Just over 70% of the interviewees have more than fifteen years of experience, while just over 50% have more than twenty years of experience.

[A] Position of the Interviewees

Given the varying titles of the interviewees, grouping them into general categories such as 'General Counsel', 'Head of Legal' or 'Senior counsel' would strip away much of the important detail conveyed by their positions, including the geographical reach of their roles. Accordingly, each interviewee's title together with the number of years he/she has been practising law are provided in Table 5.1. Presented in this manner, a more detailed picture of the interviewees who took part in the research can be provided. In the column listing the interviewees' positions, minor changes to the interviewees' job titles have been made in order to ensure that the interviewees cannot be identified.

1. A couple of words have been removed in order to ensure the interviewee's anonymity. Further, as regards the interviewee whose position was 'Head of Claims', in Table 5.1 (Interviewees' Roles and Experience) in the column entitled 'Years Practising Law' for this interviewee the number of years of experience is of handling claims.

Table 5.1 Interviewees' Roles and Experience

Interviewee's Position	*Years Practising Law (As Identified by the Interviewees)*
Senior Counsel, Dispute Resolution	10
Legal and Regulatory Counsel	21
General Counsel, Europe	30
Co-General Counsel	Over 30
General Counsel, EMEA	18
General Counsel	More than 32
Group Legal Director	28
Corporate Legal Counsel	11
Global Head Litigation Counsel	20
Global Head of Legal	14
Senior Legal Counsel	8
Senior Legal Counsel, Global Litigation	19
Head of Legal Affairs, Europe	10
Associate General Counsel	31
Head of Legal	34
Legal Counsel, Dispute Resolution	15
Head of Claims	25
Head of Litigation	18
Head of Legal (Germany)	12
Head of Litigation	20
Global Legal Head, Disputes	30

A title can, however, only convey a limited amount of information. To gain a fuller picture of the interviewees' roles, in particular regarding disputes, interviewees were asked about their involvement in their company's handling of disputes, including cross-border disputes. All of the interviewees confirmed their involvement in their company's handling of disputes, including cross-border disputes, with many emphasising the key role they played. Answers to this question included: 'I am trying to figure out where I am not involved'; 'I am responsible for all of them'; 'That's my job'; 'I am heavily involved'; 'Total involvement'; 'I managed a global team that manages the business' major disputes, very many of them are cross-border'; and 'Generally the central point of contact in the organisation.' Accordingly, the responses to this question confirmed that the interviewees were well placed to answer questions on their company's cross-border commercial disputes and their use of, and attitudes towards, mediation for such disputes.

Further, it should be noted that the majority of the interviewees were based in the UK and, more specifically, London. Of the twenty-one interviewees, seventeen were based in the UK, three in Germany and one in the Netherlands. While a greater spread of European locations would have been welcomed, the location of the interviewee is, alone, not a significant concern for this study. What matters most is the extent to which the interviewee is involved in his/her company's EU cross-border commercial disputes and can share his/her knowledge on the use of mediation for such disputes. Therefore, their confirmation, as noted above, of their involvement in and responsibility for cross-border commercial disputes together with their companies' experience of EU cross-border commercial disputes (*see* Figures 5.7 and 5.8) are the critical factors. Further, it should also be noted here that, as is demonstrated later in this chapter, the interviewees' companies had experience of EU cross-border disputes involving parties from a wide variety of EU Member States and therefore had broad experience of such disputes.[2] Finally, it should also be noted that, as stated in Chapter 4, it is unsurprising that many of the senior in-house counsel of the large multinationals who participated in this research are to be found in London given London's status as the European headquarter capital for the world's largest businesses.[3] It is important to emphasise that the research for this book was carried out before the UK left the EU and it remains to be seen whether the UK's departure will affect London's European headquarter status.

§5.03 THE INTERVIEWEES' COMPANIES

Figure 5.2 Companies' Business Sectors

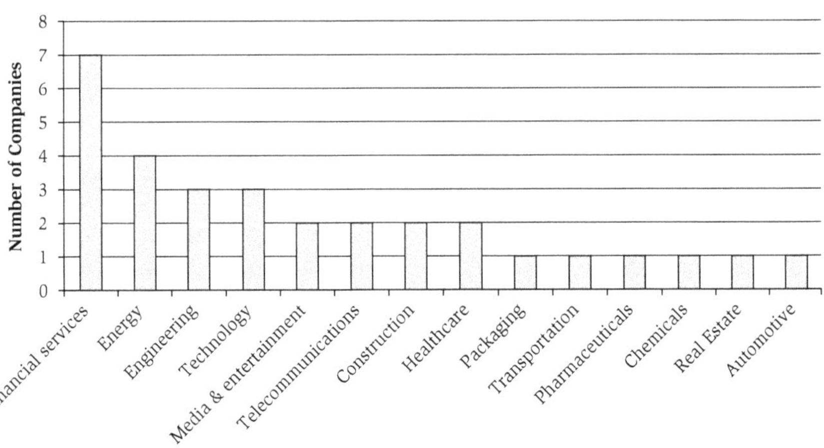

2. In the separate context of international arbitration, studies on international commercial arbitration have similarly targeted in-house counsel from multinationals. *See* Loukas Mistelis, *International Arbitration: Corporate Attitudes and Practices – 12 Perceptions Tested: Myths, Data and Analysis*, 15 The American Review of International Arbitration 526, 531 (2004).
3. As noted in Chapter 4, research by Deloitte has identified that of the largest 250 companies in the world with global or regional headquarters in Europe, 40% of those headquarters are located in London. Deloitte LLP, *London Futures, London Crowned Business Capital of Europe* (2014) <https://www2.deloitte.com/content/dam/Deloitte/uk/Documents/uk-futures/london-futures-london-crowned-business-capital-of-europe.pdf> (accessed 20 May 2020).

All of the companies represented by the interviewees are large multinational companies. Many of these companies are active across a number of business sectors and for many companies more than one business sector was relevant, accordingly more than twenty-one business sectors (specifically, a total of thirty-one sectors) are identified in Figure 5.2. Figure 5.2 includes all the business sectors identified by the interviewees as those in which their companies operate. The figure demonstrates the broad range of business sectors represented by the interviewees and their companies.

Figure 5.3 Companies' Turnover

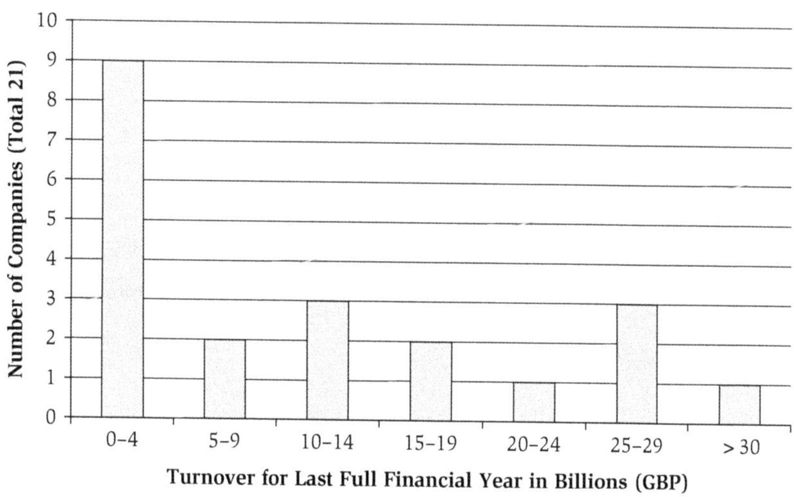

Figure 5.3 shows the significant size, by turnover, of the companies which took part in the research. Just under 50% of these companies had a turnover of more than GBP 10 billion. Given the significant spread of the companies' turnover, it is important to add further detail on the higher and lower ends of the turnover spectrum. The interviewee company represented in the highest turnover category (> GBP 30 billion) had a turnover of roughly GBP 150 billion.

Regarding the lowest turnover category (GBP 0-GBP 4 billion), as approximately 40% of the interviewees fell within this category and this category includes a significant spread of turnovers, a further figure is included at Figure 5.4 which breaks down this category into more detail.

Figure 5.4 Further Detail on the Turnover of Interviewee Companies in GBP 0-GBP 4 Billion Range

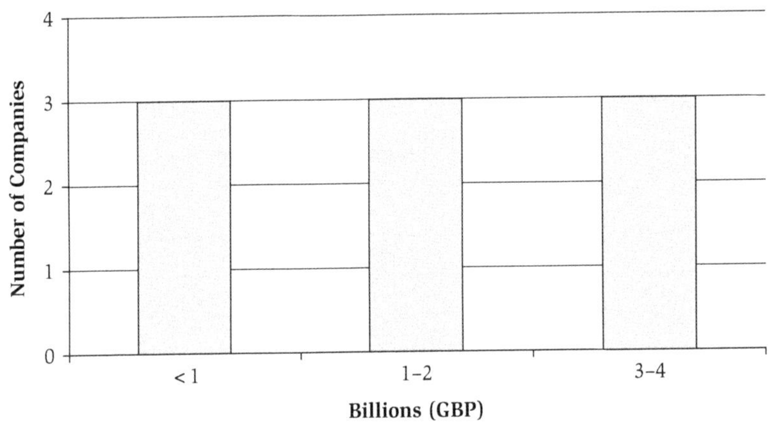

Of the three companies that had a turnover of less than GBP 1 billion, one had a turnover of roughly GBP 700 million, another of roughly GBP 350 million and the other of roughly GBP 170 million. This additional detail further conveys the significant size, by turnover, of the interviewees' companies.

[A] Geographical Reach of the Companies

When obtaining background information on the interviewees' companies, interviewees were asked whether the geographical scope of their company was national, EU or international (defined as 'the organisation's activities extend beyond the European Union'). All of the companies were international in scope and therefore had activities both within and beyond the EU.

Figure 5.5 Headquarters of the Companies

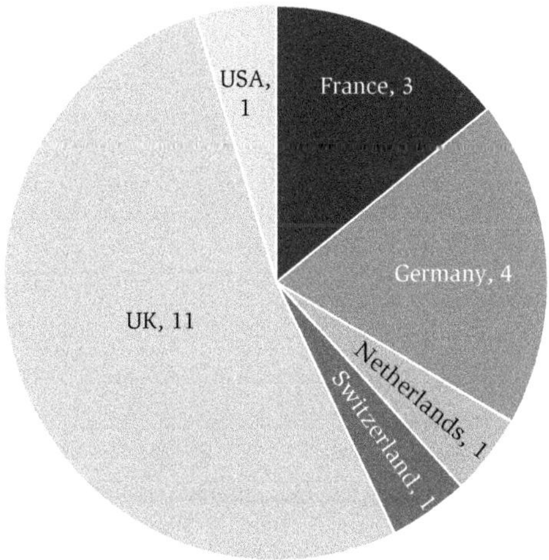

Figure 5.5 shows that a notable proportion of the interviewees' companies are headquartered in London. As acknowledged earlier, London has enjoyed the status of being the European headquarter capital for the world's largest businesses[4] and it is therefore not surprising that many of the global businesses which took part in this research have their headquarters in London.

4. As referred to in Chapter 4, research by Deloitte has identified that of the largest 250 companies in the world with global or regional headquarters in Europe, 40% of those headquarters are located in London. Deloitte, *ibid*.

Figure 5.6 Number of EU Member States (Plus UK) in Which the Companies Operate

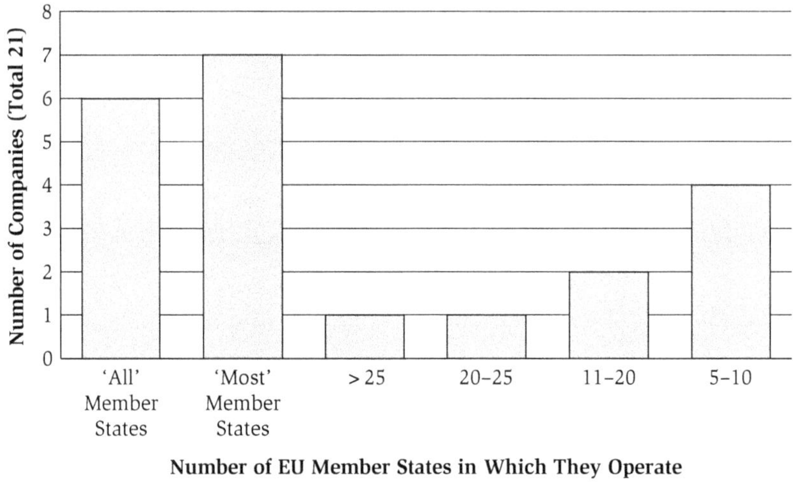

Figure 5.6 shows the number of EU Member States (plus the UK), as identified by the interviewees, in which their companies operate. The term '"Most" Member States' has been used because these words were used by some interviewees in response to the question on the number of EU Member States in which their companies operate. As regards the term '"All" Member States' used in Figure 5.6, this captures the interviewees' responses of 'All Member States' and 'Every Member State'. It should be noted here that, as the research for this book was conducted before the UK left the EU, the UK was included in the interviewees' lists of the EU Member States in which their companies operated. Therefore, the UK has been included for the purposes of Figure 5.6.

Figure 5.6 demonstrates that over three-quarters of the companies interviewed operate in eleven or more EU Member States. Further, of particular note is that two-thirds of the companies interviewed operate in all or most EU Member States.[5]

As explained in Chapter 2, one way in which to explore the particular context of EU cross-border commercial disputes is to engage with multinational companies that have activities in a number of EU Member States. Such companies may have experience of cross-border disputes involving parties from a range of EU Member States and may therefore be able to offer insights into the use of dispute resolution processes for such disputes.[6] Indeed, later in this section, Figure 5.8 validates this approach as it

5. For the purposes of this calculation, one company operating in twenty-six EU Member States (and included in the category of > 25 in Figure 5.6) is included. Further, as the UK was a member of the EU when this research was conducted, for the purposes of this calculation the UK has been included as an EU Member State.
6. Such an approach has been adopted in empirical studies on international arbitration. Empirical studies which sought to identify users' attitudes and use of international arbitration targeted general counsel or heads of legal of corporations with cross-border activities. *See* Mistelis, *supra* n. 2, at 531.

demonstrates that the interviewees' companies' collective experience of EU cross-border disputes involves parties from a wide range of EU Member States.[7] It should be repeated here that the research for this book was conducted before the UK left the EU. Accordingly, the UK is included in Figure 5.8 as some interviewees referred to the UK in their answers to the relevant question.

§5.04 EXPERIENCE OF EU CROSS-BORDER COMMERCIAL DISPUTES

In addition to obtaining information on the interviewees and the companies which they represent, questions were also included at the start of the interviews regarding the company's experience of EU cross-border commercial disputes.

As the aim of the empirical research was to gain insights from disputants on the reasons why they do, and do not, use cross-border commercial mediation within the EU, the cross-border commercial scope of the research was emphasised and explained to the participants. In particular, early in the interview, interviewees were provided with definitions of key terms to ensure that the interviewees were all addressing the same topic.[8] In accordance with the definition provided in the EU Mediation Directive, 'EU cross-border dispute' was defined as: 'a dispute in which at least two parties to the dispute are domiciled or habitually resident in different EU Member States'. Accordingly, the cross-border nature of a dispute is determined by a difference in the domicile or habitual residence of the parties.[9]

Further, to ensure that interviewees only provided information on their business-to-business disputes, they were provided with a definition for commercial dispute.[10] 'Commercial dispute' was defined broadly as 'a dispute between businesses. The term, as defined, does not include disputes between a business and a consumer nor does it include employment disputes between a business and its employees'.[11]

7. *See* Figure 5.8 later in this chapter.
8. The definitions provided to the interviewees are included at 'Section B. Definitions' of the Interview Guide at Appendix 2.
9. While other factors could be taken into account to determine the cross-border nature of a dispute, such as if the country where a substantial part of the obligations of the commercial relationship are to be performed differs from the country where the parties are domiciled or resident (drawing on the definition of 'international mediation' in section 2, Article 3, 2(b)(i) of UNCITRAL Model Law on International Commercial Mediation and International Settlement Agreements Resulting from Mediation (2018)), using a difference in the domicile or residence of the parties is a common and easily understood approach and one which is consistent with the directive from which this empirical research stems.
10. *See* Chapter 2 regarding why the focus of the empirical research is commercial disputes rather than the broader category of civil disputes.
11. *See* 'Section B. Definitions' of the Interview Guide at Appendix 2. *See* Chapter 6 for a discussion of the interviewees' interpretation of 'dispute'.

Figure 5.7 Interviewees' Companies' Experience of EU Cross-Border Commercial Disputes

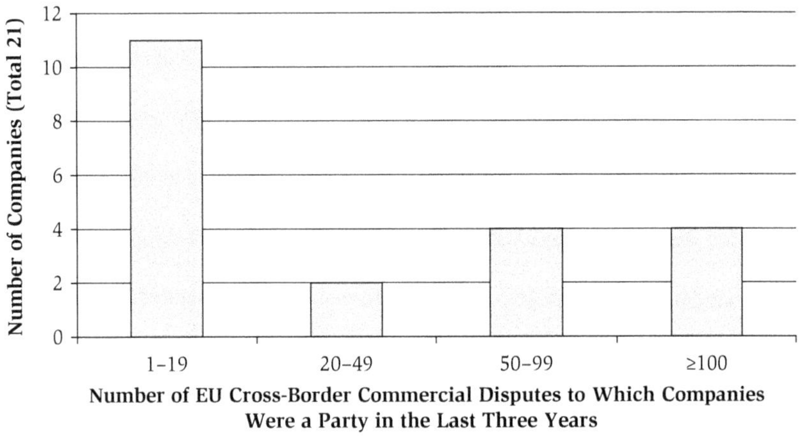

Figure 5.7 shows the number of EU cross-border commercial disputes to which the interviewees' companies have been a party, as identified by the interviewees. It demonstrates the considerable experience with EU cross-border commercial disputes of the companies which participated in the research. Just under 40% of the twenty-one companies had been a party to at least fifty EU cross-border commercial disputes and just shy of 50% of the twenty-one companies had been party to at least twenty such disputes in the past three years.[12]

The question enquired about experience with EU cross-border commercial disputes during the last three years. The timeframe of three years was chosen for two reasons. First, such a timeframe has been used for notable studies in dispute resolution.[13] Secondly, the research sought to gain an understanding of the use and perceptions of mediation following the implementation of the EU Mediation Directive. As noted in Chapter 2, the directive had to be implemented by all Member States by

12. When answering the question on how many EU cross-border commercial disputes their companies had been a party to in the last three years, a few interviewees offered answers which were not given in numbers. For example, one interviewee answered 'innumerable/countless'. The researcher therefore placed such answers in categories best reflecting the scale with, for example, 'innumerable/countless' being included in the category of '≥100'. Further, one interviewee who had only a shorter amount of time to offer for the interviews did not specify the particular number of disputes in which his company had been involved and he was not pressed on this point given time constraints. To adopt a conservative approach, that company has been placed in the smallest category i.e., 1-19.
13. For example *see* S.I. Strong, *Realizing Rationality: An Empirical Assessment of International Commercial Mediation*, 73 Washington & Lee Law Review 1973 (2016). Research participants were asked for their experience in international commercial dispute resolution in the last three years. *See also* Thomas Stipanowich and J. Ryan Lamare, *Living with ADR: Evolving Perceptions and Use of Mediation, Arbitration, and Conflict Management in Fortune 1000 Corporations*, 19 Harvard Negotiation Law Review 1, 41 (2014) for which research participants were also asked about the use of various forms of ADR in the previous three years.

May 2011. The three-year timeframe allows for a couple of years following the implementation of the directive and therefore for some time for the impact of the directive to take effect before the commencement of the three-year timeframe.

Figure 5.8 Number of Interviewee Companies Which Have Been a Party to an EU Cross-Border Commercial Dispute Involving Parties from Particular EU Member States (Plus UK)

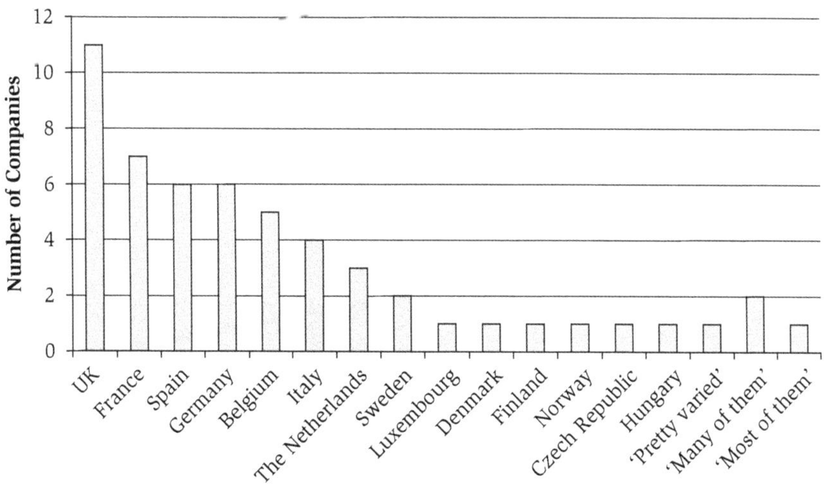

After asking the interviewees how many EU cross-border commercial disputes their companies had been involved in, interviewees were then asked from which EU Member States the parties to those disputes came. Figure 5.8 shows the number of interviewees who identified that such parties came from particular EU Member States.[14] Figure 5.8 also refers to the terms 'pretty varied', 'many of them' and 'most of them' because some interviewees offered these answers rather than identifying specific EU Member States. It should be noted here that the research for this book was conducted before the UK left the EU. Accordingly, the UK is included in Figure 5.8 as some interviewees referred to the UK in their answers to the relevant question.

Figure 5.8 demonstrates that the companies' collective experience of EU cross-border commercial disputes involves parties from a variety of EU Member States. This includes a few companies that had experience of such disputes involving parties from many or most EU Member States. The significant representation of Germany, France,

14. It should be noted that five of the interviewees did not provide such information. They either chose not to provide the requested information, did not know the information or, in the case of one interviewee, chose to state the Member States from which he did not see parties in his company's experience of EU cross-border disputes.

Italy, Spain and the UK is unsurprising given that these countries are the largest economies by gross domestic product (GDP) in Europe.[15]

§5.05 EXPERIENCE OF EU CROSS-BORDER COMMERCIAL MEDIATION

The question on whether the interviewee's company had been involved in any EU cross-border commercial disputes in the last three years was followed by a question on whether mediation had been used in any of those disputes. As Figure 5.9 demonstrates, two-thirds of the companies had not used mediation for those disputes and one-third had used mediation.

Figure 5.9 Companies' Experience of EU Cross-Border Commercial Mediation

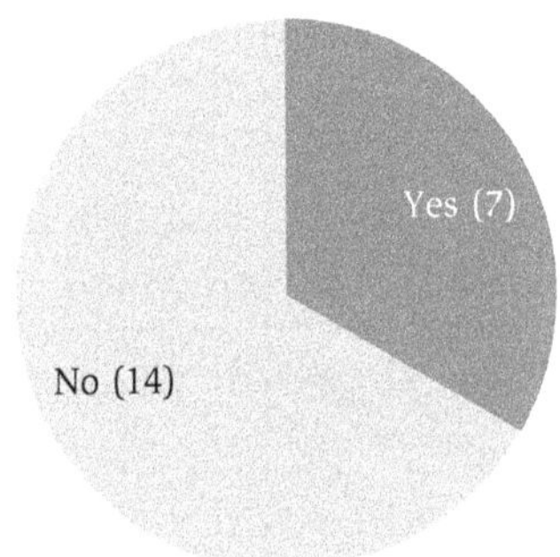

It should be noted here that, before being asked this question, interviewees were provided with the following broad definition of mediation which drew heavily on the definition in the EU Mediation Directive:

> Mediation means a consensual process, however named or referred to, in which the parties themselves attempt to reach a settlement of their dispute with the assistance of a mediator who acts as an impartial third party. 'Conciliations' are included if they fall within this definition.[16]

This broad definition captures the core component of mediation: that parties are assisted by an impartial third party in their attempts to reach a settlement. This general definition allows for differences in the mediation process across the EU Member States.[17]

---

15. The World Economic Forum's list of the largest economies by GDP by region <https://www.weforum.org/agenda/2017/03/worlds-biggest-economies-in-2017/> (accessed 20 May 2020). It should be noted here that the research for this book was carried out before the UK left the EU.
16. *See* 'Section B. Definitions' of the Interview Guide at Appendix 2.
17. Manon Schonewille and Jeremy Lack, *Mediation in the European Union and Abroad: 60 States Divided by a Common Word?* in Manon Schonewille and Fred Schonewille (eds), *The Variegated Landscape of Mediation: A Comparative Study of Mediation Regulation and Practices in Europe*

For those companies that had used mediation for their EU cross-border commercial disputes, interviewees were asked about the extent of that use. Four interviewees gave answers which can be numerically categorised. Of those four answers, two companies had been involved in one to five EU cross-border commercial mediations in the past three years and two companies had been involved in five to ten such mediations.[18] For the other three interviewees, their answers do not fit neatly into numerical categories. Two can be grouped together under the category of 'limited use'[19] while one can be attributed to the category of 'extensive use'.[20] What can be seen from these responses is that, overall, for the companies taking part in this research that had experience of mediation for EU cross-border commercial disputes during the last three years, their experience of mediation appears to be limited.

However, to gain a fuller picture, it is helpful to consider the extent of their use of mediation alongside the amount of EU cross-border disputes to which they have been a party, as shown in Table 5.2.

Table 5.2 Comparison of Number of Disputes and Number for Which Mediation Was Used

Interviewee	*Number of EU Cross-Border Commercial Disputes in the Last 3 Years for the 7 Users of Mediation (As Described by Interviewees)*	*Number of Such Disputes for Which Mediation Was Used (As Described by Interviewees)*
11	20-25	2 or 3
14	50-100	More or less 3
16	Hundreds	Half a dozen
12	100 if not more	5-10
8	A large number	There has been a limited number of mediations
5	Countless	Try to do it all of the time
3	Innumerable	We do not use it much

This additional information shows that - with the exception of Interviewee 5 - as a proportion of the amount of EU cross-border commercial disputes in which the companies have been involved, mediation has been used in only a very small proportion of such disputes.

and the World 20 (Eleven International Publishing 2013). *See* further Chapter 2 regarding the provisions of the EU Mediation Directive.

18. The categories of 1-5 and 5-10 have been used in spite of the overlap on the number 5 because of the use of such categories by a couple of the interviewees.
19. The two answers which have been placed in this category of 'limited use' are 'there has been a limited number of mediations' and 'we do not use it much'.
20. The answer captured by the category of 'extensive use' is 'try to do it all the time'.

§5.06 CONCLUSION

The information identified in this chapter demonstrates that those interviewed for the research for this book occupy very senior legal roles in their companies under which they either have responsibility for, or are involved in, their companies' cross-border disputes. They are therefore well placed to offer insights into their companies' experience of EU cross-border commercial disputes and the dispute resolution methods used for such disputes. The interviewees represent very large companies operating across numerous EU Member States and business sectors and which have considerable experience of EU cross-border commercial disputes. Further, a third of the interviewees had experience of using mediation for their EU cross-border commercial disputes, though in general mediation had been used in only a small proportion of such disputes. This appears to be consistent with the EU's view, as considered in Chapter 2, that mediation is infrequently used for EU cross-border disputes.

Against this backdrop of the characteristics and experiences of the interviewees and their companies, Chapters 6, 7 and 8 examine the content of the interviews.

CHAPTER 6

The Overlooked Role of Negotiation as a Cross-Border Commercial Dispute Resolution Process

> If one wants to know the colour distribution in a field of flowers, one first needs to establish the set of colours that are in the field; then one can start counting the flowers of a particular colour. The same is true for social facts.[1]

§6.01 EXECUTIVE SUMMARY

As addressed in Chapters 1 and 2, the empirical research conducted for this book builds upon the predominantly quantitative research which has been conducted to date on cross-border commercial mediation. The change in approach stems from a desire to explore whether any important issues have been missed or – to borrow the imagery above of Bauer and Gaskell – whether we have failed to identify a colour in the exploration of cross-border mediation. In particular, the empirical research conducted for this book seeks to broaden our understanding of why disputants do, and do not, use mediation for their EU cross-border commercial disputes.[2]

1. Martin Bauer and George Gaskel (eds), *Qualitative Researching with Text, Image and Sound: A Practical Handbook* 8 (Sage Publications 2000).
2. Steffek has emphasised the importance of the parties' perspective in the context of creating a dispute resolution taxonomy, arguing that such a taxonomy would serve to improve the regulation of dispute resolution. Felix Steffek, *The Relationship Between Mediation and Other Forms of Alternative Dispute Resolution* in European Parliament, *The Implementation of the Mediation Directive, Workshop 29 November 2016* (2016) PE 571.395, 47. Stipanowich has also identified the 'exceptional value' of the perspectives of corporate counsel as users of dispute resolution services. Thomas Stipanowich, *What Have We Learned From The Global Pound Conferences?* (Kluwer Mediation Blog, 27 November 2017) <http://mediationblog.kluwerarbitration.com/2017/11/27/learned-global-pound-conferences/?doing_wp_cron=1590503495.

This chapter identifies an interesting, and important, pattern which emerged in the interviews regarding the interviewees' understanding of mediation; in particular, the association drawn by the interviewees of mediation with negotiation. It also considers the central role, from the perspective of the interviewees, of negotiation as a dispute resolution process for cross-border commercial dispute resolution and identifies how cross-border negotiation has been absent from the quantitative research to date on cross-border commercial dispute resolution. The chapter then considers the relevance of these themes for those seeking to promote cross-border mediation such as the EU.

Chapter 7 then explores the key themes which emerge from the interview data which are relevant to the issue of why disputants use mediation for their EU cross-border commercial disputes, including the triggers for their use of mediation. Chapter 8 then explores the key themes on why mediation is not used.

§6.02 PARTIES' UNDERSTANDING OF MEDIATION

The focus of the empirical research conducted for this book is not the process of mediation but rather why mediation is, and is not, used.[3] However, during the interviews, some of the interviewees shared their understandings of mediation and an important pattern emerged in these descriptions which merits attention. Therefore, before considering the reasons why those who have experience of mediation used mediation, as will be addressed in Chapter 7, this pattern regarding the interviewees' understanding of mediation will be considered.

[A] Mediation as a Form of Negotiation

In the understandings of mediation which were provided by the interviewees, there was a notable emphasis on the relationship between mediation and negotiation. In particular, there was a pronounced pattern of interviewees displaying an understanding of mediation as a form of negotiation, with mediation being regarded as assisted or extended negotiations. It is acknowledged that this characterisation of mediation is not novel in and of itself as the literature has described mediation as assisted negotiation.[4]

401226997375488281250 0> (accessed 20 May 2020). *See also* Chapter 4 where the choice of in-house counsel as interviewees is explained.

3. Recent qualitative studies which address the process of mediation include Debbie De Girolamo, *The Fugitive Identity of Mediation* (Routledge 2013); Tamara Relis, *Perceptions in Litigation and Mediation* (Cambridge 2009).
4. For a review of the literature on mediation being characterised as assisted negotiation *see* De Girolamo *supra* n. 3, at 63-68 supporting her view of mediation as a negotiation. This is further supported by the characterisation at 63 by the mediators in her empirical ethnographic study of mediation as assisted negotiation. The focus of this empirical study differs as it is the parties' understanding, and not that of the mediators, which is the focus. *See also* Nancy A. Welsh, *Making Deals in Court-Connected Mediation: What's Justice got to do with it?*, 79 Washington University Law Quarterly 787, 799 (2001). At footnote 62 on page 799 Welsh lists key literature which describes mediation as assisted or facilitated negotiation. *See also* Chapter 8 which provides further examples from the mediation literature of mediation being described as

Rather, the relevance is that the interviewees connect the two processes of mediation and negotiation, a connection which is of particular relevance to this study on the use of mediation, as becomes apparent in Chapter 8.

For example, Interviewee 3 conveyed the link between mediation and negotiation as:

> *'What is mediation? It's getting a third party to help in bilateral negotiation, no great mystery. Having a third party is often very helpful.'*

He further noted the help which the third-party mediator can bring to the parties' negotiations in the following comments:

> *'We view mediation as one of a few levers to get people talking. Two parties can bilaterally talk but sometimes we need the help of a third party.'*
>
> *'The parties get to an agreement. It's a consensual process. Someone is helping us to get to agree.'*

Further, Interviewee 4 described mediation succinctly as '*assisted negotiation*'. In addition, Interviewee 4 explained that his company was about to use mediation because of '*an inability over the last 1.5 years to sort things out by themselves*', which further suggests his view of mediation being assisted negotiation. They were unable to resolve matters themselves so they decided to draw on the assistance of a third-party mediator.

Further, a view of mediation as being a form of negotiation, and an extension of negotiation, is also suggested by Interviewee 12's explanation that for some of their negotiations the company sometimes leapfrogs the negotiation process to use mediation:

> *'Sometimes in one third or 50% of negotiations we would immediately start with mediation rather than beginning with a negotiation.'*

Interviewee 12's explanation – that in a significant number of their *negotiations* they would start with mediation – suggests that Interviewee 12 understands mediation to be a form of negotiation. His explanation that they sometimes leapfrog negotiation to use mediation suggests a view that mediation offers something in addition to unassisted negotiation.

A similar understanding of mediation as being a form of negotiation was also conveyed by Interviewee 11 who described mediation as '*in essence a species of negotiation*'. In a similar vein, Interviewee 10 described mediation as '*a step up from decision makers sitting in a room thrashing out a deal*'.

Further, when asked for his prediction on his company's future use of mediation for their EU cross-border commercial disputes, Interviewee 10 also conveyed his understanding of mediation as being a form of negotiation when questioning why one would use mediation if there were nothing to negotiate:

---

assisted/facilitated negotiation and which explains how the relationship between mediation and negotiation, as identified by the parties to this study, is the basis for new and important findings regarding why parties do not use mediation.

> '*it depends on the nature of the dispute. If it's a cut and dry case I don't see the benefit of us using that* [mediation]. *What is there to negotiate?*'

In addition, comments made by Interviewee 8 also suggest an understanding of mediation as a form of negotiation. When asked about his company's approach to handling disputes, Interviewee 8 explained:

> '*We look into different tools. We are trying to find a negotiated solution. Mediation plays a key part in how we move forward.*'

This description of how mediation can enable them to move forward in their efforts to try to find a negotiated solution, similarly suggests a view of mediation as being a form of negotiation, and of adding something to the negotiation process.

In addition, the association of mediation with negotiation was also seen in interviewees' comments on why they did not use mediation. A pronounced theme, which will be explored fully in Chapter 8, was that there is a scepticism as to what mediation could add to the parties' own negotiation efforts. Such comments further suggest a view of mediation as being a form of negotiation, with a third party seeking to assist the parties in their negotiations. For example, when asked why his company does not use mediation for their EU cross-border commercial disputes, Interviewee 18 responded:

> '*Many disputes are already resolved through negotiations without third party assistance.*'

Similarly, Interviewee 11 explained that one of the reasons why mediation is not used for EU cross-border disputes is:

> '*People do not see the need to keep negotiating with a third party as they are already trained in being a negotiator.*'

Further, Interviewee 12 explained that the reason why his company has not used mediation for its EU cross-border disputes is:

> '*More often the opponent is not willing to enter into a mediation. It's: we're so great at negotiating that we don't need a mediator.*'

The interviewees' comments above, which suggest an understanding of mediation as a form of negotiation and, in particular, as an extension of negotiation with a third party attempting to assist parties in their negotiations, are important as they suggest an important difference between how mediation is understood in the EU Mediation Directive and how it may be understood by its users. The interviewees' comments above suggest, to borrow the words of Bush, 'an intuitive clarity about mediation's "place" in the dispute resolution universe'[5] which contrasts with the EU

5. Robert Bush, *What Do We Need a Mediator for? Mediation's Value-Added for Negotiators*, 12 Ohio Journal on Dispute Resolution 1, 5 (1996). Bush argues that mediation should not be compared to litigation but rather to negotiation either between the parties themselves or their lawyers.

Mediation Directive's approach of positioning mediation as an alternative to litigation.[6] As noted by Steffek, an understanding of mediation as an alternative to litigation leads to a focus in the directive on the relationship between mediation and judicial proceedings while the relationship between mediation and other forms of ADR is barely addressed.[7]

In particular, the pattern of the interviewees understanding mediation as a form of negotiation is important as it invites us to consider how mediation is framed and, crucially, the impact of such framing.[8] The way in which mediation is framed is important as it influences the direction in which those who seek to promote mediation look for ideas for its promotion. Understanding and presenting mediation predominantly as an alternative to litigation, as is the approach of the EU Mediation Directive, appears to have encouraged a focus of looking to litigation in the various efforts to promote mediation. For example, the directive provides for courts to invite parties to use mediation (Article 5) and, so that mediation is not regarded as the poorer alternative to court proceedings, Member States are required to ensure the enforceability of mediated settlement agreements (Recital 19 and Article 6). The trend of looking to litigation has continued in the more recent proposals to promote mediation arising from the review of the directive. These include the continued calls for mandatory mediation, a quota of the number of mediations against judicial proceedings and, more recently, the recommendation that information campaigns be conducted which raise awareness of the time and cost savings that mediation can bring compared to litigation.[9]

Further, framing mediation primarily as an alternative to litigation can encourage a promotion of mediation which relies heavily on anti-litigation rhetoric, an approach which has been criticised, among others, by Genn and Mulcahy. Genn notes that 'the case for mediation has routinely been made not so much on the strength of its special

6. It is notable that of those interviewees who offered their understandings of mediation, only one referred to mediation as an alternative to litigation in her description of mediation. Interviewee 7 stated '*Mediation is an alternative way of resolving disputes outside the court process or arbitration with an independent person facilitating a meaningful dialogue where both parties are forced to assess the merits of the case and in light of that to reassess whether they might need to compromise for settlement.*'
7. Steffek, *supra* n. 2, at 50. The focus on mediation as an alternative to litigation is a topic also addressed in Carrie Menkel-Meadow, *Dispute Resolution* in Peter Cane & Herbert M. Kritzer (eds), *The Oxford Handbook of Empirical Legal Research* 597 (Oxford 2010). Menkel-Meadow notes the more recent understanding of ADR as appropriate – rather than alternative – dispute resolution. This interpretation conveys the variety of processes available for resolution of disputes. Further, as noted by Hicks, 'To a large extent, alternative conflict resolution practices have been superimposed upon previously established methods and institutions for resolving disputes ... We can see this ... in the courthouse.' Tim Hicks, *Embodied Conflict* 100 (Routledge 2018).
8. In this context, the term 'framing' is used in its common meaning of articulation i.e., the words chosen to articulate something (*see* Oxford English Dictionary).
9. *See* Chapter 2 on the proposals to reboot the directive of mandatory mediation and a quota for the number of mediations as against the number of judicial proceedings, and also the recent recommendation for information campaigns. On the recommendation of information campaigns see in particular European Parliament, *Resolution of 12 September 2017 on the Implementation of Directive 2008/52/EC of the European Parliament and of the Council of 21 May 2008 on Certain Aspects of Mediation in Civil and Commercial Matters (the 'Mediation Directive')* [2018] OJ C337/2, para. 11.

benefits but by setting it up in opposition to adjudication and promoting it through anti-adjudication and anti-law discourse'.[10] This oppositional approach has also been criticised by Mulcahy: 'Mediation enthusiasts and lawyers alike must each be able to incorporate into their own perspectives the insights gained from the others' experience rather than set up litigation and mediation as mutually exclusive alternatives one of which is good and the other bad.'[11] Such an oppositional promotion of mediation reduces mediation simply to a way in which to avoid the courts, with no reference to the value which mediation might bring to the resolution of disputes. As Bond asks 'shouldn't it be the intrinsic quality of the mediation process and the quality of the results that make mediation attractive, not the poor quality or cost of the courts'?[12] Further, such an oppositional approach may not be applicable across all EU Member States given the varied efficiency of the courts. For example, in countries such as Germany and Belgium where the courts are renowned to be efficient and cost-effective, a promotion of mediation as a way in which to avoid the cost and time of the court system would not be relevant.[13]

In addition, framing mediation as an alternative to litigation overemphasises the extent to which litigation is used to resolve disputes. As Roberts and Palmer have noted 'in making litigation the paradigm case ... it vastly overplays the extent to which disputes – even in this culture – get anywhere near lawyers and the courts'.[14] This may

10. Hazel Genn, *Judging Civil Justice* 80 (Cambridge 2009). *See also* Hazel Genn, *What Is Justice for? Reform, ADR and Access to Justice,* 24 Yale Journal of Law and the Humanities 397, 409 (2012).
11. Varda Bondy at al., *Mediation and Judicial Review: An Empirical Research Study* 89 (The Public Law Project 2009) <http://www.nuffieldfoundation.org/sites/default/files/files/Mediation andJudicialReview.pdf> (accessed 20 May 2020). Further, Brooker notes the 'anti-litigation stance' of the Global Pound Conference (1976) in the USA. Penny Brooker, *Mediation Law* 170 (Routledge 2013).
12. Greg Bond, *Who Should Be Promoting Mediation and Why? Mediation in Germany: The Poor Cousin to the Courts* (Kluwer Mediation Blog, 24 November 2016) <http://mediationblog.kluwerarbitration.com/2016/11/24/who-should-be-promoting-mediation-and-why-mediation-in-germany-the-poor-cousin-to-the-courts/?doing_wp_cron=1590503743.97373008728027343 75000> (accessed 20 May 2020).
13. Alexander acknowledges Germany's efficient legal system and explains: 'In fact in Germany it may, in some cases, be more expensive to mediate a case successfully than to take it to court.' Nadja Alexander (ed.) *Global Trends in Dispute Resolution Vol. 1* 256 (Kluwer Law International 2006). As regards Belgium, Menkel-Meadow notes: 'Belgium ... has had a relatively efficient legal system with less delay in litigation time and has been able to structure mediation programs around the values of promoting good legal solutions.' Carrie Menkel-Meadow, *Variations in the Uptake of and Resistance to Mediation Outside of the United States,* University of California, Irvine School of Law, Research Paper No. 2015-80 [2015], 205 <https://papers.ssrn.com/sol3/papers.cfm?abstract_id=2658903> (accessed 20 May 2020).
14. Simon Roberts and Michael Palmer, *Dispute Processes, ADR and the Primary Forms of Decision-Making* 79 (2nd ed. Cambridge 2005). Similarly, Macfarlane states 'It is important to remember that the use of the legal system lies on the margins of real-life disputing, with just 10-20 percent of disputes involving over $1000 using a lawyer.' Julie Macfarlane, *The New Lawyer: How Clients Are Transforming the Practice of Law* 170 (2nd ed. UBC Press 2017). Further, Genn has also noted that 'Mediation is constantly contrasted with adjudication, even though the most common form of civil case conclusion in the UK and in many other jurisdictions is settlement.' Genn, *Judging Civil Justice, supra* n. 10, at 124-125. *See also* William Felstiner, Richard Abel and Austin Sarat, *The Emergence and Transformation of Disputes: Naming, Blaming, Claiming ...,* 15 Law & Society Review 631, 649 (1980-1981) who note: 'Unarticulated grievances, lumped claims, and bilateral disputes certainly are numerically more significant than are the cases that reach courts'.

be all the more relevant for cross-border disputes where, as noted in Chapter 2, arbitration plays a key role as a cross-border dispute resolution process.[15]

The pattern of the interviewees understanding mediation to be a form of negotiation, and in particular assisted and extended negotiation, is an important prompt to include the 'colour' of negotiation in the dispute resolution palette and, in particular, for the EU, in its efforts to promote mediation, to recognise and explore the relationship between negotiation and mediation. In so doing, this may open up the current conversation regarding how to promote mediation beyond the current focus of looking to the relationship between mediation and litigation for measures to increase the use of mediation and on criticising litigation in order to promote mediation. By looking to the relationship between mediation and negotiation, this would enable, for example, the benefits which mediation may bring to negotiation to be explored and may make parties more willing to engage in the process.

Interestingly, the interview data also revealed a further key reason why the relationship between mediation and negotiation should not be overlooked in the promotion of mediation: the centrality, as recognised by disputants, of negotiation in dispute resolution.[16] This view of the central role played by negotiation as a dispute resolution process for EU cross-border commercial disputes is consistent with the view espoused by various ADR academics that it is negotiation, and not litigation, which commonly will be used to resolve disputes and that negotiation and not litigation is the 'standard' process of dispute resolution.[17] It is to that topic which the chapter now turns.

§6.03 THE CENTRAL ROLE PLAYED BY NEGOTIATION

[A] Negotiation as a Preferred Method of Cross-Border Dispute Resolution

During the interviews, participants were asked 'What is your company's preferred method of dispute resolution for EU cross-border commercial disputes?' This question was an open question and interviewees were not given a list of options from which to

Further, regarding the English and Welsh context, *see* Pascoe Pleasance, Nigel Balmer and Tania Tam, *Civil Justice in England & Wales: Report of the 2006 English & Welsh Civil and Social Justice Survey* which found that respondents tried to obtain information from lawyers (either solicitors or barristers) for only 13.5% of their problems (*see* page 56). *See also* Christopher Hodges and Magdalena Tulibacka, *Civil Justice in England & Wales – Beyond the Courts* (2009) <https://www.law.ox.ac.uk/sites/files/oxlaw/civil_justice_in_england_and_wales_-_beyond_courts._mapping_out_non-judicial_civil_justice_mechanisms.pdf> (accessed 20 May 2020). This report sets out the non-judicial civil justice mechanisms available in England and Wales.

15. Chapter 2, text to (n. 116)-(n. 119).
16. The term 'the centrality of negotiation' is used by Menkel-Meadow in the different context of 'the centrality of negotiation in legal education' Carrie Menkel-Meadow, *Legal Negotiation: A Study of Strategies in Search of a Theory*, 8(4) American Bar Foundation Research Journal 905, 908 (1983).
17. Macfarlane, *The New Lawyer*, *supra* n. 14, at 54; Bush, *supra* n. 5, at 1, 5; John Lande, *Getting the Faith: Why Business Lawyers and Executives Believe in Mediation*, 5 Harvard Negotiation Law Review 137, 152 (2000).

choose. This contrasts with the largely quantitative relevant empirical research to date from which respondents could select their preferred method of dispute resolution from a menu of options.[18]

In their responses to this question, some interviewees answered that they did not have one preferred method of dispute resolution and their preferred method would vary on a case-by-case basis. As Interviewee 7 explained in response to this question:

> '*Would vary on a case-by-case basis. We would always look to see if it's appropriate to consider settlement. The overriding objective makes you think of settlement.*[19] *Whether every legal system requires you to do I don't know. We would certainly look at how much time and cost litigation would take us. There is no hard and fast rule. Litigation could be long and expensive but sometimes as a point of principle we should take the case – for example, to discourage further spurious cases.*'

Further, another interviewee commented that her company did not have a preferred dispute resolution method and the choice of dispute resolution process would be determined by the nature of the specific dispute.[20] These comments call to mind Menkel-Meadow's emphasis that 'the core question is not "which process is better?" but "which process is better for what and for whom?"'[21] This is an important distinction which, as the comments above suggest, may also be drawn by disputants.

However, there was a pronounced pattern in the interviewees' responses to this question on their preferred method of dispute resolution for EU cross-border commercial disputes. Of those interviewees who identified a specific type of dispute resolution as their preferred method, the most commonly identified method was negotiation.[22] In particular, there was a notable theme of parties identifying negotiation before the use

18. *See* Chapters 2 and 3 for a review of the relevant empirical research.
19. The 'overriding objective' referred to by Interviewee 7 is the overriding objective of the Civil Procedure Rules of the courts of England and Wales. The overriding objective of these rules, as stated at Rule 1.1, is to enable 'the court to deal with cases justly and at proportionate cost'. < http://www.justice.gov.uk/courts/procedure-rules/civil/rules/part01 > (accessed 20 May 2020).
20. The interviewee's words have been paraphrased rather than cited at the request of the interviewee.
21. Menkel-Meadow, *Dispute Resolution, supra* n. 7, at 600. *See also* Carrie Menkel-Meadow, *From Legal Disputes to Conflict Resolution and Human Problem Solving: Legal Dispute Resolution in a Multidisciplinary Context*, 54 Journal of Legal Education 7, 10 (2004). The same point is made by Macfarlane who cautions: 'When the zealous advocates of particular approaches or processes really get going, they veer dangerously close to suggesting that one single, preferred process works "best" for all or even most disputes ... The reality of practical conflict resolution requires responsiveness to the unique nature of each and every conflict.' Julie Macfarlane, *ADR and the Courts: Renewing our Commitment to Innovation*, 95 Marquette Law Review 927, 929 (2012).
22. Of the thirteen interviewees who identified a specific type of dispute resolution as their preferred method, eight stated negotiation was their preferred method. Others did not identify a preferred method. As already noted, some stated that they did not have a single preferred method of dispute resolution and their preference varied on a case-to-case basis. Others noted that they preferred to avoid disputes. For example, one interviewee stated '*I would say we work very closely with very large food and beverage businesses. We make a point of trying to avoid disputes. We have very few disputes.*' (Interviewee 6). And another stated: '*We tend to leave open the option of mediation or arbitration. We don't have a preferred means. We prefer not to get to that stage.*' (Interviewee 10).

of any adjudicative process (such as litigation and arbitration) as their preferred method.

For example, Interviewee 12 identified negotiation as his company's preferred method, explaining:

> *'As a rule of thumb, first it's negotiation, then mediation and if that doesn't work then escalate further.'*

Earlier in the interview, Interviewee 12 had explained that further escalation meant escalation to arbitration or litigation when he stated:

> *'We only escalate further to arbitration or litigation if the mediation fails.'*

Similarly, Interviewee 9 identified negotiation as his company's preferred method adding that if the parties cannot resolve the issue themselves then there would be an opportunity for mediation either before or alongside the litigation process. He stated:

> *'Negotiation. We are pretty proactive. We are successful in achieving an outcome. We are a pragmatic company. We do have some that go the full course and go to court.'*

Earlier, Interviewee 9 had explained:

> *'The parties try to resolve the dispute and then if they can't, there is an opportunity for mediation before or in parallel to the litigation process.'*

Similarly, Interviewee 13 explained:

> *'Our approach was always to negotiate a settlement from company to company. That was always our preference.'*[23]

Interviewee 16 also emphasised:

> *'The vast, vast majority are negotiated out. Negotiation is by far our preferred method of dispute resolution. Effectively we've taken legal advice, have outlined there are issues, have contacted the clients and outlined those issues and reached some resolution process with the client.'*

Interviewee 16 later explained that if negotiations were not successful, the dispute would then go to arbitration.[24]

Similarly, Interviewee 17 explained:

> *'We would rather get a consensual process. Normally by the time the internal client has come to use there will have been quite a lot of negotiation. All of the contractual*

---

23. Interviewee 13's later explanation of his company's policy on dispute resolution clauses clarified that by negotiation Interviewee 13 is referring to negotiation before adjudicative methods are used. Interviewee 13 described his company's policy on its dispute resolution clauses as: '*We had negotiation, escalated negotiation, and then arbitration*'.
24. Interviewee 16 later explained: '*it's difficult to factor in mediation because in insurance contracts they don't have mediation clauses, they have arbitration clauses. That's why the vast majority go to arbitration if we can't negotiate because that is the formalised process in insurance contracts*'.

stuff whether domestic or international. If it's a significant contract there will be discussion during the dispute and in the early stages.

That said, once proceedings are in place, our preferences are for different WP – without prejudice – negotiation and/or mediation.'

Further, Interviewee 14, who identified negotiation as his company's preferred method of dispute resolution for EU cross-border commercial disputes, explained: *'First we use negotiation, then mediation followed by expedited arbitration with only one arbitrator.'* In elaborating on his company's approach to handling disputes and in particular cross-border disputes, Interviewee 14 explained:

'First we try to negotiate as long as possible. In the last 29 years more or less in the licencing department I was the first person to draft the company's licencing agreement. In these 29 years, we have had 10-15 disputes and most of them were settled by mediation and arbitration. We have about 14 000 licence agreements and have had only 15 cases. 4 were in German courts and the others were mediation and arbitration. We have a lot of negotiation work. I think it was very successful. There are not so many cases.'

In addition, Interviewee 8 succinctly noted: *'Very often negotiation is key. The alternative is mediation'*[25] adding:

'We are trying to find a negotiated solution. Mediation plays a key part in how we move forward.'

Interviewee 4 identified *'commercial negotiation'* as his company's preferred method of dispute resolution for EU cross-border commercial disputes explaining, as follows, the key role which negotiation played in his company's approach to handling disputes:

'It's a mixture of the business trying to negotiate its way out of the dispute commercially and legally looking to you for guidance. When they haven't been able to work it out commercially they come to us.'[26]

As is discussed in greater detail after the following and related section on the prescription of negotiation in dispute resolution clauses, the answers to this open question on the preferred method of dispute resolution enable the role played by negotiation as a key method of cross-border commercial dispute resolution to come to light.

25. Interviewee 8's comment was not made in response to the question on what is your preferred method of dispute resolution but was made as he explained his involvement in his company's handling of disputes.
26. Interviewee 4's comment was not made in response to the question on what is your preferred method of dispute resolution but was made as he explained his company's approach to handling disputes.

[B] Prescription of Negotiation in Dispute Resolution Clauses

The importance to the interviewees of negotiation as a method of dispute resolution for their EU cross-border commercial disputes was also conveyed in the interviewees' descriptions of their companies' policies on their dispute resolution clauses. A common theme in these descriptions was the provision in these clauses that negotiation be employed first, followed by other methods of dispute resolution should negotiation not be successful.

For example, Interviewee 15 described the requirement under his company's dispute resolution clause that negotiation be attempted prior to the use of other forms of dispute resolution:

> *'We have dispute resolution clauses for cross-border contracts that will typically have a negotiation section, and obviously these clauses can be negotiated. There is negotiation and then if there's failure then it goes to arbitration. What I have been told is that the negotiation clause is never amended: it's 2 people high up in the business and usually within some time limit. 40 days is standard.'*

Further, Interviewee 12 described his company's use of the standard International Chamber of Commerce's multi-tier clause which provides for the use of negotiation as the first step:

> *'As standard in our global standard T & Cs, it's a standard ICC multi-tier DR clause: (1) negotiation, (2) before arbitration, mediation according to ICC mediation.'*

Similarly, Interviewee 13 described his company's dispute resolution clause as providing first for negotiation followed by escalated negotiation:

> *'We had negotiation, escalated negotiation, and then arbitration, and for arbitration it depended on which company it was whether the arbitration was London or New York. That was for the big procurement contracts. Then if it's a more typical supply contract it would be litigation in the courts of the country in which the product was sold.'*

In addition, Interviewee 14 explained the provision of negotiation as the first step in his company's dispute resolution clauses:

> *'Most of our licensees accept our way to handle it. We start with negotiation limited by time 30, 60 or 90 calendar days. If these negotiations fail they can start a mediation under WIPO rules or agreed rules in the same timeframe. If we have 60 days for negotiation, then it's 60 days for mediation, then we start with arbitration, expedited under WIPO rules under 9 months or we go to normal proceedings in the federal court in Germany, if not arbitration.'*

Similarly, Interviewee 18 explained that negotiation was the first step in his company's dispute resolution clause:

> *'It is a multi-tiered clause: staggered negotiation, then negotiation, then mediation and then arbitration.'*

Further, Interviewee 11 described his company's emphasis on early discussions in its dispute resolution clauses:

> *'In all of them* [model contracts] *we use pretty lengthy clauses. Generally speaking they aim to avoid litigation, they aim at an escalation process between the parties, so discussions between higher management, they ask parties to exchange information on major aspects of disputes and they ask parties to think about alternative ways to settle a case compared to litigation. Our preferred law for bigger contracts is English law and we have a preference for LCIA.'*

Interviewee 17 also identified meetings between counterparties as the first step in his company's dispute resolution clauses:

> *'There will be counterpart-to-counterpart meetings. Often either the obligation to mediate or option to do so. If fails, usually litigation.'*

In addition, Interviewee 19 explained:

> *'I am not giving away too many secrets if I say that our normal contractual template ordinarily is an escalation process before the formal DR piece. It would be: the head of the businesses meet, the senior management have two weeks to flesh out a deal.'*

The interviewees' comments above regarding the prescription of negotiation in their companies' dispute resolution clauses together with the earlier theme of negotiation being identified as the preferred method of dispute resolution for their companies' EU cross-border commercial disputes convey the value and importance which the interviewees' companies place on the dispute resolution process of negotiation. However, negotiation appears to be a 'colour' which has largely been missed in the relevant empirical research to date on cross-border commercial dispute resolution research.[27]

[C] The 'Colour' of Negotiation

Although negotiation is recognised as an important method of cross-border dispute resolution in academic literature,[28] it has received little attention in the empirical work

27. This research is considered in Chapters 2 and 3.
28. Thomas Hale, *Between Interests and Law, The Politics of Transnational Commercial Disputes* 38 (Cambridge 2015): 'commercial dispute resolution across borders may occur in a variety of processes and institutions. The most common and least institutionalized are informal negotiations between the parties'. *See also* Jacob Bercovitch and Richard Jackson, *Conflict Resolution in the Twenty-first Century, Principles, Methods and Approaches* 19 (4th ed. The University of Michigan Press 2012) which states: 'Negotiation is the most frequently employed of all methods of international conflict resolution.' *See also* Myres McDougal, *The Diversity of Contemporary Dispute Resolution: Functions and Policies,* 4(1) Journal of International Dispute Settlement 47, 50 (2013) where negotiation is described as a 'prominent form of international dispute resolution'. Further, in Eileen Carroll and Karl Mackie, *International Mediation: Breaking Business Deadlock* 14 (3rd ed. Bloomsbury Professional 2016) Carroll and Mackie note: 'Traditionally, international contracts have provided for negotiation ... by senior executives as a final negotiation stage to resolve disputes in joint ventures, distribution, licensing and similar long-term arrangements.' Further, and more recently, the Civil Mediation Council in its Interim Report on ADR and Civil Justice of October 2017 noted at page 7 that 'most disputes are resolved

on cross-border dispute resolution which has focused predominantly on the comparative use of litigation, arbitration and mediation. In the empirical research which the EU commissioned as part of its review of the EU Mediation Directive, the focus is on the relationship between litigation and mediation.[29] In Strong's research on the use and perception of international commercial mediation, negotiation is absent from the definition of international commercial dispute resolution, which is defined as 'including litigation, arbitration, mediation and conciliation in the international commercial context'.[30] In Stipanowich and Lamare's empirical research on ADR, negotiation is not listed as a 'form of ADR' in the question on which forms of ADR the respondents have used in the last three years.[31] Similarly, the IMI's research 'International Corporate Users ADR Survey'[32] focuses on mediation and arbitration and there is no reference to negotiation. In the research for the GPC Series, the dispute resolution process of negotiation also does not feature in the list of the various types of dispute resolution process.[33] Further, extensive research has been conducted by Queen Mary University of London which, while its focus is on international arbitration, also touches upon the broader topic of international dispute resolution. In the various questions which refer to international dispute resolution processes, negotiation is not specifically mentioned.[34] Further, negotiation is also not included in SIDRA's research on international

by agreement in commercial and everyday life'. < https://www.judiciary.uk/wp-content/uploads/2017/10/interim-report-future-role-of-adr-in-civil-justice-20171017.pdf > (accessed 20 May 2020).

29. *See* Chapter 2 for a review of the empirical research commissioned by the EU as part of its review of the EU Mediation Directive.
30. S.I. Strong, *Realizing Rationality: An Empirical Assessment of International Commercial Mediation*, 73 Washington & Lee Law Review 1973, 2017 (2016).
31. The forms of ADR which are listed in Stipanowich and Lamare's research are: mediation, arbitration, mediation-arbitration, fact finding, mini-trial, early neutral evaluation, early case assessment, peer review, in-house grievance system. Thomas Stipanowich and J. Ryan Lamare, *Living with ADR: Evolving Perceptions and Use of Mediation, Arbitration and Conflict Management in Fortune 1000 Corporations*, 1 Harvard Negotiation Law Review 19, 41 (2014). Stipanowich and Lamare's study is included here in the review of international empirical work as, as explained in Chapter 3, their study does not state whether or not it is confined to national mediation and, given that the respondents to the survey were Fortune 1000 companies, its reach may extend to international mediation.
32. International Mediation Institute, *IMI International Corporate Users ADR Survey* January – March 2013 < https://www.imimediation.org/2013/04/06/imi-adr-users-survey-results/ > (accessed 20 May 2020).
33. Question 3 of the Core Questions used at the Global Pound Conference Series 2016-2017 asks 'In what kinds of dispute resolution processes have you had the most experience?' The options listed are: litigation, arbitration, conciliation, mediation, adjudicative processes (defined as 'litigation & arbitration'), non-adjudicative processes (defined as 'conciliation & mediation'), approximately equal amounts of adjudicative and non-adjudicative processes, no typical process, and other < https://www.imimediation.org/research/gpc/series-data-and-reports/#core-questions > (accessed 20 May 2020).
34. In the 2018 study by the School of International Arbitration, Queen Mary University of London on *The Evolution of International Arbitration*, respondents were asked to choose from the following options to identify their preferred method of resolving cross-border disputes: 'International arbitration together with ADR'; 'International arbitration'; 'Cross-border litigation together with ADR'; and 'Cross-border litigation'. Negotiation is not specifically identified though may fall within the broad category of 'ADR' (page 5 of the 2018 study). In the 2016 study on *Pre-empting and resolving technology, media and telecoms disputes, international dispute*

dispute resolution which focuses on the more formal methods of dispute resolution of international commercial arbitration, international commercial mediation and international commercial litigation.[35]

However, there are a couple of exceptions in cross-border research conducted by mediation institutions which do refer to negotiation. As considered in Chapter 3, there is the research by CPR of in-house counsel's use of mediation and arbitration for both their domestic and cross-border disputes. In this research, 'direct negotiation' is included in the list of dispute resolution methods from which respondents can choose. As addressed in Chapter 3, CPR's research identifies 'direct negotiation' as by far the most popular method of dispute resolution for both cross-border (selected by 59% of respondents) and domestic (selected by 57% of respondents) disputes.[36]

There may also be one further exception in the specific context of intellectual property disputes. In a 2013 international study on dispute resolution in technology transactions by the Arbitration and Mediation Center of the World Intellectual Property Organisation (WIPO), respondents were asked to rank their use of various dispute resolution mechanisms for their disputes. While the relevant question does not refer explicitly to cross-border disputes, it appears that this question may apply to both cross-border disputes and national disputes as one of the options which respondents could choose was 'court litigation (in their home jurisdiction and in another jurisdiction)'.[37] Due to this reference to 'court litigation in another jurisdiction' respondents

---

resolution survey, the preferred dispute resolution mechanisms listed were 'arbitration, mediation, court litigation, expert determination'. (*See* page 20 of the 2016 study). The 2015 study on *Improvements and Innovation in International Arbitration* asks 'Over the past five years, what types of dispute resolution methods have you used for cross-border disputes?' The options from which to choose are: 'International arbitration, cross-border litigation, international arbitration together with (other ADR), mediation, cross-border litigation together with ADR.' Negotiation is not specifically identified though may fall within the broad term of 'ADR'. (*See* page 53 of the 2015 study). In the 2013 study on *Corporate Choices in International Arbitration – Industry Perspectives*, respondents were asked to 'Rank the following dispute resolution mechanisms in order of preference for your industry sector.' The list included 'Arbitration, Court litigation, Adjudication/expert determination, Mediation.' Negotiation is not listed as an option (*see* page 7 of the 2013 study). In the 2008 study on *International Arbitration: Corporate Attitudes and practices*, respondents were asked 'Does your organization have experience with the following dispute resolution mechanisms with regard to international disputes?' The options from which they could choose were 'Cross border litigation, international arbitration, mediation and other ADR mechanisms.' (*See* page 5 of the 2008 study). In the 2006 study on *International Arbitration: Corporate Attitudes and Practices*, respondents were asked for their 'Preferred mechanism(s) for resolving cross-border disputes'. The options from which they could choose were; 'International arbitration & ADR, international arbitration, international mediation & ADR, transnational litigation.' (*See* page 5 of the 2008 study). The School of International Arbitration's research reports are available at: <http://www.arbitration.qmul.ac.uk/research/> (accessed 20 May 2020).

35. SIDRA, *International Dispute Resolution Survey: 2020 Final Report* <https://sidra.smu.edu.sg/sidra-international-dispute-resolution-survey-final-report-2020> (accessed 10 August 2020).
36. CPR and CEDR, 'Insights into Alternative Dispute Resolution', Winter 2018-2019, at 3, <https://www.cpradr.org/news-publications/reports/2019-04-04-cpr-cedr-joint-insights-report-on-the-use-of-adr/_res/id=Attachments/index=0/CEDR%20CPR%20report%20040419.pdf> (accessed 20 May 2020).
37. WIPO, *Results of the WIPO Arbitration and Mediation Center International Survey on Dispute Resolution in Technology Transactions* 26 (March 2013) <https://www.wipo.int/amc/en/center/survey/results.html> (accessed 20 May 2020).

may have interpreted this question to apply to both domestic and cross-border disputes. A further indication that the results of this survey may apply to the cross-border context are that over 90% of the respondents had concluded technology-related agreements with parties from other jurisdictions.[38] The dispute resolution mechanisms from which respondents could choose included 'direct party negotiations'.[39] And it is particularly interesting to see that respondents identified direct party negotiation as the most used method of dispute resolution.[40] Accordingly, when negotiation has been included in cross-border research by mediation institutions, the key role played by negotiation as a method of dispute resolution could be identified.

Another significant exception can be found in academic empirical research on the domestic use of mediation. In such empirical research on the use of mediation in New Zealand, the research includes negotiation in its questions on which dispute resolution processes are used by the respondents. Such research consistently identifies negotiation as the most commonly used form of commercial dispute resolution in New Zealand.[41] Further, it should also be noted that in empirical research by the mediation institution, CEDR, which focused on the use of mediation in the UK,[42] respondents were asked what had happened to disputes handled in the last three years and the options from which they could choose included two options which referred to negotiation, namely: 'Settled by direct negotiation – pre litigation' and 'Settled by direct negotiation – during litigation'.[43] The outcome of 'settled by direct negotiation – pre litigation' was by far the most common outcome, with 60% of disputes having this

---

38. *See ibid.*, 4. Respondents to the survey came from sixty-three countries (*see ibid.*, 3).
39. *Ibid.*, 26. The other dispute resolution mechanisms from which respondents could choose were: court litigation, mediation, arbitration, expedited arbitration and expert determination (also listed at *ibid.*, 26).
40. *Ibid.*
41. Grant Morris and Freya McKechnie, Resolution Institute/Victoria University of Wellington, *Users of Commercial Mediation in New Zealand – Insurance Industry Report* (April 2017) <https://papers.ssrn.com/sol3/papers.cfm?abstract_id=3015041> (accessed 20 May 2020). Question 6 at page 5 of the report states 'In which of the following forms of dispute resolution does your organization most commonly participate?' Respondents could choose from: litigation, arbitration, mediation and negotiation. Negotiation was the most commonly used form of dispute resolution (*see* page 5). Negotiation is also listed alongside litigation, arbitration and mediation in Morris' earlier empirical research on commercial mediation: Grant Morris and Amanda Lamb, Resolution Institute/Victoria University, *Lawyers as Gatekeepers to Commercial Mediation in New Zealand Report* (June 2016) at question 10 page 8 <https://papers.ssrn.com/sol3/papers.cfm?abstract_id=2797995> (accessed 20 May 2020). *See also* Grant Morris and Daniella Schroder, LEADR/Victoria University, *Commercial Mediation in New Zealand Project Report* (June 2015) <https://papers.ssrn.com/sol3/papers.cfm?abstract_id=2650261> (accessed 20 May 2020) in which negotiation is also listed as one of the forms of dispute resolution which respondents can select for a question on which forms of dispute resolution they are commonly involved in (at page 8, question 13).
42. The study's focus is on the UK market as 90% of the respondents were based in the UK and only 10% were based in other jurisdictions. Further, the questions refer to 'mediation' and do not distinguish between domestic and international mediation. CEDR, 'Survey of In-House Use of Commercial Mediation', 7 March 2013, page 1 <https://www.cedr.com/docslib/In-House_Mediation_survey.pdf> (accessed 20 July 2019). This study is no longer available on CEDR's website though is on file with CEDR.
43. *Ibid.*, 2.

outcome.[44] The second most common outcome was 'settled by direct negotiation – during litigation', with 12% of the disputes having this outcome.[45] Accordingly, when negotiation is listed as an option which respondents can select, its prominence as a dispute resolution process becomes apparent. However, such a recognition of negotiation's role in dispute resolution is lacking in both the EU's research to date and the academic research on the cross-border context.

The prominent pattern in the research for this book of the interviewees identifying their preference for, and the key role played by, negotiation as a method of EU cross-border commercial dispute resolution brings negotiation clearly into view. This acknowledgement of negotiation as a favoured method of cross-border dispute resolution widens the context in which mediation is situated, from a context focused on litigation to one which recognises the contribution made by negotiation. Crucially, such recognition reorients us away from the EU's continued focus on mediation's relationship with litigation towards mediation's relationship with negotiation.

[1] Nature of the Negotiation Process

At this juncture, it may be helpful to provide a brief description of the dispute resolution process of negotiation and the way in which it differs from mediation. Negotiation is, as Roberts and Palmer explain, 'the primary, universal route to decision and action in the social world',[46] and it is used in both contentious and non-contentious issues.[47] Negotiations are 'in their simplest form ... a bilateral process of decision-making, achieved through information exchange and learning'.[48] De Girolamo identifies the essence of negotiation as: 'negotiation is about joint decision-making involving parties in conflict who strive to communicate with an opponent within a normative and psychological context about a resource they want or do not wish to give up'.[49] Models within the negotiation process have been identified, including those of Gulliver and De Girolamo, which offer detailed insights into, and enhance our understanding of, the components of the dynamic process of negotiation.[50]

44. *Ibid.*
45. *Ibid.*
46. Roberts and Palmer, *supra* n. 14, at 113. *See* De Girolamo, *supra* n. 3, at 73 for a detailed examination of the negotiation process.
47. Roberts and Palmer, *supra* n. 14, at 113.
48. *Ibid.* Similarly, Gulliver describes negotiation as 'in essence ... the process of negotiation is one of information exchange and of consequent learning and adjustment by the parties'. Phillip Hugh Gulliver, *Disputes and Negotiations: A Cross-Cultural Perspective* 81 (Academic Press 1979).
49. De Girolamo, *supra* n. 3, at 73. At 74-83 De Girolamo offers a detailed review of the literature on the negotiation process.
50. De Girolamo offers a detailed account of Gulliver's hybrid model of negotiation which is comprised of a cyclical process and a developmental process, De Girolamo, *supra* n. 3, at 78- 81, and *see also* Gulliver, *supra* n. 47, at 81, 82, 121-170. Further, drawing on her ethnographic work, at 108 De Girolamo provides her own model of the negotiation process. These models offer detailed insights into the core components which are often to be found in the dynamic, and as Gulliver calls it 'untidy', process of negotiation, Gulliver, *supra* n. 48, at 173.

There is a close relationship between negotiation and mediation, with mediation frequently described in the academic literature as an extension of the negotiation process, or as assisted or facilitated negotiation.[51] As Bercovitch and Jackson note: 'The most helpful approach to mediation sees it as an extension of negotiation, a closely related form of conflict resolution, but one with its unique features and conditions.'[52] The key distinguishing feature between mediation and negotiation is the involvement in mediation of an independent third party who assists the parties in their negotiations.[53] The presence of such a third party can give rise to subsequent differentiating factors between mediation and negotiation, such as the phases in the mediation being more structured and distinct compared to those in negotiation,[54] and a greater emphasis in mediation of an interest-based rather than a positional approach to negotiations.[55] What mediation can add to negotiation due to the involvement of a third-party neutral is considered further in Chapter 8.

§6.04 INTERPRETATION OF 'DISPUTE'

Returning to the omission of negotiation as a dispute resolution process in the academic empirical research to date on cross-border commercial disputes, such an omission suggests a narrow interpretation of the term 'dispute', and by extension 'dispute resolution', with a focus on disputes as legal cases resolved by the later, more formal third-party or third-party assisted methods of dispute resolution such as litigation, arbitration and mediation. While the relevant empirical research considered earlier in this chapter does not include a definition of 'dispute', the answers from which the research participants could choose - principally litigation, arbitration and mediation - suggest a dispute in the later, formal legal dispute stage in which a third-party

51. For example, Bercovitch and Jackson have described mediation as 'an extension of negotiation', Jacob Bercovitch and Richard Jackson, *Conflict Resolution in the Twenty-First Century* 33 (The University of Michigan Press 2009); Moore has also described mediation as 'an extension of the negotiations', Christopher Moore, *The Mediation Process* 8 (4th ed. Jossey-Bass 2014); De Girolamo states that 'negotiation lies at the heart of mediation' and has described mediation as 'a process that facilitates a negotiation', De Girolamo, *supra* n. 3, at 5; Alexander has described mediation as 'facilitated negotiation', Nadja Alexander, *International and Comparative Mediation* 25 (Wolters Kluwer 2009); Palmer and Roberts have described mediation as a 'process auxiliary to negotiation', Roberts and Palmer, *supra* n. 14, at 173.
52. Bercovitch and Jackson, *supra* n. 51, at 33. *See also* Alexander, *supra* n. 51, at 25 which states that 'mediation and negotiation are closely related processes'.
53. Alexander, *supra* n. 51, at 25; De Girolamo, *supra* n. 3, at 65. This has also been described as the difference between mediation's triadic structure compared to negotiation's dyadic structure, Bercovitch and Jackson, *supra* n. 51, at 33. *See also* Gulliver, *supra* n. 48, at 213.
54. Alexander, *supra* n. 51, at 25. Roberts and Palmer note the important role which the mediator plays in assisting with communication and thereby enhancing the information exchange and learning which lies at the core of decision-making by negotiation. Roberts and Palmer, *supra* n. 14, at 173. On a more technical note, Alexander also identifies the further distinguishing feature between mediation and negotiation that courts in a number of jurisdictions have, under certain circumstances, held that agreements to mediate were enforceable and in contrast agreements to negotiate are generally not enforceable. Alexander, *supra* n. 51, at 25.
55. Moore, *supra* n. 51, at 178. The value which a mediator can bring to unassisted negotiations is considered in Chapter 8.

specialist is involved in the resolution of the dispute.[56] The earlier stages of disputes, and the more informal, earlier methods of dispute resolution such as negotiation, appear to have been overlooked.

As suggested by Roberts and Palmer, a narrow presentation of disputes, as 'discrete, "bounded cases"',[57] as appears to be the predominant approach in the empirical research considered earlier in this chapter,[58] does not lend itself to a recognition of the role which less formal methods of dispute resolution such as simply talking with, and indeed negotiating with, the other side can play.[59] Such a narrow focus has also been identified by Menkel-Meadow who has noted the emphasis in dispute resolution on 'legally constructed "cases"' rather than the disputes which exist before such formal legal disputes.[60] Similarly, Prince has noted that 'the more formal, evidential process required by civil hearings forces the dispute narrowly to fit into the requirements of the law. This may not allow for any analysis of the underlying issues which caused the dispute itself'.[61]

Here it is appropriate to mention Felstiner, Abel and Sarat's framework of the evolution of disputes. They describe the emergence and transformation of a dispute as a process of naming, blaming and claiming.[62] More specifically, they identify the following processes: (i) a person perceives an experience to be injurious, which they call 'naming';[63] (ii) the person then blames another for the injury, thereby turning the injury into a grievance; (iii) the person then raises that grievance against the alleged perpetrator, thereby transforming it into a claim; (iv) the claim becomes a dispute when the alleged perpetrator dismisses it; and (v) finally, the dispute is transformed by lawyers to make it suitable for legal proceedings.[64] Felstiner, Abel and Sarat's framework offers an expansive conceptualisation of disputes with disputes portrayed as a continuum rather than only as distinct and detached legal cases.[65]

Returning to the empirical research for this book, the exploratory nature of this research identified an interesting pattern of interviewees recognising the ambiguity of the term 'dispute'. Of those respondents who offered their understandings of the term

56. *See* the research referred to earlier in this Chapter at text to (n. 29)-(n. 35), and also Roberts and Palmer, *supra* n. 14, at 80.
57. *Ibid.*, 80.
58. *See* text to (n. 29)-(n. 35).
59. As regards a narrow concept of disputes, Roberts and Palmer note 'the extent to which the lawyer's folk view of conflict privileges settlement-directed talking is also problematic ... – sit down talking will not necessarily be central'. Roberts and Palmer, *supra* n. 14, 80.
60. Carrie Menkel-Meadow, *From Legal Disputes to Conflict Resolution and Human Problem Solving: Legal Dispute Resolution in a Multidisciplinary Context*, 54 Journal of Legal Education 7, 12 (2004).
61. Sue Prince, *Institutionalising Mediation? An Evaluation of the Exeter Court Small Claims Mediation Pilot*, 5 Web Journal of Current Legal Issues (2007).
62. Felstiner, Abel, & Sarat, *supra* n. 14, at 635-636.
63. *Ibid.*, 635.
64. *Ibid.*, 635-637, and 645. *See also* Roberts and Palmer's summary of Felstiner, Abel and Sarat's framework in Roberts and Palmer, *supra* n. 14, at 79.
65. Roberts and Palmer note the problematic nature of a narrow conceptualisation of disputes as 'discrete, bounded "cases"' which includes the unlikelihood that talking with be used to address issues, and the separation of disputes from the flow of everyday life with a related emphasis on specialists for their resolution. Roberts and Palmer, *supra* n. 14, at 79-80.

'dispute', the tendency was to adopt an expansive understanding of this term, consistent with its presentation by Felstiner, Abel and Sarat, to include conflicts which have not yet been transformed into neat legal disputes for court or arbitral determination. Representative comments include:

> *'It is also interesting to look at the definition of a dispute. Doesn't mean parties are already fighting in court or arbitration. There might be occasions that there are cross-border disputes that are not handled by the litigation department but by the business lawyers.'*[66] (Interviewee 11)
>
> *'That's* [the number of EU cross-border commercial disputes which his company had been party to in the last 3 years] *based on a wide definition of disputes as a disagreement between two companies that they want to resolve by drawing on the legal department.'* (Interviewee 18).
>
> *'I'll take the definition to be an escalation under the DR clause.'* (Interviewee 4). (Such escalation, as explained by another interviewee, may typically be to discussions between higher management with the exchange of information on major aspects of the case. Accordingly, this reference to escalation under the dispute resolution clause suggests a wider interpretation of dispute beyond those which reach the realms of court or arbitral determination.)[67]
>
> *'this would include matters for which court proceedings have not yet started?'* (Interviewee 2)

Further, in response to the question on how many EU cross-border commercial disputes his company had been a party to, Interviewee 16 explained *'Hundreds where we've had disputes but very limited where they've been taken to a formal dispute resolution procedure.'* He then added *'The vast, vast majority are negotiated out.'* This response demonstrates an understanding of disputes as wider than those that reach a formal dispute resolution procedure such as court or arbitration.

In addition, in response to how many EU cross-border commercial disputes his company had been a party to, Interviewee 5 replied:

> *'There are so many large projects going on simultaneously and many with joint ventures. Issues keep coming up. These will be countless. We try to mediate and resolve the issue.'*

This pattern of the interviewees interpreting the term 'disputes' widely to include 'disagreements', 'issues' and 'matters' before they have been transformed into court or arbitral proceedings is consistent with the theme, identified earlier, of the important role played by negotiation in dispute resolution. A wide interpretation of disputes beyond those disputes determined by the later formal methods of dispute resolution, such as litigation and arbitration, allows for the identification of the role played by earlier and less formal methods of dispute resolution, such as negotiation. As noted earlier, the recognition of the prominent role which negotiation can play in cross-border commercial dispute resolution reorients the EU away from presenting mediation

66. Other interviewees' comments also suggested the varied ways in which the term 'disputes' could be interpreted (Interviewees 2, 4, 9, 10, 12, 14, 15, 16, 17, 18 and 21).
67. Interviewee 4 did not describe the escalation process in his company's dispute resolution clause. The explanation offered was provided by Interviewee 11.

solely as an alternative to litigation. If negotiation, rather than litigation, is the 'standard' dispute resolution process, this suggests that in its efforts to promote mediation the EU should move away from its sole focus on the relationship between mediation and litigation[68] to also consider the relationship between mediation and negotiation. While this would be a significant departure from the EU's approach to date in both its empirical research and its proposals, such an approach brings with it the opportunity to both identify and address barriers to the use of the mediation which have not previously been identified without exploring the relationship between mediation and negotiation. This is an issue to which we shall return in Chapter 8, which explores the reasons why parties do not use mediation and reveals interesting obstacles which stem from the parties' association of mediation with negotiation.

§6.05 CONCLUSION

The opening quotation of this chapter on the importance of identifying all of the colours in a field before counting their prevalence is a reminder of the importance of looking carefully at a particular setting to determine comprehensively its components. That quotation reminds us of the elicitive approach advocated by Lederach (as described in Chapter 4) which emphasises how the astute observation of what exists in a particular setting can reveal both what is already bringing about change and what may have the potential to effect further change.[69] As Lederach explains: 'Catalysts and support can come from outside, but the sustenance of change is built by keen observation of available and existing resources … and connections.'[70]

The insights provided by the interviewees of this study, all of whom are active in the setting of EU cross-border commercial disputes, enhance our understanding of this particular setting. As considered in this chapter, the interviewees' comments bring into clear sight the key role played by negotiation as a dispute resolution process in the EU cross-border commercial context. This recognition by the interviewees of the role played by negotiation contrasts with the lack of attention afforded to negotiation in the academic empirical research on cross-border commercial dispute resolution processes to date which has focused predominantly on the comparative use of litigation, arbitration and mediation.

Taken together with the prominent theme of interviewees understanding mediation as a form of negotiation, the interviewees' identification of the central role played by negotiation suggests that in the EU's efforts to determine ways in which to promote mediation it should expand upon its sole current focus on the relationship between mediation and litigation to consider and explore the relationship between mediation and negotiation.

68. As noted earlier in this chapter, and also in Chapter 2, the EU Mediation Directive focuses predominantly on the relationship between mediation and litigation and does not explore the relationship between mediation and other types of dispute resolution processes.
69. Chapter 4 explains the influence of Lederach's elicitive approach on this study.
70. John Paul Lederach, *The Moral Imagination* 94 (Oxford University Press 2005).

Such a reorientation of focus to also consider and explore the relationship between mediation and negotiation may yield fresh ideas about how to promote mediation compared to the various proposals which have been identified by looking solely to litigation for ideas on how to promote mediation (such as mandatory mediation, enforceability of mediated settlement agreements and a quota of the number of mediations compared to judicial proceedings) as has been the EU's approach to date.[71] Indeed, the relationship between mediation and negotiation is an important platform from which to explore, and understand, reasons why parties do and do not use mediation for their EU cross-border commercial disputes as are considered in detail in Chapters 7 and 8.

71. Proposals for how to promote mediation stemming from the relationship between mediation and negotiation are identified in Chapter 9.

CHAPTER 7

Why Parties Use Mediation for their EU Cross-Border Commercial Disputes

We do not see things as they are. We see things as we are.[1]

§7.01 EXECUTIVE SUMMARY

This chapter explores the key themes from the interview data which are relevant to the issue of why disputants use mediation for their EU cross-border commercial disputes, including the triggers for their use of mediation. The themes identified in this chapter confirm, challenge and expand upon the empirical research to date on why parties use mediation. Further, the themes identified regarding the triggers for the use of mediation highlight the parties' own efforts to bring about the use of mediation. An awareness of these efforts by the parties suggests that those seeking to promote mediation, such as the EU, might wish to consider how parties could be supported in their current efforts to bring about the further use of mediation.

§7.02 WHY DISPUTANTS USE MEDIATION

As noted in Chapter 5, seven out of the twenty-one interviewees had experience of mediation for EU cross-border commercial disputes. During their interviews, these interviewees shared their reasons for using such mediation, whether in response to the specific question of why their company used mediation or in their responses to other questions.[2] Various themes emerged in their answers, which are examined below.

1. Anaïs Nin, *Seduction of the Minosaur* 124 (Swallow Press 1961).
2. The reasons why companies used EU cross-border commercial mediation were specifically addressed by Question 3.1 of the interview guide: 'What were the main reasons for using mediation for EU cross-border commercial disputes?'

In the empirical research conducted to date on cross-border commercial mediation, when respondents are asked for the reasons why they use mediation, certain reasons are commonly listed from which respondents can choose.[3] These include: saves cost, saves time, preservation of relationships, control of the process and outcome, flexibility of the process and outcome, more satisfactory process, confidentiality, nature of the dispute, industry practice, expertise of the neutral, and avoidance of other methods of dispute resolution such as litigation or arbitration.[4] The same reasons also commonly appear in the empirical research on commercial mediation at the domestic level.[5] Many of these reasons were similarly identified by the interviewees as their reasons for using mediation for their EU cross-border commercial disputes. However, two reasons were particularly noticeable given their repeated occurrence in the interviewees' answers. These were the reasons of: (i) the preservation of relationships; and (ii) cost and time savings compared to using arbitration or litigation.

3. As explained in Chapter 3, the empirical research to date on cross-border commercial mediation is predominantly quantitative research using surveys from which respondents could select an answer.
4. For possible reasons why parties use mediation *see*: S.I. Strong, *Realizing Rationality: An Empirical Assessment of International Commercial Mediation*, 73 Washington & Lee Law Review 1973, 2030 and footnote 187 (2016); Question 1.2 (When parties involved in commercial disputes are choosing the type(s) of dispute resolution process(es) to use, which of the following has the most influence?) of the Core questions of the GPC Series <https://www.imimediation.org/research/gpc/series-data-and-reports/#core-questions> (accessed 20 May 2020); Thomas Stipanowich and J. Ryan Lamare, *Living with ADR: Evolving Perceptions and Use of Mediation, Arbitration and Conflict Management in Fortune 1000 Corporations*, 1 Harvard Negotiation Law Review 19, 37 (2014). Regarding the empirical research on the EU Mediation Directive commissioned by the European Parliament (namely European Parliament, *'Rebooting' the Mediation Directive: Assessing the Limited Impact of its Implementation and Proposing Measures to Increase the Number of Mediations in the EU* (2014) PE 493.042) such research focuses on the reasons of saving time and cost: *see* page 7 and pages 122-127 of the rebooting study. *See also* European Commission, *Quantifying the Cost of Not Using Mediation – a Data Analysis* (April 2011) PE 453.180; and ADR Centre (study funded by the EU), *The Cost of Non ADR – Surveying and Showing the Actual Costs of Intra-Community Commercial Litigation, Survey Data Report* (June 2010) which also focus on the time and cost savings of mediation compared to litigation.
5. *See* Grant Morris and Amanda Lamb, Resolution Institute/Victoria University, *Lawyers as Gatekeepers to Commercial Mediation in New Zealand Report* (June 2016) at 12 <https://papers.ssrn.com/sol3/papers.cfm?abstract_id=2797995> (accessed 20 May 2020); Grant Morris and Daniella Schroder, LEADR/Victoria University, *Commercial Mediation in New Zealand Project Report* (June 2015) at 16 <https://papers.ssrn.com/sol3/papers.cfm?abstract_id=2650261> (accessed 20 May 2020); John Lande, *Getting the Faith: Why Business Lawyers and Executives Believe in Mediation*, 5 Harvard Negotiation Law Review 137, 214-217 (2000); CEDR, *The Eighth Mediation Audit 2018 – A Survey of Commercial Mediator Attitudes and Experience in the UK* (10 July 2018) and in particular question 25 (What do you believe are the most common reasons why parties decide to mediate?) <https://www.research.net/r/CEDRaudit2018> (accessed 20 May 2020).

[A] Preservation of Relationships

There was a significant pattern of the interviewees identifying the preservation of relationships as a reason why they used EU cross-border mediation.[6] This is particularly interesting given that earlier empirical work on cross-border commercial mediation suggests that the preservation of relationships plays a less significant role as a reason for using mediation for cross-border disputes compared to national disputes.[7] As Interviewee 16 explained in response to the question of what the main reasons were for using mediation for EU cross-border commercial disputes:

> *'Client relationship. The cost of onboarding a new client, bringing in a new client, is so high we'd prefer to maintain relationships with our existing clients and hence we use a DR method that maintains that relationship.'*

Similarly, Interviewee 5 explained that his company has used mediation because '*We did not want to spoil the relationship*' adding that '*You don't lose customers, you don't have a bad name.*' Interviewee 11 simply identified '*Relationship*' as one of the reasons why his company uses mediation for their EU cross-border commercial disputes. In addition, Interviewee 4 explained that while his company had not been involved in any mediations in the relevant three-year timeframe, it appeared that his company would soon be involved in a mediation. The interviewee explained that the reason for the potentially imminent use of mediation was: '*an inability over the last 1.5 years to sort things out by themselves but at the same time wanting to preserve the relationship so as not to go to court*'.

Interestingly, other reasons identified by the interviewees in response to the question of why they used mediation included the opportunity to talk directly to the counterparty and confidentiality.[8] These two reasons appear to be consistent with the emphasis placed on the importance of preserving relationships.

While earlier empirical research questions the role that the preservation of relationships plays in disputants' decisions to use mediation for their cross-border disputes,[9] the insights offered above suggest that it would be premature, at least in the EU cross-border context, to discount the role which the desire to preserve relationships can play in users' decisions to use cross-border mediation.[10] It is important to emphasise that these insights are from users of EU cross-border commercial mediation

6. Three interviewees (namely Interviewees 5, 11 and 16) out of the seven interviewees who had experience of mediation for EU cross-border commercial disputes identified the preservation of relationships as their main reason, or one of their main reasons, for using mediation.
7. Strong, *supra* n. 4, at 2031. Strong notes that the ability to preserve an ongoing relationship was only the fifth most important reason for using mediation in international commercial disputes. This is in contrast to Lande's research to which Strong refers, which was national in scope and which found that 'belief in mediation is significantly related to beliefs that mediation helps preserve business relationships'. Lande, *supra* n. 5, at 205.
8. These reasons for using mediation for EU cross-border commercial disputes were identified by Interviewees 11 and 12. They also identified the further reasons of the possibility of reaching wider solutions than those available in court and being in control.
9. Strong, *supra* n. 4, at 2031.
10. It should be emphasised that both Strong's research and the research for this study explored why parties used mediation for cross-border disputes, though the scope of Strong's research was

and it is such users who are best placed to answer the question of why parties use such mediation.[11] To ask others (such as mediators, lawyers or academics) why parties use mediation, is to ask the different question of why do *you think* parties use mediation.[12]

Acknowledging the role which the desire to preserve relationships can play in a user's decision to use cross-border mediation is instructive for the EU as it seeks to promote the use of such mediation. If the preservation of relationships is a factor which influences disputants' choice to use cross-border mediation, this characteristic of mediation should be emphasised by those seeking to promote such mediation. Arguably, the EU's approach to date of focusing on the relationship between mediation and litigation[13] with the consequent association of mediation with the adversarial and adjudicative process of litigation does not assist in emphasising this characteristic. Notably, Interviewee 21 described how the differing methods of dispute resolution of mediation, litigation and arbitration can be perceived to be the same:

> *'There is a sense amongst the non-lawyers[14] that ADR is the same whether it's litigation, arbitration or mediation. There is a perception that it's not something you'd like to propose to a customer. They prefer informal ways forward ... They would be commercial discussions or without prejudice meetings. The idea of preparing thoroughly for a mediation with our customer is not something we'd like to do. This explains why we are not heavy users of mediation.'*

Interviewee 21's comment above suggests that mediation's association with formal and adversarial methods of dispute resolution, including litigation, could inhibit those in conflict from proposing the use of mediation to those whose relationship they value.

In light of the pattern identified earlier of the interviewees understanding mediation as a form of negotiation, the EU should consider altering its approach to one of at least acknowledging, if not emphasising, the relationship between mediation and negotiation. This may enable those parties for whom the preservation of relationships is an important issue to be more comfortable in both proposing and using mediation,

---

wider and addressed international commercial disputes whereas the research for this book focused only on EU cross-border commercial disputes.

11. In her empirical study on the perceptions of various parties in litigation and mediation, Relis identified the '"parallel worlds" theory', a term used to describe the different understandings held by the various actors in a dispute (e.g., the lawyers, the disputants) and its resolution. While the context of that study differs to this study (Relis' study focused on medical injury cases) such a finding supports the view that the different parties to a dispute (mediators, lawyers or the disputants themselves) may hold different views about the conflict and ways in which to address the conflict. Tamara Relis, *Perceptions in Litigation and Mediation* 9-11 (Cambridge 2009).
12. In Strong's study, the only category of respondents which could be regarded as parties were in-house counsel who were 7% of the respondents (*see* Strong, *supra* n. 4, at 2017). Further, in Strong's study it is not possible to determine how many in-house counsel participants responded to the question of why parties used international commercial mediation nor how many in-house counsel participants had experience of such mediation (*see* Strong, *supra* n. 4, at 2030 and Appendix A).
13. The EU Mediation Directive's focus on the relationship between mediation and litigation is explored in Chapter 2. *See*, in particular, text to (n. 80)-(n. 86) in Chapter 2.
14. Earlier, Interviewee 21 had referred to the *'non-lawyers in* [his company's] *businesses'*. 'Non-lawyers' is therefore understood to mean the business people.

given its association with the favoured and familiar consensual dispute resolution process of negotiation (the popularity of which is suggested by the interviewees' comments in Chapter 6 on their preferred method of dispute resolution for EU cross-border commercial disputes).

[B] Cost and Time Savings

Of the interviewees in this study whose companies had experience of using mediation for EU cross-border commercial disputes, there was also a noticeable pattern of interviewees identifying cost and/or time savings as the main reason, or one of the main reasons, for using mediation.[15] This is consistent with earlier research on cross-border mediation (though in the broader global context) which has recognised the importance of the cost and time savings which mediation can bring.[16] Interviewee 12 succinctly noted that one of the main reasons for using mediation was '*Saving time and cost from arbitration and litigation.*' Similarly, Interviewee 14 explained: '*It's mediation first because it's quite fast and cheap compared to arbitration and the federal court.*' Further, Interviewee 3 elaborated:

> '*From our point of view, it's* [mediation's] *the most sensible thing to do. Litigation is highly undesirable, unpredictable, costly and time-consuming. Would certainly like to avoid going through to trial. Don't want to use it if we can avoid it. We have litigation after negotiations have failed.*'

It may be helpful to note here that Interviewee 3's identification of mediation as a way in which to avoid the time and cost of litigation together with his association of mediation with negotiation (through the use of the term 'negotiations') suggests that the interviewees' comments in Chapter 6 on their understanding of mediation as a form of negotiation are not inconsistent with the above comments made by the interviewees on mediation being a way to avoid the time and cost of litigation and arbitration. In other words, given that mediation is a form of assisted or extended negotiation, it can enable disputants to avoid the time and cost of litigation or arbitration.

Reasons for the interviewees' use of mediation were, however, also found in their answers to other questions beyond the specific question on why they use mediation for their EU cross-border disputes. The following two themes emerged from the wider data beyond the specific question of why the interviewees used mediation.

[C] Satisfaction with Mediation

Those who had experience of EU cross-border mediation expressed satisfaction regarding their experience and expressed positive attitudes towards mediation.

15. Four interviewees (namely 3, 11, 12 and 14) out of the seven interviewees whose companies had experience of using EU cross-border commercial mediation identified cost and/or time savings as the main reason, or one of the main reasons, for using mediation.
16. Strong, *supra* n. 4, at 2031.

Accordingly, for those who had repeatedly used mediation, their satisfaction with mediation could also be a reason for their use of mediation.[17]

For example, Interviewee 5 expressed his satisfaction with mediation as follows:

> *'I love mediation and will use it most of the time ... I support mediation and try to do it all of the time and normally non-institutionalised mediation.'*

Similarly, Interviewee 3 stated: *'I have a very positive view. I am a big fan of mediation'*, adding later in the interview *'I am very positive about mediation.'*

Further, Interviewee 14 expressed his satisfaction with the high resolution rates of the disputes which his company has taken to mediation:

> *'We have had five mediations in the last 5 years. There has been a 100% success rate. It was fast and cheap and the cases settled in 1, 2 or 3 days.'*

Further, in response to the specific question on how satisfied they were with the EU cross-border mediations which they had experienced, interviewees answered that they had been satisfied with the mediations, or the vast majority of them.[18]

Looking across the dataset, beyond the data provided in response to the specific question on why mediation had been used, revealed this further reason why parties may have used mediation, namely their satisfaction with and positive view of mediation. This is consistent with the finding in earlier empirical research on the wider global cross-border commercial context that parties use cross-border mediation because they wanted to use a satisfactory process.[19]

17. *See* Chapter 5 regarding the extent of the interviewees' experience of EU cross-border commercial mediation.
18. In response to the question 'How satisfied were you with those EU cross-border commercial mediations?' Interviewees 5, 14 & 16 answered '*Yes*' or '*Satisfied*'. Interviewee 3 answered '*I like mediation. I am a big fan.*' Interviewee 12 offered a more detailed answer: '*Satisfied for the vast majority. Not satisfied with 20%. Very satisfied with 10%.*' Another (Interviewee 8) was not asked the question due to time constraints.
19. Strong's empirical research on cross-border commercial mediation found that the third highest ranked reason why parties used mediation was 'a desire for a more satisfactory process'. Strong, *supra* n. 4, at 2031. The same reason of mediation being 'a more satisfactory process' was identified in Stipanowich's 1997 Fortune 1000 Survey. *See* Stipanowich and Lamare, *supra* n. 4, at 37 which compares the findings of their 1997 study to those of the 2011 study. The findings of the 2011 study are less helpful on this particular point as the 2011 study used the umbrella term of 'ADR' rather than identify mediation specifically, which the 1997 report does. *See also* Nadja Alexander, *Global Trends in Mediation* 12, 16-17 (Kluwer 2006) for a useful summary of domestic studies which suggest high levels of user satisfaction with mediation. *See* further, on party satisfaction with mediation: Roselle Wissler, *Court-Connected Mediation in General Civil Cases: What We Know from Empirical Research,* 17 Ohio State Journal of Dispute Resolution 641, 690 (2002); Colleen Hanycz, *Through the Looking Glass: Mediator Conceptions of Philosophy, Process and Power,* 42 Alberta Law Review 819, 828 (2005). *See also* Robert Bush, *What Do We Need a Mediator for? Mediation's Value-Added for Negotiators,* 12 Ohio Journal on Dispute Resolution 1, 16 (1996) which refers to numerous studies which have found high levels of satisfaction with mediation. *See also* Hazel Genn, *What Is Civil Justice For? Reform, ADR, and Access to Justice?,* 24(1) Yale Journal of Law & the Humanities (2012) which, interestingly, notes that: 'As far as party satisfaction is concerned, evaluations of court-annexed mediation schemes show high levels of satisfaction among those who have *volunteered* to enter the process.'

[D] Sensibility to the Complexity of Disputes

Qualitative research enables the discovery of subtle, nuanced themes and one such theme emerged regarding why parties use mediation. It is an unexpected and intriguing reason. Bringing to mind Nin's quotation which opened this chapter, those who were particularly enthusiastic proponents and users of mediation displayed a particular way of thinking about disputes which might best be described as a notable sensibility to the complexity of disputes.[20] Interviewee 8 explained:

> *'in terms of theory and understanding, the legal profession is behind. What you have is lawyers who understand contractual claims, the litigation and arbitration processes. People don't understand the dynamics in dispute resolution. It's nothing to do with the law. It's about conflict management dynamics which influence how people behave. That's one of the barriers to employing mediation in a fruitful way and to settling disputes in the negotiation stage. There is a simplified way of thinking about disputes: right or wrong … Disputes are inherently complex. People look to simplify them.'*

In a similar vein, Interviewee 11 acknowledged the opportunity which mediation can bring to better understand the nature of the disputes:

> *'I think that a piece of litigation or mediation is not that important in the overall scale of things. It is more important to learn from disputes and improve how the company acts and compared to the normal way of dealing with disputes mediation gives more insights into the roots, causes of the dispute. It puts the organisation in a better place to learn from the dispute. Can learn more from it.'*

Further, Interviewee 5 acknowledged the role which behaviour plays in the creation and avoidance of disputes:

> *'My position is that ultimately big and small organisations boil down to people. If people do not know how to behave, how to maintain a relationship, this is an art. If the people are trained, then a lot of the disputes can be avoided. The training is not forthcoming. People do not know even at the initial stage: it is this is my position, take it or leave it.'*

These comments, from those who are enthusiastic users of mediation, suggest a departure from thinking about disputes as being simply about right and wrong, black and white.[21] They suggest a departure from our 'visceral tendency to cling more

---

20. The interviewees' enthusiasm for mediation is conveyed by the following comments: Interviewee 5 stated '*I … try to do it* [mediation] *all of the time*' adding later that '*We try to mediate and resolve the issue.*' Interviewee 8 explained how his company tries to '*find a negotiated solution*' and added that '*Mediation plays a key part in how we move forward.*' Interviewee 11 explained how he was the chair of his company's mediation team, the goal of which he described as being to '*use it* [mediation] *more often and of course to determine if the case is fit for mediation*'.
21. Macfarlane describes how one of the most appealing aspects of a 'rights-based approach' to disputes is for clients 'who want nothing more than to be told that they are wholly "right" and that the other side is wholly "wrong"'. Julie Macfarlane, *The New Lawyer: How Settlement Is Transforming the Practice of Law* 50 (UBC Press 2008).

tenaciously to ... our beliefs about what is real, right'[22] to a more nuanced, inquisitorial way of thinking about disputes and their resolution. While this observation is tentative, it suggests an area which would benefit from exploration in further qualitative studies. The neat and discrete reasons for using mediation which are commonly seen in empirical studies, such as saving time and cost, are undoubtedly easier to explore and quantify. However, taking a step back and exploring the type of attitude towards disputes which underpins the use of mediation could provide valuable insights into what *really* leads the parties to use mediation.[23]

A focus on how disputants' attitudes towards disputes might influence their choice of dispute resolution has been lacking in the empirical research to date.[24] Rather, the focus has tended to be on how their choice is influenced by the various characteristics of the dispute resolution processes (such as their length and cost), rather than on the characteristics of the disputants themselves. Further empirical research which expands the list of reasons why parties use mediation to allow for exploration of the issue of how disputants' attitudes towards disputes might influence their choice of dispute resolution process would afford an opportunity to gain further insights into this novel issue. For those such as the EU who are keen to promote the use of mediation, the significant challenge would then be how to cultivate any such attitudes to conflict which are conducive to the selection of mediation as a dispute resolution process.[25] Indeed, this more fundamental challenge was identified by Interviewee 18 when asked what his company needed in order to increase its use of EU cross-border commercial mediation:

> *'To be completely honest, we need a change in company culture and a change in approach to facilitated agreements and the question of the importance of being right.'*

And such a shift from the importance of being (found to be) right may not be easy to achieve for those who seek to increase the use of mediation. As Interviewee 11 explained:

> *'If parties are in dispute they are willing to pay a lot of money to say he/she is right.'*[26]

22. Tim Hicks, *Embodied Conflict* 95, and 76 (Routledge 2018).
23. In the different context of negotiation behaviour, Menkel-Meadow has identified the key influence of one's attitude of how to negotiate on negotiation behaviour: 'mind-set about how to negotiate generally was the best predictor of negotiation behaviour, regardless of the role of the parties as principals or representatives, or plaintiff or defendants'. Carrie Menkel-Meadow, *Lawyer Negotiations: Theories and Realities – What we Learn from Mediation*, 56(3) The Modern Law Review 361, 376 (1993).
24. *See*, for example, at text to (n. 4) the summary of the list of reasons why parties might use mediation included in empirical research.
25. On a related note, Hicks has noted: 'Perhaps the area of greatest opportunity, but also perhaps the greatest challenge ... is in helping the general public better understand how people tend to function in conflict so that they are better able to achieve the resolution of differences'. Hicks, *supra* n. 22, at 99-100.
26. Similarly, Prince has noted that 'Claimants generally desire a judicial authority to endorse their own opinion that they are right, and to rule them the "winner" and the other side the "loser"'.

This subtle theme of a sensibility to the complexity of disputes of those who were particularly enthusiastic proponents and users of mediation is an interesting and unexpected one. For those seeking to promote mediation, it may not be sufficient to focus only on what changes, if any, are needed to the mediation process. There may be a greater challenge of changing the way in which people view disputes, which in turn affects their choice of dispute resolution process. This, of course, is a far more significant challenge than changing elements of the mediation process.

The themes considered above regarding why parties use mediation for their EU cross-border commercial disputes confirm, challenge and expand upon the empirical research to date on why parties use mediation. The themes of cost and time savings, and user satisfaction, confirm the role which these reasons play in disputants' decisions to use mediation, as identified in earlier research on cross-border and domestic mediation. The theme of the preservation of relationships challenges the suggestion in earlier research on cross-border mediation that this reason may not be as important in the cross-border context compared to the domestic context. And the subtle theme of a sensibility to the complexity of disputes demonstrated by those who were particularly enthusiastic proponents of mediation expands upon the reasons why parties use mediation identified to date; it moves the focus from reasons regarding the characteristics of the dispute resolution process to characteristics of the disputants themselves.

§7.03 TRIGGERS FOR THE USE OF MEDIATION

In addition to asking the interviewees who had experience of EU cross-border commercial mediation why they used such mediation, such interviewees were also asked what, in particular, triggered the use of such mediation.

[A] Dispute Resolution Clauses

A trigger for the use of mediation commonly identified by these interviewees was the dispute resolution clause. A dispute resolution clause is a clause, commonly found in commercial contracts, which sets out the dispute resolution process or processes which contracting parties will use to address any disputes between them.

Interviewee 5 explained that the trigger for his company's use of EU cross-border commercial mediation was '*the dispute resolution clause in the contract*'. He added that his company's policy on dispute resolution clauses was '*we would like mediation but it depends on the context*'. Further, he described the detail of such mediation clauses:

> '*Whenever we develop a contract, we make it* [mediation] *a non-institutionalised process. It is clear: what steps, which people are involved, when they are involved, we record the mediation process.*'

Sue Prince, *Institutionalising Mediation? An Evaluation of the Exeter Court Small Claims Mediation Pilot,* 5 Web Journal of Current Legal Issues (2007).

Interviewee 12 explained that *'contractual stipulation'* was a trigger for his company's use of mediation. Further, he elaborated on his company's dispute resolution clause with its suppliers:

'As standard in our global standard T & Cs, it's a standard ICC multi-tier DR clause: (1) negotiation, (2) before arbitration, mediation according to ICC mediation ... With large suppliers in our industry we don't manage to get the multi-tier clause through. In 80% we get it in, in 20% we amend it and change it subject to what our supplier wants. It's a matter of what our negotiation power is.'

Interviewee 14 also identified the dispute resolution clause to be one of the triggers for his company's use of EU cross-border commercial mediation. He also explained his company's approach to the dispute resolution clauses and the measures taken to convince the other company to adopt their proposed clause:

'Most of our licensees accept our way to handle it. We start with negotiation limited by time, 30, 60 or 90 calendar days. If these negotiations fail they can start a mediation under WIPO rules or agreed rules in the same timeframe. If we have 60 days for negotiation, then it's 60 days for mediation, then we start with arbitration, expedited under WIPO rules under 9 months or we go to normal proceedings in the federal court in Germany, if not arbitration ... WIPO has published experiences all over the world in the last few years. You can compare some country experiences of arbitration, mediation and federal courts. It's mediation first because it's quite fast and very cheap compared to arbitration and the federal court. We send these publications to our licensees and contract parties to convince them.'

It should be noted here that the interviewees who described how mediation had been triggered by the dispute resolution clause in the contract also explained that it was in-house counsel who negotiated and drafted such dispute resolution clauses.[27]

The role which dispute resolution clauses play in triggering mediation was also suggested in the interviewees' comments on why they did *not* use mediation. A pattern emerged of interviewees identifying the lack of a mediation clause in the dispute resolution clause as a reason why mediation was not used. For example, Interviewee 6 explained that it was '*no* [to mediation] *because the contract does not provide for it*', adding that '*The thing to do is to provide for mediation in material contracts for it to be considered.*' Interviewee 2 identified '*the dispute resolution clauses*' as the reason why mediation was not used. Further Interviewee 16 explained:

'it's difficult to factor in mediation because in insurance contracts they don't have mediation clauses, they have arbitration clauses. That's why the vast majority go to

27. Interviewee 5 explained: '*We concentrate on the dispute resolution clauses and do not cut and paste them.*' When asked whether he made the final decision about the content of the dispute resolution his answer was '*Yes*'. Regarding Interviewee 12, when asked who makes the final decision about the content of the dispute resolution clause, Interviewee 12 explained: '*99% of the time it's in-house lawyers. We follow the philosophy of legal in-sourcing. We have a large group of in-house lawyers, lawyers with DR experience. We have built it in-house.*' Further, as captured in Interviewee 14's quotation preceding the text to (n. 27), Interviewee 14 described his company's approach to negotiating the dispute resolution clause which demonstrates its involvement in this process.

arbitration if we can't negotiate because that is the formalised process in insurance contracts'.

In addition, Interviewee 15 explained:

'Rarely will a mediation clause be put in. Sometimes it's very rarely put in instead of a negotiation clause. That's 1 in a million.'

The lack of a mediation clause as a reason why mediation is not used further emphasises the role played by such clauses as a trigger for the use of mediation.

The important role that dispute resolution clauses play in triggering the use of mediation in cross-border commercial disputes has been identified in earlier empirical research[28] and in the general literature.[29] In addition, it has also been recognised that such clauses play a far more significant role for commercial disputes compared to other types of disputes such as consumer or employment disputes.[30] The in-depth nature of this study builds on earlier work by revealing some interesting detail on the use of such clauses in the cross-border commercial context. In particular, two noticeable themes emerged.

[1] Heightened Importance of Dispute Resolution Clauses in Cross-Border Context

First, comments by the interviewees suggest the heightened importance of such clauses in the cross-border context compared to the domestic context. Interviewee 5, whose company liked to include mediation in its dispute resolution clauses, explained how his company adopts a more formal approach to dispute resolution clauses for EU cross-border contracts compared to national contracts:

'*In national* [contracts] *it may be simplistic. In cross-border* [contracts] *I will be more formal. And less formal if national. Our preference for dispute resolution would still apply.*'

Interviewee 5 did not elaborate on the reasons why he adopted a more formal approach to dispute resolution clauses for cross-border contracts and a less formal

28. John Lande and Peter W. Benner, *Why and How Business Use Planned Early Dispute Resolution*, 13 University of St. Thomas Law Journal 248, 274-275 (2017); Strong, *supra* n. 4, at 2026 & 2045. Both Lande and Benner, and Strong note the common provision for arbitration in such international contracts (Lande and Benner at 29, and Strong at 2028) which therefore, as Strong notes, raises doubts about the impact which court encouragement of mediation would have in the international context given that many international disputes may never reach the court but rather would be dealt with by arbitration. It should, however, be acknowledged that Strong and Lande's comments are regarding international cross-border disputes whereas this study is concerned with the narrower EU cross-border context.
29. For example, Alexander describes how useful mediation clauses are given that when parties draft them they are on good terms whereas discussions after a dispute has arisen regarding which dispute resolution process to use can be difficult and some may regard agreeing to mediation as suggesting that there are weaknesses in their case. Nadja Alexander, *International and Comparative Mediation* 171 (Wolters Kluwer 2009). Further, also at 171, Alexander notes that the validity of most mediation clauses is never challenged.
30. Stipanowich and Lamare, *supra* n. 4, at 35.

approach to national contracts. However, Interviewee 6's explanation of why his company had not used mediation for his company's EU cross-border commercial disputes may suggest why such a 'formal' approach in the cross-border context is needed. When asked why his company had not used mediation for its EU cross-border commercial disputes, Interviewee 6 answered '*Cultural issues on the other sides*'. He was then asked to elaborate on what he meant by '*cultural issues*' and answered:

> '*Suspicious, our German friends are rigid, mechanical: no because the contract does not provide for it. We have a procedure and will follow it. It's important to get in there up front and have a discussion as part of the contract rather than after the event.*'

Given, as described by Interviewees 5 and 6, the more formal approach to dispute resolution clauses and to adhering to their provisions for cross-border contracts, there may be less scope for ad hoc dispute resolution proposals (i.e., suggesting a dispute resolution process which is not referred to in the dispute resolution clause) in the cross-border context compared to the domestic context. Therefore dispute resolution clauses may play a heightened role in the triggering of mediation in the cross-border context compared to the domestic context. Those seeking to promote mediation in the commercial cross-border context may therefore wish to explore further the use of mediation clauses in cross-border contracts and, in particular, the reasons why parties may not use such clauses. The second category of insights offered by the interviewees on their dispute resolution clauses, as considered below, is instructive on this latter point.

[2] Reluctance to Include a Mediation Clause in the Dispute Resolution Clause and Reasons for such Reluctance

Secondly, the interviewees also offered insights into the resistance to the inclusion of a mediation provision in the dispute resolution clause, and the reasons for such resistance.[31] Interviewee 8 explained the resistance he has encountered when trying to include a mediation clause in the dispute resolution clauses of commercial contracts:

> '*Mediation is more mainstream now. If you have a dispute, mediation is pretty much mainstream but you don't see an increase in the numbers. We have to think about two different periods of time.*
>
> 1. *When you have a dispute: most people know about mediation. That's an easy discussion; and*
> 2. *The contract negotiation stage: there we are still behind. I say let's have a mandatory step in the contract. It's 2 step: mediation followed by arbitration or litigation. It's not that easy to get in. There's resistance. On a superficial level mediation is accepted but if I turn it into contractually binding there is more resistance.*'

31. Mediation clauses are uncommon in commercial contracts: Ewald Filler, *Commercial Mediation in Europe* 416 (Wolters Kluwer 2012); Denis Brock and Rebecca Pither, *How International Law Firms Might Approach the Subject of ADR with Their Clients* in Arnold Ingen-Housz (ed.) *ADR in Business* 282 (Wolters Kluwer 2011).

Some interviewees offered explanations for why their companies do not include a mediation provision in their dispute resolution clauses. In particular, two prominent reasons emerged in such explanations: first, the reason that mediation should be consensual and a mediation clause would be counter to this principle; and, secondly, the reason that mediation may not be appropriate for all disputes which may arise from the contract.[32]

Regarding the first reason, some interviewees noted that a mediation clause prescribing mediation would be counter to the consensual nature of mediation as it would, in effect, force parties to mediate. While entry into the mediation clause would be consensual, mediation for the specific dispute which were to arise would not be consensual as it would have been prescribed under the general dispute resolution clause.

When explaining his company's policy on dispute resolution clauses, Interviewee 3 explained:

> *'We would never require mediation. By definition it's consensual.'*

Similarly, Interviewee 21 explained:

> *'Our dispute resolution clause has escalation clauses, certain people have to have discussions at certain points. I am not for mandatory mediation. Both parties have to be willing. I am not sure it works if it is required.'*

Regarding the second reason, that mediation might not be appropriate for all disputes arising from the contract, Interviewee 21 explained:

> *'There was a situation when we had a strong case and the without prejudice offer was nowhere near close to where we were. There was no point in mediating. I don't think it is always appropriate. That is why ultimately I wouldn't want a compulsory mediation step in the contract. I don't mind a provision saying parties will consider mediation. I wouldn't want it to be a prescribed process to go through when there's a dispute. If you have a better argument, they could hold the mediation process over your head as you'd need to go through that process and cost before going to legal proceedings.'*

The concern that mediation might not be appropriate for all disputes was also identified by Interviewee 11, though in the specific sense that for some disputes mediation might be misused. When explaining his company's policy on its dispute resolution clauses, Interviewee 11 explained:

> *'We do not prescribe mediation – don't ask me whether I agree with that or not. As we are using models which should be applicable for a lot of situations, we decided not to use it as we have situations where mediation can be abused. We consider us and our counterparties grown up enough to consider mediation anyway.'*

32. It is interesting to note that the same reasons were also identified by the interviewees as reasons why interviewees did not support the EU's proposals for a type of mandatory mediation. These points about mediation being consensual and that it may not be appropriate for all disputes were also raised by interviewees as reasons why they were not in favour of mandatory mediation. Such comments were made by Interviewees 2, 3, 10, 12, 16, 19 and 21.

The interviewees' identification of the prevalence of negotiation clauses in their company's dispute resolution clauses - as considered earlier in Chapter 6 - suggests that they do not have similar concerns about being forced into the similarly consensual process of negotiation nor that the similar process of negotiation may not be appropriate for all types of dispute. Interestingly, it appears that there is a reluctance to make assisted negotiation (i.e., mediation) a formal requirement in the dispute resolution clause, which is not similarly seen for unassisted negotiation. Given the relationship between negotiation and mediation identified in Chapter 6, further research with a focus on exploring the relationship between the willingness to include negotiation clauses and the reluctance to include mediation clauses may yield important insights for those seeking to promote mediation, given the key role that mediation clauses may play as a trigger for cross-border commercial mediation. Here it is also interesting to note that there is a tendency in the literature to contrast the use of arbitration clauses with the limited use of mediation clauses.[33] For those seeking to promote the use of mediation, it may prove useful to move beyond such a focus to also explore why mediation clauses are not more frequently used in addition to negotiation clauses.

[B] Ad Hoc Suggestion by In-House Counsel

The further trigger of suggestion by in-house counsel was also identified by interviewees as a reason for their use of EU cross-border commercial mediation. Interviewee 11 explained:

> *'Mediation can come from the client but we don't see that very often. Business people do not know what it is or they have strong thoughts on it. In most experiences, if mediation is entered into it was suggested by our litigation department.'*[34]

Interviewee 12 noted:

> *'Contractual stipulation or our proposal ad hoc. In 99 out of 100 cases our company proposes to enter into ad hoc mediation.'*[35]

33. For example, Alexander describes how 'In contemporary international dispute resolution practice, arbitration clauses are increasingly making way for mediation ... clauses.' Nadja Alexander (ed.), *Global Trends in Dispute Resolution* 171 (Wolters Kluwer 2009). Further, Stipanowich and Lamare's 1997 study on the triggers for the use of ADR compared the extent to which a contractual provision triggered mediation compared to arbitration (10% of respondents identified a contractual provision as being the most frequently used trigger of mediation while 67% of respondents identified a contractual provision to be the most frequent trigger of arbitration). Stipanowich and Lamare, *supra* n. 4, at 33-34. Further, and by way of general background, Hale acknowledges that 'In much of the international law literature it is standard for scholars to claim that TCA [transnational commercial arbitration] is the dominant form of dispute resolution for international contracts.' Thomas Hale, *Between Interests and Law, The Politics of Transnational Commercial Disputes* 40 (Cambridge 2015).
34. As the interviewee is an in-house counsel, client means the in-house counsel's internal client i.e., the business team.
35. Interviewee 12.

Further, Interviewee 14 noted that recommendation by in-house counsel was a frequent trigger for the use of mediation for their EU cross-border commercial disputes.

These comments, which attribute the use of mediation to a suggestion by in-house counsel, suggest the important role which in-house counsel can play in furthering the use of mediation. The emphasis on the trigger being the parties themselves and, predominantly, the parties' in-house lawyers, differs to the finding in empirical research on international commercial mediation that one of the least likely methods of prompting the use of such mediation was suggestions from a party.[36] However, more broadly, this emphasis is consistent with findings of other empirical research, as addressed in Chapter 4, on the key role played by in-house counsel in influencing the use of dispute resolution processes in general.[37]

Indeed, both the triggers of dispute resolution clauses (included at the request of the in-house counsel, as identified earlier) and the suggestion by in-house counsel to mediate share the common feature that they are initiatives undertaken by the companies themselves. This suggests that the parties, and in particular their in-house counsel, are in a position to play a key role in influencing the use of particular dispute resolution processes. This is consistent with data from the GPC Series which found that in-house counsel is 'the group with the potential to be most influential in bringing about change in commercial dispute resolution practice'.[38] The recognition of their key role prompts those who are seeking to promote the use of mediation to consider how this group might be supported in their efforts to encourage the use of mediation. Drawing on Lederach's elicitive approach as explained in Chapter 4, Lederach advocates the ability 'to recognize and see what exists in a place that could have potential or is already building … constructive change'.[39] He elaborates:

> The greatest missed potentials of change are not those far-off things we missed because we could not envision them but those things we missed because our movement bypassed and made them invisible … When we focus on the really big things, we often miss the greatest potential of resource, insight, and change that is present right in the location where our feet are planted.[40]

Accordingly, it is important to consider how the efforts of in-house counsel to use mediation might be further supported and to draw on insights from the interviewees to do so.

36. Strong, *supra* n. 4, at 2027. The fact that in-house counsel represented only a small proportion (7%) of the participants in Strong's study may explain this difference in the identification of triggers.
37. *See* Chapter 4, §4.04[B] 'The Choice of Interviewee'.
38. IMI, Herbert Smith Freehills and PWC, *Global Pound Conference Series: Global Data Trends and Regional Differences,* at 17 <https://www.imimediation.org/research/gpc/series-data-and-reports/ - 909-reports> (accessed 20 May 2020).
39. John Paul Lederach, *The Moral Imagination* 105-106 (Oxford University Press, 2005).
40. *Ibid.*, 105.

[1] *What Else Might In-House Counsel Need?*

One of the interviewees explained how he uses certain data to encourage those who are contracting with his company to include a mediation clause in their contracts. Interviewee 14, whose company operates in the field of technology, explained:

> *'WIPO has published experiences all over the world in the last few years. You can compare some country experiences of arbitration, mediation and federal courts. It's mediation first because it's quite fast and very cheap compared to arbitration and the federal court. We send these publications to our licensees and contract parties to convince them.'*

The WIPO data which Interviewee 14 referred to appears to be WIPO's publication from March 2013 'Results of the WIPO Arbitration and Mediation Center International Survey on Dispute Resolution in Technology Transactions'.[41] The report, based on information gathered from respondents from around the world, provides data on the use of ADR in technology disputes. It includes a chart which depicts the comparative time and cost of various methods of dispute resolution processes including mediation, arbitration, litigation, and expert determination.[42] In-house counsel's use of the data produced by WIPO to convince their counterparties to provide for mediation in their contracts invites the question of whether further information may be of use to in-house counsel in their efforts to promote the use of mediation. This is an issue which is considered further in Chapter 9.

While there was recognition of the helpful information provided by WIPO for technology disputes, none of the interviewees who had experience of using EU cross-border commercial mediation attributed such use to the EU Mediation Directive nor its national implementing measures. This apparent lack of a tangible impact of the directive is consistent with the conclusion in the EU's review of the directive, together with that of numerous ADR academics, that the directive has had a limited impact.[43] Indeed, Interviewee 16 expressed his frustration with the directive and the lack of its tangible impact, explaining:

> *'We keep quoting the EU directive. That doesn't actually do anything. What you want is something that says we want to do this, this is where you go. There needs to be something like the IMI but with a more formalised role that they can go to. Like SIMC in Singapore. That does international mediation stuff. There is somewhere in Asia where you have a point of contact where everything can go through. You don't have that in Europe. First as a disputant, where do you go? Paris or London. And then the question is who deals with your dispute.'*

He later summarised this as '*a centralised platform with good mediators which is non-country specific. Seen as EU-wide which allows easy access*'.

---

41. WIPO, *Results of the WIPO Arbitration and Mediation Center International Survey on Dispute Resolution in Technology Transactions* <http://www.wipo.int/export/sites/www/amc/en/docs/surveyresults.pdf> (accessed 20 May 2020).
42. *Ibid.*, 7, 30.
43. *See* Chapter 2 regarding the limited impact of the EU Mediation Directive and the continued limited use of mediation for EU cross-border disputes.

Similar calls were made by other interviewees, including Interviewee 13 who stated:

> *'It would be good to be able to understand how it* [mediation] *could be set up. From the logistics side I would like to know where could be a good centre, a list of good mediators, the practical side. It does have its up sides but I wouldn't know what to do. I would have to go through external lawyers.'*

In a similar vein, Interviewee 17 noted:

> *'There is often a lot of toing and froing in domestic disputes on who the mediator will be – some kind of external sources for getting mediators for cross-border disputes might be helpful.'*

A similar concern regarding the difficulty in finding mediators suitable for EU cross-border disputes was expressed by Interviewee 15 when he explained his company's reluctance to include a mediation clause in their dispute resolution clauses:

> *'The reason for the lack of mediation in our templates is apparently a perceived lack of mediators who are expert enough to deal with cross-border disputes.'*

Interviewee 15 then explained that by 'expert' he meant:

> *'expertise in the sector. I have used mediators who have no expertise in pharmaceuticals but these were well-established mediators who are good enough and can learn on the job. And these were domestic mediations. For cross-border mediations we would want someone who is cognisant of pharmaceuticals and who has industry experience. That's a perception – whether it's informed or not ... If there are these people, they are difficult to find'.*

Interviewee 15's comments on the different criteria they look for in cross-border mediators compared to domestic mediators, with cross-border mediators – though not domestic mediators – expected to have specific business sector expertise, suggest that there is a higher bar regarding the expertise expected of cross-border mediators, and a difficulty in identifying such suitably qualified mediators for their cross-border disputes.[44] Further, as is considered in Chapter 8, the interviewees' comments convey a desire for more detailed information on mediators, including which mediators are commonly used and by whom, and the outcomes of the mediations.

The interviewees' comments above capture the desire for assistance, possibly by way of a centralised hub, with setting up EU cross-border mediations and in identifying suitable mediators for such mediations. They are a further indication that the EU's efforts to date to promote the use of cross-border mediation have had a limited tangible impact because they are not fully meeting the needs of users. It appears that changes

---

44. In the context of international arbitration, the very high bar expected of international arbitrators in particular has been acknowledged. *See*, for example, Catherine A. Rogers, *The Vocation of International Arbitrators*, 20 The American University International Law Review 957, 958 (2005). Rogers notes at 957 that 'International Arbitrators are exceptionally talented individuals.' At 957-958 Rogers also identifies the skills and talents which these 'elite individuals' commonly possess.

are needed to the EU's current approach, and recommendations for such changes are explored in Chapter 9.

§7.04 CONCLUSION

The insights shared by the interviewees of this study, all of whom are active in the setting of EU cross-border commercial disputes, regarding why they use mediation for their cross-border disputes confirm, challenge and expand upon the empirical research to date on why parties use mediation. In particular, the way in which the interviewees' insights challenge earlier empirical research, by suggesting that the desire to preserve relationships is a factor which influences parties' decisions to use EU cross-border mediation, builds on the recommendation identified in Chapter 6 that the EU should move beyond its key focus on the relationship between mediation and litigation to also consider the relationship between mediation and negotiation. The EU's approach to date of focusing on the relationship between mediation and litigation, with the consequent association of mediation with the adversarial and adjudicative process of litigation, may obscure the connection between mediation and the consensual and collaborative process of negotiation. A greater focus on the association of mediation with the seemingly favoured and familiar dispute resolution process of negotiation may encourage more parties for whom the preservation of their relationships is an important factor to consider using mediation.

Further, the qualitative nature of this study suggests that the topic of disputants' attitudes to disputes, which has not received any attention in the relevant empirical research to date, merits further exploration. While the neat and discrete reasons for using mediation which are commonly seen in empirical studies, such as saving time and cost, are easier to explore and measure, exploring the type of attitudes towards disputes which underpin the use of mediation may enable insights to be gained into what fundamentally leads parties to use mediation.

The interviewees' accounts of their use of EU cross-border commercial mediation highlight their companies' own efforts to bring about the use of mediation, be it by their inclusion of a dispute resolution clause or their ad hoc suggestion to the other party. An awareness of the parties' own initiatives to use mediation is a prompt for those seeking to promote the use of mediation to consider how the parties might be supported in their current efforts to bring about further use of mediation. In particular, the interviewees' comments suggest that more expertise is expected from cross-border mediators compared to domestic mediators and that assistance in identifying suitably qualified cross-border mediators would be welcomed.

In addition, given the interviewees' indication of the important role which mediation clauses may play in triggering the use of cross-border mediation, the interviewees' insights into why such clauses are not included in their contracts are valuable to those seeking to promote cross-border mediation. If they would like to increase the prevalence of mediation clauses in order to increase the use of mediation, they will need to respond to the reasons why such clauses are not used (e.g., that mediation should be consensual rather than prescribed, and that mediation may not be appropriate for all disputes). In this regard, given the interviewees' descriptions of the prevalence of negotiation clauses in their dispute resolution clauses, as considered in Chapter 6, it appears that similar reservations may not equally apply to unassisted negotiations. This suggests another reason why those seeking to promote the use of mediation may want to focus further on the relationship between mediation and negotiation and, in particular, explore why parties may be willing to prescribe negotiation though be reluctant to prescribe mediation in their dispute resolution clauses.

Finally, for those considering how to promote the use of EU cross-border commercial mediation, insights into parties' use of such mediation present only part of the picture. Of particular value are insights into why parties do *not* use such mediation and it is to that topic which the next chapter turns. It is only with an understanding of why parties both do and do not use such mediation that suggestions can be identified for how such mediation might be promoted.

CHAPTER 8

Why Parties Do Not Use Mediation for their EU Cross-Border Commercial Disputes

> Most often the greatest find is sitting right in front of your face, invisible in its obviousness ... .[1]

§8.01 EXECUTIVE SUMMARY

Following the insights provided in the previous chapter into why commercial parties use mediation for their EU cross-border commercial disputes, this chapter explores why commercial parties do not use mediation for such disputes.

At the outset, it is notable that the empirical research to date on parties' use of mediation tends to focus more on the reasons why parties use mediation rather than on why they do not use mediation.[2] For those seeking to promote mediation, such as the

1. John Paul Lederach, *The Moral Imagination* 104 (Oxford University Press, 2005).
2. *See* Thomas Stipanowich and J. Ryan Lamare, *Living with ADR: Evolving Perceptions and Use of Mediation, Arbitration, and Conflict Management in Fortune 1000 Corporations,* 19 Harvard Negotiation Law Review 1 (2014) which includes a section on the reasons why parties use mediation (at 37) but not on why they do not use mediation. Further in the GPC Series Core Questions, participants were asked what influenced their choice of dispute resolution process (Question 1.2) but not, specifically, what influenced their choice not to use a dispute resolution process <https://www.imimediation.org/research/gpc/series-data-and-reports/> (accessed 20 May 2020). Further in the EU Parliament's Rebooting study the focus is on proposed legislative and non-legislative proposals to increase the use of mediation and the issue of why parties do not use mediation is not addressed in the empirical research (for a helpful summary of the empirical research *see* European Parliament, *'Rebooting' the Mediation Directive: Assessing the Limited Impact of its Implementation and Proposing Measures to Increase the Number of Mediations in the EU* (2014) PE 493.042, at 6-10 (Rebooting Report). In addition, John Lande, *Getting the Faith: Why Business Lawyers and Executives Believe in Mediation,* 5 Harvard Negotiation Law Review 137 (2000) focuses on the reasons why parties believe in mediation. Further, SIDRA's research on international dispute resolution explores the factors which influence users' choice of mediation as a dispute resolution mechanism though does not specifically address the issue of why parties do not select mediation as a dispute resolution process. SIDRA, *International Dispute Resolution*

EU, an awareness of the reasons why parties do not use mediation is arguably more valuable than knowing why mediation is used. To encourage the use of something one needs to understand why it is not being used. In order to gain such an understanding, the interview guide for this research included a specific question on why parties did not use mediation for their EU cross-border commercial disputes. It also included a further question on what the greatest obstacles were to an increased use of mediation, which allowed for more information to be obtained on this issue. In addition, given the semi-structured nature of the interviews, interviewees offered their thoughts on why mediation was not used both in response to these questions and, at times, when elaborating on other questions.[3]

In the empirical research on both cross-border and domestic commercial mediation to date, the reasons listed for parties not using mediation focus largely on issues identified by reference to the adjudicative methods of litigation or arbitration (e.g., concerns about the enforcement of the mediated agreement, concerns about revealing litigation strategy and predictions of the likelihood of success at trial).[4] In such research, there is little focus, if any, in the list of potential reasons why parties do not use mediation to reasons identified by reference to the dispute resolution process of negotiation.[5] However, with an understanding of mediation as a form of negotiation, as

---

Survey: 2020 Final Report, 46 <https://sidra.smu.edu.sg/sidra-international-dispute-resolution-survey-final-report-2020> (accessed 10 August 2020).

3. Both interviewees who did not have experience of mediation and those who had experience of mediation offered their views on why mediation was not used. It is appropriate to include the comments made by those who had experience of mediation as they could also offer insights into decisions for mediation not to be used, including such decisions by their counterparties.
4. In Strong's research on international commercial mediation the reasons listed for parties avoidance of mediation include: 'concerns about finding an effective mediator, concerns about how to conduct a mediation effectively, concerns about revealing litigation strategy or evidence, concerns about the cost of the process, concerns about the international enforceability of an agreement to mediate, concerns about the international enforceability of a settlement award arising out of mediation, concerns about the time of the process, counsel's concerns about earning income on the dispute, counsel's lack of experience with mediation, cultural preferences for litigation or arbitration, lack of a desire to preserve ongoing relationship, and lack of experience with mediation'. S.I. Strong, *Realizing Rationality: An Empirical Assessment of International Commercial Mediation*, 73 Washington & Lee Law Review 1973, 2033 (2016). In this context counsel is understood to be external counsel given the concern about earning money from the dispute. In the domestic context, other reasons for not using mediation include that the other party is not willing to mediate, the parties have settled before mediation, the other party's claim has no merit, the party has a strong legal position and thinks he/she will succeed at trial, the desire to establish a precedent, the other party has unrealistic expectations, *see* Grant Morris and Freya McKechnie, Resolution Institute/Victoria University of Wellington, *Users of Commercial Mediation in New Zealand – Insurance Industry Report* (April 2017) 10 <https://papers.ssrn.com/sol3/papers.cfm?abstract_id=3015041> (accessed 20 May 2020). Similar reasons for not using mediation appear in Agapiou and Clark's research on Scottish construction clients' use of mediation. These include: 'costs of mediation itself, a belief in the strength of their legal case, the idea that negotiation could settle the matter and a jaundiced view that the other side would not mediate in good faith'. Andrew Agapiou and Bryan Clark, *A Follow-Up Empirical Analysis of Scottish Construction Clients' Interaction with Mediation*, 32 Civil Justice Quarterly Issue 362, 371 (2013).
5. A notable exception is Agapiou and Clark's research on mediation in Scottish construction disputes. The reasons for not using mediation listed in this research include 'the idea that negotiation could settle the matter'. Agapiou and Clark, *supra* n. 4, at 371.

was discussed in Chapter 6, further reasons can be revealed as to why mediation is not used, as will be addressed in this chapter. In particular, the interviewees' comments reveal a new barrier to the use of mediation which stems from their association of mediation with negotiation. It is a barrier regarding how the choice to use mediation might, in a very specific way, reflect negatively on the user. And this is not a reference to the concern that a party might look weak by suggesting mediation which has been acknowledged in earlier empirical research and was also identified again in this research.[6] It is a barrier that arguably is greater than that of being regarded as weak: it is a concern of being regarded as having failed, as will be explored in this chapter.

§8.02 REASONS WHY PARTIES DO NOT USE MEDIATION

[A] Parties' Own and Early Efforts to Resolve Disputes

Before considering the key themes which emerged in the interviewees' comments on why mediation is not used for EU cross-border commercial disputes, it is important to note a key absence from the interviewees' comments. When providing their reasons for not using mediation for their EU cross-border commercial disputes, none of the interviewees cited a preference for the dispute resolution processes against which mediation is so frequently compared, and at times criticised, namely arbitration and litigation.[7]

---

6. The concern that a party who proposes mediation could be regarded by their counterparty as being weak was identified by respondents as an additional reason beyond those which were listed in the survey in Strong's research on international commercial mediation, Strong, *supra* n. 4, at 2035. This obstacle to the use of mediation was also identified in the empirical research for this book with Interviewee 19 explaining: '*One of the obstacles is that people are reluctant to be the first person to suggest it – makes me look weak- it's a weird Mexican stand-off. For the judge to suggest it saves face for the parties.*' However another interviewee, Interviewee 17, held a different view, noting that at least as regards the UK context: '*I think that a willingness to mediate is not relied on by the other side as a sign of weakness.*' Such a concern has also been identified in the academic literature. *See* Eileen Carroll and Karl Mackie, *International Mediation: Breaking Business Deadlock* 45 (3rd ed. Bloomsbury 2016). Further, Mackie and others note that the fear that suggesting ADR will be interpreted as a lack of confidence in their case is one of the key difficulties which a party faces when trying to suggest ADR. *See* Karl Mackie and others, *The ADR Practice Guide, Commercial Dispute Resolution* 188 (3rd ed. Tottel Publishing 2007).
7. Interestingly, a similar finding was found in recent research by Grant Morris and Amanda Lamb regarding the use of commercial mediation in New Zealand, though it should be emphasised that Morris and Lamb's research was on commercial lawyers rather than commercial users of dispute resolution processes. Morris notes that in response to the question of why clients do not use mediation, only a few commercial lawyers mentioned other forms of dispute resolution. The dispute resolution processes mentioned were negotiation, meeting with chief executives or the broader description of 'other forms of dispute resolution (for example adjudication)'. *See* Grant Morris and Amanda Lamb, Resolution Institute/Victoria University, *Lawyers as Gatekeepers to Commercial Mediation in New Zealand Report* (June 2016) at 13 <https://papers.ssrn.com/sol3/papers.cfm?abstract_id=2797995> accessed 20 May 2020.
   It should also be noted that the interviewees' lack of reference to a preference for litigation or arbitration as a reason why they do not use EU cross-border commercial mediation is a notable difference to earlier research which identifies a preference for litigation or arbitration as the most important reason why parties do not use mediation for their international commercial disputes, according to respondents who were inexperienced in international commercial mediation.

Rather than identify a preference for adjudicative processes as a reason why they did not use mediation, a key theme in the interviewees' answers as to why they did not use mediation was their own and early efforts to resolve disputes, including by way of negotiation.[8] This is consistent with the GPC Series' research which identified a significant interest in early dispute resolution.[9] This is also consistent with the theme, as identified in Chapter 6, of parties interpreting the term 'dispute' widely to include those matters which have not yet reached the stage of court or arbitral proceedings.

For example, Interviewee 18 explained that his company did not use mediation because negotiations usually work:

> *'Many disputes are already resolved through negotiations without third party assistance. It's still really common in our industry. It's really a small industry – there are not a lot of customers. There are not that many and you want to work together later on. You usually don't go beyond structured negotiation where ultimately the CEOs decide.'*

Similarly, in response to the question of why his company did not use mediation for its EU cross-border commercial disputes, Interviewee 10 explained his company's focus on its efforts to resolve disputes early:

> *'Our outlook is that it is better to avoid any form of dispute. Almost anything can be resolved by talking to the other side. It doesn't have to be formalised. This is outside the US – it is different there, they will enter into arbitration and mediation frequently. For us when it's going beyond escalation it is a sign that the relationship has broken down and that is something we try to avoid.'*

Further, when asked for the reasons why his company did not use mediation for its EU cross-border commercial disputes, Interviewee 6 – whose company's preferred method of dispute resolution was the avoidance of disputes[10] – acknowledged the key role played by bilateral negotiations:

Strong's research found that the most important reason why parties do not use mediation for international commercial disputes, as identified by respondents who were inexperienced in international commercial mediation, is a cultural preference for litigation or arbitration (*see* Strong, *supra* n. 4, 2034 and Appendix D). However, only a small proportion of respondents in Strong's research could be categorised as users of international commercial dispute resolution processes (i.e., in-house counsel who accounted for 7% of the respondents) and the majority of the respondents were others giving their views on the users' reasons for not using mediation.

8. As regards the avoidance or early management of disputes, Stipanowich and Lamare's research on the use of mediation, arbitration and conflict management in Fortune 1000 corporations found a 'growing emphasis on addressing conflict at its roots'. Stipanowich and Lamare, *supra* n. 2, at 32.
9. In answer to the question 'To improve the future of commercial dispute resolution, which of the following processes and tools should be prioritised?' the most popular choice (at 51%) was 'preventative pre-dispute or pre-escalation processes'. Another popular, and associated, choice was 'non-adjudicative resolution methods' (at 43%). IMI, Herbert Smith Freehills and PWC, *Global Pound Conference Series, Global Data Trends and Regional Differences*, at 13 <https://www.imimediation.org/research/gpc/series-data-and-reports/> (accessed 20 May 2020).
10. Earlier in the interview, in response to the question on what his company's preferred method of dispute resolution for EC cross-border commercial disputes was, Interviewee 6 explained: '*I would say we work very closely with very large food and beverage businesses. We make a point of trying to avoid disputes. We have very few disputes.*'

'Clearly we would try to find a solution by bilateral discussions but if that doesn't work we would use mediation.'

In the same vein, Interviewee 9 explained how his company's teams felt capable of finding a resolution through bilateral negotiations, without the assistance of a third party:

'The supply and sales teams will feel confident enough that they can get the best deal rather than get a mediator in … Resolving the dispute is like starting up a new commercial deal with the threat of litigation so people don't lose focus … If parties continue to think they can resolve things themselves, that's more likely to continue.'[11]

The prominent theme of parties identifying their own, and early, negotiation efforts as a reason why mediation is not used is a further indication of the central role played by negotiation as a dispute resolution method, as considered in Chapter 6.

In its efforts to promote mediation, the EU has focused on understanding mediation to be an alternative to litigation and has therefore focused on the relationship between mediation and litigation, looking to litigation for ideas on how to promote mediation's use (such as mandatory mediation, an enforcement mechanism for mediated settlement agreements, a quota of the number of mediated cases compared to litigated cases and raising awareness of the time and cost which mediation can save compared to litigation).[12] A recognition of the central, and valued, role played by negotiation as a dispute resolution method reorients us away from a focus on the relationship between mediation and litigation towards the relationship between mediation and negotiation. This is not a relationship which the EU has considered in its work to date on the encouragement of the use of mediation. With a focus on this relationship between mediation and negotiation, important reasons why disputants do not use mediation can be revealed, as will now be addressed.

[B] Failure

An awareness of the key role played by negotiation in dispute resolution and the consequent shift which this encourages to focus on the relationship between mediation and negotiation enables a new and intriguing reason why parties do not use mediation to be found.[13] This reason is a concern of being regarded – to draw on the words of the interviewees – as having failed if one were to need to use mediation to resolve the dispute. Put another way, viewed through the disputants' perspective, proceeding to mediation draws attention to the fact that they were unable to resolve the dispute themselves in their own and unassisted negotiations.

11. Interviewee 9.
12. *See* text to (n. 9) in Chapter 6.
13. As noted in Chapter 4, qualitative research is particularly suited to the discovery of new insights. As Patton has recognised regarding qualitative research: 'It's not how many said something that matters. It's the import, wisdom, relevance, insightfulness, and applicability of what was said, by many or by a few.' Michael Quinn Patton, *Qualitative Research & Evaluation Methods* 632 (4th ed. Sage 2015).

The theme of failure appeared in the interviewees' comments regarding both the initial step of sending the dispute to mediation and then the later stage of settling the dispute at mediation. First, regarding entering into the mediation process, interviewees noted that suggesting or sending a dispute to mediation could reflect negatively on the business people who have been trying to resolve the dispute through commercial negotiations. Interviewee 4 explained:

> '*The business see going to mediation as an admission of failure. They haven't been able to deal with it commercially. With the court and with legalese, that's a specialised forum. Senior managers have tried to resolve it.*'

Further, when explaining why parties do not use mediation, Interviewee 11 recognised the sensitivity needed when proposing mediation to the business people who have been negotiating the matter to ensure that they do not interpret the proposal as a suggestion that they have failed:

> '*if have professional people and negotiations have failed, then let's continue with a 3rd party. If you don't wrap it carefully, it's perceived that I didn't do a great job*'.

By way of important context, Interviewee 11 had explained earlier in the interview that in most cases, if mediation is entered into, it is at the suggestion of the litigation team to the business people.[14] Accordingly, the 'professional people' who, according to Interviewee 11, may perceive a suggestion to mediate to imply that they had failed to do a good job in their negotiations are understood to be the business people.

The interviewees' comments above capture a concern that the referral of a dispute to mediation, under which a third party will assist disputants with their negotiations, draws attention to the disputants' inability to resolve the dispute themselves through their own negotiations.

Secondly, the theme of failure appeared again in a further comment regarding the later stages of settlement in a mediation. When explaining why mediation usage is not greater, Interviewee 18 explained:

> '*A lot of management saying if I go to mediation and then settle I might get shot at for agreeing a bad deal. If I let it get ruled by court I can say that they got it all wrong. I'm kind of exculpated.*'

Put another way, the management's fear of 'getting shot at for agreeing a bad deal' suggests a fear of making an unsatisfactory deal and thus being regarded as having failed in the mediation. By sending the dispute to court, they would be relieved of such a fear; someone else would be to blame.

Concerns about failing, both as regards how sending a dispute to mediation emphasises their failure to resolve the dispute with negotiation and later as regards the settlement which might be reached in the mediation, brings to mind the quotation

14. When asked what the trigger was for his company's use of mediation, Interviewee 11 explained: '*Mediation can come from the client but we don't see that very often. Business people do not know what it is or they have strong thoughts on it. In most experiences, if mediation is entered into it was suggested by our litigation department.*'

which opened this chapter: 'Most often the greatest find is sitting right in front of your face, invisible in its obviousness.'[15] With the identification of this new theme regarding why parties may not use mediation, it seems unsurprising that concerns about being regarded as having failed may inhibit the use by commercial parties of mediation. Drawing on Lederach's words which opened this chapter, it is an issue which may have lain invisible in its obviousness. Concerns about how choosing to use mediation might reflect badly on the individuals involved in the earlier negotiations may loom large in the parties' minds.[16]

Further, in the particular commercial context which is the focus of this study, given that negotiating plays a key role in the work of business people as they frequently negotiate both non-contentious and contentious matters in their everyday work, this finding is perhaps, with hindsight, unsurprising as business people may be particularly sensitive to any suggestion that they were not competent negotiators.[17] This also suggests that context matters. While the EU has focused on a broad promotion of mediation for civil and commercial disputes, there may be issues which are specific to particular contexts which would need a tailored rather than a general approach. For example, the concern about being perceived as having failed may not apply equally outside of the commercial context to civil disputes, such as for example family disputes, given that for such parties they may not be as sensitive to suggestions that they were not good enough negotiators given that negotiating may not be something which forms a key part of their everyday work.

This issue of failure has not been identified in earlier empirical research on mediation nor, it appears, has it been suggested in the academic literature on mediation. Its identification is an important contribution to the continued discussions on how to promote the use of commercial mediation. An awareness of this factor is the first step in exploring how prevalent this issue might be and also how such an issue might be addressed.[18]

At this juncture, it may be helpful to note that the issue of being perceived as weak has been identified in earlier research as a reason why parties do not use mediation.[19] A concern that the suggestion to mediate may make the proposing party look weak or suggest that they regard their case to be weak was one of the reasons for

15. Lederach, *supra* n. 1, at 104, and 102: 'respect for what is naturally in place accompanies their every step'.
16. Interestingly, in Lande's earlier empirical research in the USA on business lawyers and executives' belief in mediation, 55% of in-house counsel did not believe that the increased use of ADR would increase their opportunities for advancement (Lande's study does not focus exclusively on mediation, *see* footnote 12 at 142) Lande, *supra* n. 2, at 181. However, in light of the findings in the empirical research for this book one wonders whether the fear of being perceived as having failed either in the negotiations preceding a mediation or regarding the outcome of the mediation might go some way to explain why a majority of in-house counsel felt that the use of ADR would not lead to opportunities for advancement.
17. Genn notes the tendency that business people will be experienced negotiators: 'Many business people who find themselves in the middle of a dispute are experienced negotiators and understandably believe that if they have not been able to negotiate a settlement, then a mediator is unlikely to be able to assist.' Hazel Genn, *Judging Civil Justice* 110 (Cambridge 2010).
18. In Chapter 9 recommendations are identified for the promotion of mediation.
19. *See* (n. 6).

the CPR Pledge.[20] It is interesting to compare the issue of weakness with the issue of failure identified by this research.[21]

As regards weakness, as captured by the rationale for the CPR Pledge, this is a concern about how one (and one's case) looks to others outside of one's company, i.e., those to whom one suggests mediation. However, regarding the theme of failure in this particular context of EU cross-border commercial dispute resolution, and drawing on the interviewees' comments above, this appears predominantly to be a concern about how one is perceived internally, i.e., within one's company. The concern is of being viewed by others in one's company as having been unable to resolve the dispute through unassisted negotiations and, separately, of failing to get a good deal in the mediation. Recall here Interviewee 11's concern, as set out above, regarding how the suggestion from the litigation department to the business people in their company to try mediation after their failed negotiations may be interpreted by the business people as suggesting that they had not done a good job at negotiating. Recall, too, Interviewee 18's comment that management is concerned about pursuing mediation because they may be criticised for agreeing to a bad deal. Such criticism is internal (i.e., from within the company). Given that the concern relates to how one is perceived internally within one's company, it appears that internal measures may be needed to address this issue.[22]

[C] Responsibility

It is appropriate here to consider a further reason why parties do not use mediation which is related to the theme of failure identified by the interviewees: the avoidance of responsibility. Building on his comment cited earlier, Interviewee 18 explained how management might seek to avoid responsibility and noted that a management which assumes control and responsibility is needed for there to be an increase in the use of mediation:

> *'I have an insight for you. I think the usage of mediation, will be much more usage if there is a general change – and I see that coming – in a change in company culture. Resolving by mediation rather than non-consensual methods requires a certain amount of accountability and let's say a certain management type. A lot of*

20. CPR has explained that 'the Pledge sends the message that willingness to negotiate or mediate is not a sign of weakness, but company policy. By conveying a message that a company will routinely consider negotiation, mediation where appropriate, the Pledge makes it clear that the exercise of such choices does not reflect a lack of confidence in the company's bargaining position. Put another way, the Pledge may be viewed as a mechanism for taking the onus off those who wish to start the ball rolling on negotiations, or respond positively to a similar request from another company'. <https://www.cpradr.org/resource-center/adr-pledges/pledges-faqs/1002-how-does-the-pledge-benefit-companies-and-their-counsel> (accessed 20 May 2020).
21. It may be helpful to emphasise that this comparison between the concepts of weakness and failure relates to the interviewees' comments on the specific context of this study (i.e., the use of mediation in EU cross-border commercial disputes). This analysis therefore does not consider what these terms may mean more broadly in the psychology literature.
22. In Chapter 9 recommendations are identified for the promotion of mediation which draw on the themes identified in Chapters 6, 7 and 8.

management saying if I go to mediation and then settle I might get shot at for agreeing a bad deal. If I let it get ruled by court I can say that they got it all wrong. I'm kind of exculpated. You need to have management that – excuse my French – has balls. I take that risk because it is the best solution for the company.

If moving to a company culture which is more entrepreneurial ... in my industry it's very much administration in the [[23]] industry, very state owned and they try to hedge bets and try to avoid responsibility for conclusions. Once it's more entrepreneurial there will be more mediation.'

This theme of responsibility was also suggested by Interviewee 8. In describing his company's emphasis on early dispute resolution and the key role which mediation played in '*mov[ing] forward to find a negotiated solution*', he explained the importance of encouraging business ownership of disputes and noted how the business would like to be relieved of their involvement in handling disputes given that a dispute is an event in the past:

'*You need to have an owner* [of the dispute] *in the business. The business would love the lawyers to run with it – a dispute is in the past.*'

Further, Interviewee 11 hinted at the appeal of avoiding responsibility when, in response to the question of why mediation was not used, he explained: '*People want an independent person to give an opinion.*'

The influence which a disputant's appetite for responsibility can have on the choice of dispute resolution mechanism has also been identified by each of Roberts and Lande in their empirical research, though the focus of their research and the type of interviewees differed from those of this study. Lande's research involved interviews with internal and external counsel as well as business executives regarding their attitudes towards litigation rather than mediation. Lande's research identified that many business executives welcomed the lack of control which litigation offered as it relieved them of responsibility and therefore of any subsequent blame.[24] Further, in Roberts' interviews with mediators, Andrew Ackland shared his view that using an adjudicative process was a way of 'ducking responsibility'.[25]

While the ADR literature has noted that mediation requires parties to continue to take responsibility for their disputes,[26] with the associated risk which that brings, it is

23. The type of industry has been removed to ensure anonymity.
24. John Lande, *Failing Faith in Litigation? A Survey of Business Lawyers' and Executives' Opinions*, 3 Harvard Negotiation Law Review 1, 20 (1998). Lande shares the words of one in-house counsel who explained: 'One of the things that I find here inside our corporation is that frequently there are a lot of people who would just as soon [have] the lawyers make all of the decisions, because it saves [effort] for them to do that. And then there's always somebody else to blame.'
25. Marian Roberts, *Developing the Craft of Mediation* 81 (Jessica Kingsley Publishers 2007). Ackland explained: 'Let me stick my neck out here. I think going to courts to adjudicate a commercial dispute is a way of ducking responsibility for the issues which you have created. Now I'm sure there are very good practical and pragmatic reasons for doing it. But on the whole people benefit from taking responsibility for sorting out their own problems and not giving them to somebody else to deal with.'
26. Eijsbouts has noted that while retaining control of the conflict by continuing negotiations with the assistance of mediation may increase the chances that a commercial solution may be found,

valuable to hear from the disputants themselves that their appetite for taking responsibility for the resolution of the dispute is a factor which can influence their willingness to use mediation. Their comments are also a further challenge to the assumption that mediation is for those who are risk-averse, or even weak, while litigation continues to be for the courageous.[27] Importantly, the recognition of what is required of parties in opting for mediation, namely that they continue to take responsibility for their disputes and their resolution, can help in determining how parties might be supported in choosing, and pursuing, mediation.[28]

[D] Why Mediate When You Have Already Negotiated?

At this juncture it is helpful to recall, as addressed in Chapter 6, the pattern of the interviewees associating mediation with negotiation and, in particular, understanding mediation to be a form of negotiation. When the interviewees explained why they did not use mediation for their EU cross-border commercial disputes, a recurrent theme was a scepticism as to what the mediation process could add to their efforts to resolve the dispute through negotiation, and in particular their early efforts to negotiate (i.e., pre-litigation or arbitration).[29] Interviewee 11 explained:

---

retaining control also requires the party to maintain responsibility for the resolution of the conflict. Jan Eijsbouts, *Mediation as Management Tool in Corporate Governance* in Ingen-Housz (ed.), *ADR in Business, Practice and Issues Across Countries and Cultures*, Vol. II. 76 (Wolters Kluwer 2011). Hicks has also noted that 'Resorting to position litigation can feel safer and easier than entering into a collaborative process of uncertain outcome in which one must take responsibility for the conflict and its resolution.' Tim Hicks, *Embodied Conflict* 153 (Routledge 2018).

27. Macfarlane explains how the assumption that going to court is 'the way of the warrior' while mediation or negotiation is for those who are risk-averse is inconsistent with what has been learnt from the Prisoner's Dilemma. Macfarlane explains that the Prisoner's Dilemma suggests that proposing negotiations – and 'offering to cooperate without any certainty regarding the other side's good faith' – is the riskier option while litigation is the safer option. Julie Macfarlane, *The New Lawyer* 86 and 87 (UBC Press 2008). By way of explanation of the Prisoner's Dilemma game to which Macfarlane refers, two prisoners are kept in different rooms and are each given the choice of confessing or not confessing to a crime they committed. If neither confesses, they will both be imprisoned for a year. If they both confess, they will both be imprisoned for three years. If one confesses and the other does not, the confessor will go free and the non-confessor will be imprisoned for 5 years. *See* Howard Raiffa, John Richardson and David Metcalfe *Negotiation Analysis* 67 (Harvard University Press 2007) and Julie Macfarlane, *The New Lawyer* 79 (UBC Press 2008).
28. In Chapter 9 recommendations are identified for the promotion of mediation which draw on the themes identified in Chapters 6, 7 and 8.
29. In Robert Bush, *What Do We Need a Mediator for? Mediation's 'Value-Added' for Negotiators*, 12 Ohio State Journal on Dispute Resolution 1, 4 (1996), Bush explores the value added by mediation to negotiation in response to an imagined scenario where a business person questions the use of mediation as follows: 'If mediation is simply, as you put it, assisted negotiation, then why do we need it at all? Why do we need a mediator? We ourselves, as businesspeople are experienced negotiators'. Bush's imagined scenario bears striking resemblance to actual comments made by some of the interviewees in this research. The literature on the value added by mediation to negotiation is considered later in this chapter.

> *'The key one: unfamiliarity with the process or closely related to that is a misconception of what it* [mediation] *is. People do not see the need to keep negotiating with a third party as they are already trained in being a negotiator.'*[30]

Such negotiations are understood to be early negotiation (i.e., before the use of adjudicative methods such as litigation or arbitration) as, earlier in the interview, Interviewee 11 had explained how his company's dispute resolution policy prescribed an escalation process between the parties with discussions between members of higher management from the parties, consistent with the policy's aim of avoiding litigation.[31]

Similarly, when asked why mediation was not used for his company's EU cross-border commercial disputes, Interviewee 9 explained:

> *'There is not a decent knowledge of how to go about it and what it brings. People will think that because we went through a period of running through the internal process that the only alternative is court.'*

Regarding Interviewee 9's reference to 'the internal process', this is understood to be negotiation as Interviewee 9 had earlier in the interview explained that his company's preferred method of dispute resolution for EU cross-border commercial disputes was negotiation and had added that if negotiations were not successful then the next step would be court.[32] He later added:

> *'The supply and sales team will feel confident enough that they can get the best deal rather than get a mediator in ... Resolving the dispute is like starting up a new commercial deal with the threat of litigation so people don't lose focus ... If parties continue to think they can resolve things themselves, that's more likely to continue.'*

Further, Interviewee 4 whose company's preferred method of dispute resolution was 'commercial negotiations',[33] explained the business' reluctance to send the dispute to mediation after failed attempts '*to deal with it commercially*' noting '*Why compound an already bad situation when can go to a more structured process in court?*' His description of mediation as '*compound[ing] an already bad situation*' suggests a view of mediation as adding nothing to his company's (failed) negotiation efforts.

30. Interestingly, this interviewee's comments resemble Genn's assertion that many business people who find themselves in a dispute are experienced negotiators and will think that if they could not resolve a dispute then a mediator would not be able to help. Genn, *supra* n. 17, at 110.
31. Interviewee 11 described his company's policy on the dispute resolution clauses included in its commercial contracts as: '*In all of them* [the company's model contracts] *we use pretty lengthy clauses. Generally speaking they aim to avoid litigation, they aim at an escalation process between the parties, so discussions between higher management, they ask parties to exchange information on major aspects of disputes and they ask parties to think about alternative ways to settle a case compared to litigation.*'
32. As stated in Chapter 6, when asked what his company's preferred method of dispute resolution was for EU cross-border disputes, Interviewee 9 answered: '*Negotiation. We are pretty proactive. We are successful in achieving an outcome. We are a pragmatic company. We do have some that go the full course and go to court.*'
33. Earlier in the interview, Interviewee 4 described his company's approach to handling disputes as '*It's a mixture of the business trying to negotiate its way out of the dispute commercially and legally looking to you for guidance. When they haven't been able to work it out commercially they come to us* [the legal department].'

In addition, Interviewee 12 perhaps most emphatically expressed this point regarding the scepticism as to what mediation could add to the parties' own negotiation efforts. Interviewee 12 explained his company's approach to dispute resolution for EU cross-border commercial disputes as: '*As a rule of thumb, first its negotiation, then mediation and if that doesn't work then escalate further [to arbitration or litigation].*' He then identified the main reason why his company has not used mediation for its EU cross-border commercial disputes as the tendency of parties to regard themselves to be great negotiators and therefore to not need a mediator and to underestimate the speed which a mediator could bring to their negotiations:

> '*Probably because our opponent doesn't want to. They think: let's negotiate because I am the best negotiator in the world. And also there are cases when we overstate our negotiation skills. It's on both sides. More often the opponent is not willing to enter into a mediation. It's: we're so great at negotiating that we don't need a mediator ... I hear it and feel it all the time. I find it irrational. There is a recent study in Germany on the low quality of negotiation skills of lawyers and non-lawyers in Germany. They overstate their negotiation skills and underestimate the speediness that a mediator can bring.*[34] *It's ignorance of people. I am fully aware that is my opinion – I have to wait.*'

In addition, the view that mediation does not add anything to negotiation was indirectly expressed by Interviewee 15 in his explanation of why his company's preferred method of dispute resolution is negotiation, and if negotiations fail then arbitration is used:

> '*To my mind, cost is obviously woven into it. Negotiation costs nothing: you need authorisation to make a deal and sit around a table and follow it. Arbitration sits next to negotiation. Arbitration is so expensive that it puts cost pressure on negotiation. If then you add mediation then there is a sense that the dispute might not get resolved without recourse to court or arbitration. Negotiation and arbitration sit rather nicely together. If you stick mediation in the middle it's another hoop.*'

Interviewee 15's description of mediation after negotiation and before arbitration as being 'another hoop' to go through, together with the view that ultimately arbitration or litigation may well be needed to resolve the dispute, suggests a perception that mediation adds nothing to the negotiation process.[35]

This scepticism of what mediation can add to the parties' own negotiation efforts is a reason which emerges only by reference to the dispute resolution process of

34. On a related note, Interviewee 14 attributed the low level of use of mediation in the German courts to judges' overestimating their ability to settle disputes and doubting the value which mediation can bring. He explained: '*How many % of judges use mediation, what do you think? ... In Bavaria less than 1%. That's the same picture all over Germany. Judges often say that's not my way to handle problems. I'm a very good judge. I try to settle disputes, that's my daily business. If I didn't have success, a mediator will not have success. We have mediator judges who are meant to be involved with the normal judges but they are not involved as the normal judges are superstitious and don't see the advantage of mediation.*'
35. Interestingly, Interviewee 15's comment bears striking resemblance to a comment made to Robert Bush by one of his former students as captured in his article of over 20 years ago: 'As far as I am concerned it's [mediation's] just another hoop you have to jump through and an additional expense. Tell me, am I missing something?' Bush, *supra* n. 29, at 5.

negotiation. Negotiation is a key comparator for the disputants in considering whether to use mediation. Similarly, the reason considered earlier in this chapter of not using mediation because of a fear of being regarded as having failed also stems from the relationship between mediation and negotiation. These are novel insights into why parties do not use mediation which have not been identified nor explored by the EU in its continued efforts to promote mediation.

In particular, the parties' scepticism as to what mediation could add to their own negotiation efforts suggests that the EU's focus in conveying the usefulness of mediation is too narrow. In the EU's recommendations, the usefulness of mediation is anchored in an understanding of mediation as an alternative to litigation. Specifically, the European Parliament's resolution of 12 September 2017 calls on Member States 'to boost awareness of how useful mediation is'[36] and in particular mediation's 'advantages in terms of economising time and money'.[37] Accordingly, mediation's usefulness is portrayed as the time and cost which mediation can save compared to litigation. For those disputants who do not want to use mediation because of their doubts as to what mediation can add to their own negotiation efforts, information on mediation's usefulness in terms of time and cost savings determined by reference to litigation will not address their specific concerns. Indeed, mediation would require those who have not been able to resolve their disputes by negotiation to spend more time and money in negotiations, albeit assisted negotiations. Rather, such parties would require information on how mediation might add value to their negotiation efforts. Demonstrating that mediation is efficient as compared to litigation does not necessarily demonstrate that mediation is effective compared to the parties' unassisted negotiations, and in particular the early negotiation efforts which are so valued by parties.[38]

It should also be repeated here that, as stated in Chapters 2 and 6, presenting mediation as a way in which to avoid costly and lengthy litigation may not be relevant in all EU Member States with, for example, the court systems of Germany and Belgium being renowned for being swift and accessible.[39] If the court system is swift and cheap, why would disputants use mediation if the only message they are being given is that mediation is a way to save time and cost compared to litigation? However, if it were possible to demonstrate that mediation was effective compared to unassisted negotiation, parties may be willing to use mediation even where the court systems are efficient. This, of course, raises the question of whether mediation adds value to unassisted negotiations.

36. European Parliament, *Resolution of 12 September 2017 on the Implementation of Directive 2008/52/EC of the European Parliament and of the Council of 21 May 2008 on Certain Aspects of Mediation in Civil and Commercial Matters (the 'Mediation Directive')* [2018] OJ C337/2, para. 11.
37. *Ibid.*
38. On a related note, Clark has argued 'many of the key benefits which participants may derive from mediation may be lost in an efficiency-driven species of the process'. Bryan Clark, *Lawyers and Mediation* 142, and also 164 (Springer 2012).
39. *See* Chapter 2 and in particular text to (n. 124) and (n. 125).

[1] *Mediation's Added Value to Unassisted Negotiation?*

Much has been written on why mediation might work where unassisted negotiations have failed.[40] In order to determine the value which mediation might add to unassisted negotiations, it is first necessary to understand why unassisted negotiations may fail. An awareness of why unassisted negotiations might fail sets the scene for understanding what mediation might add to such negotiations.

The ways in which mediation might add value to unassisted negotiation relate to how mediation can address three broad categories of barriers which arise in unassisted negotiation, namely strategic, cognitive and structural barriers.[41] Before considering these categories of barriers, it should be noted that 'failed' negotiations may be of two types. Failed negotiations might be - and this is the more obvious category - those which do not result in any agreement.[42] Failed negotiations may, however, also be those for which an agreement is reached though how the agreement was reached was sub-optimal (e.g., the time and cost incurred) or, and more importantly, the terms of the agreement were sub-optimal.[43]

By way of a very brief overview of each of these barriers, strategic barriers (also referred to as tactical barriers)[44] refer to actions taken by a party such as concealing information or providing misleading information in the hope of maximising that party's share of the pie.[45] The dispute is seen as a zero-sum game in which a gain by one party

40. *See* Bush, *supra* n. 29; Robert Mnookin, *Why Negotiations Fail: An Exploration of Barriers to the Resolution of Conflict* in Kenneth Arrow and others (eds), *Barriers to Conflict Resolution* 22-23 (W.W. Norton & Company 1995); Carrie Menkel Meadow, *When Dispute Resolution Begets Disputes of Its Own: Conflicts among Dispute Professionals,* 44 UCLA Law Review 1871, 1898-1899 (1996-1997); Peter Wolfe, *How a Mediator Enhances the Negotiation Process,* 46 New Hampshire Bar Journal 38 (2005); Mackie and others, *supra* n. 6 and in particular Chapter 2; Carroll and Mackie, *supra* n. 6 and in particular Chapter 3. *See also* William Ury, *The Third Side* (Penguin 2000).
41. The three broad categories of negotiation barriers are described by Arrow and others, *see supra* n. 40 and in particular at Chapter 1. Mnookin recognises that the classification into three groups of types of barriers is rather arbitrary given the interrelated nature of some of the barriers, though adds that this broad categorisation is helpful to convey the different types of factors which can affect the dispute resolution process (at 7). *See also* Menkel-Meadow, *When Dispute Resolution Begets Disputes of Its Own, supra* n. 40, at 1898-1899; Carrie Menkel-Meadow, *From Legal Disputes to Conflict Resolution and Human Problem Solving: Legal Dispute Resolution in a Multidisciplinary Context,* 54 Journal of Legal Education 7, 23 (2004); Wolfe, *supra* n. 40. Wolfe also explains how mediation addresses these barriers (at 40-47). *See* Bercovitch who identifies five categories of barriers to successful negotiations, namely structural, strategic, psychological, institutional and cultural barriers, *See also* Jacob Bercovitch and Richard Jackson, *Conflict Resolution in the Twenty-First Century* 28-29 (4th ed., The University of Michigan Press 2012). On cognitive biases in negotiation, *see also* Roy Lewicki, David Saunders and Bruce Barry, *Essentials of Negotiation* 122-128 (5th ed., McGraw-Hill 2011).
42. Bush, *supra* n. 29, at 8.
43. *Ibid. See also* Bercovitch and Jackson, *supra* n. 41, at 28; Menkel-Meadow, *From Legal Disputes to Conflict Resolution, supra* n. 41, at 23.
44. Arrow and others, *supra* n. 40, at 6; Menkel-Meadow, *From Legal Disputes to Conflict Resolution, supra* n. 41, at 23.
45. Arrow and others, *supra* n. 40, at 6; Bush, *supra* n. 29, at 8; Wolfe, *supra* n. 40, at 38. *See also* Bercovitch and Jackson, *supra* n. 41, at 28; Menkel-Meadow, *From Legal Disputes to Conflict Resolution, supra* n. 41, at 23; Menkel Meadow, *When Dispute Resolution Begets Disputes of Its Own, supra* n. 41, at 1899.

is at the expense of the other,[46] a perception which underpins tactics of concealment or deception. This has also been described as 'positional negotiating' in which you distrust the other party and you use tactics to try to come away with a greater portion of the pie.[47] There is an understandable concern than being open and honest may mean relinquishing one's advantage and handing that over to the other side.[48] However, the lack of information, or of reliable information, resulting from such tactical behaviour can lead to sub-optimal outcomes for each party.[49]

Another category of barriers to successful negotiation is cognitive barriers.[50] Cognitive barriers are the cognitive biases to which we are all susceptible and which affect the way in which we process and prioritise information.[51] These biases have been described as 'regular and identifiable departures from rationality'[52] which affect the way in which we receive and act on information.[53] They affect us in all of our interactions, and negotiations are no exception.[54] Such biases include loss aversion bias (under which we attach greater weight to future losses than to gains), overconfidence bias (under which we overestimate the likelihood that we are right), confirmation bias (under which we favour information which confirms our view and ignore information which challenges it) and reactive devaluation (under which we devalue an offer made by a person with whom we are in conflict).[55]

The third category of barriers is structural barriers.[56] The way in which a negotiation is structured may serve as a barrier to successful negotiation.[57] A key

46. Wolfe, *supra* n. 40, at 38.
47. Mackie and others, *supra* n. 6, at 22. Mackie and others provide examples of the types of tactics used in positional bargaining which include the concealment of information and making threats or bluffs.
48. Bush, *supra* n. 29, at 8.
49. Wolfe, *supra* n. 40, at 39; Menkel-Meadow, *From Legal Disputes to Conflict Resolution*, *supra* n. 41, at 23; Bush, *supra* n. 29, at 8. *See also* Robert Mnookin, *Beyond Winning* 21-25 (Harvard University Press 2000) on information asymmetries and strategic opportunism.
50. Menkel Meadow, *When Dispute Resolution Begets Disputes of Its Own*, *supra* n. 41, at 1898-1899.
51. Arrow and others, *supra* n. 40, at 6. Bush, *supra* n. 29, at 10.
52. Bush, *supra* n. 29, at 10.
53. Arrow and others, *supra* n. 40, at 6; Wolfe, *supra* n. 40, at 40-41. On cognitive biases *see* Daniel Kahneman and Amos Tversky, *Conflict Resolution; A Cognitive Perspective* in Arrow and others, *supra* n. 40; Amos Tversky and Daniel Kahneman, *Judgment under Uncertainty; Heuristics and Biases* in Terry Connolly, Hal Arkes and Kenneth Hammond, (eds) *Judgment and Decision Making* (2nd ed. Cambridge University Press 2000); Daniel Kahneman, *Thinking, Fast and Slow* (Penguin 2011).
54. Mnookin describes how a negotiation is 'an interactive social process, one in which parties make attributions and inferences not only about each other's proposals, but also about each other's motives and character'. Arrow and others, *supra* n. 40, at 6.
55. Robert Mnookin, *Beyond Winning* 156-167 (Harvard University Press 2000); Bercovitch and Jackson, *supra* n 41, at 28-29; Hicks, *supra* n. 26, at 64; Kahneman, *Thinking Fast and Slow*, *supra* n. 53, on loss aversion *see* 282-286, anchoring *see* 119-128, on confirmation bias *see* 80-81 and on overconfidence *see* 261-265. On reactive devaluation *see* Hicks, *supra* n. 26, at 64. A detailed examination of cognitive biases is beyond the scope of this chapter; the point which this part of the chapter is exploring is the key reasons why negotiation fail in order to set the scene for how mediation can add value to unassisted negotiations.
56. Arrow and others, *supra* n. 40, at 6; Menkel-Meadow, *The Lawyer as Problem Solver and Third-Party Neutral: Creativity and Non-Partisanship in Lawyering*, 72 Temple Law Review 785, 796 (1999); Wolfe, *supra* n. 40, at 38.
57. Wolfe, *supra* n. 40, at 38; Bercovitch and Jackson, *supra* n. 41, at 28.

example of a structural barrier is the use of an agent (e.g., a lawyer) to represent the principal in negotiations.[58] If the agent's interests differ from those of the principal, this can impede negotiations. For example, in a negotiation scenario where the agent is a lawyer, the principal and agent's interests could differ if the lawyer's interest lies in continuing with litigation (and continuing to be remunerated by the hour for such work) while the principal would benefit from earlier resolution of the dispute.[59] This barrier may be more prevalent when external counsel is engaged due to their common system of payment per hour and their billable hour targets which might encourage the continuation of litigation.[60] In contrast, the interests of in-house counsel and business representatives may be more closely aligned given that a comprehensive understanding of the business, and of what is important to the business, and acting accordingly is regarded as essential to performing well as an in-house counsel.[61]

The recognition of these barriers is the first step in identifying how the involvement of a third-party mediator may help to overcome such barriers and thereby add value to parties' unassisted negotiations.[62] Many have written on the value which the involvement of a mediator can bring to negotiation by addressing these barriers to successful negotiations.[63] By way of brief overview, the ways in which a mediator may add value include: (i) improving the flow of information between the parties by, for example, creating an environment which is conducive to the sharing of information (such as a requirement that parties do not interrupt one another), and sharing information he/she has received from one party in a caucus with the other party, subject to having authority to do so; (ii) helping parties to identify and share their underlying interests and thereby increasing the size of the proverbial pie from which they can take their slices; (iii) encouraging a problem-solving approach; (iv) reframing language and issues; (v) assisting parties to challenge assumptions by making them aware of their assumptions and exploring their validity; (vi) reality testing options

58. Wolfe, *supra* n. 40, at 38; Arrow and others, *supra* n. 40, at 19.
59. Arrow and others, *supra* n. 40, at 20-21. Wolfe, *supra* n. 40, at 38, 46.
60. Prashant Dubey and Eva Kripalani, *The Generalist Counsel* 37 (Oxford 2013) which explains that in law firms success is measured by the amount of billable hours. Dubey and Kripalani also explain at 97 how during their interviews they 'heard frequent expressions of frustration about the resistance of law firms to adapt their business models to address client needs and general dissatisfaction about law firm/client relationships'. It has been acknowledged that some lawyers might consider 'ADR' to stand for alarming drop in revenue. *See* Don Peters, *To Sue Is Human; To Settle Divine: Intercultural Collaborations to Expand the Use of Mediation in Costa Rica,* 17 Florida Journal of International Law 9, 13 (2005).
61. Dubey and Kripalani, *supra* n. 60, at 104-105.
62. Some of these barriers and the value which mediation can bring to addressing them were acknowledged by GE in its Singapore Mediation Lecture 2014. Brad Berensen for GE explained that however competent the negotiators may be there are times when disputes will not be resolvable via direct negotiations though may be resolvable with the assistance of a third-party mediator. Singapore Mediation Lecture 2014, *The Mediation Imperative: Why successful companies cannot afford to ignore mediation,* at 7 <https://www.imimediation.org/wp-content/uploads/2018/06/Singapore-Mediation-Lecture-2014.pdf> (accessed 20 May 2020).
63. *See* Bush, *supra* n. 29; Mackie and others, *supra* n. 6, in particular pages 24- 35; Wolfe, *supra* n. 40, at 38; Robert Mnookin & Lee Ross, *Introduction* in Arrow and others, *supra* n. 40; Carroll and Mackie, *supra* n. 6, Chapter 3. Further, *see* Debbie De Girolamo, *The Fugitive Nature of Mediation* 65 (Routledge 2013) for a helpful summary of how a mediator might overcome barriers in the negotiation process.

identified by the parties; (vii) ensuring that the principal is at the table to ensure that his/her needs can be identified and that the person with authority to agree to a resolution is present; and (viii) identifying who else may need to be at the table.[64] In essence, and as summed up by mediators themselves in their descriptions of their role, a mediator's job is to make others 'be more productive than they would be without a third party there'.[65] Similarly, Bush describes the mediator's role as: 'she can help you understand your situation – and your options and each other – better and more fully than you do now, and better than you will if you continue working on your own'.[66]

Empirical work suggests the value which mediation can bring to unassisted negotiations, though it is important to recognise that such work focuses on the particular context of settlement negotiations once litigation has commenced, which have been called 'litigotiation',[67] and not the type of earlier negotiations favoured by many of the interviewees in this research project. As noted by Menkel-Meadow, while

64. These ways in which a mediator may assist parties to overcome the barriers arising in unassisted negotiations have been identified from a review of the literature listed in (*supra* n. 63). *See also* Craig McEwen and Roselle Wissler, *Finding Out If it Is True: Comparing Mediation and Negotiation Through Research,* 1 Journal of Dispute Resolution 131, 136-138 (2002). On a broader note, *see also* The American Bar Association Section of Dispute Resolution, *Report of the task force on research on mediator techniques* (12 June 2017) <https://www.americanbar.org/content/dam/aba/administrative/dispute_resolution/med_techniques_tf_report.pdf> (accessed 20 May 2020), which explores the effects of various mediator actions on mediation outcomes. It should also be noted that in the non-contentious context of deal facilitation, the similar value which a third party facilitator can bring to parties' negotiations has also been identified. *See* Scott Peppet, *Contract Formation in Imperfect Markets: Should We Use Mediators in Deal?,* 19(2) Ohio State Journal on Dispute Resolution 283 (2004); Manon Schonewille and Kenneth Fox, *Moving Beyond 'Just' a Deal, a Bad Deal or No Deal* in Arnold Ingen-Housz (ed.) *ADR in Business: Practice and Issues across Countries and Cultures,* Vol. II (Kluwer Law International 2010); L. Michael Hager and Robert Pritchard, *Deal Mediation: How ADR Techniques Can Help Achieve Durable Agreements in the Global Markets,* 14(1) ICSID Review – Foreign Investment Law Journal 1 (1999).
65. Marian Roberts, *supra* n. 25, at 81.
66. Bush, *supra* n. 29, at 14.
67. The term 'litigotiation' is used by McEwen and Wissler in McEwen and Wissler, *supra* n. 64, at 133. For example, research by McEwen, Rogers and Maiman on mandatory divorce mediation found that mediation was useful because it 'improves negotiation' because 'it increases efficiency, decreases communication problems, enhances client involvement and understanding of the process, increases information for attorneys and dignifies the divorce process for many clients'. Craig McEwen, Nancy Rogers and Richard Maiman, *Bring in the Lawyers: Challenging the Dominant Approaches to Ensuring Fairness in Divorce Mediation,* 79 Minnesota Law Review 1317, 1379 (1994-1995). It should however be noted that this finding was based on the views of the lawyers present at the mediations rather than the parties themselves. Further, there have been numerous studies on mediation's effect on settlement rates in litigated cases. Notable such studies include: The Rand study which evaluated mediation schemes used in six US federal district courts (*see* James Kakalik and others, *An Evaluation of Mediation and Early Neutral Evaluation under the Civil Justice Reform Act* (Rand 1996)); the evaluation of Ontario's mandatory mediation programme (*see* Robert Hann and Carl Baar, *Evaluation of the Ontario Mandatory Mediation Program (Rule 24.1): Executive Summary and Recommendations* (12 March 2001) <http://www.ontla.on.ca/library/repository/mon/1000/10294962.pdf> (accessed 20 May 2020); and mediation schemes in the Central London County Court (*See* Executive summary of Hazel Genn and others, *Twisting Arms: Court Referred and Court Linked Mediation under Judicial Pressure* (May 2007) <https://webarchive.nationalarchives.gov.uk/20110201151141/http://www.justice.gov.uk/publications/docs/Twisting-arms-mediation-report-Genn-et-al.pdf> (accessed 20 May 2020).

there is data available on court-connected mediation programmes, there is 'almost no reliable data'[68] on the type of private mediation offered by private providers and associations (such as CEDR in the UK).[69] It is such private mediation that might involve mediation of matters which have not yet made it to court and therefore occur before the parties' negotiations have been transformed into litigotiation. Research of mediations conducted at such bodies therefore may offer the opportunity to gain insights specifically on what mediation might add to parties' earlier negotiation efforts *before* the dispute is transferred to litigation. Such a focus may be particularly valuable as, as explained earlier, an important theme identified in the research for this book regarding why parties do not use mediation is a scepticism as to what mediation can add to the parties' own and early negotiation efforts before the dispute has been transferred to an adjudicative process.[70] In essence, their view is that mediation cannot add value to their own negotiation efforts so they may as well proceed straight to court or arbitration rather than try mediation after their own negotiation efforts. To change this approach and adopt mediation, they would need to be assured of the value which mediation can add to what they themselves have already done.

Further, it is also important to note that much of the large body of empirical research on court-connected mediation tends to focus on the rather crude measurement of settlement rates to assess mediation's value.[71] For example, the rate and speed of settlement in mediated court cases (with the associated cost of resolution) has been compared with non-mediated court cases.[72] Such data shows that the rate of settlement

68. Carrie Menkel-Meadow, *Variations in the Uptake of and Resistance to Mediation outside of the United States*, University of California, Irvine School of Law, Research Paper No. 2015-80 [2015], 189, 197 <https://papers.ssrn.com/sol3/papers.cfm?abstract_id=2658903> (accessed 20 May 2020).
69. *Ibid.*
70. *See* the earlier section in this Chapter §8.02[D] Why Mediate When You have Already Negotiated?
71. On the challenges presented in trying to assess the contribution of mediation *see* Bercovitch and Jackson, *supra* n. 41, at 45-46. As Bercovitch notes at 46, mediation can still be regarded as successful even if the dispute remains unresolved post mediation: 'Even if a conflict remains unresolved, mediation – in any form – can do much to change the way disputants feel about each other and lead, however indirectly, to both a long-term improvement in the parties' relationship and a resolution of the conflict.' Further, in one of the studies by the European Commission on the implementation of the EU Mediation Directive, the study acknowledged that even when mediation had not been successful it had helped the parties to reach closer positions and led to less acrimonious subsequent judicial proceedings. European Commission *Study for an Evaluation and Implementation of Directive 2008/52/EC – the Mediation Directive* (16 March 2016) 69. *See also* Jacob Bercovitch, *Mediation Success or Failure: A Search for the Elusive Criteria*, 7 Cardozo Journal of Conflict Resolution 289 (2005-2006).
72. As regards mediation's effect on settlement rates in litigated cases, notable such studies and their findings include: The Rand study which evaluated mediation schemes used in six US federal district courts and which found that the use of mediation or neutral evaluation programmes increased the proportion of cases with a monetary settlement (*see* James Kakalik and others, *supra* n. 67, at page xxxii, pages 4 and 50); the evaluation of Ontario's mandatory mediation programme which found that the introduction of mandatory mediation had a significant impact on the proportion of cases which settled earlier in the litigation process (*see* Hann and Baar, *supra* n. 67, at 12; and mediation schemes in the Central London County Court (*See* Executive summary of Hazel Genn and others *Twisting Arms*, *supra* n. 67). A study of the voluntary mediation scheme in the Central London County Court from 1996-1998 found that 'Compared with non-mediated cases, mediated cases had a higher settlement rate overall,

has been higher and quicker in mediated cases compared to those which were not mediated, thereby suggesting mediation's apparent value.[73] However, such settlement data cannot explain *why* this may be the case. In other words, settlement rates record but do not explain the potential value of mediation. Further, as noted by Brooker and Lavers, 'a proper appraisal of the effects of mediation should include outcomes which cannot be understood by reference to a settlement rate'.[74] Given the theme identified earlier regarding disputants' scepticism of what mediation can add to their own efforts to resolve the dispute through negotiation, further exploration on what mediation might add to disputants' own efforts at resolution would be a useful contribution to those seeking to promote mediation, such as the EU.

Above all, however, the focus of this large body of empirical work on court-connected mediation is on mediation within the litigation context and it therefore does not specifically address what mediation might add to the parties' own negotiation efforts *before* the dispute is transferred to litigation. There is far less empirical research which focuses on the particular issue of what mediation might add to negotiations outside of the litigation context. This is unsurprising given the likely difficulties of identifying and accessing such types of mediation, though the private providers of mediation mentioned earlier might be an important avenue to access such mediations. Outside of the litigation context, there is research by Bazerman et al. which explores the effect of third parties (both agents and mediators) on the outcomes of negotiation.[75] While their study found that 'The results generally support our predictions concerning the impact of mediators and agents on impasse rates: agents hurt and mediators

---

whether or not settlement was achieved at the mediation appointment.' *Twisting Arms*, *supra* n. 67, at 22. There are numerous empirical studies on court-connected mediation which address topics beyond settlement rates though none focuses on the topic of what mediation might add to the parties' unassisted negotiation efforts. *See* for example, Colleen Hanycz, *Looking Through the Looking Glass: Mediator Conceptions of Philosophy, Process and Power*, 42 Alberta Law Review 819 (2005); Roselle Wissler, *Court-Connected Mediation in General Civil Cases: What We Know from Empirical Research*, 17 Ohio State Journal on Dispute Resolution 641 (2002); Julie Macfarlane, *Culture Change? A Tale of Two Cities and Mandatory Court-Connected Mediation*, 2 Journal of Dispute Resolution 241 (2002). It should be noted that there is research by McEwen and others regarding mandatory divorce mediation which found that 'mediation improves negotiation' though the relevant negotiations were external lawyer-external lawyer negotiations rather than those between the parties themselves. Further such mediations and negotiations were of divorce cases which is a different context to the commercial disputes which are considered in this book. *See* Craig McEwen, Nancy Rogers and Richard Maiman, *Bring in the Lawyers: Challenging the Dominant Approaches to Ensuring Fairness in Divorce Mediation*, 79 Minnesota Law Review 1317, 1379-1385 (1995).

73. *See*, *supra* n. 72 on findings regarding settlement rates in mediation.

74. Penny Brooker and Anthony Lavers, *Mediation Outcomes: Lawyers' Experience with Commercial and Construction Mediation in the United Kingdom*, 5 Pepperdine Dispute Resolution Law Journal 161, 213 (2005). *See also* Jacob Bercovitch, *Mediation Success or Failure: A Search for the Elusive Criteria*, 7 Cardozo Journal of Conflict Resolution 289, 293 (2005-2006) which explains: 'Perhaps the clearest concrete indication of a mediation success is the quality of effectiveness. Effectiveness is a measure of results achieved, change brought about, or behavioural transformation. Conflict management and mediation are processes of change.'

75. Max Bazerman et al., *The Effect of Agents and Mediators on Negotiating Outcomes* in Terry Connolly, Hal Arkes and Kenneth Hammond (eds), *Judgment and Decision Making* 443 (Cambridge University Press 2000).

help',[76] there is a limitation in the methodology of their study which challenges the reliability of its finding on mediation's apparent value. The negotiations used for this research were negotiation simulations carried out by MBA students and, crucially, those who were acting as mediators had not been trained as mediators.[77] Accordingly, any findings regarding the students' impact as mediators are limited given that the students were not mediators. More research which explores what mediation might add to disputants' own and early negotiation efforts would be helpful. This appears to be an important area of focus for those seeking to promote the use of mediation given disputants' reluctance to use mediation due to a view than it would add nothing to their own and early negotiation efforts.

This issue of what mediation could add to the parties' own negotiation efforts was a theme which emerged following the analysis of the data received in the interviews. It was therefore not a topic on which questions were asked during the interviews. However, some comments made by the interviewees suggest there is value that mediation can bring to the parties' early negotiation efforts.

For example, Interviewee 19 described mediation as being 'far more successful' than early negotiations between the parties:

> *'My personal preference is undoubtedly mediation. And the other pieces are negotiation, pre-action escalations, without prejudice negotiations. They do work but mediation is far more successful.'*[78]

Further, Interviewee 12 described how his company sometimes bypasses negotiation to go straight to mediation. The fact that his company leapfrogs unassisted negotiation to go straight to mediation suggests that mediation might be able to offer more to the parties compared to unassisted negotiation:

> *'We only escalate further to arbitration or litigation if the mediation fails. Usually we only enter mediation when we have experienced that negotiation was not effective. Sometimes in one third or 50% of negotiations we would immediately start with mediation rather than beginning with a negotiation. As a rule of thumb, first it's negotiation, then mediation and if that doesn't work then escalate further.'*

In addition, Interviewee 6's explanation that when the parties' discussions fail, his company would use mediation, which he described as 'positive and worthwhile', suggests that mediation can bring value to the parties' own efforts to resolve the dispute. Interviewee 6 stated:

76. *Ibid.*, 450. Max Bazerman et al. however emphasise the tentative nature of the finding as regards the impact which mediators have on impasse rates and provides various explanations for this.
77. Max Bazerman et al. note that 'Another explanation of why the effect for mediation was not significant is that the participants in this study were not trained in mediation techniques.' *Ibid.*, 450.
78. Interviewee 19 explained that there is an escalation process comprised of meetings between the senior management before formal dispute resolution processes are pursued: '*I am not giving away too many secrets if I say that our normal contractual template ordinarily is an escalation process before the formal DR piece. It would be: the head of the businesses meet, the senior management have two weeks to flesh out a deal. I've seen it work and I've seen people just going through the motions.*'

> *'Clearly we would try to find a solution by bilateral discussions but if that doesn't work we would use mediation. My experience is that mediation is a positive and worthwhile process.'*

It should be added that such bilateral discussions are understood to be early negotiations between the parties given Interviewee 6's explanation during the interview that his company tries to avoid disputes.[79]

Further, Interviewee 18 identified a specific way in which mediation can bring value to unassisted negotiation: the greater compliance rates of agreements resulting from mediation compared to those from unassisted negotiation. By way of important context, earlier in the interview, Interviewee 18 had described his company's dispute resolution policy as being first negotiation, followed by mediation and then arbitration.[80] He also explained, just before stating the following quotation, that many disputes are resolved through negotiations between CEOs and without any third-party assistance.[81] Accordingly, the references to negotiation in the following quotation are understood to be negotiations before any litigation proceedings have commenced. Interviewee 18 explained:

> *'There have been mediations before the 3 years. Both parties, we've complied with them. Compliance rate is 100%. Although, we have settlement agreements not from mediation but from negotiation. There the compliance rate is not 100%, it's 80 or 90%. One of the best parts of mediation is you have a third party who does not vet the result of the settlement but a good mediator should say have we addressed everything. Sometimes I get to look at settlements: why didn't you address that? Why is that so ambiguous? The third party can help you to take stock. We've thought of everything. The compliance rate outside the mediation system is lower at about 80 to 90%.'*

On a more general note, the interviewees' general satisfaction with mediation, as considered in Chapter 7, suggests that mediation can bring value to negotiation. It is

---

79. In response to the question of what his company's preferred method of dispute resolution was for EU cross-border commercial disputes, Interviewee 6 answered: '*I would say we work very closely with very large food and beverage businesses. We make a point of trying to avoid disputes. We have very few disputes.*'
80. In response to the question of whether his company had a policy on the dispute resolution clauses in its commercial contracts, Interviewee 18 answered: '*Yes it does have a policy on DR. What it clearly provides is a final resort to arbitration as opposed to state courts. It strongly recommends to include a mediation clause. It is a multi-tiered clause: staggered negotiation, then negotiation, then mediation and then arbitration.*' Later, when asked whether his company's multi-tiered DR clause applied equally to cross-border and national disputes, Interviewee 18 answered that he did not see any 'strategic reason' to distinguish between international and domestic clauses for the DR clause. Accordingly, negotiation plays a key role in the DR clauses and policy of his company for cross-border disputes.
81. Immediately before stating the text which follows above, Interviewee 18 explained that one of the main reasons why his company does not use mediation for its EU cross-border commercial disputes is '*Many disputes are already resolved through negotiations without third party assistance. It's still really common in our industry. It's really a small industry – there are a lot of customers. There are not that many and you want to work together later on. You usually don't go beyond structured negotiation where ultimately the CEOs decided.*'

unlikely that users would be satisfied with mediation if they felt that it added nothing to their own negotiation efforts.[82]

If, as identified earlier, a reason why parties do not use mediation is their doubt as to what mediation can add to their own, early negotiation efforts, further research is needed in order to explore the value which mediation might bring to such efforts.[83] While the interviewees' comments above suggest that there is value which mediation might bring to such negotiations before the dispute has been transferred to litigation, further empirical work needs to be done to gain more detailed insights into what mediation may add to such negotiations.

Such further research would be a significant departure from the EU's recent focus on information measures which seek to highlight the usefulness of mediation not in terms of what it can add to negotiation but rather in terms of the time and cost savings it can bring compared to litigation.[84] As stated earlier, demonstrating that mediation is efficient as compared to litigation does not necessarily demonstrate that mediation is effective compared to the parties' early and unassisted negotiations.

In addition, a focus on what mediation can add to negotiation may also address the further barrier to the use of mediation which was considered earlier: the concern of being regarded as having failed for not having been able to resolve the matter in unassisted negotiation. If mediation can bring value to unassisted negotiation and if

82. *See* Chapter 7, §7.02[C] Satisfaction with Mediation.

83. It should be noted that it appears that such early mediation does occur as recognised in particular by Interviewee 12's comments that his company frequently bypasses negotiations to go straight to mediation. Further, the Civil Mediation Council has recently noted that mediation is being more frequently used at the earlier stages of the dispute and in particular in high value disputes. The CMC's report notes: 'It is clear that parties in higher value disputes, often unbidden by their lawyers or even without contacting their lawyers, are agreeing to mediate well in advance of proceedings.' Civil Justice Council ADR Working Group, *ADR and Civil Justice, Interim Report*, October 2017, at 25 <https://www.judiciary.uk/wp-content/uploads/2017/10/interim-report-future-role-of-adr-in-civil-justice-20171017.pdf> (accessed 20 May 2020).

84. In the *European Parliament's Resolution of 12 September 2017, supra* n. 36, at para. 11 the Parliament recommends that Member States use information campaigns to convey the time and money savings which mediation can bring. There have been numerous empirical studies which have explored time and cost differences between mediation and the process against which it is most commonly compared: litigation. These include, for example: the European Parliament's, *Rebooting Report, supra* n. 2 which includes a section on the time and cost of mediation as compared to litigation, *see* pages 122-128; a study on a mandatory mediation programme in Ontario, Canada for which *see supra* n. 67. *See also* on the Ontario programme, Colleen Hanycz, *Through the Looking Glass: Mediation Conceptions of Philosophy, Process and Power*, 42(3) Alberta Law Review 819 (2005); the study by the Rand Corporation of the use of ADR and case management measures in federal courts in the US, *see* James Kakalik and others, *supra* n. 67 and also Hazel Genn and others *Twisting Arms, supra* n. 67, at 22. However, it should be emphasised that, as Carrie Menkel-Meadow has explained, empirical studies which compare the efficacy of different dispute resolution processes are inherently problematic as the same dispute cannot be subjected to two different dispute resolution processes and therefore a direct comparison of which process might be better cannot be achieved. The important refinement which Menkel-Meadow identifies is that empirical studies of this comparative nature can, at best, only compare *similar* cases which have been subjected to *different* dispute resolution processes. Carrie Menkel-Meadow, *Dispute Resolution* in Peter Cane, Herbert Kritzer (eds), *The Oxford Handbook of Empirical Legal Research* 599 (Oxford University Press 2010). It is interesting to note though that the same dispute could be subject to the two different dispute resolution processes of negotiation and mediation, if the negotiation process is not successful.

disputants can be made aware of such value, this may challenge disputants' view that opting for mediation suggests that they had failed.[85] Rather, this would suggest that it is not because they were in some way incompetent negotiators that their negotiations had failed but that there are limitations to what unassisted negotiations can achieve, however competent the negotiators.[86]

[E] Lack of Awareness

Earlier empirical research on the use of international commercial mediation has identified parties' lack of experience with mediation as the most likely reason why parties do not use mediation.[87] The insights provided in this research, which has focused on the EU context and on data provided by the users themselves,[88] suggest that it might be helpful to take a step back and consider the more fundamental issue of a lack of awareness of mediation.[89] A lack of awareness of mediation was a recurrent theme in the interviewees' comments on why mediation is not used.[90] For example, Interviewee 4 explained:

> *'I still get 100% blank looks from clients as I did 18 years ago about DR. They know what going to court is. Arbitration, adjudication, mediation, conciliation – they don't care about the difference. It's commercial adjudication and litigation.'*

Similarly, Interviewee 9 explained that one of the main reasons why mediation is not used is:

85. It is interesting to note in this regard that while they do not refer to the particular psychological barrier of being regarded as a failure, Barendrecht and De Vries suggest that better information about the benefits and costs of the dispute resolution options may reduce psychological barriers to choosing a process. Maurits Barendrecht and Berend R. de Vries, *Fitting the Forum to the Fuss with Sticky Defaults: Failure in the Market for Dispute Resolution Services,* 7 Cardozo Journal of Conflict Resolution 83, 106 (2005).
86. Here it is appropriate to recall the types of barriers which can arise in unassisted negotiation as were addressed earlier in this chapter.
87. Strong, *supra* n. 4, at 2034, 2036.
88. Only 7% of the respondents to Strong's research were in-house counsel. Strong, *supra* n. 4, at 2017.
89. The theme identified in the interviewees' comments of their lack of awareness and knowledge about mediation is consistent with commentary in the field that the infrequent use of mediation, or ADR more generally, is due to parties' lack of knowledge. Frank Sander, *The Future of ADR: The Earl F. Nelson Memorial Lecture,* 1 Journal of Dispute Resolution 3, 5 (2000) and Barendrecht and de Vries, *supra* n. 85, at 92.
90. A lack of awareness of mediation has also been acknowledged as a reason for its limited use in various publications in the review of the EU Mediation Directive. See the recommendation in the European Parliament's recent resolution for Member States to undertake information campaigns to boost awareness of mediation (*European Parliament Resolution of 12 September 2017, supra* n. 36 at para. 11; European Commission, *Study for an Evaluation and Implementation of Directive 2008/52/EC, supra* n. 71, at VI & 70; and European Parliament, *The Mediation Directive – European Implementation Assessment* (December 2016) PE 593.789, 24. Further, in its final report on ADR and Civil Justice, the UK Civil Mediation Council at section 2.4 identified raising awareness of ADR as 'probably the most important, and also the most difficult challenge'. The report also notes at section 4.4 that 'public awareness of ADR was acutely limited'. <https://www.judiciary.uk/wp-content/uploads/2018/12/CJC-ADR-Report-FINAL-Dec-2018.pdf> (accessed 20 May 2020).

> *'both in our company and other state-owned companies there is a big amount of ignorance about what mediation is. I had it the other day with the director of a large infrastructure project the questions; what does the mediator say and what is the mediator's decision? Like that'.*

Further, Interviewee 4 explained that the main reason why mediation was not used was '*Lack of awareness by the business*' while Interviewee 11 explained: '*the key one: unfamiliarity with the process or closely linked to that is a misconception of what it is*'. Interviewee 17 also identified a lack of '*familiarity of the parties to the process*' as an obstacle to the increased use of mediation.

Interviewee 14 even noted the lack of awareness of mediation in circles in which one might expect those present to be well acquainted with mediation:

> *'There was a talk by a German minister in the Ministry of Justice. The subject was the German way to handle disputes. First it is litigation and second it is arbitration. Nobody mentioned mediation. A law professor and me stood up and said there are dispute boards, mediation, adjudication, conciliation.'*

Further, Interviewee 1 described a general failure in the selling of mediation, noting that many lawyers would not have heard of mediation. Similarly, Interviewee 19 explained that what his company needed in order to increase its use of EU cross-border commercial mediation was '*Greater publicity about it, particularly on the continent*'.

In addition, linked to this theme of a lack of awareness of mediation, a couple of interviewees identified the type of information of which they would like to be aware in order to increase their use of mediation. When asked what the greatest obstacles were to the increased use of mediation in EU cross-border commercial disputes, Interviewee 2 answered:

> *'Lack of information on cost of the process and the seniority and experience of mediators. Also wider acceptance amongst peer group. We need more knowledge and awareness of current case outcomes. A big challenge in adopting mediation is knowing how well trusted that route is.'*

He later added:

> *'We would like insight into real cases that are resolved. There is certainty in precedent. Which panel or mediator was used and what their experience really is. It's key how able a particular mediator is.'*

Interviewee 2's comments suggest that an awareness of who is using mediation, which mediators are being used and the outcomes of the mediations are needed in order for disputants to feel more comfortable in opting for mediation.

Similarly, Interviewee 15 noted the importance of information on mediators and an awareness of the outcomes of mediations. When asked what his company needed in order to increase its use of EU cross-border commercial mediation, Interviewee 15 answered:

> *'If there was a real hot bed of experience and the same companies use the same mediators with good success rates and if word gets round.'*

These comments suggest that efforts to promote mediation may need to go beyond simply raising awareness of mediation in general to also include more detailed information on who is using mediation, which mediators are being used and the outcomes of mediations. Inspiration could be drawn from Arbitrator Intelligence, a significant data initiative in international arbitration, for ideas on how to gather and share data on mediators and their mediations.[91]

Further, on the theme of awareness of mediation, it should also be noted that a number of interviewees referred to a differing level of awareness, and indeed use, of mediation between the UK and some countries within the EU. Interviewee 19 explained the scepticism with which a proposal to mediate was viewed by French counterparties:

> *'In my previous life, I had experience outside of the UK in France. We suggested it* [mediation]. *There was a cross-border issue. The other side had virtually never heard of mediation. They thought it was a fast trick we were trying to play on them. In the UK everyone knows it. It was viewed with scepticism in that instance.'*

In addition, when asked why his company has not used mediation for their EU cross-border commercial disputes, Interviewee 19 noted '*my sense is that it's* [mediation's] *less well-known and utilised in Europe than in the UK*'. Interviewee 11 also described:

> *'If we look at the EU, the actual use* [of mediation] *is limited. I see a clear difference on the one hand between the UK and the rest of the EU. I see that mediation is already much more developed and used in the UK.'*

Further, when Interviewee 3 was asked about the obstacles to an increased use of mediation for EU cross-border disputes, he explained that as London is a hub for litigation in his company's industry there is an increased knowledge in the UK of the various options for dispute resolution:

> *'For the financial services industry globally, leaving aside Asia, so dominated by New York and London and that is where most of the litigation is. Other countries are far less down the road, there is a lack of understanding, there is less knowledge of what is available.'*

The interviewees' comments about the varied awareness and use of mediation across the EU accord with similar conclusions in the review of the EU Mediation Directive on the variegated use of mediation across the EU.[92] The Rebooting Report identified the countries with the greatest number of mediations (more than 10,000 mediations estimated per year) as Germany, Italy, UK and the Netherlands, and those with the lowest number (less than 500 mediations estimated per year) as Bulgaria,

91. For a detailed description of Arbitrator Intelligence *see* Catherine Rogers, *Arbitrator Intelligence: from Intuition to Data in Arbitration Appointments*, 11(2) New York Dispute Resolution Lawyer (Spring 2018).
92. *See* Rebooting Report, *supra* n. 2, at 6 which includes a table comparing the number of mediations in various EU Member States. *See also* Guiseppe De Palo and Mary Trevor (eds), *EU Mediation, Law and Practice* (Oxford 2012) and in particular pages 2-3. For a more recent review of the mediation laws and regimes in each of the EU Member States *see* Nadja Alexander, Sabine Walsh and Martin Svatos (eds), *EU Mediation Law Handbook* (Wolters Kluwer 2017).

Croatia, Cyprus, Czech Republic, Estonia, Finland, Greece, Latvia, Lithuania, Luxembourg, Malta, Portugal and Sweden.[93] Accordingly, in the EU's continued efforts to promote cross-border mediation, some countries may have a further distance to go than others.

Returning to the theme of a lack of awareness of mediation identified by the interviewees, the question which this theme invites is how should awareness be raised. And by 'how' this does not mean the *measures* to be used to raise awareness (such as education initiatives) but rather the more fundamental issue of how mediation should be presented. In particular, how might mediation be presented in a way which is relevant to, and resonates with, potential users? The first step in answering this question is to get to know the particular audience to whom you seek to present mediation so that mediation can be presented in a way which is tailored to that audience.[94] The reasons identified in this chapter of why commercial parties do not use mediation for their EU cross-border disputes offer an important opportunity to gain more understanding of the particular audience of potential users of EU cross-border commercial mediation. A better understanding of that audience affords the opportunity to present mediation in a manner which resonates with, and is relevant to, them.

In particular, gaining a deeper understanding of why interviewees do not use mediation, as is revealed by the themes identified in this chapter, suggests that in the EU's efforts to raise awareness of mediation it may be effective to differentiate mediation from negotiation rather than only focusing on differentiating mediation from litigation as the EU has tended to do (i.e., presenting mediation as cheaper and quicker than litigation).[95] Given the themes considered in this chapter - of the central role played by the parties' own negotiation efforts, a scepticism as to what mediation can add to mediation, and an associated fear of being perceived as having failed for not resolving the matter in unassisted negotiations - for a promotion of mediation to resonate with potential commercial users it will need to address these reservations. And in order to do so, the raising of awareness of mediation will need to differentiate mediation from negotiation.

On an associated point, when some of the interviewees were asked what they needed in order to increase their use of EU cross-border commercial mediation, some identified the need for an awareness of the benefits which such mediation can bring. They spoke of such benefits generally.[96] To be effective, the presentation of mediation's benefits will need to respond to the reservations which potential users have

93. Rebooting Report, *supra* n. 2, at 6.
94. In his article on the promotion of mediation in the 'East' compared to the 'West', Sean Izor notes: 'it is important to know your audience when promoting mediation and then to target that audience'. Sean Izor, *Selling Mediation in the East? Is There an Asian Way?* Asian Journal on Mediation 1, 12 (2013).
95. As noted earlier, the *European Parliament Resolution of 12 September 2017*, *supra* n. 36, at para. 11 calls on Member States to provide citizens and legal persons with information regarding the advantages of mediation as regards saving time and money.
96. For example, Interviewee 16 answered: '*Increased willingness and understandings of the benefits of cross-border mediation.*' Interviewee 4 answered: '*Greater awareness of its advantages and confidence that it could be delivered cheaply.*' A similar call for information on the benefits of mediation was also found in research by Queen Mary University. Empirical research

about using mediation.[97] For example, if such potential users are sceptical as to what mediation can add to negotiation, then the benefits of mediation which they would need to see would be that mediation can add something to negotiation. Raising awareness of mediation simply by presenting mediation as a quick and cheap alternative to litigation, which has tended to be the EU's approach to date, will not resonate with those who are sceptical as to what mediation can add to their own negotiation efforts.

§8.03 AN ENHANCEMENT OF MEDIATION

In seeking to differentiate mediation from negotiation, in addition to further empirical research which explores what mediation might add to parties' own and early negotiation efforts, those who are seeking to promote mediation might also wish to consider how they might be able to further enhance what mediation can add to negotiation. Put simply, are there opportunities to further differentiate mediation from negotiation? In light of interviewees' comments on both the value which they place on confidentiality for dispute resolution and their concerns regarding the confidentiality which attaches to cross-border negotiation and mediation, one area which merits further attention is the issue of confidentiality. This is a topic which has not been considered by the EU in its efforts to enhance the EU Mediation Directive.[98]

[A] The Importance to Disputants of Confidentiality and the EU Mediation Directive's Confidentiality Provision

During the interviews, as will be explored further in this section, interviewees highlighted the importance to them of confidentiality in their choice of dispute resolution process. Given the apparent value to disputants of confidentiality, one way in which those who seek to promote mediation might make mediation more attractive to potential users is to offer an enhanced confidentiality regime compared to that which is available for unassisted negotiations.

conducted by the School of International Arbitration, Queen Mary University of London identified that some interviewees believed that a lack of understanding of the benefits of mediation was the cause of its limited use. School of International Arbitration, Queen Mary University of London, *Improvements and Innovations in International Arbitration* (2015), at 31 <http://www.arbitration.qmul.ac.uk/media/arbitration/docs/2015_International_Arbitration_Survey.pdf> (accessed 20 May 2020).

97. The EU's current focus is only on the advantages which mediation can bring in terms of saving time and cost by avoiding litigation. For the purpose of enhancing the impact of the EU Mediation Directive, the *European Parliament Resolution of 12 September 2017, supra* n. 36, at para. 11 calls on Member States to conduct information campaigns to raise awareness of how useful mediation is as regards 'its advantages in terms of economising time and money'.
98. In particular, in the European Parliament's latest recommendations on how to improve the EU Mediation Directive, none of its recommendations relate to the issue of confidentiality. *See* the *European Parliament Resolution of 12 September 2017, supra* n. 36, at paras 11-15.

A focus on an enhanced confidentiality regime seems particularly relevant given that the EU Mediation Directive has been criticised, as noted in Chapter 2, for ambiguities and inadequacies in its provision on confidentiality.[99] Confidentiality is regarded as essential in enabling parties to share information during mediation free from the fear that such information could later be used against them in court or arbitral proceedings.[100] It has been argued that uncertainty regarding confidentiality can undermine mediation's role as a method of dispute resolution.[101] Further, as regards the particular commercial context which is the focus of this book, Brooker has noted that confidentiality may be particularly attractive to commercial parties who want to keep their disputes private.[102] The EU Mediation Directive has been criticised because, for the purposes of any subsequent court or arbitration proceedings, the confidentiality obligation does not apply to the disputing parties. Rather, it only applies to mediators and 'those involved in the administration of the mediation process'.[103] As the General Council of the Bar of England and Wales has noted 'the omission in Article 7 is that it is silent as to the position between the parties themselves in respect of the confidentiality of the mediation process. This has been described as a fundamental flaw'.[104] Further, as Bosnak has explained:

> Because the directive provides only minimum norms, it only addresses the mediator's privilege and that of his support staff, and not, as in the UNCITRAL Model Law and the Unified Mediation Act, also that of the parties or others involved in the mediation. Many respondents to the 'Green Paper' questionnaire were opposed to this minimalist approach.[105]

---

99. *See* Chapter 2, §2.03[B] which identifies these ambiguities in Article 7 (Confidentiality) of the EU Mediation Directive.
100. Bar Council of England and Wales, *Response to the Commission's Public Consultation on the Application of Directive 2008/52/EC on Certain Aspects of Mediation in Civil and Commercial Matters* at 2 < https://www.barcouncil.org.uk/media/407911/bar_council_response_to_the_european_commission_consultation_paper_-_the_application_of_directive_200852ec_on_certain_aspects_of_mediation_in_civil_and_commercial_matters.pdf > (accessed 20 May 2020); Felix Steffek, 'Mediation in the European Union: An Introduction' at 11 < https://e-justice.europa.eu/fileDownload.do?id = b3e6a432-440d-4105-b9d5-29a8be95408f > (accessed 20 May 2020). *See also* Michel Kallipetis, *Mediation Privilege and Confidentiality and the EU Directive* in Arnold Ingen-Housz (ed.), *ADR in Business, Practice and Issues Across Countries and Cultures* 184 (Wolters Kluwer 2011).
101. In their article on confidentiality in mediation in the UK, Agapiou and Clark note that 'uncertainty and confusion' regarding confidentiality in mediation 'may in turn undermine the very nature of mediation as a means of dispute settlement'. Andrew Agapiou and Bryan Clark, *The Practical Significance of Confidentiality in Mediation*, 37(1) Civil Justice Quarterly 74, 82 (2018).
102. Penny Brooker, *Mediation Law* 185 (Routledge 2013).
103. EU Mediation Directive, Article 7(1). Kallipetis has noted: 'The inexplicable omission in Article 7 is that it is utterly silent as to the position between the parties themselves in respect to the confidentiality of the mediation process.' Kallipetis, *supra* n. 100, at 205. *See also* Brooker, *supra* n. 102, at 208-213.
104. Bar Council, *supra* n. 100, at 2.
105. John Bosnak, *The European Mediation Directive: More Questions than Answers* in Arnold Ingen-Housz (ed.), *ADR in Business, Practice and Issues Across Countries and Cultures* 651 (Wolters Kluwer 2011). Bosnak adds that as in some countries privilege is only given to a small and select group of professionals, giving privilege to the parties to mediation would have been too big a step for such countries (also at 651).

In light of the interviewees' comments on the value which they place on confidentiality and, as Bosnak has described, the 'minimalist' approach to confidentiality in the directive, in its review of the directive it appears that the EU may have missed a key opportunity to enhance what has been called the 'critical'[106] characteristic of mediation.

In the interviewees' answers to various questions in the interviews, a pronounced theme which emerged was the importance that confidentiality plays in their selection of a dispute resolution process. As regards mediation, the importance of confidentiality was identified by Interviewee 10 when, in response to the question of what his company would need in order to increase its use of EU cross-border commercial mediation, the interviewee answered:

> *'With my limited knowledge, confidentiality – we would want to be sure that the protections offered under that are at least the regime of such obligations which are enforceable in the UK. We would want to know that anything that's agreed, would want that to be watertight.'*

Further, Interviewee 10 later explained: *'I don't know the detail of the directive and I don't know how broad that provision on confidentiality is.'*

However, the importance of confidentiality to the interviewees in their selection of a dispute resolution process was most prominently displayed in their comments on the importance which confidentiality plays in their decision to use arbitration. This further suggests the value to disputants of confidentiality.[107] For example, Interviewee 3 explained:

> *'Arbitration is very dependent on the quality of the arbitrator. It can be as time consuming as litigation, and I don't trust it as much as a court. Its value is confidentiality.'*

Similarly, Interviewee 6 explained:

> *'I would say that the starting point is arbitration because of privacy but the costs tend to be as high if not higher than the court.'*

Further, Interviewee 15 explained:

> *'We like arbitration because of confidentiality and we are not overly trusting of some courts in Europe.'*

---

106. Brooker notes 'Some mediation advocates argue that confidentiality is so "critical that without it the process will not work" because it encourages the parties to make concessions and compromise proposals or even admissions as to liability when exploring settlement options.' Brooker, *supra* n. 102, at 212. Brooker also notes as regards the UK regulations which implemented the EU Mediation Directive, 'Commentators regret...the lost opportunity for enhancing mediation confidentiality'. Brooker, *supra* n. 102, at 212.
107. This is consistent with research by the School of International Arbitration, Queen Mary University of London, which found that in-house counsel highly value the confidentiality and privacy which arbitration affords. *See 2018 International Arbitration Survey: The Evolution of International Arbitration*, at 7 and 27. <http://www.arbitration.qmul.ac.uk/media/arbitration/docs/2018-International-Arbitration-Survey---The-Evolution-of-International-Arbitration-(2).PDF> (accessed 20 May 2020).

Interviewee 15 later added:

> *'for insurance contracts, these are all arbitration. We place great stress on confidentiality – we do not want insurance cover exposed in court … I don't think expense has anything to do with it anymore. Court can be cheaper. For big commercial disputes, arbitration is the norm and the mainstay of that is confidentiality – the parties don't like their relationships exposed. Sometimes there are quite juicy issues'.*

And, again, Interviewee 21 explained:

> *'For all international disputes, even beyond the EU, it would be international arbitration because of the confidentiality and privacy that those proceedings will have. We don't like our disputes determined by the courts where we can avoid it.'*

The interviewees' comments above capture the value which they place on confidentiality when dealing with their disputes. Considered together with the deficiencies of the EU Mediation Directive regarding confidentiality (which are considered earlier and also addressed in Chapter 2), it appears that in its continued efforts to promote mediation it may be prudent for the EU to further consider the directive's provision on confidentiality in order to meet disputants' needs. As Kallipetis warned prior to the implementation date of the directive:

> The one issue that currently frequently emerges is the question of confidentiality and privilege. Leading mediators are often asked about the status of documents disclosed for, or statements made in, mediation if there are subsequent court or arbitration proceedings. At present it is difficult to give an accurate reply and certainly there is no answer that would apply in all the Member States.[108]

The lack of attention given to the issue of confidentiality during the review of the directive is surprising, particularly as concerns regarding the directive's confidentiality provision issue were raised during the public consultation on the application of the directive. For example, as noted earlier, the General Council of the Bar of England and Wales highlighted that Article 7 does not address the issue of confidentiality for the parties themselves (but rather only attaches to the mediator and 'those involved in the administration of the mediation process')[109] and suggested a heightened common approach to confidentiality.[110] In particular, the Bar Council suggested that the provision on confidentiality be revised to reflect what they termed the 'following principle':[111]

108. Kallipetis, *supra* n. 100, at 208. *See also* Alexander, Walsh and Svatos, *supra* n. 92, which describes the mediation laws in each EU Member State including the provisions on confidentiality. Further, at the national UK level, concern has been expressed that there is also confusion regarding confidentiality in mediation. Agapiou and Clark have noted that the operation of confidentiality in mediation 'is surrounded with uncertainty and confusion which may in turn undermine the very nature of mediation as a means of dispute settlement'. Agapiou and Clark, *supra* n. 101, at 81.
109. EU Mediation Directive, Article 7.
110. Bar Council, *supra* n. 100, at paras 10-12.
111. *Ibid.*, para. 12.

> that nothing which is communicated in any form between the parties to a dispute themselves and between them and the mediator before, during or after a mediation, and whether in private or joint meetings, in connection with the process of mediating that dispute, may be used outside the mediation without the written consent of all the parties and the mediator except in identified situations.[112]

The interviewees' comments highlight the value which they place on dealing with their disputes confidentially. If the EU can alleviate any concerns which potential users of mediation may have regarding the confidentiality of their cross-border mediations, mediation may become a more attractive method of dispute resolution. At the narrower national level, similar calls are being made for an enhanced confidentiality provision for mediation in order to make mediation more attractive to disputants. Agapiou and Clark have argued that, in the specific UK context, legislative provisions are needed to enhance confidentiality in mediation given that the current system of relying on the without prejudice rules results in confusion as such rules do not always apply in mediation, which may discourage parties from using mediation.[113] Further, at the broader, international level, SIDRA's research also suggests a need for the improvement of the confidentiality provision for international commercial mediation. As noted in Chapter 3, SIDRA's preliminary report shows that while 55% of users of international commercial mediation identified confidentiality as an 'absolutely crucial' factor influencing their decision to use such mediation, only 38% of users were 'very satisfied' with the confidentiality of such mediation.[114] These figures show that some users who identified confidentiality as an 'absolutely crucial' factor in their decision to use international commercial mediation were not 'very satisfied' with this characteristic of such mediation. It seems, therefore, that there is room for improvement as regards this valued characteristic of mediation which has been notably absent from the focus of recent measures and discussions to foster the increased use of international commercial mediation.

The provision of a broader confidentiality regime for mediation across the EU would also help to distinguish mediation from unassisted negotiation. The data suggests a concern regarding confidentiality for cross-border unassisted negotiation. Some interviewees who did not identify negotiation as their preferred method of cross-border dispute resolution raised concerns regarding the confidentiality of their negotiations. In particular, their comments capture the lack of a consistent approach regarding confidentiality for cross-border negotiations across EU Member States. For example, Interviewee 7 explained that for bilateral negotiations regarding an EU cross-border dispute, the UK-based in-house counsel of her company did not attend

112. *Ibid.* Further, as noted by Agapiou and Clark 'those crafting any general provision applying to confidentiality in mediation in general must grapple with the potential conflict between encouraging mediation through promises of confidentiality, providing certainty in the confidentiality regime and also ensuring that unconscionable conduct which too stringent controls on disclosure would facilitate is not permitted'. Agapiou and Clark, *supra* n. 101, at 95.
113. Agapiou and Clark, *supra* n. 101, at 88-89.
114. SIDRA, *International Dispute Resolution Survey: Currents of Change, 2019 Preliminary Report*, 11 <https://sidra.smu.edu.sg/international-dispute-resolution-survey-currents-change-2019-preliminary-report> (accessed 10 August 2020). Please *see* Chapter 3, n. 84 which explains why some data from SIDRA's preliminary report, rather than its final report, has been cited.

negotiations in the Netherlands as they had been advised that the discussions would not be treated as without prejudice:[115]

> *'In the one [the dispute] involving The Netherlands, we have lawyers speaking to each other. We have asked if it would help for us to come out. It would not be treated as without prejudice so that is not an option. We would always look to see a sensible discussion.'*

Further, Interviewee 21 also identified a concern about the confidentiality which attaches to the outcomes of without prejudice cross-border negotiations, whether outside of or within mediation.[116] When asked what the greatest obstacles were to the increased use of mediation for EU cross-border commercial disputes, Interviewee 21 explained:

> *'More generally across the sectors and from discussions with lawyers in civil law jurisdictions the whole without prejudice offers to settle is not the same. They would be shown to the court. This is not specifically confined to mediation. They certainly wouldn't want to make concessions, they would want to hold firm lines.'*

Interviewee 21's identification that disputants are concerned about the confidentiality which applies not only to cross-border mediation but more broadly to other types of cross-border without prejudice negotiations suggests that this may be an area where mediation could differentiate itself from unassisted negotiation. If there were a robust confidentiality regime for EU cross-border mediation this would be a way in which mediation could be differentiated from, and add value to, disputants' unassisted cross-border negotiations. There is certainly no standardised, regulated approach to confidentiality for cross-border unassisted negotiations which applies across the EU. The pan-European platform for cross-border mediation provided by the EU Mediation Directive is a platform upon which a broader confidentiality provision could be built.

In summary, given the identification by the interviewees of the value which they place on confidentiality and their concerns over the confidentiality which attaches to cross-border negotiations, be those within or outside of mediation, a more substantial confidentiality provision for EU cross-border commercial mediation may be an important way in which to differentiate such mediation from cross-border negotiation and thereby promote such mediation. In light of the apparent weakness in the directive's confidentiality provision regarding, as discussed earlier, the application of confidentiality only to the mediator and to 'those involved in the administration of the mediation process'[117] with no reference to the confidentiality for the parties themselves, there is clear scope for its enhancement.

---

115. In common law countries, without prejudice protection means that negotiations between disputing parties regarding the dispute cannot later be disclosed should the dispute proceed to court. Brooker, *supra* n. 102, at 187. The concept of privilege is not part of civil law jurisdictions, *see* Kallipetis, *supra* n. 100, at 184.
116. As Brooker, and Agapiou and Clark have noted, in England confidentiality in mediation is generally achieved through the without prejudice rules. Brooker, *supra* n. 102, at 186 and Agapiou and Clark, *supra* n. 101, at 88.
117. EU Mediation Directive, Article 7.

Finally, Interviewee 21's comment above suggests that he is not aware of the EU's specific provision on confidentiality for mediation. Interviewee 21 refers only to without prejudice protection for mediation, and he makes no reference to the specific mediation confidentiality for cross-border mediation provided by the EU Mediation Directive. This confidentiality provision is separate from the without prejudice protection available in common law jurisdictions.[118] Accordingly, if the EU were to enhance the confidentiality provision in the EU Mediation Directive in order to add value to unassisted cross-border negotiations, such a change would need to be accompanied with efforts to make disputants aware of such a change. Changes in the regulatory framework for mediation would need to be publicised; there would be little impact if disputants were unaware of a broader confidentiality provision for mediation.

§8.04 NOTABLE ABSENCES FROM THE INTERVIEWEES' ANSWERS

In addition to noting key themes which emerged in the interviewees' comments on why they did not use mediation for their EU cross-border commercial disputes, it is also informative to note any relevant themes which were absent. Of particular note is the absence of a reference to the lack of a direct enforcement mechanism for settlement agreements arising from cross-border mediation. None of the interviewees identified such a lack as a reason for not using EU cross-border commercial mediation.[119]

Such an absence is significant given the interest both at EU and the broader international level for a direct enforcement mechanism for cross-border mediated settlement agreements. It has been argued that the reason why cross-border commercial mediation is not more popular is because, unlike arbitration, it does not have the type of international convention on the recognition and enforcement of the outcome of the process which arbitration enjoys.[120] However, it has also been noted that the consensual nature of mediation (which differs from the adjudicative nature of arbitration) means that parties are likely to adhere to their mediated settlement agreements.[121]

118. Agapiou and Clark argue that a type of specific legislative provision on confidentiality in mediation similar to that provided in the EU Mediation Directive would be a way in which to enhance confidentiality in mediation in the UK which currently largely relies on the without prejudice rules. Agapiou and Clark, *supra* n. 101, at 90.

119. It should be noted that one interviewee acknowledged the role played by enforceability in arbitration for disputes with countries beyond the EU such as China and other sovereigns (Interviewee 3). Another interviewee (Interviewee 17) explained that while his company did not tend to use arbitration for cross-border disputes, arbitration has the benefit of enforceability.

120. Edna Sussman, *A Path Forward: A Convention for the Enforcement of Mediated Settlement Agreements* at 1 <https://www.transnational-dispute-management.com/article.asp?key=2295> (accessed 20 May 2020); S.I. Strong, *Beyond International Commercial Arbitration? The Promise of International Commercial Mediation*, 45 Washington University Journal of Law & Policy 11, 31-32 (2014). *See also* Menkel-Meadow, *Variations in the Uptake of and Resistance to Mediation*, *supra* n. 68, at 220. Menkel-Meadow notes that a major issue which must be studied and dealt with is an appropriate international legal authority for enforcement decisions of mediated agreements and also of decisions to mediate.

121. Simon Roberts and Michael Palmer, *Dispute Processes ADR and the Primary Forms of Decision-Making* 215 (2nd ed. Cambridge 2005); Edna Sussman, *The Final Step: Issues in Enforcing the Mediation Settlement Agreements*, at 2 & 3 <https://sussmanadr.com/docs/

UNCITRAL members have worked hard over recent years to create an enhanced enforcement mechanism for cross-border mediation. Their efforts resulted in the Singapore Convention which opened for signature on 7 August 2019 in Singapore and entered into force on 12 September 2020.[122] At EU level, the European Parliament has recommended that the European Commission conducts a detailed study on the barriers to the 'free circulation' of settlement agreements arising from EU cross-border settlement agreements and the options to address such barriers.[123] One such option could be, as proposed by Esplugues and Iglesias, to either revise the directive or create a new legal instrument which enables the direct enforcement of an EU cross-border mediated settlement agreement in all EU Member States without the need for any judicial ratification or further procedural steps.[124] This recommendation by the Parliament, drawing on the work and proposals of Esplugues and Iglesias,[125] is an unexpected development as the European Parliament had previously dismissed suggestions for a type of direct enforcement instrument across the EU due to the additional standards regarding the mediation process which this would require and the Parliament's view

Enforcement_Fordham_82008.pdf> (accessed 20 May 2020); Laurence Boulle, *International Enforceability of Mediated Settlement Agreements: Developing the Conceptual Framework*, 7 Contemporary Asia Arbitration Journal 35, 57 (2014). Further, Boulle has acknowledged that there is not a problem in practice regarding compliance with mediated settlement agreements, Winnie Jo-Mei Ma and others, *Enforcing Cross-Border Mediated Settlement Agreements: Colloquium held at Bond University Faculty of Law on November 2013*, 7(1) Contemporary Asia Arbitration Journal 3, 8 (2014).

122. UNCITRAL, 'Singapore Convention Signing Ceremony' <https://uncitral.un.org/en/07.08.2019> (accessed 20 May 2020). Following the ratification of the convention by Singapore, Fiji and Qatar, the convention entered into force on 12 September 2020 <https://www.singaporeconvention.org/convention/about-convention/> (accessed 16 September 2020).

123. *European Parliament Resolution of 12 September 2017*, *supra* n. 36, at recommendation 14. The topic of the enforcement of settlement agreements arising from EU cross-border mediations first received attention in November 2016 in a paper prepared by Carlos Esplugues and Jose Luis Iglesias. Their paper provides a detailed review of the relevant legal instruments in the EU on enforcement and notes that there is no general system for direct enforcement (i.e., without further procedural steps involving courts or authorities). It is helpful to recall here that Article 6 (enforceability of agreements resulting from mediation) of the EU Mediation Directive requires that Member States ensure that parties can request that a court or competent authority enforce settlement agreements arising from cross-border mediation. There is, however, no requirement on Member States to ensure direct enforceability of the settlement agreements i.e., without any further procedural steps. One of the measures which Esplugues and Iglesias propose in order to increase the use of cross-border mediation is the development of an instrument which allows for the direct enforcement of an EU cross-border settlement agreement arising from mediation in all EU Member States without the need for any judicial ratification or further procedural steps. In suggesting this proposal they refer to the developments at UNCITRAL level on an instrument on the enforcement of international commercial settlement agreements resulting from mediation. *See* Carlos Esplugues and Jose Luis Iglesias, *Mediation and Private International Law: Improving Free Circulation of Mediation Settlement Agreements Across the EU* in European Parliament, *The Implementation of the Mediation Directive* (29 November 2016) PE 571.395, 73-75. *See also* Haris Meidanis, *International Enforcement of Mediated Settlement Agreements: Two and a Half Models – Why and How to Enforce International Mediated Settlement Agreements*, 85(1) Arbitration 49, 56-58 (2019) which contains a helpful summary of the system of enforcement available under the EU Mediation Directive.

124. Esplugues and Iglesias, *supra* n. 123, at 75.

125. Esplugues and Iglesias, *supra* n. 123.

that this would not be supported by the Member States.[126] It is also a surprising development given that neither the EU nor its Member States were signatories of the Singapore Convention at its opening for signature on 7 August 2019 and have yet to sign the convention.[127]

Towards the end of the interviews, interviewees were asked for their thoughts on the EU's recent interest in a direct enforcement mechanism for mediated settlement agreements (under which there would be no need for any judicial ratification or further procedural steps in order to enforce the agreement). Of those interviewees who did not welcome the proposal (namely Interviewees 3, 7, 9, 11, 12, 16, 18, 20), a couple of noticeable themes emerged in their responses.[128]

First, many noted that they did not see a need for such a mechanism given that they had not experienced, nor did they have any concerns about, any problems with compliance of settlement agreements arising from EU cross-border mediation. For example, Interviewee 3, whose company had experience of EU cross-border commercial mediation, explained:

> *'It would make no difference to our use of mediation the fact that it was more easily enforceable. We have never had to litigate a settlement agreement.'*

Similarly, Interviewee 7 explained:

> *'I am not sure how much benefit that would add. We have never had an issue where we settled something and then it didn't happen ... I have never known any agreement not to be blessed.'*

In addition, Interviewee 12 described issues with compliance with the settlement agreements arising from EU cross-border commercial mediations as '*the largest of myths*' and added '*We would never mediate with a party if we sensed that they wouldn't comply with the outcome.*' He also added '*enforceability is not a practical issue*'.

---

126. European Parliament, *The Mediation Directive, European Implementation Assessment*, *supra* n. 90, at 18.
127. Information on the signatories to the convention and ratification by such signatories can be found at: < https://uncitral.un.org/en/texts/mediation/conventions/international_settlement_agreements/status > (accessed 20 May 2020).
128. For completeness, it should be added that the interviewees who welcomed the proposal were Interviewees 2, 6, 10, 13, 15, 17, 19. Interviewee 4 was ambivalent about the proposal and Interviewee 21 did not have a view on the proposal. Further, it was difficult to discern Interviewee 14's view on the proposal. Early in his interview, Interviewee 14 explained that there was not the equivalent for mediation of UNCITRAL rules for arbitration enforcement and that this was a problem. Later in the interview when asked for his thoughts on the various proposals to increase the use of EU cross-border commercial mediation, including a direct enforcement mechanism, Interviewee 14 answered '*All of these are not very ... they do not become true.*' He then added that '*These ideas are nice to have but not reality.*' As regards enforcement, he explained: '*There must be a way, especially only in Europe as a starter there should be a way in the civil procedure law very fast to enforce such mediation settlements. That's the way to do it and bring better acceptance.*' This appears to be a different approach to the direct enforcement mechanism suggested in the proposals put to the interviewees. It is also interesting to note that those who welcomed the proposal for a direct enforcement mechanism did not have experience of EU cross-border commercial mediation and therefore would not have had any experience regarding compliance with the outcomes of mediated cross-border settlement agreements.

Similarly, Interviewee 16 responded:

'I can understand if people feel it's necessary but, as mentioned before, from the insurance perspective we don't see any benefit ... if you have done it, your view will be there's no need.'

Interviewee 11 also queried the need for such an enforcement mechanism:

'Enforceability: the EU is very much against an alternative for the New York convention for agreements reached in mediation. Don't know why they would be in favour of such a regime in the EU. If the question were do you really see the need for such a mechanism for the enforceability of agreements, we do not have that on top of the list.'

The interviewees' views that that there is no practical need for a direct enforcement mechanism are consistent with the literature which notes that, due to the consensual nature of mediation, parties are likely to adhere to their mediated settlement agreements.[129] This calls into question the need for an enforcement mechanism for mediation of the type which is available for international arbitration.

As an important aside, it should also be noted here that of those interviewees who, in contrast, welcomed the proposal for a direct enforcement mechanism, there was a prominent theme of such interviewees welcoming the proposal to the extent that it was needed, rather than identifying an actual need for such a proposal. In other words, it was a qualified 'yes' to the proposal i.e., if it were needed. For example, Interviewee 6 noted:

'Enforcement is a good point to the extent that people had problems of enforcement, they would clearly want a degree of confidence. We haven't had any problems.'

Similarly, Interviewee 15 noted:

'Yes that makes sense; I don't know how problematic the judicial enforcement is – but anything to make it easier.'

And Interviewee 19 explained:

'The last one makes sense to me, although it's never really been a concern to me.'

Accordingly they appear to be welcoming the proposal on the assumption that there are problems with enforcement generally, though they themselves have not experienced any such issues.

Secondly, when considering such a proposal for a direct enforcement mechanism, there was a pronounced pattern of the interviewees drawing an analogy between settlement agreements reached in mediation and those reached in negotiation. For example, Interviewee 9 responded:

'[It] sounds sensible but I wouldn't have seen it as an issue. I don't have a settlement agreement from a mediation but I do have settlement agreements from negotiations. I haven't been concerned about it.'

---

129. *See supra* n. 121.

In addition, Interviewee 21 explained:

'I haven't had any issues for enforcing settlement agreements from negotiation or mediations. These normally require payment to another party and then the other party doesn't proceed to legal proceedings.'

Further, Interviewee 12 queried why settlement agreements reached through mediation should be treated differently to those reached through negotiation, which suggests his view of the similar nature of such settlements:

'I don't think it's a good proposal. First it treats settlements reached in mediation differently to those reached in negotiation.'

The interviewees' comments above suggest that they draw an analogy between the outcomes of mediation and those of negotiation. The comparator they choose when considering the proposal for a direct enforcement mechanism is negotiation and not arbitration. This calls into question the suitability of borrowing an enforcement mechanism from arbitration to be used in the very different dispute resolution process of mediation. Interestingly, such doubts were suggested by some of the interviewees who noted that the very nature of the types of agreements which can be reached in mediation might make a direct enforcement mechanism, borrowed from arbitration, unsuitable. For example, Interviewee 3 explained that such an enforcement mechanism would not be appropriate for some of the types of agreement which can arise as a result of mediation given that interpretation would be needed:

'And enforceability: this is a solution in search of a problem. I can theoretically see the benefit because effectively when you've settled because of a mediation you take a stamp and stamp it and say you did it because of mediation. But it kind of missed the point that interpretation is required – this is easy when it is money. But what about when the agreement is that I will not go and poach employees. That becomes a factual question on whether I tried to poach someone. Having something readily enforceable isn't going to help you. It's also misconceived – the settlement might include non-poaching clauses which an arbitration and court proceedings wouldn't have. It's a solution in search of a problem. It is also misconceived.'

He added:

'The focus on enforceability strikes me as a bit odd. The parties get to an agreement. It's a consensual process. Someone is helping us to get to agree – then it's a contract. It represents a significant change to the rule of contract and strikes me as weird. When you have a settlement agreement it does not say that it was the result of mediation. It's a settlement agreement. By definition mediation is bringing two parties together. Arbitration is different. It's a quasi court proceeding.'

In a similar vein, Interviewee 7 expressed a concern that such a mechanism might inhibit the types of solutions which could be reached in a settlement:

'I am worried if directly enforceable, would that impact on the way that you document the settlement and not just the mechanics. At the moment you can draft a settlement agreement in any way you want … At the moment you can agree on what you want to do. Could you frustrate the process with direct enforceability? The

settlements are not just based on money. Could be you will put up a press release, you can share this information.'

The identification by these interviewees of the unsuitability of borrowing the enforcement approach used in arbitration for mediation together with, as identified earlier, the analogy which the interviewees' draw between the outcomes of mediation and negotiation further emphasises the EU's failure to explore the relationship between mediation and negotiation in its continued efforts to promote cross-border mediation. A significant comparator which the interviewees have chosen when considering the proposal of a direct enforcement mechanism is negotiation, and not arbitration. As explained earlier, in failing to explore the relationship between mediation and negotiation, certain barriers to the use of mediation have lain undiscovered. In addition, such a failure to explore this relationship means that further ideas on how to promote mediation, such as an enhanced confidentiality regime for cross-border mediation beyond that which is available for cross-border negotiation, have not been considered.

§8.05 CONCLUSION

The key proposals to increase the use of cross-border mediation in the EU (such as the recent recommendations to raise awareness of the time and cost savings which mediation can offer, and the repeated proposals for mandatory mediation)[130] focus on the relationship between mediation and litigation. In particular, the proposals are anchored in an understanding of mediation as an alternative to litigation. This sole focus on mediation's relationship with litigation means that certain obstacles to an increased use of mediation have been missed.

The key themes identified by the interviewees regarding why they do not use mediation for their EU cross-border commercial disputes reorient us away from a sole focus on mediation's relationship with litigation towards an appreciation of the relationship which interviewees have drawn between mediation and negotiation. In particular, they view mediation in terms of their earlier negotiations and not solely as a way in which to avoid future litigation. Crucially, the themes identified by the interviewees (such as a scepticism as to what mediation can add to negotiation and a concern about being regarded as having failed for not having been able to resolve the dispute in unassisted negotiations) suggest that the relationship drawn between mediation and negotiation can affect parties' willingness to use mediation.

The relationship between mediation and negotiation is frequently acknowledged in the mediation literature with mediation being described as assisted or extended negotiation.[131] However, what appears not to have been considered is how this

130. European Parliament, *A Ten-Year-Long 'EU Mediation Paradox'. When an EU directive Needs to be More … Directive,* (November 2018) PE 608.847.

131. *See* Nancy Welsh, *Making Deals in Court-Connected Mediation: What's Justice Got to Do with It?,* 79 Washington University Law Quarterly 787, 799 (2001). At footnote 62 on page 799 Welsh lists key literature which describes mediation as assisted or facilitated negotiation. *See also* Roberts and Palmer, *supra* n. 121, at 173; Jacob Bercovitch, *Mediation Success or Failure: A Search for the Elusive Criteria,* 7(2) Cardozo Journal of Conflict Resolution 289, 290 (2006);

relationship between mediation and negotiation may affect parties' willingness to use mediation. Rather, some of the ways in which the relationship between mediation and negotiation has been explored include theoretical and empirical accounts of how the mediator affects the negotiation process (including, for example, how the mediator can contribute to the negotiation process, and the extent to which the mediator him/herself becomes a party to the negotiations).[132] The relationship between mediation and negotiation has also underpinned accounts of how lawyers can contribute in the mediation process (including identifying the skills which litigators need to maximise the chances of a successful mediation).[133] It appears that what has not been considered to date, neither theoretically nor empirically, is how the relationship between mediation and negotiation can affect disputants' proclivity to use mediation. This is a new finding which has emerged from this qualitative study.

Drawing on the themes identified in the interviews, the relationship between mediation and negotiation reveals a paradox: in mediation's close association with negotiation lie both an opportunity for and an obstacle to mediation's increased use. There is an opportunity because mediation is associated with a dispute resolution process with which parties are familiar and which they favour. And there is an obstacle because mediation's close association with negotiation leads to barriers to the use of mediation (notably a scepticism as to what mediation can add to unassisted negotiation, and an associated concern of being regarded as having failed for not having been able to resolve the dispute in unassisted negotiations). An awareness of these barriers and indeed this paradox is an important step in determining how to address them. These obstacles are revealed through an appreciation of the relationship between mediation and negotiation and an acknowledgement of the key role which negotiation

---

Debbie De Girolamo, *A View from Within: Reconceptualising Mediator Interactions*, 30 Windsor Yearbook of Access to Justice 103, 109 (2012); Lisa Blomgren Amsler, *Dispute System Design and the Global Pound Conference 2016 Symposium: Where Do We Come From: What Are We – Where Are We Going: Keynote*, 18 Cardozo Journal of Conflict Resolution 621, 627 (2017); Alan Limbury, *Should Mediation be an Evidentiary Black Hole*, 35 University of New South Wales Law Journal 914, 916 (2012); Don Peters, *Can we Talk – Overcoming Barriers to Mediating Private Transborder Commercial Disputes in the Americas*, 41(5) Vanderbilt Journal of Transnational Law 1251, 1252 (2008); McEwen and Wissler, *supra* n. 64, at 132; Bobette Wolski, *Arb-Med-Arb (and MSAs): A Whole Which Is Less Than, Not Greater than, the Sum of Its Parts*, 6(2) Contemporary Asia Arbitration Journal 249, 252 (2013); Bobette Wolski, *On Mediation, Legal Representatives and Advocates*, 38(1) University of New South Wales Law Journal 5, 9 at footnote 25 (2015); Jacqueline Nolan-Haley, *Lawyers, Clients and Mediation*, 73 Notre Dame Law Review 1369, 1371 (1997-1998).

132. As regards empirical studies of how the mediator affects the negotiation process, *see* Debbie De Girolamo's ethnographic study of commercial mediations, *supra* n. 63, in particular at 208-209 and De Girolamo, *A View from Within*, *supra* n. 131. As regards theoretical accounts of how the mediator affects the negotiation process *see* Roberts and Palmer, *supra* n. 121, at 173-177; Howard Raiffa, *Negotiation Analysis, The Science and Art of Collaborative Decision Making* (2007 Harvard University Press) Chapter 17, 311-327 and in particular tables 17.1 and 17.2 at 318 and 319 respectively; Christopher W. Moore, *The Mediation Process* (4th ed. Jossey-Bass 2014) 177-178 and Chapter 6; Peters, *supra* n. 131, at 1253; Chris Guthrie, *The Lawyer's Philosophical Map and the Disputant's Perceptual Map: Impediments to Facilitative Mediation and Lawyering*, 6 Harvard Negotiation Law Review 145, 177 (2001).

133. James K. L. Lawrence, *Mediation Advocacy: Partnering with the Mediator*, 15 Ohio State Journal of Dispute Resolution 425 (2000).

can play as a dispute resolution process. And now that these obstacles have come to light, drawing on the words of Lederach which opened this chapter, they seem to have lain 'invisible in [their] obviousness'.[134]

The following chapter, Chapter 9, will draw on the findings identified in Chapters 6, 7 and 8 to conclude and to identify recommendations for the EU in its continued efforts to promote the use of cross-border mediation. Chapter 9 will also suggest areas for further exploration.

134. Lederach, *supra* n. 1, at 104.

CHAPTER 9
Changing the Frame; Framing the Changes

> Because we have been framing the problem incorrectly, we have been finding flawed solutions.[1]

> Catalysts and support can come from outside, but the sustenance of change is built by keen observation of available and existing resources, space, *and connections*.[2] (emphasis added)

§9.01 EXECUTIVE SUMMARY

This chapter brings together the findings identified in Chapters 6, 7 and 8 to argue that the EU's continued focus on mediation's relationship with litigation, to the exclusion of other methods of dispute resolution, has resulted in recommendations which are insufficient to address fully the barriers to the use of mediation. In particular, by changing the frame to view the use of mediation through the disputants' perspective, this in turn leads to a change in the framing of mediation from an alternative to litigation (as has been the EU's focus to date) to an extension of what parties already do (i.e., negotiation). Such an understanding of mediation reveals barriers to the use of mediation which have not been considered by the EU to date in its efforts to promote mediation. An awareness of such barriers leads to a recognition of what is being *asked of* disputants in pursuing mediation which differs to the EU's approach of emphasising what mediation enables disputants to *avoid* (i.e., litigation). Framing the use of mediation in this way presents the changes which are needed in its promotion. This chapter identifies recommendations for the EU in its continued efforts to promote mediation. It then closes with reflections on this research and recommends further research to support the reframing of cross-border mediation.

1. Johann Hari, *Lost Connections* 161 (Bloomsbury 2018).
2. John Paul Lederach, *The Moral Imagination* 94 (Oxford University Press 2005).

§9.02 CHANGING THE FRAME; FRAMING THE CHANGES

In the EU Mediation Directive, mediation is understood and presented as an alternative to litigation.[3] Such an understanding has led to a continued focus on the relationship between mediation and litigation in identifying proposals to achieve the directive's as yet unfulfilled aim of increasing the use of cross-border mediation in the EU. As discussed in Chapter 2, these include forms of mandatory mediation, quotas of the number of mediations compared to litigated cases and, more recently, the European Parliament's recommendation for information measures which convey the time and cost savings which mediation can bring compared to litigation. The continued focus on mediation's relationship with litigation, to the exclusion of other methods of dispute resolution, has resulted in recommendations which are insufficient to address fully the barriers to the use of mediation.

The interviews conducted for this book with key users of dispute resolution processes for EU cross-border commercial disputes reveal the prominent role which negotiation, and in particular, negotiation pre-litigation or arbitration, plays as a dispute resolution process for such disputes. As considered in Chapter 6, a key and unexpected theme which emerged from the interviews was the interviewees' preference for such negotiation as a dispute resolution process for their EU cross-border commercial disputes. This is an important insight as negotiation has been neglected in the academic empirical research on commercial cross-border dispute resolution processes to date which has focused predominantly on the comparative use of litigation, arbitration and mediation.[4] The qualitative nature of this research, conducted by way of semi-structured interviews, enabled the valued and central role played by negotiation in EU cross-border commercial disputes to come to light.[5] The interviewees' emphasis on negotiation as a valued method of cross-border dispute resolution sets the scene for important findings regarding the relationship between mediation and negotiation and its impact on the use of mediation, as are explored below.

Against this backdrop of negotiation's prominent role as a dispute resolution process for EU cross-border commercial disputes can be placed another key theme which emerged from the interviews: the interviewees' association of mediation with negotiation and, in particular, understanding mediation to be an extended and assisted form of negotiation. As addressed in Chapter 6, associating mediation with negotiation would be a significant departure from the EU's understanding and portrayal of mediation by reference to litigation, as an alternative to litigation. Importantly, an understanding of mediation as an extension of negotiation, rather than simply as an alternative to litigation, influences the direction in which those who seek to promote mediation might look for measures to further its use. Such an understanding prompts them to look more widely beyond those measures which have been identified to date by reference to litigation.[6]

---

3. *See* further Chapter 2.
4. *See* Chapter 6.
5. *See* Chapter 6.
6. *See* §9.02 for the measures which have been identified by reference to litigation.

Further, and as explored in Chapter 6, such an understanding also encourages us to consider the impact of presenting mediation as an assisted form of negotiation rather than as an alternative to litigation. Given the central and favoured role played by negotiation as a dispute resolution process for EU cross-border commercial disputes, the research findings suggest that it may be more effective for the EU to emphasise the connection between mediation and negotiation, rather than between mediation and litigation. This becomes particularly relevant given a further theme which emerged regarding how the preservation of relationships is a factor which influences disputants' choice to use cross-border mediation. As considered in Chapter 7, arguably, the EU's approach to date of focusing on the relationship between mediation and litigation,[7] with the consequent association of mediation with the adversarial and adjudicative process of litigation, does not assist in emphasising this characteristic of mediation. An emphasis in the promotion of mediation on the association between mediation and negotiation, with negotiation being a consensual process, familiar to and favoured by the parties, may encourage those disputants for whom the preservation of relationships is an important issue to both use and propose mediation. Further, given the apparent familiarity of commercial parties with negotiation and, according to the interviewees, their general lack of awareness of mediation, associating mediation with negotiation may be a useful association for those seeking to raise awareness of mediation.

It is, however, intriguing to note that mediation's association with negotiation – with mediation being, in essence, extended and assisted negotiation – also raises obstacles to the increased use of mediation. As considered in Chapter 8, the relationship between mediation and negotiation reveals a paradox: such a relationship raises both an opportunity and an obstacle. The opportunity is that mediation is associated with a dispute resolution process which is familiar to and favoured by disputants. And the obstacle is that mediation's association with negotiation leads to barriers to the use of mediation. Such barriers, identified in the research for this book, include a scepticism as to what mediation can add to negotiation, an associated fear of being regarded as having failed for not having been able to resolve the dispute through negotiation, a reluctance to maintain responsibility for the resolution of the dispute (which disputants are required to do if they continue to mediation and of which they can be absolved if they send the dispute to an adjudicative process such as litigation or arbitration) and an associated concern about being criticised for failing to get a good deal in the mediation. Such barriers come into clear sight through an appreciation of the relationship between mediation and negotiation. They do not emerge from a focus on understanding mediation as an alternative to litigation, a focus which has led the EU to emphasise the time and cost savings which mediation can bring compared to litigation. While mediation is commonly referred to as assisted negotiation in the mediation literature, a key finding from the research conducted for this book, and which has not been explored to date from the disputants' perspective in the cross-border context, is how the relationship between mediation and negotiation can affect disputants' proclivity to use mediation.

---

7. The EU Mediation Directive's focus on the relationship between mediation and litigation is considered in Chapter 2. *See*, in particular, text to (n. 80)-(n. 87) in Chapter 2.

Of particular note is the theme of failure both as regards the parties' fear of being regarded as having failed for not having been able to resolve the dispute in unassisted negotiations, and their fear of being regarded as having failed for getting a deal in the mediation which others might consider to be unsatisfactory. This issue appears not to have been identified in earlier research in this context and it is a new and important contribution to furthering our understanding of why parties may not use mediation. As noted in Chapter 8, it is interesting to compare the issue of failure with the issue of weakness, which has been identified in earlier research and was, again, identified in this research. The CPR Pledge sought to address the concern that a suggestion to mediate may make the proposing party look weak or suggest that they regard their case to be weak.[8] As was explored in Chapter 8, the issue of weakness relates to how one looks to others outside of one's company, i.e., those to whom one suggests mediation. However, the theme of failure identified in the research for this book relates to how one is perceived within one's company, i.e., others in your company regard you as having failed for needing to use mediation rather than resolving the dispute yourself in unassisted negotiation, and then regarding you as having failed to get a good deal in the mediation if it is used.

Indeed, a focus on the relationship between mediation and negotiation may be, to use one of Lederach's concepts described in Chapter 4, the critical yeast in the promotion of mediation. The critical yeast is that little thing that makes the difference; it is the catalyst which makes other things grow exponentially. In his work as a mediator, Lederach identified the critical yeast in bringing about change in protracted conflicts to be the 'who' rather than the 'how many'. It was identifying the small set of people who, when brought together, created the quality of the platform which brought about change, rather than simply focusing on bringing together large quantities of people. In Lederach's work, it was who these people were *in relationship* to one another which offered the potential for exponential change in profound and protracted conflicts.[9]

Returning to the context of the promotion of mediation, the critical yeast appears not to be Lederach's 'who in relationship to one another' but rather 'what in relationship to what'. What mediation and negotiation are in relationship to each other is an important, and as yet overlooked, focus in the EU's continued efforts to promote mediation. A focus on the relationship between mediation and negotiation may offer a platform for the promotion of mediation which may prove to be more effective than simply focusing on seeking to hastily generate an increase in the number of mediations by way of measures identified through mediation's relationship with litigation, such as mandatory mediation which, as explained in Chapter 2, is more problematic in the cross-border context. Recommendations which stem from the relationship between mediation and negotiation are identified later in this chapter. Drawing on Hari's words which opened this chapter, changing the frame from understanding mediation to be an alternative to litigation to understanding mediation to be a form of assisted and extended negotiation frames the changes for mediation's promotion. In other words, if

8. *See* Chapter 8 for details of the CPR Pledge.
9. *See* Chapter 4 for a detailed description of Lederach's concept of the critical yeast.

the EU were to change the way it views and presents mediation by framing it as assisted and extended negotiation, this would enable the identification of reasons which have not been explored to date by the EU regarding why parties might not use mediation, which may then lead to different approaches to its promotion of mediation.

It is important to recognise that framing mediation as a form of extended and assisted negotiation, as we are prompted to do by the interviewees' insights, moves us away from understanding and presenting mediation to be the avoidance of something (i.e., litigation), as the EU has done to date, to see it as an extension of what disputants already frequently do (i.e., negotiation) and to appreciate what such an extension asks of those disputants. As the research findings suggest, for disputants mediation is not simply the avoidance of litigation but rather mediation asks disputants: to accept that engaging a third party to assist in their negotiations may add value to their own, unassisted negotiation efforts; to continue to take responsibility for resolving their disputes; to risk being regarded as having failed for not having been able to resolve the dispute through unassisted negotiations; to risk being criticised for the outcome achieved in mediation; and to adopt a more nuanced inquisitorial way of thinking about disputes rather than a right or wrong, black or white approach to disputes. This is certainly asking a lot of the parties. Indeed, further uncomfortable demands which mediation makes of its users have been identified by Hicks, including that mediation 'asks parties to see the issue from the other's point of view, when each wants to believe that they see the situation accurately'[10] and 'asks parties to move from the security of strongly held positions to the discomfort and uncertainty of focusing on interests'.[11] An acknowledgement of what is being asked of parties when they mediate – rather than simply focusing on what they are avoiding (i.e., litigation) – directs those who seek to promote mediation to consider how they might encourage and support such parties in selecting and using mediation given what they are asking parties to *do*, rather than to *avoid*, by choosing mediation.

To sum up, viewing mediation through the frame of the disputants' perspective leads to framing mediation not as an alternative to litigation but rather as assisted and extended negotiations. Such an understanding of mediation reveals barriers to the use of mediation which have not been considered by the EU to date in its efforts to promote mediation. An awareness of such barriers leads to a recognition of what is being *asked of* disputants in pursuing mediation which differs to the EU's approach of emphasising what mediation enables disputants to *avoid* (i.e., litigation). Framing the use of mediation in this way presents the changes which are needed in its promotion. To promote mediation in a way which resonates with potential users, such a promotion will need to acknowledge what is being asked of disputants by pursuing mediation, for example, by conveying what mediation might add to disputants' own negotiation efforts and by supporting those who may choose to use it. Such an approach would be a marked change to that which has been employed by the EU to date with its focus on

10. Tim Hicks, *Embodied Conflict* 154 (Routledge 2018).
11. *Ibid*. Further, Hicks explains that collaborative conflict resolution processes, such as mediation, require parties to overcome or control their core neural responses to conflict.

mediation's relationship with litigation and in particular how mediation enables disputants simply to avoid the cost and time of litigation.

Finally, and on a broader note, a promotion of mediation which draws on the relationship between mediation and negotiation, rather than simply focuses on how mediation enables parties to avoid the cost and time of litigation, could be a more principled one if it could promote mediation on the basis of what mediation can bring to the parties' own negotiation efforts. In the context of the UK's continued focus on the encouragement of mediation instead of litigation, including calls for mandatory mediation, Genn has argued that a more principled justification for mediation policy is needed:

> I believe that policy on mediation requires more in the way of principled justification. Who needs mediation and what for? Is it to reduce expenditure on courts? Is it to provide more access to justice? Is it simply access to quicker settlement? Or is it about encouraging harmony and moral growth?[12]

Or is it to assist those who would like to continue to negotiate to do so? A promotion of mediation which recognises the key role played by negotiation, which appreciates all that is being asked of parties in using mediation, and could demonstrate what mediation can add to negotiation may well be a more principled one. If further focus on this issue cannot convincingly determine the value which mediation can add to negotiation, this of itself would be an important finding which would suggest that those in the field of mediation would need to enhance what mediation can offer to disputants before further promoting it.[13]

In short, under a principled promotion, the case must be made for mediation's effectiveness as compared to unassisted negotiations rather than the EU's continued sole focus on mediation's efficiency compared to the courts.[14] Such a promotion would have at its core a focus on achieving (what mediation might add to the parties' own and early negotiation efforts) rather than avoiding (the time and cost of court).[15] Simply put, such a promotion would be *for* rather than simply *against* something.

---

12. Hazel Genn, *Judging Civil Justice* 123-124 (Cambridge 2010).
13. One way in which the field of mediation may enhance what it can offer to disputants is, as suggested by Tim Hicks, to draw upon the increasing knowledge of how the brain functions to explain why people behave as they do when they are in conflict and to refine conflict resolution practices. Hicks, *supra* n. 10, at 159.
14. Steffek argues for a principled approach to the regulation of dispute resolution which would enable disputants to select the dispute resolution process most suitable for their dispute. He describes that such an approach would require 'coherence and a systematic structure within forms of dispute resolution, across different forms of resolving conflicts and in cross-border conflicts'. Felix Steffek, *The Relationship Between Mediation and Other Forms of Alternative Dispute Resolution* in European Parliament, *The Implementation of the Mediation Directive, Workshop 29 November 2016* (2016) PE 571.395, 47, 43, 47 & 49.
15. This distinction between a focus on achieving compared to avoiding was inspired by the terms from psychology of promotion focus and prevention focus. Under a promotion focus, 'people are oriented toward opportunities and accomplishing aspired goals and generally engage in approach-related behaviours toward positive end states, such as acquiring or consuming desired objects ... people operating under a prevention focus are oriented toward security and responsibilities and generally engage in avoidance-related behaviours away from negative outcomes, such as withdrawing from harmful situations and rejecting aversive end states'.

§9.03 RECOMMENDATIONS

Drawing on the conclusions set out above and the findings included in Chapters 6, 7 and 8, the following recommendations have been identified for the EU in its continued review of the EU Mediation Directive.

[A] Understand and Present Mediation as Extended and Assisted Negotiation Rather Than Only as an Alternative to Litigation

The EU Mediation Directive does not mention the dispute resolution process of negotiation. The only reference in the directive to negotiation is not to the dispute resolution process of negotiation but rather to non-contentious 'pre-contractual negotiations',[16] with the preamble to the directive explaining that the directive does not apply to such negotiations. With its reference to mediation as 'alternative dispute resolution'[17] and its focus on the relationship between mediation and litigation,[18] the directive presents mediation only as an alternative to the courts. Prompted by the interviewees' insights into the central and valued role which negotiation plays as a dispute resolution process for their EU cross-border commercial disputes, their reference to negotiation and not litigation as their comparator when considering whether to use mediation, together with their indications of the value which mediation can bring to unassisted negotiation, the EU should consider referring to and emphasising the relationship between mediation and negotiation, rather than focusing solely on the relationship between mediation and litigation. The starting point is a change in the terminology used.

Further, such a change of terminology and consequently in how mediation is framed, from an alternative to litigation to a form of advanced negotiation, invites a shift in focus away from what mediation enables the parties to *avoid* (i.e., the time and

---

Matthijs Baas, Carsten K.W. De Dreu, Bernard A. Nijstad, *When Prevention Promotes Creativity: The role of Mood, Regulatory Focus, and Regulatory Closure*, 100(5) Journal of Personality and Social Psychology 794, 794 (2011). *See also* Ronald Friedman, Jens Förster, *Effects of Motivational Cues on Perceptual Asymmetry: Implications for Creativity and Analytical Problem Solving*, 88(2) Journal of Personality and Social Psychology 263, 265 (2005); Marieke Roskes, Carsten K.W. De Dreu, Bernard A. Nijstad, *Necessity Is the Mother of Invention: Avoidance Motivation Stimulates Creativity through Cognitive Effort*, 103(2) Journal of Personality and Social Psychology 242, 242-243 (2012). This literature also suggests that the type of focus used (i.e., whether a promotion or prevention focus is used) can influence the way in which people then engage in the particular activity, with a promotion focus encouraging creative thinking. Given that creative thinking is an important element in the mediation process, the adoption of a promotion focus in the promotion of mediation (under which there would be an emphasis of what mediation could achieve rather than avoid) could help to foster the use of such thinking.

16. EU Mediation Directive, Preamble 11 states: 'This Directive should not apply to pre-contractual negotiations'.
17. EU Mediation Directive, Article 1(1).
18. For example, the focus on the relationship between mediation and the courts is seen in EU Mediation Directive Article 1's reference to 'a balanced relationship between mediation and judicial proceedings', Article 5 on court encouragement of mediation (Article 5) and Recital 19 and Article 6 on the enforceability of mediated settlement agreements so that mediation is not 'regarded as a poorer alternative to judicial proceedings'.

cost of litigation) to what mediation *is asking of* the disputants, as identified earlier in this chapter. Currently, in the EU's various efforts to promote mediation, there is no recognition of what is required of disputants when they engage in mediation. Recognising what mediation asks of its users is, for those who seek to promote its use such as the EU, essential to promoting mediation in a way which resonates with potential users. If much is being asked of disputants in using mediation, much must be offered to them to sufficiently support and encourage them in taking that step. The following recommendations are potential ways in which to do so.

In addition, it should be emphasised that as the points identified above arose from the study of commercial mediation and appear to be of particular relevance to that field (rather than the EU Mediation Directive's broader scope of commercial and civil mediation), the following recommendations relate specifically to the promotion of commercial mediation. Accordingly, it is recommended that the EU considers a tailored approach to the promotion of commercial mediation rather than the broader category of civil and commercial mediation.

[B] Further Explore the Value Which Mediation Can Add to Unassisted Negotiation, i.e., How Mediation Can Advance Negotiation

In its latest recommendations, the EU has called on Member States to conduct information campaigns to convey the usefulness of mediation in terms of the time and cost savings it can bring compared to litigation.[19] In light of this book's research findings, it appears that presenting mediation's usefulness only in terms of the time and cost savings it can bring to litigation will be insufficient to address users' reservations about using mediation. Given the theme of disputants not using mediation because of a scepticism as to what it can add to their own negotiation efforts, a focus on what mediation can add to such negotiations is also needed. Put another way, disputants would need assurance that mediation can advance their own negotiation efforts. Information is therefore needed regarding how effective mediation can be compared to unassisted negotiations rather than only how efficient it can be compared to court or arbitral proceedings. As noted earlier, demonstrating mediation's efficiency in relation to litigation does not necessarily demonstrate mediation's effectiveness in relation to unassisted negotiations. Such information on mediation's effectiveness could, for example, include insights from EU cross-border disputants regarding their views of what mediation added to their own unassisted negotiations before engaging in litigation, including both the likelihood of resolving the dispute and the quality of the outcome, and what in particular led to those outcomes, i.e., *why* those outcomes were achieved compared to the outcome of unassisted negotiations.

As noted in Chapter 8, there is considerable theoretical work on how mediation can add value to unassisted negotiation by addressing three broad categories of barriers

19. European Parliament, *Resolution of 12 September 2017 on the Implementation of Directive 2008/52/EC of the European Parliament and of the Council of 21 May 2008 on Certain Aspects of Mediation in Civil and Commercial Matters* (the 'Mediation Directive') [2018] OJ C337/2, para. 11.

which can arise in unassisted negotiation, namely strategic, cognitive and structural barriers. But will disputants feel compelled to use mediation based on theory? As Bush has noted 'Explaining that mediation will "enrich the decisionmaking [sic] environment" is fine in theory, but will this explanation seem relevant to the parties – to put it bluntly, will it "sell"?'[20] In order to offer a more compelling and convincing promotion of mediation to disputants, further empirical work is needed in order to determine, and then convey, the value which mediation might add to disputants' own unassisted negotiation, and in particular early negotiation which is a key dispute resolution method for disputants. While findings from the research for this book suggest the value which mediation can add to such negotiation, this particular issue was not a focus of this research and further research is needed.[21] In particular, more research is needed, ideally with disputants, regarding what mediation can (or indeed cannot) add to the disputants' own negotiation efforts for their EU cross-border disputes, including whether or not a resolution is reached, the quality of the resolution, and crucially the reasons why particular resolutions were (or were not) reached. Central to such research will be the involvement of the disputants. Insights into how other disputants consider mediation to add value to negotiation will be far more compelling and convincing for those disputants considering whether to use mediation than insights from mediators or other dispute resolution professionals who have tended to dominate the EU's research to date in this area.[22] The challenge will be gaining the involvement of disputants in such research as this is notoriously difficult to achieve. However, this is a challenge worth pursuing given the unique insights which can be obtained from these essential participants.

Such an approach would be an important addition to the EU's current sole focus on information campaigns on the time and cost savings of mediation compared to litigation. It would also be an important addition to the type of data provided by WIPO on its comparison of the various dispute resolution processes such as mediation, litigation, arbitration and expert determination.[23] If the EU could demonstrate the value which mediation could bring to parties' own negotiation efforts, such information could be helpful to those commercial parties who are already trying to encourage their counterparties to use mediation either by way of inserting a mediation provision into the dispute resolution clause or by way of ad hoc suggestion. If they can point to

20. Robert Bush, *What Do We Need a Mediator for? Mediation's 'Value-Added' for Negotiators*, 12 Ohio State Journal on Dispute Resolution 1, 15 (1996).
21. Interestingly, in the UK context in the Final Report of the Civil Justice Council's ADR Working Group on ADR and Civil Justice, the group noted the desire for better statistical analysis of what is happening in ADR so that 'the success story' could be used to promote ADR. *See* para. 4.7 <https://www.judiciary.uk/wp-content/uploads/2018/12/CJC-ADR-Report-FINAL-Dec-2018.pdf> (accessed 20 May 2020).
22. *See* Chapter 2 for a summary of the research commissioned by the EU for its review of the EU Mediation Directive.
23. As mentioned in Chapter 7, one of the interviewees referred to using data provided by WIPO which compares arbitration, mediation and litigation. Such data appears to be WIPO's *Results of the WIPO Arbitration and Mediation Center International Survey on Dispute Resolution in Technology Transactions* <http://www.wipo.int/export/sites/www/amc/en/docs/surveyresults.pdf> (accessed 20 May 2020).

research which suggests the value which mediation can bring to negotiation, parties may be more willing to accept such proposals to mediate following negotiation.

Further, such research would also be an opportunity to improve mediation were it to identify the need for improvements. If the results of the research were to query the value which mediation can add to negotiation then this would be an important opportunity for those who seek to promote mediation to ensure that mediation is improved before it is further promoted.

[C] Consider How the Value Which Mediation Can Offer to Unassisted Negotiations May Be Enhanced

In addition to exploring the value which mediation might bring to unassisted negotiations, the EU may also want to consider how such value might be enhanced. As considered in Chapter 8, given the importance to disputants of confidentiality, one such possibility may be to create a more robust confidentiality regime for EU cross-border mediation. In particular, as is discussed in Chapters 2 and 8, an enhancement of the EU's current approach to mediation confidentiality would be to ensure that confidentiality is extended to the parties to the disputes rather than only applying to the mediator and his/her administrators.[24] Suggested revised wording for the confidentiality provision in the EU Mediation Directive is to expand the current confidentiality provision to apply not only to 'mediators' and 'those involved in the administration of the mediation process' (as currently provided by Article 7 of the EU Mediation Directive) but also to 'the disputing parties and their representatives'.

An enhanced approach to mediation confidentiality for EU cross-border mediation could be a way to add value to the parties' unassisted EU cross-border negotiation efforts for which there is not a standardised, consistent approach to confidentiality across the EU.

[D] Increase the Visibility of Mediation and Mediators

An important way in which to promote mediation would be to demonstrate that key players are using mediation for their cross-border disputes.[25] As noted in Chapter 8, some interviewees commented that they would be more likely to use EU cross-border mediation if they knew that others were using mediation and also which mediators they were using. In its latest recommendations, the EU has recommended that the Commission should consider the creation and maintenance of 'national registers of

24. For further detail on the confidentiality provision in the EU Mediation Directive *see* Chapters 2 and 8.
25. In spite of the recognised limited use of EU cross-border mediation, as addressed in Chapter 2, it appears from this research study that well-known companies are using EU cross-border commercial mediation. Obviously their names cannot be disclosed due to the anonymity given to the participants of this study. However, this suggests that there would be some data with which to start any such initiative to raise the visibility of cross-border mediation.

mediated proceedings'.[26] The recommendation states that such registers 'could be a source of information for the Commission but also used by national mediators to benefit from best practices across Europe'. Building upon the EU's recommendations, such registers could also serve another important function: to raise the visibility of mediation, i.e., to enable others to see that mediation is being used and by whom. While the process of mediation is confidential, if the parties were to agree to be listed in the register as users of mediation this could be a useful way in which to raise awareness of who is using mediation.

Further, given the theme identified in this research of disputants being reluctant to use mediation given the concern that it suggests that they had failed to resolve the dispute through their own negotiation attempts, seeing that others are willing to use mediation to resolve their disputes may go some way to addressing, and indeed alleviating, this concern.[27] In addition, seeing that others are using mediation may indirectly convey the value which mediation can bring to the parties' own efforts to resolve their disputes.

Those who use mediation may well be willing to contribute to such a register given: the general satisfaction expressed by those interviewees who have experience of mediation; the frustration expressed by some of the interviewees who have used mediation regarding the limited use of mediation; and their own efforts to encourage others to use mediation. Recall for example from Chapter 8, Interviewee 12's frustration regarding the reluctance of others to engage a mediator: '*They overstate their negotiation skills and underestimate the speediness that a mediator can bring. It's ignorance of the people. I am fully aware that this is my opinion. I have to wait.*' Recall as well Interviewee 14's use of the WIPO data to try to convince his counterparties to include a mediation clause in the dispute resolution clause. Accordingly, there may be a willingness from those who have used mediation to contribute to the register if it will assist in generating information which may, in turn, help them in their own efforts to encourage others to use mediation.

Further, if such a register could capture, in an anonymised way in order to preserve the confidential nature of mediation, the key outcomes of the mediation and also the users' views on the mediation, this would be an invaluable source of information for those seeking to promote mediation. It would offer both an opportunity to capture what mediation can do and to identify how mediation may need to be improved.

In addition, given, as noted in Chapter 2, the cross-border scope of the EU Mediation Directive, it would seem prudent for there to be a coordinated pan-European initiative for any such registers rather than the separate national registers recommended by the EU. This would ensure that, consistent with the directive's scope,

26. *European Parliament Resolution of 12 September 2017*, *supra* n. 19, at para. 13.
27. In the UK context, the Civil Justice Council Alternative Dispute Resolution Working Group has recommended the use of a website to offer information on the ADR processes which are available. Further it suggests that examples of the successful use of ADR in settling disputes be included. *See supra* n. 21, at Recommendation 9. In light of the findings of this research, it is suggested that information on the relationship between mediation and negotiation be included on any such website.

cross-border rather than purely domestic data could be captured and, crucially, would allow for consistency in the collection of data across the EU.

As noted in Chapter 8, some interviewees commented that they would be more likely to use EU cross-border mediation if they knew which mediators were commonly being used. The type of pan-European register proposed could be one way in which to capture such information on mediators. This would be a significant extension to the current type of information which is available on mediators, with Article 9 of the EU Mediation Directive only encouraging Member States to provide contact details for mediators and mediation organisations. As mentioned in Chapter 8, inspiration could be drawn from Arbitrator Intelligence, a significant data initiative in international arbitration, for ideas on how to gather and share data on mediators and their mediations.[28] Further information on mediators appears particularly important in the cross-border context given the suggestion arising from the interview data of a higher bar and expectations being applicable for cross-border mediators compared to their domestic counterparts, as addressed in Chapter 7.

Finally, the register could be an important source for the EU's proposed information campaigns considered earlier at Recommendation B. As such, it would be useful for the EU to regard its information campaigns and its recommendation for mediation registers to be coordinated measures rather than the separate initiatives which they currently appear to be. In other words, the data obtained in the registers should be used to inform the information campaigns.

[E] Expand Current Initiatives

As mentioned in Chapter 8, mediation pledges have been used to promote the use of mediation by addressing the concern that suggesting mediation may make the proposing party look weak or imply that its case is weak. For example, under the CPR Pledge signatories commit to exploring the use of ADR for their disputes.[29] Other organisations

28. For a detailed description of Arbitrator Intelligence *see* Catherine Rogers, *Arbitrator Intelligence: From Intuition to Data in Arbitration Appointments*, 11(2) New York Dispute Resolution Lawyer (Spring 2018).
29. More than 4,000 companies have signed the CPR pledge: <https://www.cpradr.org/programs/pledges> (accessed 20 May 2020). The wording of the pledge is: 'We recognize that for many disputes there is a less expensive, more effective method of resolution than the traditional lawsuit. Alternative dispute resolution (ADR) procedures involve collaborative techniques which can often spare businesses the high costs of litigation. In recognition of the foregoing, we subscribe to the following statements of principle on behalf of our company and its domestic subsidiaries: In the event of a business dispute between our company and another company which has made or will then make a similar statement, we are prepared to explore with that other party resolution of the dispute through negotiation or ADR techniques before pursuing full-scale litigation. If either party believes that the dispute is not suitable for ADR techniques, or if such techniques do not produce results satisfactory to the disputants, either party may proceed with litigation.' The pledge can be found at: <https://www.cpradr.org/resource-center/adr-pledges/21st-century-pledge> (accessed 20 May 2020). CPR's mediation pledge is also promoted by CEDR in the UK: <https://www.cpradr.org/news-publications/press-releases/2013-08-20-cpr-and-cedr-enter-into-groundbreaking-agreement-to-jointly-promote-the-cpr-21st-century-pledge-in-united-kingdom-signatories-to-be-announced-november-12th-press/_res/id=Attachments/index=0/CEDR-UK-Agreement-Press-Release.pdf> (accessed 20 May 2020).

offer similar pledges such as WIPO.[30] In light of the findings of this research, those seeking to encourage the use of mediation, such as the EU, may wish to consider adopting an expanded version of such pledges which also addresses the concerns that parties may have about how choosing to use mediation may reflect negatively on them within their companies. Such concerns may include that pursuing mediation emphasises that they could not resolve the dispute themselves in unassisted negotiations, that using mediation requires them to continue to take responsibility for the resolution of the dispute and opens them up to criticism should they resolve the dispute in a way which others deem inappropriate. Accordingly, the standard type of mediation pledge could be expanded to include a section which provides that: companies do not view the use of mediation following negotiations as a reflection of their employees' ability to resolve the dispute in unassisted negotiations; that seeking the assistance of a third-party mediator is not a reflection of any lack of negotiation ability on the part of their employees; that they recognise what mediation requires of their employees, including continuing to take responsibility for the resolution of the dispute; and that they support their employees in the furtherance of their negotiations through the use of mediation.

Further, given, as explained in Chapter 7, the heightened role which dispute resolution clauses can play in the commercial cross-border context in triggering the use of mediation, mediation pledges could also be used to encourage greater use of mediation clauses in contractual dispute resolution clauses. Such pledges could state that parties will explore the inclusion of a mediation provision in their commercial contracts. Such an approach can be found in the mediation pledge for intellectual property and technology disputes by WIPO which was launched on 7 November 2018.[31] Under the WIPO mediation pledge, signatories commit to exploring the use of mediation clauses in the contracts which they enter into and, in the absence of such clauses, to consider exploring the use of mediation to resolve their disputes.[32] Those seeking to promote cross-border mediation in the EU may wish to consider a similar approach for an EU-wide mediation pledge though with a broader scope beyond that of WIPO's scope of intellectual property disputes to encompass all types of commercial disputes.

It should be added here that the type of information on the value which mediation can bring to negotiation, as is addressed in Recommendation B above, may also be another way in which to encourage parties to include a mediation clause in their dispute resolution clauses.

30. The World Intellectual Property Organisation's mediation pledge is available at <https://www.wipo.int/amc/en/mediation/join.html> (accessed 20 May 2020).
31. The launch of WIPO's mediation pledge was announced on its Twitter account on 7 November 2018: <https://twitter.com/WIPO> (accessed 20 May 2020).
32. WIPO's mediation pledge provides: 'We are prepared to explore the inclusion of mediation clauses in contracts and agreements we are party to. In the absence of such clauses, we are prepared to explore the resolution of existing disputes through mediation.' The pledge can be found at: <http://www.wipo.int/amc/en/mediation/pledge_annoucement.html> (accessed 20 May 2020).

[F] An Initiative to House the Other Initiatives

Given the EU's continued aim of encouraging cross-border mediation, the lack of a body dedicated to cross-border mediation in Europe is a significant omission in the EU's various efforts and suggestions. This omission is particularly noticeable given the proliferation of centres focused on the promotion of cross-border mediation in other corners of the world. Key examples include the Japan International Mediation Centre[33] and the Singapore International Mediation Centre.[34] Further, others have taken steps to establish such international centres or expressed their intention to do so. In May 2017, the US state of New Jersey enacted the New Jersey International Arbitration, Mediation and Reconciliation Act aimed at establishing New Jersey as a hub for international dispute resolution. The law enables the creation of centres focused on the resolution of international disputes through mediation, arbitration, conciliation and other forms of dispute resolution other than litigation.[35] In addition, the government of Hong Kong has announced that it will establish 'a unique, fair, impartial and internationally recognised dispute resolution centre for the Belt and Road Initiative to provide dispute resolution services for state-owned enterprises and small and medium-sized enterprises of various countries'.[36] Such centres also facilitate the parties' selection of a mediator for their cross-border disputes, with panels of mediators selected specifically for cross-border disputes.[37] Such a tailored selection is consistent with the seemingly higher bar expected of cross-border mediators compared to their domestic peers, as suggested by the interview data and as mentioned earlier for Recommendation D.

It is also interesting to note that many of these centres have links with academic institutions. The Japan International Mediation Center is located in Doshisha University,[38] and the Singapore International Mediation Centre has hosted events with SIDRA which is based at the School of Law, Singapore Management University.[39] As regards New Jersey, the International Arbitration, Mediation and Reconciliation Act refers to

33. The Japan International Mediation Center was launched on 20 November 2018. Information on the centre can be found at <https://www.jimc-kyoto.jp/about> (accessed 20 May 2020).
34. The Singapore International Mediation Centre was launched in November 2014. Information on the centre can be found at <http://simc.com.sg> (accessed 20 May 2020).
35. The New Jersey International Arbitration, Mediation and Reconciliation Act came into force on 7 May 2017 and can be found at: <ftp://www.njleg.state.nj.us/20162017/AL17/1_.HTM> (accessed 20 May 2020).
36. Government of the Hong Kong Special Administrative Region Press Release of 16 May 2018: <https://www.info.gov.hk/gia/general/201805/16/P2018051600873.htm> (accessed 20 May 2020).
37. For example, regarding the Belt and Road Initiative, China and Singapore have announced the establishment of an international panel of mediators for disputes arising out of this initiative. Siong O, *Singapore, China to Set up International Mediator Panel for Belt and Road Projects* (Channel News Asia, 24 January 2019) <https://www.channelnewsasia.com/news/singapore/singapore-china-belt-road-project-mediator-panel-11161414> (accessed 20 May 2020). Similarly, the Japan and Singapore international centres also have panels of mediators specifically for international disputes.
38. The 'About JIMC-Kyoto' section on the Japan International Mediation Centre's describes how the centre is located in one of Japan's leading universities: the University of Doshisha. *See* further the centre's website <https://www.jimc-kyoto.jp/about> (accessed 20 May 2020).
39. For more information on SIDRA and the events it has hosted with the Singapore International Mediation Centre *see* <https://sidra.smu.edu.sg/about-us> (accessed 20 May 2020).

the use of New Jersey's public research universities as potential homes for the international dispute resolution centres.[40] Such links between mediation hubs and academic institutions facilitate the opportunity for further research into cross-border mediation which can then be used to both enhance and promote such mediation.

The creation of a cross-border mediation body in the EU would offer a forum from which the various recommendations outlined above could be coordinated. It could be a central point which could, for example, coordinate research on cross-border mediation, provide disputants with data on such mediation including the users and mediators involved, and develop the promotion and provision of mediation in a way which responds to disputants' needs.

§9.04 RELEVANCE OF FINDINGS BEYOND THE EU CONTEXT

The research for this book focused on the particular context of EU cross-border commercial disputes and the use of mediation for such disputes. While it would be prudent not to generalise too widely from this specific context,[41] some of the findings appear to have wider resonance and relevance. In particular, the importance of the relationship between mediation and negotiation and, specifically, how the association between mediation and negotiation can affect parties' willingness to use mediation is a theme which may be of relevance in other commercial contexts, including both domestic commercial contexts and other cross-border commercial contexts (such as cross-border contexts beyond the EU). As regards domestic EU commercial contexts, there appears to be no reason why this theme would not equally apply in these narrower EU domestic contexts. However, in other different commercial contexts, such as domestic or cross-border commercial contexts beyond the EU, while the finding that the association between mediation and negotiation can affect parties' willingness to use mediation may also be relevant, the way in which such an association might affect parties' receptivity to mediation may differ. Put another way, while the finding may be relevant across contexts, *how* it applies may differ. Therefore further research in those specific contexts would be needed.

For example, we could consider both the domestic and cross-border context of Asian commercial disputes. The greater significance of 'face-saving'[42] is sometimes attributed to Asian countries.[43] Some therefore assume that such countries will be particularly receptive to the use of mediation due to the avoidance of win-or-lose

40. The New Jersey International Arbitration, Mediation and Reconciliation Act, 7 May 2017, s. 3.
41. The importance of the specificity of a particular context is noted by Menkel-Meadow who states 'the use of mediation in both "other" (foreign to us) nations and at the international level remains somewhat dependent on the specifics of local legal and social culture'. Carrie Menkel-Meadow, *Variations in the Uptake of and Resistance to Mediation Outside of the United States*, University of California, Irvine School of Law, Research Paper No. 2015-80, 189, 213 (2015). <https://papers.ssrn.com/sol3/papers.cfm?abstract_id=2658903> (accessed 20 May 2020).
42. 'Face-saving' has been described as 'the preservation of respect and avoidance of shame within one's reference group.' Sean Ivor, *Selling Mediation in the East. Is there an Asian Way?* Asian Journal of Mediation 1, 5 (2013).
43. Ivor, *supra* n. 42, at 5. *See also*: Joel Lee and Teh Hwee Hwee (eds) *An Asian Perspective on Mediation* 59 (Academy Publishing 2009); Menkel-Meadow, *supra* n. 41, at 216.

outcomes and the preservation of relationships which mediation can offer.[44] However, it would also be interesting to consider whether a greater tendency to value face-saving could also serve as an impediment to the uptake of mediation. Viewed through the lens of the association between negotiation and mediation, could there be a concern that the very suggestion to those with whom one has been negotiating of engaging a mediator may result in the loss of face to those parties who are negotiating?[45] In other words, by asking your counterparty to engage a mediator could this be interpreted as a suggestion that your counterparty is not sufficiently capable as a negotiator to resolve the matter on his/her own? Such a suggestion could result in a loss of face, something which Asian parties might be keener to avoid. So, in this case, the concern would be that a suggestion to mediate could be viewed as a criticism of one's counterparty's negotiation ability. Accordingly, this demonstrates that while the theme which has emerged from this study – that the relationship between negotiation and mediation can affect parties' proclivity to use mediation – may be relevant in different contexts, we must not, however, assume that it applies in the same way in different contexts. This theme does however present us with a new lens through which to explore the use of mediation in different contexts.

§9.05 REFLECTIONS ON THIS RESEARCH

As this books draws to a close, it is important to reflect on its approach, what it did and did not do, and what should now follow.

As explained in Chapter 2, the EU Mediation Directive applies to the broad category of civil and commercial disputes. The research for this book focused only on commercial disputes and the reasons for this choice are explained in Chapter 2. These include the central role of commercial activities in the EU's internal market and the EU's consequent focus on studies on the use of ADR for commercial disputes.[46] In focusing only on commercial disputes, reasons why parties do and do not use mediation for such disputes have come to light which are of particular relevance to the context of commercial disputes, rather than to the broader category of civil disputes.

In particular, the impact which the association between negotiation and mediation appears to have on parties' willingness to use mediation, as identified in this book, may be of greater relevance to commercial disputes due to the notable role played by negotiation in commercial dealings. Given that commercial parties use negotiation both in their everyday course of business dealings as well as for dispute resolution, the reasons discovered in the research for this book of why they do not use mediation (such as their scepticism as to what mediation can add to their own negotiation efforts) may

44. Menkel-Meadow, *supra* n. 41, at 216-217.
45. Parties will try to both preserve their own face as well as that of the other parties. Ivor, *supra* n. 42, at 5. Accordingly, a party may choose not to suggest mediation both as this could result in a loss of face to themselves (through the implication that they could not resolve the matter through negotiations) and also a loss of face to the other parties (through the implication that they, too, were unable to resolve the matter through negotiations).
46. *See* further Chapter 2.

be of specific relevance to the commercial context. It cannot be assumed that such reasons apply equally in the broader civil context.

Further, the important role which dispute resolution clauses can play in triggering the use of mediation may not be equally applicable in the wider category of civil disputes given that certain categories of such disputes, such as family disputes, may not be contractual disputes. The findings which have arisen from focusing on commercial disputes suggest that, as noted earlier, it would be beneficial for those seeking to promote mediation, such as the EU, to adopt a tailored approach which enables matters to be addressed which are specific to that particular context rather than the wider civil and commercial context (which is the scope of the EU Mediation Directive).

In addition, while, as addressed in Chapter 3, the literature on cross-border mediation pays significant attention to the cross-cultural nature of such mediation, culture was not a theme which emerged in the interviews regarding the interviewees' use of mediation. It may be that such a theme did not appear because the interviewees' companies are large multinational companies and the interviewees may therefore be used to, and comfortable with, working and negotiating across numerous cultures. However, issues related to culture may be of significant relevance in other contexts such as for smaller commercial entities or outside of the commercial context.

More broadly, it is important to emphasise, as set out in detail in Chapter 5, that the interviewees' companies are companies with high turnovers, which operate in a variety of EU Member States (and indeed beyond the EU) and which have experience of EU cross-border commercial disputes. The findings from this research may not apply to smaller companies who may not engage in cross-border activities nor have experience of cross-border disputes or who may have smaller value disputes given that they are smaller commercial entities.

Further, as explained in Chapter 4, the research for this book sought to gain the views of the users of dispute resolution processes and, within this category of 'user', the chosen focus was in-house lawyers. The findings warrant further exploration with other actors in the process, including business representatives of the companies who may offer a different perspective on the perception and use of cross-border dispute resolution processes. As Clarke has noted, in-house counsel may continue to have a 'cultural opposition to mediation given the educational background and professional norms and ideology they share with external attorney colleagues'.[47] The perspective of business representatives may therefore differ from that of in-house, and external, counsel. As a researcher it may, however, prove difficult to identify the business representatives in a range of companies who have experience of cross-border disputes and would therefore be well placed to take part in such research. However, further research with business representatives, even if challenging, should be done given the differing perspectives it may reveal.

Finally, this research highlights the central importance of how the association between mediation and negotiation affected disputants' willingness to use mediation. This finding warrants further exploration. The section below on recommendations for

47. Bryan Clark, *Mediation and Lawyers* 39 (Springer 2012).

future research outlines the ways in which our understanding of this central finding can be deepened and nuanced.

§9.06 RECOMMENDATIONS FOR FUTURE RESEARCH

An important area to explore further is the theme, which emerged in this study, that the commercial disputants' association of mediation with negotiation can affect their willingness to use mediation. Reasons why this association can affect disputants' appetite to use mediation include: their scepticism of what mediation can add to negotiation; their concern about being regarded as having failed for having been unable to resolve the dispute in their own negotiations; the requirement that mediation makes of them to continue to take responsibility of the dispute and to risk being criticised for failing to get a good outcome if mediation is used. Further quantitative research which explores the extent to which such factors may affect parties' willingness to use commercial mediation would be an important contribution to the field.

In addition, another valuable contribution would be further qualitative research which explores in-depth this theme of how the association between mediation and negotiation can affect commercial parties' willingness to use mediation. In particular, further questions related to this theme which would be informative to ask include: why disputants think mediation would not add anything to their own efforts to resolve the dispute via negotiation; and what would be needed to demonstrate to them that mediation could offer something beyond what is already offered by unassisted negotiation. While such further qualitative research could be conducted by way of further interviews, the opportunity to spend time in the legal departments of the international companies in order to observe and record cross-border disputants' views on and use of EU cross-border dispute resolution processes would offer particularly rich insights.

Further, given, as identified in Chapter 7, the important role which dispute resolution clauses can play in triggering the use of EU cross-border commercial mediation, qualitative research which explores why parties appear to be comfortable in including a negotiation clause, though not a mediation clause, in their dispute resolution clauses may yield interesting insights for those seeking to promote mediation.

In addition, some of the reasons why parties do not use mediation identified in the interview data and which stem from the association which disputants make between mediation and negotiation suggest that another area which deserves further exploration is the extent to which cognitive biases may affect parties' choice of whether or not to use mediation. For example, given the reasons of disputants' scepticism as to what mediation adds to negotiation and their associated fear of being regarded as having failed for not having been able to resolve the dispute through unassisted negotiations, the cognitive biases of overconfidence, loss aversion and anticipated regret come to mind.[48] While much has been written on how cognitive biases can affect parties during the mediation process,[49] less attention has been given to how such cognitive biases may affect the very entry into the process, i.e., whether or not to use mediation.[50] Barendrecht and De Vries suggest the need for empirical work on this specific issue.[51] For those seeking to promote mediation, a better understanding of the influences at play when parties choose whether or not to use mediation may yield interesting, new insights. As Hicks has explained:

> As a third party, it can be helpful to understand the neural basis for the resistance parties may experience entering into a collaborative, interest-based conflict resolution process ... Understanding the neural basis for resistance that parties may experience can help third parties pay more attention to what may be needed to bring parties to the table and to help them participate effectively once they are at the table.[52]

Finally, following the finding that those who were particularly enthusiastic proponents and users of mediation displayed a notable sensibility to the complexity of disputes, research into the type of attitude towards disputes held by those who do – and indeed who do not – use mediation is also recommended. While, as explained in Chapter 7, the neat and discrete reasons for using mediation which are commonly seen in empirical studies, such as saving time and costs, are undoubtedly easier to explore and quantify, further insights into what *really* leads parties to use, or not to use, mediation may be particularly interesting and useful for those seeking to promote mediation's use.

---

48. By way of brief description of these cognitive biases, as regards the cognitive bias of overconfidence this is the inclination to overestimate the likelihood that we are right. As regards the bias of loss aversion this is the tendency to attach greater weight to future losses than to gains, and as regards the cognitive bias of anticipated regret this is the inclination to anticipate the painful emotion of regret. *See* Daniel Kahneman, *Thinking Fast and Slow* (Penguin 2011) 261-265 on overconfidence, 282-286 on loss aversion, and 346-349 on anticipated regret.
49. On how cognitive biases may influence and inhibit the negotiation process see, for example: Robert Mnookin and Lee Ross, *Introduction* in Kenneth Arrow et al., (eds), *Barriers to Conflict Resolution* 6 (W.W. Norton & Company 1995); Robert Mnookin, *Beyond Winning* 156-167 (Harvard University Press 2000); Jacob Bercovitch & Richard Jackson, *Conflict Resolution in the Twenty-First Century* 28-29 (4th ed. The University of Michigan Press 2012).
50. On this issue of whether the cognitive barriers at play in the resolution of disputes also affect the selection of a dispute resolution process *see* Maurits Barendrecht, Berend R. de Vries, *Fitting the Forum to the Fuss with Sticky Defaults: Failure in the Market for Dispute Resolution Services*, 7 Cardozo Journal of Conflict Resolution 83, 95 (2005). It is a topic also addressed by Don Peters, *Can we Talk – Overcoming Barriers to Mediating Private Transborder Commercial Disputes in the Americas*, 41(5) Vanderbilt Journal of Transnational Law 1251 (2008). Further, as regards the different dispute resolution process of arbitration, Strong has examined how cognitive biases may affect the use of arbitration and how such biases might be addressed. S.I. Strong, *Truth in a Post-Truth Society: How Sticky Defaults, Status Quo Bias, and the Sovereign Prerogative Influence the Perceived Legitimacy of International Arbitration*, University of Illinois Law Review 533 (2018), and *see* pages 576-578 which explain how the 'Reversal Test' heuristic could be used to address the status quo bias for litigation.
51. Barendrecht and De Vries note: 'Is it likely that the barriers to dispute resolution also stand in the way of deciding on the appropriate method of dispute resolution? Unfortunately, we do not know of empirical research answering this question.' Barendrecht and de Vries, *supra* n. 50, at 95.
52. Hicks, *supra* n. 10, at 153.

In closing, not only this section but the book as a whole, the following words attributed to Viktor E. Frankl come to mind:

> Between stimulus and response there is a space. In that space is our power to choose our response. In our response lies our growth and our freedom.[53]

It is hoped that the findings from this study will expand the space upon which disputants can draw when choosing how to address their differences.

53. These words are frequently attributed to Viktor E. Frankl though they do not appear in Frankl's famous *Man's Search for Meaning* (Rider 2004). Rather, they appear in a preface written by Stephen Covey to *Lead or Get Off the Pot! The Seven Secrets of a Self-Made Leader* xiv (Simon & Schuster 2004).

Appendices

APPENDIX 1

Information Sent to Interviewees Before the Interviews

Research study by Anna Howard on EU cross-border commercial mediation

Thank you for kindly agreeing to speak with me regarding my PhD research on cross-border commercial mediation in the EU. The principal purpose of this research is to gain insights from in-house counsel on their experience of, and views on, cross-border commercial mediation in the EU.

There has been much discussion on how to improve the European Mediation Directive on Civil and Commercial Matters (2008/52/EC). My interest is in bringing the voice of the users, and potential users, into this discussion and, more broadly, into the discussion of how to promote mediation. To date, the users' perspective has been notably lacking in much of the relevant research.

Some of the topics which I will explore during our discussion include: your company's use, or lack of use, of commercial EU cross-border mediation; the reasons for using, or not using, mediation; the relationship between the use of mediation for national commercial disputes and its use in EU cross-border commercial disputes; and what you consider to be the greatest obstacles and opportunities for an increased use of EU cross-border commercial mediation.

At this stage, I'd like to mention a few important procedural points:

- This research is aimed only at in-house counsel who have experience of EU cross-border commercial disputes. You do not, however, need experience of mediation.
- Your involvement in my research is on an *anonymous* basis. At the beginning of our discussion, I will ask you some general questions on your company (including its sector, turnover and the countries in which it operates). If you are happy for me to do so, I will refer to your company in my thesis and any related publications with this general information.

- The data which I obtain will be used for my PhD and for any publications arising from it. The data will be treated as strictly confidential and handled in accordance with the Data Protection Act 1998 (England & Wales).
- Ethical approval has been granted for this research from Queen Mary University of London. Should you have any concerns about the way in which the research is conducted, in the first instance please let me know. You may also contact the Secretary at the Queen Mary Ethics of Research Committee at research-ethics@qmul.ac.uk.
- Finally, I will take verbatim notes of our discussion and, on the next working day following our discussion, I will send you my notes for any comments you may have on them.

Thank you again for your time. Our discussion should take no more than 20 minutes.

APPENDIX 2

Interview Guide

Initial points to share with the interviewee

Thank you very much for taking the time to speak with me. As outlined in the note which I sent you before our meeting/call, the principal purpose of this research is to gain insights from in-house counsel on their experience of, and views on, cross-border commercial mediation in the EU.

I will make detailed notes of our discussion and will send you my notes. Please do let me know if you would like me to make any amendments to these.

The Interview

A. Background information on you and your company

Your answers are on an *anonymous* basis. It would however be very helpful to refer to your company by sector, size and the location of its activities. Would you be happy to provide me with that information?

- Sector:
- Turnover for the last full financial year:
- Geographic scope of your organisation:
  - National
  - European Union
  - International (your organisation's activities extend beyond the European Union)
- Headquarters:
- In which EU member states does your organisation operate?
- And now some information about you:
  - Your primary role:
  - May I ask how many years you have been practising law?
  - And in which country are you based:

  - And your involvement in your company's handling of disputes, both cross border and national disputes?
- By way of background information, what is your company's corporate structure for handling disputes, particularly cross-border disputes (for example are decisions about how to handle disputes taken by a team, a person, the business team or the legal team?)

Meaning of Mediation:

At the outset, I'd be very interested in your view of what mediation is.

B. Definitions

A few key terms are frequently used in my questions. In order to ensure that all participants are talking about the same thing, I will share these brief definitions with you:
An *EU cross-border dispute* is a dispute in which at least two parties to the dispute are domiciled or habitually resident in different EU Member States (this definition is based on the definition in the EU Mediation Directive on Civil and Commercial Matters).
A *national dispute* is a dispute in which all parties to the dispute are domiciled or habitually resident in the same EU Member State.
A *commercial dispute* is a dispute between businesses. It does not include disputes between a business and a consumer nor does it include employment disputes between a business and its employees.
Mediation means a consensual process, however named or referred to, in which the parties themselves attempt to reach a settlement of their dispute with the assistance of a mediator who acts as an impartial third party. 'Conciliations' are included if they fall within this definition.

C. QUESTIONS

1. Use of EU cross-border commercial mediation and other dispute resolution processes

1.1 (a) During the past 3 years, approximately how many EU cross-border commercial disputes has your company been a party to?
(b) And which EU Member States were the parties to these disputes from?
1.2 In roughly how many of those disputes did your organisation use EU cross-border commercial mediation?
1.3 If your company used EU cross-border commercial mediation, how satisfied were you with the mediation/s?
1.4 If your company used EU cross-border commercial mediation, did your company use mediation in combination with another type of dispute resolution method (e.g. arbitration, court proceedings)?
1.5 What is your company's preferred method of dispute resolution for EU cross-border commercial disputes?

1.6 Do you have a policy on the dispute resolution clauses to be included in your commercial contracts?
- (a) If YES, how long has that policy been in operation?
- (b) What form does that policy take? (for example is it a formal written policy or an informal understanding)?
- (c) Which dispute resolution method or methods does your policy promote?
- (d) Does your policy on dispute resolution clauses differ depending on whether the commercial contract is national or cross-border in scope?
- (e) If YES, how does it differ?

1.7 Are there any notable differences in your company's level of use of mediation for EU cross-border commercial disputes compared to your company's level of use of mediation for national commercial disputes?

1.8 Is your decision to use mediation for EU cross-border disputes influenced by your use of mediation for national disputes? If so, how?

2. Triggers for EU cross-border commercial mediation

2.1 Drawing on your experience over the past 3 years, how has your use of mediation for EU cross-border commercial disputes been triggered?

2.2 If by a dispute resolution clause in a contract, how many of your disputes are contractual disputes?

2.3 And who makes the final decision about the content of that clause?

2.4 Do parties tend to adhere to the specific type of dispute resolution process stated in the dispute resolution clause?

2.5 Have you used mediation for national commercial disputes?
If YES, are the triggers for the use of mediation for the national disputes the same as for EU cross-border disputes?

3. Reasons for using mediation

Part 1: Reasons for using mediation for EU cross-border commercial disputes

(If NO experience of EU cross-border commercial mediation move to 3.3)

3.1 What were the main reasons for using mediation for EU cross-border commercial disputes?

3.2 (a) Have you used mediation for national disputes?
(b) If so, did your main reasons for using mediation for national disputes differ to your main reasons for using mediation in EU cross-border commercial disputes?

For those who have NOT used mediation for EU cross-border commercial disputes:

3.3 What are the main reasons why your company has NOT used mediation for EU cross-border commercial disputes?
3.4 And do these reasons also apply to your decisions to NOT use mediation for national commercial disputes?

4. Compliance with outcome of mediation

4.1 Over the past 3 years or so, for the EU cross-border commercial disputes which were settled using mediation, what was the approximate compliance rate by the parties with the settlement agreements?
4.2 How does the compliance rate with settlement agreements reached in the mediation of EU cross-border commercial disputes compare with the compliance rates for the outcomes of (i) arbitration and (ii) litigation for such cross-border commercial disputes?
4.3 And now to national commercial disputes: over the past 3 years or so, for the national commercial disputes which were settled using mediation, what was the approximate compliance rate by the parties with the settlement agreements?

5. Trends in the use of mediation

EU cross border commercial disputes

5.1 Over the past 3 years or so, have there been any changes in the level of use of mediation for EU cross-border commercial disputes by (a) your company or (b) in your industry sector in general?
5.2 What are your predictions for your company's future use of mediation for EU cross-border commercial disputes? And for your industry sector in general?
5.3 Over the past 3 years or so, have you witnessed any trends in the use of EU cross-border commercial mediation for particular types of dispute (e.g. IP disputes, joint venture disputes, partnership disputes, competition disputes)?
5.4 Over the past 3 years or so, have any industry changes influenced your company's use of EU cross-border commercial mediation (changes in the industry could for example include a change in the major players in the industry, a change in the type of business conducted or an increase in joint ventures)?

Domestic disputes

5.5 And now turning to national disputes, have there been any changes in the level of use of mediation for national commercial disputes (a) by your company and (b) in your industry sector in general

5.6 And what are your predictions for your company's future use of mediation for national disputes, and for your industry sector in general?

6. Users' needs

6.1 What does your company need in order to use/increase its use of EU cross-border commercial mediation?
6.2 What would you want to see in the process of mediation?
6.3 What do you consider to be the greatest obstacles to the increased use of mediation in EU cross-border commercial disputes?
6.4 What do you consider to be the greatest opportunities for an increase in the use of mediation for EU cross-border commercial disputes?

7. Current proposals to amend the directive and promote the use of EU cross-border mediation

I would be very interested in your thoughts on some of the recent legislative proposals to promote EU cross-border mediation. These include:

- mandatory initial mediation sessions: before a dispute can be filed with the court, parties would be required to have an initial mediation session with a trained mediator.
- In the alternative, Member States would be required to meet a quota of the number of mediations compared to the number of judicial proceedings. The latest suggestion has been of a quota of more than one mediation for every two court proceedings; and
- A direct enforcement mechanism for settlement agreements arising from the mediation of EU cross-border disputes: under this approach, which has been referred to as an 'EU Mediation Settlement Certificate', a mediation settlement agreement entered into in one EU Member State would be directly enforceable in another Member State without the need for any judicial ratification.

8. Finally

8.1 What question should I have asked you?

Would you know any in-house counsel who might be willing to speak with me?

Bibliography

Abramsom H L, *Time to Try Mediation of International Commercial Disputes*, 4 Journal of International and Comparative Law 323 (1997-1998).

Adler P, Lovaas, K. and Milner N, *The Ideologies of Mediation: The Movement's Own Story*, 10 Law and Policy 317 (1988).

ADR Centre, *The Cost of Non-ADR – Surveying and Showing the Actual Costs of Intra-Community Commercial Litigation* (June 2010) 5 <https://www.adrcenterfordevelopment.com/wp-content/uploads/2018/06/Survey-Data-Report.pdf> (accessed 10 June 2020).

Agapiou A and Clark B, *Scottish Construction Lawyers and Mediation: An Investigation into Attitudes and Experiences*, 3(2) International Journal of Law in the Build Environment 159 (2011).

Agapiou A and Clark B, *A Follow-Up Empirical Analysis of Scottish Construction Clients' Interaction with Mediation*, 32(3) Civil Justice Quarterly 362 (2013).

Agapiou A, *The Factors Influencing Mediation Referral Practices and Barriers to Its Adoption: A Survey of Construction Lawyers in England and Wales*, 7(3) International Journal of Law in the Built Environment 231 (2015).

Agapiou A and Clark B, *The Practical Significance of Confidentiality in Mediation*, 37(1) Civil Justice Quarterly 74 (2018).

Alberstein M, *The Jurisprudence of Mediation: Between Formalism, Feminism and Identity Conversation*, 11 Cardozo Journal of Conflict Resolution 1 (2009-2010).

Alexander N, *Mediation in Practice: Common Law and Civil Law Perspectives Compared*, 6 International Trade and Business Law Annual 1 (2001).

Alexander N, *What's Law Got To Do With It? Mapping Modern Mediation Movements in Civil and Common Law Jurisdictions*, 13(2) Bond Law Review 5 (2001).

Alexander N (ed), *Global Trends in Mediation* (Kluwer Law International 2006).

Alexander N, *The Mediation Metamodel: Understanding Practice*, 26(1) Conflict Resolution Quarterly 97 (2008).

Alexander N, *International and Comparative Mediation, Global Trends in Dispute Resolution*, Vol. 4 (Kluwer Law International 2009).

Alexander N, *Nudging Users Towards Cross-border Mediation: Is it Really About Harmonised Enforcement Regulation?* 7(2) Contemporary Asia Arbitration Journal 405 (2014).

Alexander N, Walsh S, and Svatos M (eds), *EU Mediation Law Handbook* (Kluwer 2017).

Alexander N and Chong S, *The Singapore Convention on Mediation – A Commentary* (Wolters Kluwer 2019).

American Bar Association Section of Dispute Resolution, *Report of the Task Force on Research on Mediator Techniques* (12 June 2017) <https://www.americanbar.org/content/dam/aba/administrative/dispute_resolution/med_techniques_tf_report.pdf> (accessed 10 June 2020).

Amsler L B, *Dispute System Design and the Global Pound Conference 2016 Symposium: Where Do We Come From: What Are We: Where Are We Going: Keynote,* 18 Cardozo Journal of Conflict Resolution 621 (2017).

Andrews N, *Mediation: International Experience and Global Trends,* 4(2) Journal of International and Comparative Law 217 (2017).

Apollon G, *Cross-Cultural Deal Mediation as a New ADR Method for International Business Transactions,* 20 Law & Business Review of the Americas 255 (2014).

Arrow K J and others (eds), *Barriers to Conflict Resolution* (W.W. Norton & Company 1995).

Association for International Arbitration (ed.), *The New EU Directive on Mediation, First Insights* (Maklu 2008).

Avruch K and Black P W, *A Generic Theory of Conflict Resolution Theory,* 3(1) Negotiation Journal 87 (1987).

Avruch K, *Culture and Conflict Resolution* (United States Institute of Peace Press 1998).

Avruch K, *Culture and Negotiation Pedagogy,* 16 Negotiation Journal 339 (2000).

Avruch K, *Context and Pretext in Conflict Resolution,* 2 Journal of Dispute Resolution 353 (2003).

Avruch K, *Type I and Type II Errors in Culturally Sensitive Conflict Resolution Practice,* 20 Conflict Resolution Quarterly 351 (2003b).

Avruch K, *Culture as Context, Culture as Communication: Considerations for Humanitarian Negotiators,* 9 Harvard Negotiation Law Review 391 (2004).

Avruch K, *Context and Pretext in Conflict Resolution* (Paradigm Publishers 2013).

Baas M, De Dreu C K W and Nijstad B A, *When Prevention Promotes Creativity: The Role of Mood, Regulatory Focus, and Regulatory Closure,* 100(5) Journal of Personality and Social Psychology 794 (2011).

Bar Council of England & Wales, Bar Council's Response to the Commission's Public Consultation on the Application of Directive 2008/52/EC (dated 11 December 2015) <https://www.barcouncil.org.uk/media/407911/bar_council_response_to_the_european_commission_consultation_paper_-_the_application_of_directive_200852ec_on_certain_aspects_of_mediation_in_civil_and_commercial_matters.pdf> (accessed 10 June 2020).

Barendrecht M and de Vries B R, *Fitting the Forum to the Fuss with Sticky Defaults: Failure in the Market for Dispute Resolution Services,* 7 Cardozo Journal of Conflict Resolution 83 (2005).

Barkai J, *What's a Cross-Cultural Mediator to do? A Low-Context Solution for a High-Context Problem*, 10 Cardozo Journal of Conflict Resolution 43 (2008-2009).

Bauer M and Gaskel G (eds), *Qualitative Researching with Text, Image and Sound: A Practical Handbook* (Sage Publications 2000).

Bazerman M and others, *The Effect of Agents and Mediators on Negotiating Outcomes* in Connolly T, Arkes H and Hammond K (eds), *Judgment and Decision Making* (Cambridge University Press 2000).

Bercovitch J, *Mediation Success or Failure: a Search for the Elusive Criteria*, 7 Cardozo Journal of Conflict Resolution 289 (2005-2006).

Bercovitch J and Elgström O, *Culture and International Mediation: Exploring Theoretical and Empirical Linkages*, 6 International Negotiation 3 (2001).

Bercovitch J and Jackson R, *Conflict Resolution in the Twenty-first Century: Principles, Methods and Approaches* (4th ed. The University of Michigan Press 2012).

Berensen B, *The Mediation Imperative: Why Successful Companies Cannot Afford to Ignore Mediation*, Singapore Mediation Lecture 2014 <https://www.imimediation.org/wp-content/uploads/2018/06/Singapore-Mediation-Lecture-2014.pdf> (accessed 10 June 2020).

Berger K P, *Private Dispute Resolution in International Business: Negotiation, Mediation, Arbitration* (3rd ed. Kluwer Law International 2015).

Billiet P and Kurlanda E, *An Introduction to the Directive on Certain Aspects of Mediation in Civil and Commercial Matters* in *Association for International Arbitration* (ed), *The New Directive on Mediation, First Insights* (Maklu, 2008).

Birch E, *The Historical Background to the EU Directive on Mediation*, 72(1) Arbitration 57 (2006).

Blackaby N and others, *Redfern and Hunter on International Arbitration* (6th ed. Oxford University Press 2015).

Blanke G, *The Mediation Directive: What Will It Mean For Us?* 74(4) Arbitration 441 (2008).

Bolskey J B, *The Proper Role of the Mediator: Rational Assessment, Not Pressure*, 10 Negotiation Journal 367 (1994).

Bond G, *Mediation and Culture: The Example of the ICC International Commercial Mediation Competition*, 29(3) Negotiation Journal 315 (2013).

Bond G, *Who Should Be Promoting Mediation and Why? Mediation in Germany: The Poor Cousin to the Courts* (*Kluwer Mediation Blog*, 24 November 2016) <http://mediationblog.kluwerarbitration.com/2016/11/24/who-should-be-promoting-mediation-and-why-mediation-in-germany-the-poor-cousin-to-the-courts/> (accessed 10 June 2020).

Bondy V, Mulcahy L and others, *Mediation and Judicial Review: An Empirical Research Study* (The Public Law Project 2009) <http://www.nuffieldfoundation.org/sites/default/files/files/MediationandJudicialReview.pdf> (accessed 10 June 2020).

Born G B, *International Commercial Arbitration* (2nd ed. Kluwer Law International 2014).

Bosnak J, *The European Directive: More Questions than Answers* in Ingen-Housz A (ed), *ADR in Business* Vol. II (Wolters Kluwer 2011).

Boulle L, *Mediation: Principles, Process, Practice* (Butterworths 1996).

Boulle L, *International Enforceability of Mediated Settlement Agreements; Developing the Conceptual Framework,* 7 Contemporary Asia Arbitration Journal 35 (2014).

Brady A, *Mediation Developments in Civil and Commercial Matters Within the European Union,* 75(3) Arbitration 390 (2009).

Brady A, *Time for Reflection,* New Law Journal (29 July 2011).

Braun V and Clarke V, *Using Thematic Analysis in Psychology,* 3 Qualitative Research in Psychology 77 (2006).

Braun V and Clarke V, *Teaching Thematic Analysis: Overcoming Challenges and Developing Strategies for Effective Learning,* 26(2) The Psychologist 120 (2013).

Brock D and Pither R, *How International Law Firms Might Approach the Subject of ADR with Their Clients* in Arnold Ingen-Housz (ed), *ADR in Business* (Wolters Kluwer 2011).

Brooker P and Lavers A, *Commercial and Construction ADR: Lawyers' Attitudes and Experience,* 20 Civil Justice Quarterly 327 (2001).

Brooker P and Lavers A, *Mediation Outcomes: Lawyers' Experience with Commercial and Construction Mediation in the United Kingdom,* 5 Pepperdine Dispute Resolution Law Journal 161 (2005).

Brooker P and Wilkinson S, *Mediation in the Construction Industry: An International Perspective* (Spon Press 2010).

Brooker P, *Mediation Law: Journey Through Institutionalism to Juridification* (Routledge 2013).

Bryman A, *Social Research Methods* (5th ed. OUP 2016).

Bryson A and McConville S, *The Routledge Guide to Interviewing* (Routledge 2014).

Buhring-Uhle, C, Kirchhoff L and Scherer G, *The Arbitrator as Mediator: Some Recent Empirical Insights,* 20(1) Journal of International Arbitration 81 (2003).

Buhring-Uhle C, Kirchhoff L and Scherer G, *Arbitration and Mediation in International Business* (2nd ed. Kluwer Law International 2006).

Burns S, *Thinking about Fairness and Achieving Balance in Mediation,* 35 Fordham Urban Law Journal 39 (2008).

Bush, R A B, *What Do We Need a Mediator For? Mediation's Value-Added for Negotiators,* 12 Ohio State Journal on Dispute Resolution 1 (1996-1997).

Bush, R A B and Folger J, *The Promise of Mediation* (Revised ed. Jossey-Bass 2005).

Bush, R A B, *Staying in Orbit, or Breaking Free: The Relationship of Mediation to the Courts over Four Decades,* 84 North Dakota Law Review 705 (2008).

Bush, R A B and Folger J, *Mediation and Social Justice: Risks and Opportunities,* 27 Ohio State Journal on Dispute Resolution 1 (2012).

Bush, R A B and Folger J, *Reclaiming Mediation's Future: Re-Focusing on Party Self-Determination,* 16 Cardozo Journal of Conflict Resolution 741 (2014).

Cane P and Kritzer H (eds), *The Oxford Handbook of Empirical Legal Research* (OUP 2010).

Carroll E and Mackie K, *International Mediation – The Art of Business Diplomacy* (Tottel Publishing 2006).

Carroll E and Mackie K, *International Mediation: Breaking Business Deadlock* (3rd ed. Bloomsbury Professional 2016).

Centre for Effective Dispute Resolution (CEDR), *Survey of In-House Use of Commercial Mediation* (7 March 2013) <https://www.cedr.com/docslib/In-House_Mediation_survey.pdf> (accessed 20 July 2019). This study is no longer available on CEDR's website though is on file with CEDR.

Centre for Effective Dispute Resolution (CEDR), *The Eighth Mediation Audit – A Survey of Commercial Mediator Attitudes and Experience in the UK* (10 July 2018) <https://www.research.net/r/CEDRaudit2018> (accessed 10 June 2020).

Chua E, *The Future of International Mediated Settlement Agreements: of Conventions, Challenges and Choices,* Tan Pan Online: A Chinese-English Journal on Negotiation 1 (2015).

Chua E, *The Singapore Convention on Mediation – A Brighter Future for Asian Dispute Resolution,* 9(2) Asian Journal of International Law 195 (2019).

Civic Consulting, *Study on the Use of Alternative Dispute Resolution in the European Union* (16 October 2009) (submitted to DG SANCO, European Commission) <http://www.civic-consulting.de/reports/adr_study.pdf> (accessed 10 June 2020).

Civil Justice Council, *'ADR and Civil Justice' Interim Report* (October 2017) <https://www.judiciary.uk/wp-content/uploads/2017/10/interim-report-future-role-of-adr-in-civil-justice-20171017.pdf> (accessed 10 June 2020).

Civil Justice Council, *'ADR and Civil Justice' Final Report* (November 2018) <https://www.judiciary.uk/wp-content/uploads/2018/12/CJC-ADR-Report-FINAL-Dec-2018.pdf> (accessed 10 June 2020).

Civil Procedure Rules of England and Wales <http://www.justice.gov.uk/courts/procedure-rules/civil/rules/part01> (accessed 10 June 2020).

Clancy M and Walde T, *Efficiency in Mediation: Solving a Complex Cross-Border Energy Infrastructure Dispute in the Shadow of Three Moving Regulatory Regimes,* 5 Journal of World Investment and Trade 257 (2004).

Clark B, *Lawyers and Mediation* (Springer 2012).

Cloke K, *The Dance of Opposites* (Goodmedia Press 2013).

Coben J R and Thompson P N, *Disputing Irony: A Systematic Look at Litigation about Mediation,* 11 Harvard Negotiation Law Review 43 (2006).

Coben J R, *Barnacles, Aristocracy and Truth Denial: Three Not So Beautiful Aspects of Contemporary Mediation,* 16 Cardozo Journal of Conflict Resolution 779 (2014-2015).

Cohen A J, *Debating the Globalization of U.S. Mediation: Politics, Power, and Practice in Nepal,* 11 Harvard Law Review 295 (2006).

Cohen A J, *Dispute Systems Design, Neoliberalism, and the Problem of Scale,* 14 Harvard Negotiation Law Review 51 (2009).

Cohen A J, *Revisiting Against Settlement: Some Reflections on Dispute Resolution and Public Values,* 78 Fordham Law Review 1143 (2009-2010).

Constantino C A and Lewis M R, *What Dispute Systems Design Can Learn from Project Management,* 31(3) Negotiation Journal 175 (2015).

Council of Europe, European Commission for the Efficiency of Justice, *Mediation Development Toolkit* <https://www.coe.int/en/web/portal/-/the-cepej-adopts-a-toolkit-to-strengthen-the-implementation-of-the-cepej-guidelines-on-mediation> (accessed 10 June 2020).

Council of the European Union, *Action Plan of the Council and the Commission on How Best to Implement the Provisions of the Treaty of Amsterdam on an Area of Freedom, Security and Justice* [1999] OJ C-19.

Covey S, *Lead or Get off the Pot! The Seven Secrets of a Self-Made Leader* (Simon & Schuster 2004).

Creutzfeld N, *Trusting the Middle-Man: Impact and Legitimacy of Ombudsmen in Europe* (June 2016) <https://www.law.ox.ac.uk/trusting-middle-man-impact-and-legitimacy-ombudsmen-europe> (accessed 10 June 2020).

Curran D, *The Role of Mediation in the Resolution of Two Industrial Disputes in Ireland,* 36(5) Employee Relations 496 (2014).

D'Alessandro E, *Enforcing Agreements Resulting from Mediation Within the European Judicial Area: A Comparative Overview from an Italian Perspective* (1 October 2011) <https://papers.ssrn.com/sol3/papers.cfm?abstract_id=1950988> (accessed 10 June 2020).

De Castro I and Chalkias P, *Mediation and Arbitration of Intellectual Property and Technology Disputes,* 24 Singapore Academy of Law Journal 1059 (2012).

De Girolamo D, *Seeking Negotiated Order Through Mediation: A Manifestation of Legal Culture?* 5(2) Journal of Comparative Law 118 (2010).

De Girolamo D, *A View from Within: Reconceptualising Mediator Interactions,* 30 Windsor Yearbook of Access to Justice 103 (2012).

De Girolamo D, *The Fugitive Identify of Mediation* (Routledge 2013).

De Girolamo D, *Rhetoric and Civil Justice: a Commentary on the Promotion of Mediation Without Conviction in England and Wales,* 35(2) Civil Justice Quarterly 162 (2016).

De Hoon M W, *Making Mediation Work in Europe: What's Needed Is a New Balance Between Mediation and Court Proceedings,* 20 Dispute Resolution Magazine 23 (2013-2014).

Deloitte LLP, *London Futures, London Crowned Business Capital of Europe* (2014) <https://www2.deloitte.com/content/dam/Deloitte/uk/Documents/uk-futures/london-futures-london-crowned-business-capital-of-europe.pdf> (accessed 10 June 2020).

De Palo G and Costabile L, *Promotion of International Commercial Arbitration and Other Alternative Dispute Resolution Techniques in Ten Southern Mediterranean Countries,* 7 Cardozo Journal of Conflict Resolution 303 (2005).

De Palo G and Trevor M B (eds), *EU Mediation, Law and Practice* (OUP 2012).

De Palo G, *Mandatory Mediation is Back in Italy with New Parliamentary Rules,* 22 October 2013 <http://www.mondoadr.it/cms/articoli/mandatory-mediation-italy-parliamentary-rules.html> (accessed 10 June 2020).

De Palo G and Canessa R, *Sleeping? Comatose? Only Mandatory Consideration of Mediation Can Awake Sleeping Beauty in the European Union,* 16 Cardozo Journal of Conflict Resolution 713 (2014).

De Palo G, *Mediation as Alternative Dispute Resolution (the Functioning of Directive 2008/52/EC on Certain Aspects of Mediation in Civil and Commercial Matters)*, in European Parliament, *Cross-Border Activities in the EU – Making Life Easier for Citizens* 2015, PE 510.003.

De Palo G and D'Urso L, *Achieving a Balanced Relationship Between Mediation and Judicial Proceedings in Mediation and Private International Law: Improving Free Circulation of Mediation Agreements Across the EU*, in European Parliament, *The Implementation of the Mediation Directive – 29 November 2016, Compilation of In-depth Analyses* <http://www.europarl.europa.eu/RegData/etudes/IDAN/2016/571395/IPOL_IDA(2016)571395_EN.pdf> (accessed 10 June 2020).

Dezalay Y and Garth B G, *Dealing in Virtue: International Commercial Arbitration and the Construction of a Transnational Legal Order* (University of Chicago Press 1996).

Dress T P, *International Commercial Mediation and Conciliation*, 10 Loyola of Los Angeles International and Comparative Law Journal 569 (1988).

Dubey P and Kripalani E, *The Generalist Counsel, How Leading General Counsel Are Shaping Tomorrow's Companies* (OUP 2013).

Drahozal C and Naimark R (eds), *Towards a Science of International Arbitration: Collected Empirical Research* (Kluwer 2005).

Dyson Lord, *A Word on Halsey v Milton Keynes*, 77(3) Arbitration 337 (2011).

Ecorys, *Study on the Use of Alternative Dispute Resolution for Business to Business Disputes in the European Union* (15 October 2012) <https://www.adrcenterfordevelopment.com/wp-content/uploads/2018/06/ADR-Final-Report-151012-1.pdf> (accessed 10 June 2020).

Eijsbouts J A J, *Mediation as Management Tool in Corporate Governance* in Ingen-Housz (ed) *ADR in Business, Practice and Issues Across Countries and Cultures*, Vol. II. (Wolters Kluwer 2011).

Epstein J, *The Use of Comparative Law in Commercial International Arbitration and Commercial Mediation*, 75(4) Tulane Law Review 913 (2000-2001).

Epstein L and Martin A D, *An Introduction to Empirical Legal Research* (Oxford 2014).

Esplugues C and Marquis L (eds.), *New Developments in Civil and Commercial Mediation, Global Comparative Perspectives* (Springer 2015).

Esplugues C and Iglesias J L, *Mediation and Private International Law: Improving Free Circulation of Mediation Agreements Across the EU* in European Parliament, *The Implementation of the Mediation Directive – 29 November 2016, Compilation of In-Depth Analyses* <http://www.europarl.europa.eu/RegData/etudes/IDAN/2016/571395/IPOL_IDA(2016)571395_EN.pdf> (accessed 10 June 2020).

European Code of Conduct for Mediators <http://ec.europa.eu/civiljustice/adr/adr_ec_code_conduct_en.pdf> (accessed 20 July 2019).

European Commission, *Green Paper on Alternative Dispute Resolution in Civil and Commercial Law* COM (2002) 196.

European Commission, *Summary of Responses to the Green Paper on Alternative Dispute Resolution in Civil and Commercial Law* JAI/19/03.

European Commission, *Proposal for a Directive of the European Parliament and of the Council on Certain Aspects of Mediation in Civil and Commercial Matters* COM (2004) 718.

European Commission, *Business-to-Business Alternative Dispute Resolution in the EU* (November 2012) <http://ec.europa.eu/commfrontoffice/publicopinion/flash/fl_347_en.pdf> (accessed 10 June 2020).

European Commission, *Study for an Evaluation and Implementation of Directive 2008/52/EC – the 'Mediation Directive'*, October 2013, <https://publications.europa.eu/en/publication-detail/-/publication/6c84b6a6-913e-4231-a677-55f8fa9ccbb6> (accessed 10 June 2020).

European Commission, *Study for an Evaluation and Implementation of Directive 2008/52/EC – the 'Mediation Directive'*, Updated report – 16 March 2016 <https://publications.europa.eu/en/publication-detail/-/publication/bba3871d-223b-11e6-86d0-01aa75ed71a1> (accessed 10 June 2020).

European Commission, *Report from the Commission to the European Parliament, the Council and the European Economic and Social Committee on the Application of Directive 2008/52/EC of the European Parliament and of the Council on Certain Aspects of Mediation in Civil and Commercial Matters,* COM (2016) 0542.

European Council, *Tampere European Council 15 and 16 October 1999, Presidency Conclusions* <http://www.europarl.europa.eu/summits/tam_en.htm> (accessed 10 June 2020).

European Council, *Lisbon European Council 23 and 24 March 2000, Presidency Conclusions* <http://www.europarl.europa.eu/summits/lis1_en.htm> (accessed 10 June 2020).

European Council and Commission, *Action Plan of the Council and the Commission on How Best to Implement the Provisions of the Treaty of Amsterdam on an Area of Freedom, Security and Justice,* [1999] OJ C19/01.

European Economic and Social Committee, *Opinion of the European Economic and Social Committee on the Proposal for a Directive of the European Parliament and of the Council on Certain Aspects of Mediation in Civil and Commercial Matters,* [2005] OJ C286/1.

European Parliament, *Report on the Proposal for a Directive of the European Parliament and of the Council on Certain Aspects of Mediation in Civil and Commercial Matters*, A6-0074/2007.

European Parliament, *Lessons Learnt from the Implementation of the EU Mediation Directive: the Business Perspective*, (2011) PE 453.173.

European Parliament, *Quantifying the Cost of Not Using Mediation – a Data Analysis* (2011) PE 453.180.

European Parliament, *A European Framework for Private International Law: Current Gaps and Future Perspectives* (2012) PE 462.487.

European Parliament, *Resolution of 13 September 2011 on the Implementation of the Directive on Mediation in the Member States, its Impact on Mediation and its Take-Up by the Courts,* [2013] OJ CE51/17.

European Parliament, *'Rebooting' the Mediation Directive: Assessing the Limited Impact of Its Implementation and Proposing Measures to Increase the Number of Mediations in the EU*, (2014) PE 493.042.

European Parliament, *The Implementation of the Mediation Directive – Workshop 29 November 2016*, (2016) PE 571.395.

European Parliament, *The Mediation Directive – European Implementation Assessment* (2016) PE 593.789.

European Parliament, *Report on the Implementation of Directive 2008/52/EC of the European Parliament and of the Council of 21 May 2008 on Certain Aspects of Mediation in Civil and Commercial Matters*, A8-0238/2017.

European Parliament, *Resolution of 12 September 2017 on the Implementation of Directive 2008/52/EC of the European Parliament and of the Council of 21 May 2008 on Certain Aspects of Mediation in Civil and Commercial Matters (the 'Mediation Directive')* [2018] OJ C337/2.

European Parliament, *A Ten-Year-Long 'EU Mediation Paradox'. When an EU Directive Needs to be More … Directive* (2018) PE 608.847.

Farcas A, '*Implications of the Constitutional Court Decision No. 266/2014 in the Field of Dispute Resolution Through Mediation' (November 10, 2014)*, Romanian Case Law Review Issue 5/2014 <https://ssrn.com/abstract=2520935> (accessed 10 June 2020).

Felstiner W, Abel R and Sarat A, *The Emergence and Transformation of Disputes: Naming, Blaming and Claiming …*, 15(3-4) Law & Society Review 631 (1980-1981).

Filler E, *Commercial Mediation in Europe, An Empirical Study of the User Experience* (Wolters Kluwer 2012).

Fisher R, Ury W and Patton B, *Getting to Yes: Negotiating an Agreement Without Giving In* (3rd ed. rh Business Books 2012).

Folberg J and Taylor A, *Mediation: A Comprehensive Guide to Resolving Conflicts Without Litigation* (1984 Jossey Bass).

Friedman R and Förster J, *Effects of Motivational Cues on Perceptual Asymmetry: Implications for Creativity and Analytical Problem Solving*, 88(2) Journal of Personality and Social Psychology 263 (2005).

Fuller L, *Mediation – Its Forms and Functions*, 44 Southern California Law Review 305 (1970-1971).

Gadlin H, *Conflict Resolution, Cultural Differences, and the Culture of Racism*, 10(1) Negotiation Journal 33 (1994).

Gadlin H, *Remembrance of Pleasures Past: Reflections of a Practitioner* in Ian Macduff (ed) *Essays on Mediation, Dealing with Disputes in the 21st Century* (Wolters Kluwer 2016).

Garth B G, *Taking Dispute Resolution Theory Seriously at Home and Abroad: Prospects and Limitations*, 2 Journal of Dispute Resolution 377 (2003).

Gaultier T, *Cross-Border Mediation: A New Solution for International Dispute Settlement?* 26(1) New York State Bar Association International Law Practicum 38 (2013).

Geertz C, *The Interpretation of Cultures* (Basic Books 1973).

Genn H, Partington M and Wheeler S, *Law in the Real World: Improving Our Understanding of How Law Works* (2006, The Nuffield Inquiry on Empirical Legal Research).

Genn H, *Hazel Genn and Paths to Justice* in Halliday S and Schmidt P, *Conducting Law and Society Research* (Cambridge 2009).

Genn H, *Judging Civil Justice* (Cambridge 2009).

Genn H and others, *Twisting Arms: Court Referred and Court Linked Mediation under Judicial Pressure* (Ministry of Justice Research Series 1/07, May 2007) <https://webarchive.nationalarchives.gov.uk/20110201151141/http://www.justice.gov.uk/publications/docs/Twisting-arms-mediation-report-Genn-et-al.pdf> (accessed 10 June 2020).

Genn H, *What Is Civil Justice for? Reform, ADR, and Access to Justice*, 24 Yale Journal of Law and the Humanities 397 (2012).

Gladwell M, *The Tipping Point* (Abacus 2000).

Global Pound Conference Series, Core Questions, available at: <https://www.imimediation.org/research/gpc/series-data-and-reports/> (accessed 10 June 2020).

Golbert R, *An Anthropologist's Approach to Mediation*, 11 Cardozo Journal of Conflict Resolution 81 (2009-2010).

Golbert R, *The Global Dimension of the Current Economic Crisis and the Benefits of Alternative Dispute Resolution*, 11 Nevada Law Journal 502 (2010-2011).

Government of the Hong Kong Special Administrative Region, Press Release of 16 May 2018: <https://www.info.gov.hk/gia/general/201805/16/P2018051600873.htm> (accessed 10 June 2020).

Grillo T, *The Mediation Alternative: Process Dangers for Women*, 100(6) The Yale Law Journal 1545 (1991).

Gulliver P H, *Disputes and Negotiations; A Cross-Cultural Perspective* (Academic Press 1979).

Guthrie C, *The Lawyer's Philosophical Map and the Disputant's Perceptual Map: Impediments to Facilitative Mediation and Lawyering*, 6 Harvard Negotiation Law Review 145 (2001).

Hager L M and Pritchard R, *Deal Mediation: How ADR Techniques Can Help Achieve Durable Agreements in the Global Markets*, 14 ICSID Review – Foreign Investment Law Journal 1 (1999).

Hale T, *Between Interests and Law, The Politics of Transnational Commercial Disputes* (Cambridge University Press 2015).

Halliday S and Schmidt P (eds), *Conducting Law and Society Research* (Cambridge 2009).

Hann R G and Baar C, Evaluation of the Ontario Mandatory Mediation Program (Rule 24.1): Executive Summary and Recommendations (12 March 2001) <http://www.ontla.on.ca/library/repository/mon/1000/10294962.pdf> (accessed 10 June 2020).

Hanycz C M, *Looking Through the Looking Glass: Mediator Conceptions of Philosophy, Process and Power*, 42(3) Alberta Law Review 819 (2005).

Hari J, *Lost Connections* (Bloomsbury 2018).

Harrington C B and Merry S E, *Ideological Production: The Making of Community Mediation*, 22 Law & Society Review 709 (1988).

Henderson D A, *Mediation Success: An Empirical Analysis*, 11 Ohio State Journal on Dispute Resolution 105 (1996).

Hensler, D R, *Suppose it's Not True: Challenging Mediation Ideology*, 1(5) Journal of Dispute Resolution 81 (2002).

Herbert W A and others, *International Commercial Mediation,* 45 The International Lawyer 111 (2011).

Heron J and Reason P, *The Practice of Co-Operative Inquiry: Research with Rather than on People* in Reason P and Bradbury H (eds) *Handbook of Action Research: Participative Inquiry and Practice* (Sage 2000).

Hicks T, *Embodied Conflict* (Routledge 2018).

Hodges C and Tulibacka M, *Civil Justice in England & Wales – Beyond the Courts* (2009) <https://www.law.ox.ac.uk/sites/files/oxlaw/civil_justice_in_england_and_wales_-_beyond_courts._mapping_out_non-judicial_civil_justice_mechanisms.pdf> (accessed 10 June 2020).

Hodges C, Benohr I, and Creutzfeldt-Banda N, (eds), *Consumer ADR in Europe* (Hart Publishing 2012).

Hodges C, *Delivering Dispute Processes* (Hart 2019).

Hoffman D, *Exploring the Boundaries and Terrain of ADR Practice,* 14 Dispute Resolution Magazine 4 (2007-2008).

Honeyman C, McAdoo B and Welsh N, *Not Quite Protocols: Toward Collaborative Research in Dispute Resolution,* 19(1) Conflict Resolution Quarterly 75 (2001).

Hopt K J and Steffek F, (eds) *Mediation – Principles and Regulation in Comparative Perspective* (Oxford University Press 2013).

Howell-Richardson P, *The European Mediation Directive and some Thoughts on the Principles Involved in Dealing with the Problems Surrounding Mediation Confidentiality,* in Association for International Arbitration (ed), *The New Directive on Mediation, First Insights* (Maklu 2008).

Ingen-Housz A (ed), *ADR in Business: Practice and Issues Across Countries and Cultures,* Vol. II (Kluwer Law 2010).

International Institute for Conflict Prevention and Resolution (CPR) ADR Pledge <https://www.cpradr.org/resource-center/adr-pledges> (accessed 10 June 2020).

International Institute for Conflict Prevention and Resolution (CPR) and the Centre for Effective Dispute Resolution (CEDR), *Insights into Alternative Dispute Resolution,* Winter 2018-2019, <https://www.cpradr.org/news-publications/reports/2019-04-04-cpr-cedr-joint-insights-report-on-the-use-of-adr/_res/id=Attachments/index=0/CEDR%20CPR%20report%20040419.pdf> (accessed 10 June 2020).

International Mediation Institute, Inter-Cultural Certification, <https://imimediation.org/intercultural-certification-criteria> (accessed 10 June 2020).

International Mediation Institute, idrgroup.org and CEDR, *Shaping the Future of International Dispute Resolution* (29 October 2014) <https://www. imimediation.org/wp-content/uploads/2018/11/London-2014-Final-data.pdf> (accessed 10 June 2020).

International Mediation Institute, *How Users View the Proposal for a UN Convention on the Enforcement of Mediated Settlements* (December 2014) <https://www.imimediation.org/wp-content/uploads/2018/06/IMI-UN-Convention-on-Enforcement-Survey-Summary-final-27.11.14.pdf> (accessed 10 June 2020).

International Mediation Institute, *The 2016 IMI International Mediation and ADR Survey: Census of Conflict Management Stakeholders and Trends* <http://www.odreurope.com/assets/site/content/IMI_survey_2016.pdf> (accessed 10 June 2020).

International Mediation Institute, Herbert Smith Freehills and PWC, *Global Pound Conference Series: Global Data Trends and Regional Differences* <https://www.imimediation.org/research/gpc/series-data-and-reports/> (accessed 10 June 2020).

Irvine C, *What Do 'Lay' People Know About Justice? An Empirical Enquiry,* 16(2) International Journal of Law in Context 146 (2020).

Izor S, *Selling Mediation in the East? Is there an Asian Way?* Asian Journal on Mediation 1 (2013).

Jarren B, *The Future of Mediation: A Sociological Perspective,* 1 Journal of Dispute Resolution 49 (2009).

Kahneman D and Tversky A, *Conflict Resolution; A Cognitive Perspective* in Arrow K and others (eds), *Barriers to Conflict Resolution* (W.W. Norton & Company 1995).

Kahneman D, *Thinking, Fast and Slow* (Penguin 2011).

Kakalik J S and others, *An Evaluation of Mediation and Early Neutral Evaluation under the Civil Justice Reform Act* (Rand 1996).

Kallipetis M, *Mediation Privilege and Confidentiality and the EU Directive* in Ingen-Housz A (ed), *ADR in Business, Practice and Issues Across Countries and Cultures* (Wolters Kluwer 2011).

Katz L V, *Compulsory Alternative Dispute Resolution and Voluntarism: Two-Headed Monster or Two Sides of the Coin?* 1 Journal of Dispute Resolution 22 (1993).

King N and Horrocks C, *Interviews in Qualitative Research* (Sage Publications 2010).

Kirk J and Miller M L, *Reliability and Validity in Qualitative Research* (Sage Publications 1986).

Klerman D and Klerman L, *Inside the Caucus: An Empirical Analysis of Mediation from Within,* 12(4) Journal of Empirical Legal Studies 686 (2015).

Kovach K K, *The Vanishing Trial: Land Mine on the Mediation Landscape or Opportunity for Evolution: Ruminations on the Future of Mediation Practice,* 7 Cardozo Journal of Conflict Resolution 27 (2005-2006).

Kovach K K, *The Mediation Coma: Purposeful or Problematic,* 16 Cardozo Journal of Conflict Resolution 755 (2014-2015).

Kvale S and Brinkmann S, *Interviews, Learning the Craft of Qualitative Research Interviewing* (2nd ed. Sage 2009).

Lande J, *Failing Faith in Litigation? A Survey of Business Lawyers' and Executives' Opinions,* 3 Harvard Negotiation Law Review 1 (1998).

Lande J, *Getting the Faith: Why Business Lawyers and Executives Believe in Mediation,* 5 Harvard Negotiation Law Review 137 (2000).

Lande J and Benner P W, *Why and How Business Use Planned Early Dispute Resolution,* 13 University of St. Thomas Law Journal 248 (2017).

Larana E, Johnston H and Gusfield J R, (eds) *New Social Movements* (Temple University Press 1994).

Lawrence J K L, *Mediation Advocacy: Partnering with the Mediator,* 15 Ohio State Journal of Dispute Resolution 425 (2000).

Leathes M, *Negotiation: Things Corporate Counsel Need to Know But Were Not Taught* (Wolters Kluwer 2017).

Law Society of England & Wales, *Response of the Law Society of England and Wales to the Public Consultation on the Application of Directive 2008/52/EC* <http://www.lawsocieties.eu/download?ac=19208> (accessed 10 June 2020).

LeBaron M, *Bridging Troubled Waters* (Jossey Bass 2002).

Lederach J P, *Preparing for Peace: Conflict Transformation Across Cultures* (Syracuse University Press 1995).

Lederach J P, *Building Peace: Sustainable Reconciliation in Divided Societies* (United States Institute of Peace Press 1997).

Lederach J P, *Building Mediative Capacity in Deep-Rooted Conflict,* 26 Fletcher Forum of World Affairs 91 (2002).

Lederach J P, *The Little Book of Conflict Transformation* (Good books 2003).

Lederach J P, *The Moral Imagination* (Oxford University Press 2005).

Lederach J P, *Reconcile* (Herald Press 2014).

Lee J and Hwee T H (eds), *An Asian Perspective on Mediation* (Academy Publishing 2009).

Lewicki, R J, Saunders D M and Barry B, *Essentials of Negotiation* (5th ed. McGraw-Hill 2011).

Limbury A, *Should Mediation be an Evidentiary 'Black Hole'?* 35 University of New South Wales Law Journal 914 (2012).

Lipsky D B and Seeber R L, *The Appropriate Resolution of Corporate Disputes: A Report on the Growing Use of ADR by U.S. Corporations, Scheinman Institute on Conflict Resolution, Cornell University ILR School* <http://digitalcommons.ilr.cornell.edu/cgi/viewcontent.cgi?article=1003&context=icrpubs> (accessed 10 June 2020).

Litov L, Sepe S and Whitehead C, *Lawyers and Fools: Lawyer-Directors in Public Corporations* [2014] Cornell Law Faculty Publications 673 <https://scholarship.law.cornell.edu/facpub/673> (accessed 10 June 2020).

Lo, C-F, *Desirability of a New International Legal Framework for Cross-Border Enforcement of Certain Mediated Settlement Agreements,* 7 Contemporary Asia Arbitration Journal 119 (2014).

Lofland J and others, *Analyzing Social Settings: A Guide to Qualitative Observation and Analysis* (4th ed. Wadsworth 2004).

Ma, W J-M and others, *Enforcing Cross-Border Mediated Settlement Agreements: Colloquium Held at Bond University Faculty of Law on 4 November 2013,* 7 Contemporary Asia Arbitration Journal 3, 15 (2014).

Macduff I (ed), *Essays on Mediation: Dealing with Disputes in the 21st Century* (Wolters Kluwer 2016).

Macfarlane J, *Culture Change? A Tale of Two Cities and Mandatory Court-Connected Mediation,* 2 Journal of Dispute Resolution 241 (2002).

Macfarlane J and Keet M, *Civil Justice Reform and Mandatory Civil Mediation in Saskatchewan: Lessons from a Maturing Program,* 42 Alberta Law Review 677 (2004-2005).

Macfarlane J, *The New Lawyer: How Settlement is Transforming the Practice of Law* (UBC Press 2008).

Macfarlane, J, *ADR and the Courts: Renewing our Commitment to Innovation,* 95 Marquette Law Review 927 (2012).

Macfarlane, J, *The New Lawyer: How Clients are Transforming the Practice of Law* (2nd ed. UBC Press 2017).

Mackie K and others, *The ADR Practice Guide, Commercial Dispute Resolution* (3rd ed. Tottel Publishing 2007).

Marsh B, *A Heart-Felt Plea to the UNCITRAL Drafters* (*Kluwer Mediation Blog,* 17 March 2016) <http://mediationblog.kluwerarbitration.com/2016/03/17/6443/?doing_wp_cron=1592476856.8090310096740722656250> (accessed 10 June 2020).

Marsh B, Oddy A and O'Neill J, *England and Wales* in Alexander N, Walsh S and Svatos M (eds), *EU Mediation Law Handbook* (Wolters Kluwer 2017).

Marzocco A M, and Nino M, *The EU Directive on Mediation in Civil and Commercial Matters and the Principle of Effective Judicial Protection,* 19 Lex ET Scientia International Journal 105 (2012).

Mason P E, *What's Brewing in the International Commercial Mediation Process,* 66(1) Dispute Resolution Journal 64 (2011).

Masucci D and Leathes M, *The Urgent Need for Data: Are the Needs of Users and the Dispute Resolution Market Misaligned?* (*Kluwer Mediation Blog,* 5 November 2014) <http://mediationblog.kluwerarbitration.com/2014/11/05/the-urgent-need-for-data-are-the-needs-of-users-and-the-dispute-resolution-market-misaligned-2/> (accessed 10 June 2020).

Masucci D, *The Global Pound Conference: The Journey to Determine the Needs of Users has Started,* 9(2) New York Dispute Resolution Lawyer 27 (2016).

Matz D E, *Mediator Pressure and Party Autonomy: Are They Consistent with Each Other?* 10(4) Negotiation Journal 359 (1994).

McAdoo B, Welsh N A and Wissler R, *Institutionalization: What do Empirical Studies Tell us about Court Mediation?* 21 GPSolo 34 (2004).

McConville M and Chui W H, *Research Methods for Law* (Edinburgh 2007).

McDermott E P and Obar R, *What's Going on in Mediation: an Empirical Analysis of the Influence of a Mediator's Style on Party Satisfaction and Monetary Benefit,* 9 Harvard Negotiation Law Review 75 (2004).

McDougal M S, *The Diversity of Contemporary Dispute Resolution: Functions and Policies,* 4(1) Journal of International Dispute Settlement 47 (2013).

McEwen C A, *Managing Corporate Disputing: Overcoming Barriers to the Effective Use of Mediation for Reducing the Cost and Time of Litigation,* 14 Ohio State Journal on Dispute Resolution 1 (1998).

McEwen C A and Wissler R L, *Finding Out If it's True: Comparing Mediation and Negotiation Through Research,* 1 Journal of Dispute Resolution 131 (2002).

McEwen C A, Rogers N H and Maiman R J, *Bring in the Lawyers: Challenging the Dominant Approaches to Ensuring Fairness in Divorce Mediation,* 79 Minnesota Law Review 1317 (1994-1995).

McFadden D, *Developments in International Commercial Mediation: U.S., UK, Asia, India and EU,* 8(2) Contemporary Asia Arbitration Journal 299 (2015).

McGregor L, *Alternative Dispute Resolution and Human Rights: Developing a Rights-Based Approach through the ECHR*, 26(3) European Journal of International Law 607 (2015).

McIlwrath M, *Ignoring the Elephant in the Room: International Arbitration – Corporate Attitudes and Practices*, 74(4) Arbitration 424 (2008).

McIlwrath M and Savage J, *International Arbitration and Mediation: A Practical Guide* (Kluwer Law International 2010).

Meidanis, H, *International Enforcement of Mediated Settlement Agreements: Two and a Half Models – Why and How to Enforce International Mediated Settlement Agreements*, 85(1) Arbitration 49 (2019).

Menkel-Meadow C, *Legal Negotiation: A Study of Strategies in Search of a Theory*, 8(4) American Bar Foundation Research Journal 905 (1983).

Menkel-Meadow C, *Toward Another View of Legal Negotiation: The Structure of Problem Solving*, 31 University of California Los Angeles Law Review 754 (1984).

Menkel-Meadow C, *Pursuing Settlement in an Adversary Culture: A Tale of Innovation Co-Opted or 'The Law of ADR'*, 19(1) Florida State University Law Review 1 (1991).

Menkel-Meadow C, *Whose Dispute Is It Anyway? A Philosophical and Democratic Defence of Settlement (in Some Cases)*, 83 Georgetown Law Journal 2663 (1995).

Menkel-Meadow C, *When Dispute Resolution Begets Disputes of Its Own: Conflicts Among Dispute Professionals*, 44 University of California Los Angeles Law Review 1871 (1996).

Menkel-Meadow C, *Introduction: What Will We Do When Adjudication Ends? A Brief Intellectual History of ADR*, 44 University of California Los Angeles Law Review 1613 (1996-1997).

Menkel-Meadow C, *The Lawyer as Problem Solver and Third-Party Neutral: Creativity and Non-Partisanship in Lawyering*, 72 Temple Law Review 785 (1999).

Menkel-Meadow C, *Mothers and Fathers of Invention: The Intellectual Founders of ADR*, 16 Ohio State Journal of Dispute Resolution 1 (2000-2001).

Menkel-Meadow C, *And Now a Word About Secular Humanism, Spirituality and the Practice of Justice and Conflict Resolution*, 28 Fordham Urban Law Journal 1073 (2001).

Menkel-Meadow C, *Correspondences and Contradictions in International and Domestic Conflict Resolution: Lessons from General Theory and Varied Contexts*, Journal of Dispute Resolution 319 (2003).

Menkel-Meadow C, *From Legal Disputes to Conflict Resolution and Human Problem Solving: Legal Dispute Resolution in a Multidisciplinary Context*, 54 Journal of Legal Education 7 (2004).

Menkel-Meadow C and Wheeler M, *What's Fair? Ethics for Negotiators* (Jossey-Bass 2004).

Menkel-Meadow C, *Remembrance of Things Past: The Relationship of Past to Future in Pursuing Justice in Mediation*, 5(2) Cardozo Journal of Conflict Resolution 97 (2004).

Menkel-Meadow C, *Is the Adversary System Really Dead? Dilemmas of Legal Ethics as Legal Institutions and Roles Evolve* in Jane Holder (ed), *Current Legal Problems* (OUP 2005).

Menkel-Meadow C, *Exporting and Importing ADR*, 12 Dispute Resolution Magazine 5 (2005-2006).

Menkel-Meadow C, *Peace and Justice: Notes on the Evolution and Purposes of Legal Processes*, 94 The Georgetown Law Journal 553 (2006).

Menkel-Meadow C, *Why Hasn't the World Gotten to Yes? An Appreciation and Some Reflections*, 22(4) Negotiation Journal 485 (2006).

Menkel-Meadow C, *Maintaining ADR Integrity*, UC Irvine School of Law Research Paper No. 2009-6 <https://ssrn.com/abstract=1340185> accessed 20 July 2019.

Menkel Meadow C, *Are There Systemic Ethics Issues in Dispute System Design? And What We Should [Not] Do About it: Lessons from International and Domestic Contexts*, 14 Harvard Negotiation Law Review 195 (2009).

Menkel-Meadow, C, *Dispute Resolution* in Cane P and Kritzer H M (eds), *The Oxford Handbook of Empirical Legal Research* (OUP 2010).

Menkel-Meadow C, *Mediating Multiculturally: Culture and the Ethical Mediator* in Ellen Waldman (ed), *Mediation Ethics: Cases and Commentaries* (Jossey-Bass 2011).

Menkel-Meadow C, *The Historical Contingencies of Conflict Resolution*, 1(1) International Journal of Conflict Engagement and Resolution 32 (2013).

Menkel-Meadow C, *Cultural Variations in Restorative/Transitional Justice: Process Pluralism, Not One Size Fits All*, 68 UC Irvine School of Law Legal Studies Research Paper Series 1 (2014).

Menkel-Meadow C, *Alternative and Appropriate Dispute Resolution in Context: Formal, Informal, and Semiformal Legal Processes*, School of Law, University of California Irvine School of Law Research Paper No. 2015-26, 10 <https://papers.ssrn.com/sol3/papers.cfm?abstract_id=2584188> (accessed 10 June 2020).

Menkel-Meadow C, *Variations in the Uptake of and Resistance to Mediation Outside of the United States*, University of California, Irvine School of Law, Research Paper No. 2015-80, 189 [2015] <https://papers.ssrn.com/sol3/papers.cfm?abstract_id=2658903> (accessed 10 June 2020).

Menkel-Meadow C, *Mediation, Arbitration, and Alternative Dispute Resolution (ADR)* in *International Encyclopedia of the Social and Behavioral Sciences* (Elsevier Ltd 2015) and UC Irvine School of Law Research Paper No. 2015-59 <https://papers.ssrn.com/sol3/papers.cfm?abstract_id=2608140> (accessed 10 June 2020).

Menkel-Meadow C, *Chartered Institute of Arbitrators 8th Symposium on Mediation, October 15: The Case for Mediation: the Things that Mediators Should Be Learning and Doing*, 82(1) Arbitration 22 (2016).

Menkel-Meadow C, *The Future of Mediation Worldwide: Legal and Cultural Variations in the Uptake of or Resistance to Mediation* in Ian Macduff (ed), *Essays on Mediation: Dealing with Disputes in the 21st Century* (Wolters Kluwer 2016).

Merry S E, *Disputing Without Culture*, 100 Harvard Law Review 2057 (1987).

Mistelis L, *International Arbitration – Corporate Attitudes and Practices. 12 Perceptions Tested: Myths, Data and Analysis,* 15 The American Review of International Arbitration 525 (2014).

Mnookin R H, *Why Negotiations Fail: An Exploration of Barriers to the Resolution of Conflict* in Arrow K and others (eds), *Barriers to Conflict Resolution* (W.W. Norton & Company 1995).

Mnookin R H, Peppet S P and Tulumello A S, *Beyond Winning, Negotiating to Create Value in Deals and Disputes* (The Belknap Press of Harvard University Press 2000).

Moore C W, *The Mediation Process* (4th ed. Jossey-Bass 2014).

Morek R, *Mandatory Mediation in Italy – Reloaded* (Kluwer Mediation Blog, 9 October 2013) <http://mediationblog.kluwerarbitration.com/2013/10/09/mandatory-mediation-in-italy-reloaded/?doing_wp_cron=1592478336.1362919807434082031250> (accessed 10 June 2020).

Morris G and Schroder D, LEADR/Victoria University, *Commercial Mediation in New Zealand Project Report* (June 2015) <https://papers.ssrn.com/sol3/papers.cfm?abstract_id=2650261> (accessed 10 June 2020).

Morris G and Lamb A, Resolution Institute/Victoria University, *Lawyers as Gatekeepers to Commercial Mediation in New Zealand Report* (June 2016) <https://papers.ssrn.com/sol3/papers.cfm?abstract_id=2797995> (accessed 10 June 2020).

Morris G and McKechnie F, Resolution Institute/Victoria University of Wellington, *Users of Commercial Mediation in New Zealand – Insurance Industry Report* (April 2017) <https://papers.ssrn.com/sol3/papers.cfm?abstract_id=3015041> (accessed 10 June 2020).

Mulcahy C, *The Changing Face of Disputes in the Liquefied Natural Gas Market,* 33 Journal of Energy and Natural Resources Law 271 (2015).

Mulcahy L, *The Collective Interest in Private Dispute Resolution,* 33(1) Oxford Journal of Legal Studies 59 (2013).

Neuberger D, *Keynote Address: A View From On High* (Civil Mediation Conference 2015, London, 15 May 2015) <https://www.supremecourt.uk/docs/speech-150512-civil-mediation-conference-2015.pdf> (accessed 10 June 2020).

Neumann R K and Krieger S H, *Empirical Inquiry Twenty-Five Years after the Lawyering Process,* 10 Clinical Law Review 349 (2003-2004).

Niemeijer B and Pel M, *Court-Based Mediation in the Netherlands: Research, Evaluation and Future Expectations,* 110 Penn. State Law Review 345 (2005).

Noce D, Bush R, Folger J, *Clarifying the Theoretical Underpinnings of Mediation: Implications for Practice and Policy,* 3 Pepperdine Dispute Resolution Law Journal 39 (2002-2003).

Nolan-Haley J, *Lawyers, Clients and Mediation,* 73 Notre Dame Law Review 1369 (1997-1998).

Nolan-Haley J, Lawyers, *Non-Lawyers and Mediation: Rethinking the Professional Monopoly from a Problem-Solving Perspective,* 7 Harvard Negotiation Law Review 235 (2002).

Nolan-Haley J, *The Merger of Law and Mediation: Lessons from Equity Jurisprudence and Roscoe Pound,* 6 Cardozo Journal of Conflict Resolution 57 (2004-2005).

Nolan-Haley J, *Self-Determination in International Mediation: Some Preliminary Reflections,* 7 Cardozo Journal of Conflict Resolution 277 (2005-2006).

Nolan-Haley J, *Teaching Comparative Perspectives in Mediation: Some Preliminary Reflections,* 81 St. John's Law Review 259 (2007).

Nolan-Haley J, *Consent in Mediation,* 14 Dispute Resolution Magazine 4 (2007-2008).

Nolan-Haley J, *Mediation Exceptionality,* 78 Fordham Law Review 1247 (2009-2010).

Nolan-Haley J, *Evolving Paths to Justice: Assessing the EU Directive on Mediation* (October 2011) Fordham Law Legal Studies Research Paper No. 1942391, 2-5 <http://ssrn.com/abstract=1942391> (accessed 10 June 2020).

Nolan-Haley J, *Is Europe Headed Down the Primrose Path with Mandatory Mediation?* 37 North Carolina Journal of International Law & Commercial Regulation 981 (2012).

Nolan-Haley J, *Mediation: the 'New Arbitration',* 17 Harvard Negotiation Law Review 61 (2012).

Nolan-Haley J, *Mediation: The Best and Worst of Times,* 16 Cardozo Journal of Conflict Resolution 731 (2014-2015).

Noone M A and Ojelabi L A, *Ensuring Access to Justice in Mediation Within the Civil Justice System,* 40(2) Monash University Law Review 528 (2014).

Patton M Q, *Qualitative Research & Evaluative Methods* (4th ed. Sage 2015).

Peppet S, *Contract Formation in Imperfect Markets: Should We Use Mediators in Deals?* 19(2) Ohio State Journal on Dispute Resolution 283 (2004).

Peters D, *Can We Talk – Overcoming Barriers to Mediating Private Transborder Commercial Disputes in the Americas,* 41 Vanderbilt Journal of Transnational Law 1251 (2008).

Peters D, *To Sue Is Human; to Settle Divine: Intercultural Collaborations to Expand the Use of Mediation in Costa Rica,* 17 Florida Journal of International Law 9 (2015).

Petsche M, *Mediation as the Preferred Method to Solve International Business Disputes? A Look into the Future,* 4 International Business Law Journal 251 (2013).

Piers M, *Is Europe Skipping a Step? Exploring the Harmonization of ADR Agreements,* 20 Maastricht Journal of European and Comparative Law 506 (2013).

Piers M, *Europe's Role in Alternative Dispute Resolution: Off to a Good Start?* 2 Journal of Dispute Resolution 269 (2014).

Pleasance P, Balmer N and Tam T, *Civil Justice in England & Wales: Report of the 2006 English & Welsh Civil and Social Justice Survey* <https://webarchive.nationalarchives.gov.uk/20110215121414/http://lsrc.org.uk/publications/2010CSJSAnnualReport.pdf> (accessed 10 June 2020).

Pound R, *The Causes of Popular Dissatisfaction with the Administration of Justice,* 8 Baylor Law Review 1 (1956).

Prince S, *An Evaluation of the Effectiveness of Court-Based Mediation Processes in Non-Family Civil Proceedings at Exeter and Guildford County Court,* (2006) Department of Constitutional Affairs <https://ore.exeter.ac.uk/repository/handle/10036/22735> (accessed 10 June 2020).

Prince S, *Institutionalising Mediation? An Evaluation of the Exeter Court Small Claims Mediation Pilot,* 5 Web Journal of Current Legal Issues (2007).

Prince S, *Mandatory Mediation: the Ontario Experience*, 26 Civil Justice Quarterly 79 (2007).

Prince S, *Mediating Small Claims: Are We on the Right Track?* 26 Civil Justice Quarterly 328 (2007).

Raiffa H, Richardson J and Metcalfe D, *Negotiation Analysis, The Science and Art of Collaborative Decision Making* (The Belknap Press of Harvard University Press 2002).

Raiffa H, Richardson J and David Metcalfe, *Negotiation Analysis* (Harvard University Press 2007).

Reif L C, *The Use of Conciliation or Mediation for the Resolution of International Commercial Disputes*, 45 The Canadian Business Law Journal 20 (2007).

Relis T, *Perceptions in Litigation and Mediation: Lawyers, Defendants, Plaintiffs and Gendered Parties* (Cambridge University Press 2009).

Rhode D L, *Legal Scholarship*, 115(5) Harvard Law Review 1327 (2002).

Riskin L, *Understanding Mediators' Orientations, Strategies and Techniques: a Grid for the Perplexed*, 1(7) Harvard Negotiation Law Review 7 (1996).

Riskin L, *Decision-Making in Mediation: The New Old Grid and the New New Grid System*, 79(1) Notre Dame Law Review 1 (2003).

Roberts M, *Developing the Craft of Mediation* (Jessica Kingsley Publishers 2007).

Roberts S, *Alternative Dispute Resolution and Civil Justice: An Unresolved Relationship*, 56 Modern Law Review 452 (1993).

Roberts S and Palmer M, *Dispute Processes ADR and the Primary Forms of Decision-Making* (2nd ed. Cambridge 2005).

Roberts S, *A Court in the City: Civil and Commercial Litigation in London at the Beginning of the 21st Century* (Wildy, Simmonds & Hill Publishing 2013).

Rogers C, *The Vocation of International Arbitrators*, 20 The American University International Law Review 957 (2005).

Rogers C, *Arbitrator Intelligence: From Intuition to Data in Arbitration Appointments*, 11(2) New York Dispute Resolution Lawyer (Spring 2018).

Roskes M, De Dreu C K W and Nijstad B A, *Necessity Is the Mother of Invention: Avoidance Motivation Stimulates Creativity through Cognitive Effort*, 103(2) Journal of Personality and Social Psychology 242 (2012).

Rubino-Sammartano M, *Domestic, Transnational, Foreign and International Mediations: Legal Issues*, 81(4) Arbitration 381 (2015).

Rutledge P B, *Convergence and Divergence in International Dispute Resolution*, 1 Journal of Dispute Resolution 49 (2012).

Sako M, *General Counsel with Power?* Said Business School, University of Oxford <http://eureka.sbs.ox.ac.uk/4560/1/General_Counsel_with_Power.pdf> (accessed 10 June 2020).

Sander F E A and Goldberg S, *Fitting the Forum to the Fuss: A User Friendly Guide to Selecting an ADR Procedure*, 10 Negotiation Journal 49 (1994).

Sander F, *The Future of ADR: The Earl F. Nelson Memorial Lecture*, 1 Journal of Dispute Resolution 3 (2000).

Sander F, *Achieving Meaningful Threshold Consent to Mediation Style(s)*, 14 Dispute Resolution Magazine 8 (2007-2008).

Sander F, *A Dialogue Between Professors Frank Sander and Mariana Hernandez Crespo: Exploring the Evolution of the Multi-Door Courthouse*, 5(3) University of St. Thomas Law Journal 665 (2008).

Schnabel T, *The Singapore Convention on Mediation: A Framework for the Cross-Border Recognition and Enforcement of Mediated Settlement Agreements,* 19 Pepperdine Dispute Resolution Law Journal 1 (2019).

Schonewille M and Fox K, *Moving Beyond 'Just' a Deal, a Bad Deal or No Deal* in Arnold Ingen-Housz (ed.), *ADR in Business: Practice and Issues Across Countries and Cultures,* Vol. II (Kluwer Law International 2010).

Schonewille M and Lack J, *Mediation in the European Union and Abroad: 60 States Divided by a Common Word?* in Schonewille M and Schonewille F (eds), *The Variegated Landscape of Mediation: A Comparative Study of Mediation Regulation and Practices in Europe and the World* (Eleven International Publishing 2013).

Schonewille M and Schonewille F (eds), *The Variegated Landscape of Mediation: A Comparative Study of Mediation Regulation and Practices in Europe and the World* (Eleven International Publishing 2013).

School of International Arbitration, Queen Mary University of London, *Corporate Attitudes and Practices* (2006) <http://www.arbitration.qmul.ac.uk/media/arbitration/docs/IAstudy_2006.pdf> (accessed 10 June 2020).

School of International Arbitration, Queen Mary University of London, *Corporate Attitudes: Recognition and Enforcement of Foreign Awards* (2008) <http://www.arbitration.qmul.ac.uk/research/2008/> (accessed 10 June 2020).

School of International Arbitration, Queen Mary University of London, *Choices in International Arbitration* (2010) <http://www.arbitration.qmul.ac.uk/research/2010/> (accessed 10 June 2020).

School of International Arbitration, Queen Mary University of London, *Current and Preferred Practices in the Arbitral Process* (2012) <http://www.arbitration.qmul.ac.uk/research/2012/> (accessed 10 June 2020).

School of International Arbitration, Queen Mary University of London, *Corporate Choices in International Arbitration* (2013) <http://www.arbitration.qmul.ac.uk/research/2013/> (accessed 10 June 2020).

School of International Arbitration, Queen Mary University of London, *Improvements and innovations in International Arbitration* (2015) <http://www.arbitration.qmul.ac.uk/research/2015/> (accessed 10 June 2020).

School of International Arbitration, Queen Mary University of London, *An Insight into Resolving Technology, Media and Telecoms Disputes* (2016) <http://www.arbitration.qmul.ac.uk/research/2016/> (accessed 10 June 2020).

School of International Arbitration, Queen Mary University of London, *The Evolution of International Arbitration* (2018) <http://www.arbitration.qmul.ac.uk/research/2018/> (accessed 10 June 2019).

Sertillanges A D, *The Intellectual Life: Its Spirits, Conditions and Methods* (Mary Ryan tr, Mercier Press 1978).

Shapira O, *Exploring the Concept of Power in Mediation: Mediator's Sources of Power and Influence Tactics*, 24 Ohio State Journal on Dispute Resolution 535 (2008-2009).

Singapore International Dispute Resolution Academy, *International Dispute Resolution Survey: Currents of Change 2019, Preliminary Report* < https://sidra.smu.edu.sg/sites/sidra.smu.edu.sg/files/documents/SIDRA2019_IDR_Survey_Preliminary_Report.pdf > (accessed 10 June 2020).

Singapore International Dispute Resolution Academy, *International Dispute Resolution Survey: 2020 Final Report* < https://sidra.smu.edu.sg/sidra-international-dispute-resolution-survey-final-report-2020 > (accessed 10 August 2020).

Singapore Ministry of Law, *Singapore Launches First International Dispute Resolution Survey* (23 January 2019) < https://www.mlaw.gov.sg/news/press-releases/singapore-launches-first-international-dispute-resolution-survey > (accessed 20 June 2020).

Siong O, *Singapore, China to Set Up International Mediator Panel for Belt and Road Projects* (*Channel News Asia*, 24 January 2019) < https://www.channelnewsasia.com/news/singapore/singapore-china-belt-road-project-mediator-panel-11161414 > (accessed 20 June 2020).

Smith S and Martinez J, *An Analytic Framework for Dispute Systems Design*, 14 Harvard Negotiation Law Review 123 (Winter 2009).

Steele B, *Enforcing International Commercial Mediation Agreements As Arbitral Awards Under the New York Convention*, 54 University of California Los Angeles Law Review 1385 (2006-2007).

Steffek F, *Mediation in the European Union: an Introduction* (June 2012) < https://www.fomentonet.eu/mediation/ > (accessed 20 June 2020).

Steffek F and others (eds), *Regulating Dispute Resolution – ADR & Access to Justice at the Crossroads* (Hart Publishing 2013).

Steffek F, *The Relationship Between Mediation and Other Forms of Alternative Dispute Resolution* in European Parliament, *The Implementation of the Mediation Directive – Workshop 29 November 2016, Compilation of In-Depth Analyses* < http://www.europarl.europa.eu/RegData/etudes/IDAN/2016/571395/IPOL_IDA(2016)571395_EN.pdf > (accessed 20 June 2020).

Stipanowich T J, *ADR and the 'Vanishing Trial': the Growth and Impact of Alternative Dispute Resolution*, 1 Journal of Empirical Legal Studies 843 (2004).

Stipanowich T J, *Arbitration: the 'New Litigation'*, 1 University of Illinois Law Review 1 (2010).

Stipanowich T J and Lamare J R, *Living with ADR: Evolving Perceptions and Use of Mediation, Arbitration, and Conflict Management in Fortune 1000 Corporations*, 19 Harvard Negotiation Law Review 1 (2014).

Stipanowich T J, *The International Evolution of Mediation: A Call for Dialogue and Deliberation*, 46 Victoria University of Wellington Law Review 1191 (2015).

Stipanowich T J, *Living The Dream of ADR: Reflection on Four Decades of the Quiet Revolution in Dispute Resolution (Symposium Keynote)*, 18 Cardozo Journal of Conflict Resolution 513 (2017).

Stipanowich T, *What Have We Learned From The Global Pound Conferences?* (*Kluwer Mediation Blog*, 27 November 2017) <http://mediationblog.kluwerarbitration.com/2017/11/27/learned-global-pound-conferences/> (accessed 10 June 2020).

Strong S I, *Beyond International Commercial Arbitration? The Promise of International Commercial Mediation*, 45 Washington University Journal of Law & Policy 11 (2014).

Strong S I, *Use and Perception of International Commercial Mediation and Conciliation: a Preliminary Report on Issues Relating to the Proposed UNCITRAL Convention on International Commercial Mediation and Conciliation*, University of Missouri, School of Law Legal Studies Research Paper No 2014-28 <https://papers.ssrn.com/sol3/papers.cfm?abstract_id=2526302> (accessed 10 June 2020).

Strong S I, *Clash of Cultures: Epistemic Communities, Negotiation Theory and International Lawmaking at the United Nations Commission on International Trade Law (UNCITRAL)*, 50 Akron Law Review 495 (2016).

Strong S I, *Realizing Rationality: An Empirical Assessment of International Commercial Mediation*, 73 Washington & Lee Law Review 1973 (2016).

Strong S I, *Truth in a Post-Truth Society: how Sticky Defaults, Status Quo Bias, and the Sovereign Prerogative Influence the Perceived Legitimacy of International Arbitration*, 2 University of Illinois Law Review 533 (2018).

Stulberg J, *Fairness and Mediation*, 13 Ohio State Journal on Dispute Resolution 909 (1997-1998).

Stulberg J, *Questions*, 17 Ohio State Journal of Dispute Resolution 531 (2001-2002).

Stulberg J, *Mediation and Justice: What Standards Govern?* 6 Cardozo Journal of Conflict Resolution 213 (2004-2005).

Stulberg J, *Honoring our Past, Celebrating our Future*, 14 Dispute Resolution Magazine 27 (2007-2008).

Susskind R, *Tomorrow's Lawyers* (2nd ed. OUP 2017).

Sussman E., *The New York Convention through a Mediation Prism*, 15 Dispute Resolution Magazine 10 (2008-2009).

Sussman E, *The Final Step: Issues in Enforcing the Mediation Settlement Agreement Conference paper for Fordham Law School Conference* <https://sussmanadr.com/docs/Enforcement_Fordham_82008.pdf> (accessed 10 June 2020).

Sussman E, *A Path Forward: A Convention for the Enforcement of Mediated Settlement Agreements* <http://www.sussmanadr.com/docs/UNCITRAL Enforcing settlement agreements TDM.pdf> (accessed 10 June 2020).

Titi C and Gómez K F (eds), *Mediation in International Commercial and Investment Disputes* (Oxford University Press 2019).

Toulmin J, *Cross-Border Mediation and Civil Proceedings in National Courts*, 10 ERA Forum 551 (2009).

Tromans R, *Challenging the Conflict Culture: Mediation's Struggle for Acceptance in Europe*, 68 The European Lawyer 19 (2007).

Tversky A and Kahneman D, *Judgment under Uncertainty; Heuristics and Biases* in Connolly T, Arkes H R and Hammond K R (eds), *Judgment and Decision Making* (2nd ed. Cambridge University Press 2000).

UNCITRAL Working Group II, *Secretariat's Note on International Commercial Conciliation: Preparation of an Instrument on Enforcement of International Commercial Settlement Agreements Resulting from Conciliation*, A/CN.9/WG.II/WP.198.

Ury W L, Brett J M and Goldberg S B, *Getting Disputes Resolved: Designing Systems to Cut the Costs of Conflict* (Program on Negotiation at Harvard Law School 1993).

Ury W L, *Conflict Resolution among the Bushmen: Lessons in Dispute Systems Design*, 11(4) Negotiation Journal 379 (1995).

Ury W, *The Third Side* (Penguin 2000).

Van Gestel R and Micklitz H-W, *Why Methods Matter in European Legal Scholarship*, 20(3) European Law Journal 292 (2014).

Van Hoecke M (ed), *Methodologies of Legal Research: Which Kind of Method for What Kind of Discipline?* (Hart Publishing 2013).

Von Kunberg W, *The Future for Mediation in Europe*, 72(1) Arbitration 62 (2006).

Walde T W, *Efficient Management of Transnational Disputes: Mutual Gain by Mediation or Joint Loss in Litigation*, 22(2) Arbitration International 205 (2006).

Webley L, *Qualitative Approaches to Empirical Legal Research* in Cane P and Kritzer H (eds), *The Oxford Handbook of Empirical Legal Research* (OUP 2010).

Welsh N, *The Thinning Vision of Court Annexed Mediation: The Inevitable Price of Institutionalization?* 6 Harvard Negotiation Law Review 17 (2001).

Welsh N, *Making Deals in Court-Connected Mediation: What's Justice Got to do With It?* 79 Washington University Law Quarterly 787 (2001).

Welsh N, *Stepping Back Through the Looking Glass: Real Conversations with Real Disputants about Institutionalized Mediation and Its Value*, (2004) 38 Ohio State Journal on Dispute Resolution 573.

Welsh N, *I Could Have Been a Contender: Summary Jury Trial as a Means to Overcome Iqbal's Negative Effects upon Pre-Litigation Communication, Negotiation and Early Consensual Dispute Resolution*, 114(4) Pennsylvania State Law Review 1149 (2010).

White S, *Directive 2008/52 on Certain Aspects of Mediation in Civil and Commercial Matters: a New Culture of Access to Justice?* 79(1) Arbitration 52 (2013).

Wong C, *46 Countries Sign International Mediation Treaty Signed after Singapore*, The Straits Times (Singapore, 7 August 2019) <https://www.straitstimes.com/singapore/key-facts-about-the-singapore-convention-on-mediation> (accessed 10 June 2020).

World Economic Forum, 'The World's Biggest Economies in 2017' <https://www.weforum.org/agenda/2017/03/worlds-biggest-economies-in-2017/> accessed 20 July 2019.

World Intellectual Property Organisation, Arbitration and Mediation Center, *International Survey on Dispute Resolution in Technology Transactions* (March 2013) <https://www.wipo.int/amc/en/center/survey/results.html> (accessed 20 June 2020).

Wissler R, *The Effects of Mandatory Mediation: Empirical Research on the Experience of Small Claims and Common Pleas Courts*, 33 Willamette Law Review 565 (1997).

Wissler R, *Court-Connected Mediation in General Civil Cases: What We Know from Empirical Research*, 17 Ohio State Journal on Dispute Resolution 641 (2002).

Wissler R, *Representation in Mediation: What We Know from Empirical Research*, 37 Fordham Urban Law Journal 419 (2010).

Wissler R, *Judicial Settlement Conferences and Staff Mediation: Empirical Research Findings*, 17 Dispute Resolution Magazine 18 (2010-2011).

Wolcott H, *Writing Up Qualitative Research* (Sage 1990).

Wolfe P Y, *How a Mediator Enhances the Negotiation Process*, 46 New Hampshire Bar Journal 38 (2005).

Wolski B, *Recent Developments in International Commercial Dispute Resolution: Expanding the Options*, 13(2) Bond Law Review 1 (2001).

Wolski B, *Using Dispute Systems Design to Identify, Explain and Predict Trends in the Settlement of International Commercial Disputes: The UNCITRAL and ICC ADR Initiatives*, 6(2) International Journal of Private Law 132 (2013)

Wolski B, *Arb-Med-Arb (and MSAs): A Whole Which is Less Than, Not Greater Than, the Sum of its Parts?* 6 Contemporary Asia Arbitration Journal 249 (2013).

Wolski B, *Enforcing Mediated Settlement Agreements (MSAs): Critical Questions and Directions for Future Research*, 7 Contemporary Asia Arbitration Journal 87 (2014).

Wolski B, *On Mediation, Legal Representatives and Advocates*, 38(1) University of New South Wales Law Journal 5 (2015).

Zartman W, *Ripe for Resolution: Conflict and Intervention in Africa* (updated edition, OUP 1989).

Table of Cases

Table of Legislation

Index

H

I

J

L

M

GLOBAL TRENDS IN DISPUTE RESOLUTION

1. Nadja Alexander (ed.), *Global Trends in Mediation*, Second Edition, 2006 (ISBN 978-90-411-2571-2).
2. Giuseppe De Palo and Mary B. Trevor (eds), *Arbitration and Mediation in the Southern Mediterranean Countries*, 2007 (ISBN 978-90-411-2684-9).
3. Lars Kirchhoff, *Constructive Interventions – Paradigms, Process and Practice of International Mediation*, 2008 (ISBN 978-90-411-2685-6).
4. Nadja Alexander, *International and Comparative Mediation: Legal Perspectives*, 2009 (ISBN 978-90-411-2684-9).
5. Ewald A. Filler, *Commercial Mediation in Europe: An Empirical Study of the User Experience*, 2012 (ISBN 978-90-411-3116-4).
6. Ian Macduff (ed.), *Essays on Mediation: Dealing with Disputes in the 21st Century*, 2016 (ISBN 978-90-411-8366-8).
7. Nadja Alexander, Sabine Walsh and Martin Svatos (eds), *EU Mediation Law Handbook: Regulatory Robustness Ratings for Mediation Regimes*, 2017 (ISBN 978-90-411-5859-8).
8. Nadja Alexander and Shouyu Chong, *The Singapore Convention on Mediation: A Commentary*, 2019 (ISBN 978-94-035-1481-9).
9. Anna Howard, *EU Cross-Border Commercial Mediation: Listening to Disputants – Changing the Frame; Framing the Changes*, 2021 (ISBN 978-94-035-1753-7).

www.ingramcontent.com/pod-product-compliance
Ingram Content Group UK Ltd.
Pitfield, Milton Keynes, MK11 3LW, UK
UKHW020247290926
15470UKWH00002B/787

9 789403 517537